Indonesian Syariah

The **Institute of Southeast Asian Studies (ISEAS)** was established as an autonomous organization in 1968. It is a regional centre dedicated to the study of socio-political, security and economic trends and developments in Southeast Asia and its wider geostrategic and economic environment. The Institute's research programmes are the Regional Economic Studies (RES, including ASEAN and APEC), Regional Strategic and Political Studies (RSPS), and Regional Social and Cultural Studies (RSCS).

ISEAS Publishing, an established academic press, has issued almost 2,000 books and journals. It is the largest scholarly publisher of research about Southeast Asia from within the region. ISEAS Publishing works with many other academic and trade publishers and distributors to disseminate important research and analyses from and about Southeast Asia to the rest of the world.

Indonesian Syariah

Defining a National School of Islamic Law

M.B. HOOKER

LSEAS

INSTITUTE OF SOUTHEAST ASIAN STUDIES
Singapore

First published in Singapore in 2008 by
ISEAS Publishing
Institute of Southeast Asian Studies
30 Heng Mui Keng Terrace
Pasir Panjang
Singapore 119614

E-mail: publish@iseas.edu.sg
http://bookshop.iseas.edu.sg

The responsibility for facts and opinions in this publication rests exclusively with the author and his interpretations do not necessarily reflect the views or the policy of the Institute or its supporters.

ISEAS Library Cataloguing-in-Publication Data

Hooker, M. B. (Michael Barry), 1939-
    Indonesian syariah : defining a national school of Islamic law.
    1. Islamic law—Indonesia—Interpretation and construction.
    2. Islam—Customs and practices.
    I. Title
KNW480 H78   2008

ISBN 978-981-230-801-6 (soft cover)
ISBN 978-981-230-802-3 (hard cover)
ISBN 978-981-230-803-0 (PDF)

Edited and typeset by Beth Thomson, Japan Online, Canberra
Indexed by Alan Walker, Sydney
Printed in Singapore by Utopia Press Pte Ltd

Contents

Tables, Figures and Appendices

TABLES

FIGURES

APPENDICES

Preface:
Indonesian Syariah: A Work in Progress

In its classical sense syariah means 'path to water'—hence, allegorically, to life, and this means duty to God. But what that duty is, how it is to be defined, who does the defining and for whom it is being defined is a matter of intense and often divisive debate in Indonesia as elsewhere. Duty, in the context of the real, temporal world, has a myriad reference points. These include the classical *fiqh*; local Muslim and pre-Muslim practice; the politics of religion; national state codes and texts; philosophies; political commentary; public orthopraxy; and the ever-present weight of history, about which there is no consensus in Indonesia. The syariah is not now one path, if it ever were. Instead, many paths are offered. The essays in this book are likewise offered as examples from one place at one time to illustrate what choices have been made and to try and judge whether those choices are in reality viable routes to attaining the purpose of the journey, which is fidelity to revelation.

The concept of a distinctly Indonesian school of legal thought (*mazhab*) is necessarily complementary to the definition of syariah; we are talking about a specific syariah that is 'national' because it is 'Indonesian'. Movement towards defining and establishing a national *mazhab* began with the rise of nationalist aspirations in the 1930s, and became especially focused in the 1940s with the successful achievement of independence and the debates as to what the proper foundation of the new state should be. As it happened, that foundation turned out to be secular principles, not the syariah. However, this did not prevent the parallel discussion of a national *mazhab* from continuing and may even, in reaction, have intensified it. By the late 1960s and early 1970s the idea of a national *mazhab*—a specifically Indonesian syariah—was being debated in sophisticated terms by the late Professor Hazairin. His proposals were resisted by both the (secular) state authority and the religious scholars ('*ulamā*') and went nowhere. The climate of the times was against him.

The 1940s and 1960s are now behind us. However, the debates of those times still resonate strongly, and for this reason I begin with the 1940s, a period of political turmoil in Indonesia. This obviously had serious repercussions for law generally and for syariah in particular. Indeed, some would hold that the past half-century has seen the destruction of Indonesia's legal system. On the other hand, it has also seen the development of a formal syariah to a degree unimaginable in pre-independence times (Chapter 1). Similarly, I believe that we can now identify five schools of syariah philosophy (Chapter 2), although I do not claim that each is wholly discrete. The overall impression is of ambiguity and uncertainty, but there is nothing to be afraid of in this situation. It is normal in all systems of law, and an overemphasis on certainty, while uncomfortable for policy makers, is always damaging. As the history of any law tradition clearly shows, pluralism in the philosophy of law is natural and beneficial, and this includes the orientalism debate.

The next two essays (Chapters 3 and 4) are both concerned with how syariah is transmitted from one generation to the next. Part of the process is to define the object being communicated. Any such process has to: (a) convey basic principles; (b) explain them; and (c) present them in a coherent and justifiable form. I have chosen two examples. The first is the syariah curricula used in Indonesia's Islamic colleges and universities (Chapter 3). They cover formal instruction in the principles of syariah, as well as reasoning about syariah. The various curricula are consciously and specifically defined for Indonesian needs and circumstances. As such they are always controversial and generate considerable tension at the national and local levels. Argument over content and method is continuous. The second example is the *khutbah*, the Friday sermon (Chapter 4). Although it may appear simpler in content, it is equally important because it is a public expression of syariah values and reaches many millions of Muslims each week. Of course, working from written collections is less than ideal. The whole theatre of *khutbah* presentation is lost, but the collections at least allow us to see how syariah values are transmitted to the ordinary person. They also give us a permanent record of the issues, addressed critically, through time.

Chapter 5 takes us into the Department of Religion (established in 1946). In direct contrast to the *khutbah*, which is completely independent of the state, the department is a total syariah bureaucracy. Its formal structure is not my direct concern here; instead, I take one of its most important duties—the pilgrimage (*hajj*)—as an illustration of how the department works. This also gives us the chance to see how the modern *hajj* is constructed.

The final essay (Chapter 6) takes us into regional varieties of syariah values, with examples from Aceh, West Sumatra and South Sulawesi. In this chapter, I also examine the proposal for a national syariah criminal code. Each code in its own way aims to express syariah values through the use of compulsion. It is noticeable that the major, indeed sole, emphasis in 'implementing syariah' is on conduct in public. This includes dress, 'proper' behaviour (that is, male–female relations), recitation of the Qur'ān and payment of *zakat*. Penalties up to and including physical mutilation are proposed or recommended. There seems to be a somewhat naive belief that orthopraxy will make the person a 'better' Muslim. However, it is too easy to criticize: values issues always appear naive to those who prefer so-called pragmatism, which is really just shorthand for expediency or, in extreme cases, amorality and political opportunism.

The thesis put forward in this book is that there is a syariah that has been formulated to meet the needs of Islam in Indonesia on its own terms. I am speaking of an indigenous originality in which there is a high degree of public trust (which is more than can be said for the general secular state system). However, the significance of the Indonesian originality has wider implications. First, for general studies in Islamic law, Indonesia gives us a version of the classical inheritance that has been adapted so as to reflect (via selection) the social, political and intellectual structures in one place at one time (the 1940s to 2006). To anticipate, we find that the classical inheritance is fundamental but not primary for public or private law. This is an important lesson for generalist studies of 'Islamic law today'.

Second, in the wider world of comparative law, local studies such as this act as necessary correctives to the tendency to construct grand theories about the nature of law itself. Until recently comparative law was largely Euro-American-centric, and the laws of the East, including syariah, were pretty much dismissed as pre-modern, irrelevant or, at worst, only marginally law at all. Fortunately this has now changed, and Islamic law in both its classical and modern versions is now emphatically recognized as part of international comparative law.

Having said this, it is still true that contemporary comparative law has difficulty with modern Islamic law because, as a general class, syariah has within itself so many variant references as to make it quite amorphous. That is a challenge for comparative law theory. It is also a vital challenge for the modern world, where 'sharia' is used by the media, in Muslim and non-Muslim countries, in a wholly indiscriminate way. I hope that the Indonesian material may act as some corrective in this respect (see also the epilogue).

I must stress that this book is very much a work in progress; in this it reflects the Indonesian syariah, which has always been a work in progress. I make no pretence to completeness; other scholars of Islam and syariah in Indonesia will have their own personal sets of significant issues. I do claim, however, a reasonable degree of comprehensiveness so far as formal syariah structures are concerned. What these formal structures are and what they mean is the subject of this book. I am aware that the essays in this book raise more questions than they provide answers, but that too is my intention—to initiate debate and suggest a framework within which it might take place.

M.B. Hooker
Faculty of Law, Australian National University
'Kuala Pilah', Braidwood, NSW
December 2007

Acknowledgments

The research on which this book is based was funded by two Australian Research Council Discovery grants, the first with Professor Timothy Lindsey (University of Melbourne) and the second with Professor Virginia Hooker (Australian National University). I am very grateful to the ARC and to my two colleagues for their contributions in data collection and discussions on Indonesian syariah.

My colleagues in Indonesia were unfailingly generous with their time and advice. In particular, I acknowledge with gratitude the assistance of Drs. H. Suryadi, now Chief Judge of the Islamic High Court in Banten, and Professor Azyumardi Azra, formerly Rector of UIN Syarif Hidayatullah Jakarta. Drs. Yasrul Huda M.A., IAIN Imam Bonjol, and Akh. Muzakki M.Phil., IAIN Sunan Ampel, provided a great mass of primary material for which I am most grateful. For detailed discussions I am indebted to Dr H. Al Yasa Abubakar, Head of Dinas Syariat, Aceh, and Dr Khoiruddin Nasution, UIN Sunan Kalijaga, Yogyakarta.

In Australia, Ms Helen Pausacker and Mr Rowan Gould (both from the University of Melbourne) made translations and summaries of very difficult legal–bureaucratic material. Their care and competence are beyond praise. Mr Jeremy Kingsley and Ms Katheryn Taylor, also from Melbourne, and Ms Jemma Parsons and Mr Ismatu Ropi (both from the ANU) gave me considerable assistance. I am especially grateful to Ms Linda Elford of the ANU Law Library for searching out and alerting me to relevant material.

Initial formatting was done by Mrs Claire Smith with unfailing good humour. The editing and final formatting was done by Ms Beth Thomson and I am most fortunate to have had the benefit of her considerable technical skills. Mr Alan Walker compiled the index. I join a long list of authors who owe him a huge debt for the material improvement he has made to our books.

Mrs Triena Ong and her staff at the Institute of Southeast Asian Studies have been most helpful. I hope this book can take a place in the now well-established ISEAS Islamic series.

Materials, Dates and Spelling

Much of the material in the book is from primary sources. A collection has been lodged with the Asian Law Centre, University of Melbourne, much of it now online or in the process of going online (see http://www.law.unimelb.au/alc/bibliography).

Dates are always a problem in Indonesian law generally, and for syariah as well. The practice of cross-referencing and back-referencing laws, regulations, instructions, decisions and letters is a minefield for anyone fixated on certainty of time(s). No doubt I have made errors, and for this reason I give dates as well as I can throughout each chapter rather than a comprehensive or final date for the whole law. I do not believe the latter is possible at the moment.

My guide to Indonesian spelling has been:

Alan M. Stevens and A. Ed. Schmidgall-Tellings (2004), *A Comprehensive Indonesian–English Dictionary*, Athens OH: Ohio University Press.

The main problem is that transliterations from Arabic are still not standardized in Indonesia, although there is a consistent trend towards following the system adopted in *Studia Islamika*. I use its system of transliteration except in cases of doubt, where I use that of *Encyclopaedia of Islam* (second edition). I have tried to strike a balance between fidelity to the primary sources and standard usage that directs the reader to the correct (Arabic) technical classes. However, the reader must accept that inconsistency is the norm.

Translations from the Qur'ān are taken from:

Abdallah Yousuf Ali (1934), *The Glorious Kur'an*, Lahore: Call of Islam Society

and

M.A.S. Abdel Haleem (2004), *The Qur'an*, Oxford: Oxford University Press.

The former may appear archaic to the modern reader, although to those brought up on the King James version of the Old and New Testaments it has a sort of comfortable resonance. Haleem (2004: xxvi ff.) provides a good short introduction to the issues involved in translating the Qur'ān into English. For some striking examples of just how much translations can differ, the reader may wish to consult Ruthven (2006: 100–3).

Glossary

adab	civilization, culture
adat	customs, customary laws
ahkam	system of prescription
ahl al-Kitab	'People of the Book'; term used in the Qur'ān to refer to Jews and Christians, who, like Muslims, have scriptures recognized as having been revealed by God
ahlus sunnah waljamaah	'those who follow the tradition of the Prophet and the [consensus of the] community'; long-hand term for the majority Sunni branch within Islam, though some self-ascribed Sunni groups use the term in a narrow and exclusivist way
ahwal al-shakhisiyah	Islamic civil law
akhlak / akhlaq	ethics, character
'alim	singular of *'ulamā'*
aqidah	creed, religious belief, theology
Arafah	the name of a plain 27 kilometres southwest of Mecca where all pilgrims must assemble on the ninth day of the pilgrimage month to perform *wukuf*
azan	the call to prayer
Badan Wakaf Indonesia	Indonesian Wakaf Board
bahtsul masail	forum for the examination of disputed issues
Baitulmal/*bait ul-mal*	'State Treasury', a centralized institution for administering *zakat*
BAZ	Badan Amil Zakat (Zakat Collection Board)
BPAH	Badan Pengelola Asrama Haji (Board for Management of Hajj Accommodation)
BPH	*biro perjalanan haji* (*hajj* travel agency)
BPHI	Balai Pengobatan Hajj Indonesia (Hall for the Medical Care of Indonesian Pilgrims)
CE	Common Era

dakwah	outreach, proselytizing
Dana Abadi Umat	Islamic Community Perpetual Fund
dar ul-harb	'realm of war'; non-Muslim lands
dhimmi	non-Muslims accorded protection of life and property in Muslim lands
din	religion, faith; more specifically, living in obedience to God (for which one will be held accountable on the Day of Judgment
do'a	prayers
DPR	Dewan Perwakilan Rakyat (People's Representative Council); also known as the House of Representatives or parliament
DPRD	Dewan Perwakilan Rakyat Daerah (regional assembly)
dzikir / dzikr	'remembrance'; repetition of phrases containing the name of God, chanted repeatedly to 'remember' or be mindful of God
Dzulhijjah	the last month in the Muslim calendar; the *hajj* is performed during this month
ekonomi Islam	Islamic economics
ekonomi syariah	syariah economics
farā'id	rules on inheritance set down in the Qur'ān and Hadith
fatāwā	plural of *fatwā*
fatwā	ruling on a point of law or dogma given by a scholar who has the authority to do so
fiqh	formal rules of classical law, prescriptions
fitnah	deviation
fitrah	payment required at the end of Ramadan
five pillars of Islam	(1) profession of faith (*shahadah*); (2) performance of ritual prayers (*shalat*); (3) fasting (*sawm*); (4) payment of the wealth tax (*zakat*); and (5) performance of the pilgrimage (*hajj*)
FPI	Front Pembela Islam (Islamic Defenders Front)
Guided Democracy	the system of government during the Soekarno era (1945–65)
Hadith	report or account of the words and deeds of the Prophet Muhammad transmitted through an accepted chain of narrators
Hajar Aswad	the Black Stone (in the Ka'bah)
hajj / haji	the annual pilgrimage to Mecca (and one of the five pillars of Islam)
halal	lawful, permitted

haram	forbidden, something prohibited by *fiqh*
Haramain	the cities of Mecca and Medina
Hijiri	the Islamic calendar
Hijrah	the Prophet's flight from Mecca to Medina (622 CE); New Year; the base date for the Muslim calendar
hikmah	underlying rationale for a new case (see *'illa, qiyas*); wisdom, insight
HTI	Hizbut Tahrir Indonesia (Liberation Party of Indonesia)
hudud	plural of Arabic *hadd* ('limit', 'prohibition'); a legal term for the offences and punishments set out in the Qur'an and Hadith, with the prescribed penalties ranging from various forms of corporal punishment to death
hukum negara	law state, law-based state
IAIN	Institut Agama Islam Negeri (State Islamic Institute); provides degrees at tertiary level
ibadah	worship, prescribed ritual duty
Idul Adha	religious festival celebrated during the *hajj*, commemorating Abraham's willingness to sacrifice his son for God
Idul Fitri	religious festival at the end of Ramadan
ihram	a state of ritual purity for pilgrims before beginning the *hajj* and *umrah*, signified by special dress and behaviour
ijma'	consensus of expert legal opinion
ijtihad	independent judgment, based on recognized sources of Islam, on a legal or theological question (in contrast to *taqlid*, judgment based on tradition or convention)
'illa	effective cause for the extension of an existing principle to a new case/circumstance
imam	an Islamic leader, often the leader of prayers in a mosque
iman	faith
Isra'	the Night Journey (of the Prophet)
istihsan	finding the right principle from texts by exercising reason
jamrah/*jamarat*	see *lontar jamrah*
jihad	'to strive', 'to exert', 'to fight'
jilbab	head covering, headscarf (for women)
jinayah	criminal matters

Ka'bah	cube-like building located in the Grand Mosque (Masjid Haram) in Mecca
kabupaten	district, region
kalam	dialectical theology/philosophy
kecamatan	subdistrict
khatib	preacher at a mosque, mosque official
KHI	Kompilasi Hukum Islam (Compilation of Islamic Law)
khilafah Islamiya	Islamic caliphate
khutbah	the Friday sermon
kitab kuning	'yellow books' (a reference to the colour of the pages);commentaries on the Qur'ān and Islamic law used as teaching texts in *pesantren*
kloter	*kelompok terbang* (travel group)
kota	city, municipality
KPPSI	Committee for the Enforcement of Islamic Syariah (Komite Penegakan Syari'at Islam)
KPSI	Committee for the Preparation of Enforcement of Islamic Syariah (Komite Persiapan Penegakan Syari'at Islam)
KUA	Kantor Urusan Agama (Religious Affairs Office)
KUHP	Kitab Undang-Undang Hukum Perdata (Civil Code)
kyai	religious expert, title for the head of a *pesantren* (Java)
Lailatul Qadar	the Night of Power (during Ramadan)
Landraad	civil native court (Dutch period)
LAZ	Lembaga Amil Zakat (Zakat Collection Agency)
LIPI	Lembaga Ilmu Pengetahuan Indonesia (Indonesian Institute of Sciences)
lontar jamrah	ritual 'stoning of the devil' during the *hajj* at Mina
mabit	waiting, staying; one of the rites of the *hajj* and *umrah*
madrasah	Islamic school
Mahkamah Agung	Supreme Court
Mahkamah Syariah	Syariah Court
Majlis Tarjih	Majlis Tarjih dan Pengembangan Pemikiran Islam (Council on Law-making and Development of Islamic Thought); founded by Muhammadiyah in 1927
maqasid al-syariah	the five purposes or aims of syariah: protection of religion, protection of life (self), protection of

	generations (family), protection of property and protection of intellect
masālah al-mursalah	public interest, the public good
masjid	mosque
Masjid Haram	the Grand Mosque (in Mecca)
Masjid Nabawi	the Prophet's Mosque (in Medina)
maslahah	benefit, the public good (see *masālah al-mursalah*)
Masyumi	Majelis Syuro Muslimin Indonesia (Indonesian Muslim Consultative Council)
mazhab	'direction'; school of legal thought; the four main schools in Sunni Islam are Shafi'i, Maliki, Hanafi and Hanbali, distinguished from each other by their different methods of jurisprudential reasoning
mazhab nasional	a national school of legal thought
mazhab syariah	a national syariah
Mi'raj	the Ascension (of the Prophet, during the Night Journey)
MKDK	Mata Kuliah Dasar Keahlian (Basic Skills Subjects)
MKDU	Mata Kuliah Dasar Umum (General Basic Subjects)
MKK	Mata Kuliah Keahlian (Specialist Skills Subjects)
MMI	Majelis Mujahidin Indonesia (Council of Indonesian Mujahideen)
MPR	Majelis Permusyawaratan Rakyat (People's Consultative Assembly)
MPU	Majlis Permusyawaratan Ulama (Consultative Council of Ulama) (Aceh)
mu'amalat	principles of law dealing with non-ritual human/ social relations, especially contracts
muballigh	itinerant or lay preacher or speaker (male)
muballighah	itinerant or lay preacher or speaker (female)
Muhammadiyah	modernist Islamic organization founded in 1912
MUI	Majelis Ulama Indonesia (Indonesian Council of Ulama)
New Order	the Soeharto era (1966–98)
NU	Nahdlatul Ulama (Revival of the Religious Scholars); traditionalist Islamic organization founded in 1926
Nuzulul Qur'ān	the day on which the Qur'ān was first revealed to the Prophet (in Indonesia, the 17th day of Ramadan)

Old Order	the Soekarno era (1945–65)
P-4	Pedoman Penghayatan dan Pengamalan Pancasila (Guidelines for Instilling and Experiencing Pancasila) (official government publications)
Pancasila	the five guiding principles of the Indonesian state (belief in God, humanitarianism, national unity, democracy and social justice)
pengadilan agama	religious court
peraturan	regulation, decree
perda	*peraturan daerah* (regional regulation)
perna	*peraturan nagari* (district regulation, West Sumatra)
Persis	Persatuan Islam (Islamic Association); reformist Islamic organization founded in 1923
pesantren	traditional Islamic boarding school
PKI	Partai Kommunis Indonesia (Indonesian Communist Party)
PPIH	Panitia Penyelenggaraan Ibadah Haji (Hajj Management Committee)
PPOH	Panitia Pelaksanaan Operasional Haji (Committee for the Operational Implementation of the Hajj)
Priesteraad	priests' court (Dutch period)
puskesmas	*pusat keselamatan massa* (community health centre)
qanun	regional statute or regulation (Aceh)
qath'iy	a definitive or categorical principle in the Qur'ān or Hadith whose meaning cannot be negotiated or reinterpreted
qisas	retribution through compensation as punishment for capital crimes and assault, the extreme form of compensation being 'a life for a life'
qiyas	in Islamic law, reasoning by analogy to solve a new issue
Qur'ān	God's word revealed to the Prophet Muhammad and the supreme source and absolute authority for Islam
Ramadan	ninth month of the Islamic calendar during which fasting is required
riba	interest, increase on capital
sa'i	'seeking', 'trying'; one of the rites of the *hajj* and *umrah*
salat	see *shalat*

Shafi'i	one of the four main schools in Sunni Islam and the dominant school in Southeast Asia
shalat	the prescribed ritual prayer to be performed five times a day
Shi'a	second largest branch of Islam after Sunni
siyasah	policy, the practical application of the Qur'ān and Sunnah in the world
siyasah–jinayah	constitutional and public law
SK	*surat keterangan* (letter of instruction)
STAIN	Sekolah Tinggi Agama Islam Negeri (State Islamic College)
Sufism	mysticism; its doctrine
Sunnah	custom, usage; established custom and normative precedent in Islam based on the example of the Prophet Muhammad
Sunni	following or followers of early established traditions; the majority branch of Islam; in law, it means the law schools (Shafi'i, Maliki, Hanafi, Hanbali)
syariah	Islamic law in the broadest sense, concept of law
ta'zir	punishment administered at the discretion of the judge, as opposed to *hudud* or *hadd* (punishments for certain offences fixed by the Qur'an or Hadith)
tafsir	exegesis of the Qur'an
taqlid	close following of accepted texts/authority of one of the four Sunni schools, unquestioning acceptance
taqwa	consciousness of God, fear of God
tasawwuf	Mysticism
tauhid	the doctrine of the unity of God; in Sufism, merging with the unity of the universe
tawaf	circumambulating the Ka'bah seven times during the *hajj* and *umrah*
UIN	Universitas Islam Negeri (State Islamic University)
'ulamā'	Islamic scholars (plural of *'alim*)
ummah	the Islamic community in the sense of 'all Muslims'
umrah	a pilgrimage to Mecca that can be undertaken at any time of the year [delete]
undang	law, law text
ustadz	teacher (male)
ustadzah	teacher (female)

wakaf	donation for pious purposes
wali	guardian
waris	heir
Wilayatul Hisbah	the syariah police authority in Aceh
wukuf	'stopping' or 'staying' on the plain of Arafah; one of the obligatory rites of the *hajj*
yurisprudensi	decision of a court
zakat maal	general calculation of *zakat* based on disposable income
zakat	'wealth tax', the payment of which is one of the five pillars of Islam

1   Syariah in the State: The New *Fiqh*

In the contemporary world of Islam we have by now become accustomed to the
fact that the formal expression of syariah differs from region to region. In practice
this means that we have to be specific as to place and time when answering the
question, 'What is syariah and how is it known?' At the level of nations—Egypt,
Tunisia, Saudi Arabia, India, Malaysia and so on—we can give a specific reply
to this question, but for the Islamic world as a whole there is no answer except
at some almost meaningless level of generality. It is also possible to answer the
question in terms of Western forms of law, that is, civil and common law reformulations which show, for example, that Malaysia and India have quite a lot in
common whereas Malaysia and Indonesia do not, despite their similar languages
and culture. In short, syariah in practice is various, not homogenous.

These comments should not be read as saying that the formal rules of positive
law (*fiqh*) in the classical texts are no longer of any significance. It is easy to suppose this because of the nineteenth and twentieth-century state reformulations of
'Islamic' or 'Muslim' law, but it is wrong. Perhaps the best way of putting it is to
say that the classical *fiqh* texts are *fundamental* but no longer *primary* on a day-
to-day basis. This is not a paradox but, I believe, a plain assessment of fact.

The idea that *fiqh* is no longer important has come about because of the
dominance of Western forms of law. However, as I argue below, that dominance
is by no means uncontested. The main characteristic of state dominance is *selection*: the practice of taking from the classical (Arabic) legal thought that which
is held to be appropriate for a particular state at a given time. The motives for
particular selections vary according to the political circumstances of the time
and place. But whatever the motives are, they all have in common a belief in the
inevitability of the process. Even the contemporary calls for an 'Islamic state',
while generally vague as to the substance of the law, do admit the necessity for
modern bureaucratic structures and some degree of legal borrowing from outside the syariah.

The result of selection is a change in the character of the syariah. This is
well marked in Indonesia, no less than in other Muslim countries. For example,
the pre-modern law texts of the Malay and Javanese world exhibit three sorts of

1

changes in the received syariah tradition. First, the Java ('Agama') texts took nothing from *fiqh*. Instead, the name/title Allah was used to give legitimacy to the entire content of the law. Second, at about the same time (the late seventeenth century), the Melaka laws incorporated clearly identifiable passages of *fiqh*, but just as clearly subordinated them to local regulations.[1] These were the *adat negeri*—the customs of the country. We can call this a positive selection, but one that gave *fiqh* a subordinate value. Third, slightly later, in the mid-eighteenth century, the Minangkabau texts from West Sumatra show us that the authors recognized a conflict in principle between *fiqh* and local custom, and attempted not just to reconcile difference but actually to explain it away. While the arguments were specious, they were also useful from a practical point of view because they allowed room for obfuscation.[2]

In all these examples, the syariah has certainly changed character. Equally important is the fact that the main texts show a sophisticated grasp of technical legal reasoning. Selection and variation involve not just the acceptance or rejection of the content of a rule, but also the manipulation of *methods* of legal reasoning. This is significant, because it shows technically intelligent selection. Unfortunately this last point was lost on nineteenth-century European scholarship (the Dutch in the Netherlands East Indies and the British in the neighbouring Malay states).

The implications of this failure were immense and are still with us today in that area of study that we now call orientalism. What this has meant for the indigenous law texts was that they were seen as 'corrupted', that is, as deviating from the classical Middle Eastern (Arabic) originals. It followed, therefore, that they were not 'law', and that Indonesian Islam was 'impure' and not true. It followed, further, that Indonesian Muslims were only 'nominal' Muslims and that the syariah was not and never could be an appropriate system of law for them.

We return to these points later, but for now we need to pursue the idea of variety a little further. The issue can be stated simply: the law texts existed and called themselves 'law texts' (*undang*), but they were not in a form recognized by European scholars and administrators. The latter defined or selected texts that were law according to their own training and practice (in nineteenth-century Europe). At best, the *undang* of Muslim Southeast Asia were seen as corruptions of 'pure' syariah; they were a variant form. The scholarship of the period followed from this view. We can see now that the idea of variant form and variety of expression came from the educational background of the scholar or administrator. That person was the key to the formation of later colonial policy. He (and all were male) was taught the classical *fiqh*, even though the classical texts were not much in evidence in Indonesia. In this lay the origin of the 'Great Tradition—little tradition' debate. Essentially at issue was whether, for law, the Southeast

---

1   For a full range of examples for the pre-modern period, see Hooker (1986).

2   For detailed argument, see Hooker (1986: 356 ff.).

Asian texts were 'copies' or 'distortions' of the Greater (Indian, Islamic, Chinese) originals. We now know that they were not. There was a regional originality or, rather, many originalities. This was not apparent to the nineteenth and twentieth-century scholars, who were blinded both by their own education and by imperial duty. It was thus the colonial civil servants who were selecting and inventing their own variant forms.

Whether derived from Islamic scholarship or the imposition of European definitions of law, selection and variant forms have a long history in Indonesian syariah texts. Post-independence, there have been further examples of selection, each with its accompanying variation of syariah. We now trace the development of this new *fiqh* through the religious courts, the Compilation of Islamic Law (Kompilasi Hukum Islam; KHI), some aspects of finance and some contemporary rulings on points of law or dogma (*fatāwā*).[3] These are what the state means by syariah; from the state's point of view, together they constitute a distinctly Indonesian school of legal thought—that is, an Indonesian national *mazhab*.

1   SYARIAH AND THE STATE

From the nineteenth century, as European dominance over Muslim lands spread, God was displaced as the sole source of authority and as the only legitimate foundation for rule and sovereignty. To put it bluntly, He was no longer necessary as prime mover. Instead, various forms of secular constitutionalism became the operative principle. The first example I look at here is syariah under the colonial state.

Syariah under the Colonial State

In the Netherlands East Indies, syariah was selected out. This meant that it had no independent existence within the colonial legal system. In political terms, the syariah was suppressed; it was not even in the selection race. In the language of the time, it had never been 'received' by Indonesian Muslims as valid prescription. As we would say now, it did not pass the test of efficacy so as to truly constitute a legal system (Raz 1970). As a result it fell into a sort of limbo, with its very existence conditional on some sort of acknowledgment by customary laws (*adat*). This is the reception theory (*teori recepsie*) much anathemized by later generations of Indonesian syariah scholars as *teori iblis*—a 'theory of the Devil' (Hazairin 1951). How did it come about that nearly 1,300 years of jurisprudence were dismissed so summarily? Why did not the evidence of the pre-modern texts suggest to the Dutch scholars and administrators that the syariah was in

---

3   In this book I follow the Indonesian and Arabic in using *fatwā* for the singular and *fatāwā* for the plural.

fact known (commented on with considerable originality) and alive, making it a candidate for selection or recognition? There are two interconnected answers that, between them, respond to these questions. The period of importance here is the 1850s to 1920s, though I do not suggest that these dates are absolutely fixed. This was a period of high colonialism for the Dutch in the Netherlands East Indies—as it was for the British and French elsewhere. But by 1900 or even earlier, the justification for European imperialism was in question. The violent oscillations that were occurring in colonial policy, including legal policy, were an essential context for syariah in these years.

The first answer is the obvious one, that until quite late in the nineteenth century the Dutch in fact knew very little about Islam in general and syariah in particular. The Dutch East India Company (Verenigde Oostindische Compagnie; VOC) was not interested except insofar as 'political Islam' impinged on its activities, and to a large extent this remained true well into the nineteenth century. But, as is usual, politics eventually forced the Dutch to pay attention to Islam and, by extension, to syariah. In addition, the demands of efficient colonial administration for the extensive Dutch-controlled and indirectly administered territories made the acquisition of such knowledge imperative. Courses in 'Muhammadan law' proliferated in special institutions, the official Office for Native and Arab Affairs and universities (Fasseur 1993). This was not 'pure' learning for its own sake—it was always directed towards the purposes of imperialism, which is where the roots of orientalism lie. Just as important for our purposes here is the *type* of knowledge about syariah acquired in these institutions. The syariah was taught in its classical (Arabic) form, which was not its form as generally understood by Muslims in the Netherlands East Indies (the small and confined circle of religious scholars, or *'ulamā'*, excepted). Local practices believed by Indonesian Muslims to be 'Islamic' were thus dismissed by Dutch scholarship as at best corrupted versions of the classical canon.[4] Indonesian Muslims were therefore 'nominal' rather than 'real' Muslims; it followed that the (classical) syariah was inapplicable or inappropriate. In this way scholarship provided an intellectual backing for the formal colonial legal policy, which we conventionally date from 1854.[5]

The second answer to what happened to the syariah lies in the colonial administration's legal policy, which had as its fundamental premise that the laws for the population of the Netherlands East Indies should appropriately be determined on a racial basis. For the Dutch or persons assimilated to that status, this meant the Dutch law; for native Indonesians it meant one of the various *adat* laws. The syariah, as such, had no independent or recognized status within this system. By syariah was meant the classical canon. However, as a practical concession, some

---

4   The 'Great Tradition—little tradition' debate referred to earlier (see Wolters 1982).
5   This is the year in which the reformed Constitution for the Netherlands East Indies was promulgated (see Burns 1988).

localized version of syariah in family matters was recognized to the extent that it was acknowledged in *adat*, that is, to the extent that it could be proved to have been received by customary practice as a viable working principle. Whatever one might think now, the fact remains that the syariah, in whatever distorted form, was dependent, a far cry from its status in pre-colonial Muslim states. Another aspect of this dependency is found in the priests' court (Priesteraad) established by the Dutch for Java and Madura in 1882. This court was given a limited jurisdiction (over dowries and marriage), but its decisions could only be enforced with the consent of the civil court for natives (Landraad).[6] The later reform of the Priesteraad (in 1937) actually limited its jurisdiction even further. Thus, syariah was doubly dependent: it was dependent on *adat* reception and it was also dependent on civil law process.

In short, the syariah was effectively selected out of the formal legal system. Did this mean that the classical canon disappeared in the Netherlands East Indies? The answer is that it did not. It remained in the Islamic boarding schools (*pesantren*), where the Arabic texts were taught as an essential and often quite sophisticated element of the curriculum (van Bruinessen 1990). From the 1890s and especially the 1920s, it also remained in *fatāwā* (Kaptein 1995; Hooker 2003a). It had an independent existence, but one that was outside the formal colonial legal structure. Its outsider status was part of the legal life of the Netherlands East Indies until 1942 and has remained to plague succeeding generations from the 1950s. Also from that time, we can see attempts to reverse this selected-out dependency.

The Rise of Political Islam

As World War II drew to a close, nationalists, both Muslim and non-Muslim, were united in a common desire to achieve independence. However, they were in serious disagreement as to whether the foundations of the new state of Indonesia should be Islamic or secular. That disagreement went well back into the 1930s and has been fully documented by Noer (1973) among others. Briefly, on one side one had prominent modernists like Mohammad Natsir and Ahmad Hassan arguing that revelation was primary.[7] The implication of such a view was that society had to be reformed through the implementation of syariah, which was both a tool and an end in itself. The secular nationalists argued that this was impractical and that it would be a retrograde step in the circumstances of the contemporary world.

The argument was, and remains, unresolvable; there was no common ground or middle position from which one could proceed. However, this has not stopped

---

6   For details, see Hooker (1984: 249 ff.).

7   On the *fatāwā* of Ahmad Hassan, see Hooker (2003a).

the issue from being raised, generation after generation, and it continues today without resolution. But although resolution is not really possible in the sense of being able to invent a coherent legal system that satisfies both secular and Islamic demands, steps towards an *accommodation* are feasible given the requisite political will. This depends, however, on mutual understanding of what a nation-state is and what it does. In the 1940s that understanding was even more bitterly contested than it is today.

After much wrangling, the Islamic and nationalist leaders agreed on a secular constitution based on five principles (Pancasila), the first of which was belief in one God.[8] Controversially, however, seven words that would have obliged Muslims to implement syariah were excluded from the preamble to the Constitution (the Jakarta Charter) when it was promulgated in August 1945. The context of these events is important: the Japanese occupation (1942–45), the independence war (1945–49) and the undefined nature of 'syariah'. Despite the lack of consensus on what it actually meant, *syariah* was a factor (for many, *the* factor) in the formation of the new state, and therefore a crucial political factor in the 1945 Constitution. All constitutions are of course about power, but they are also technical–legal documents about how the distribution of power is to operate. Many 'secular state' constitutions refer to God but operate perfectly well in His effective absence. Poorly drafted though it is, the 1945 Constitution also has this capacity in the important distributive–technical areas.[9] Although written in Indonesian, its language is conceptually European in that the key concepts are derived from Dutch, German and French constitutional thought. This is not a facile observation, nor is it a criticism. It is an acknowledgment that formal drafting must always be read for and in its time—here, 1945.

As one would expect, the 'God reference' is tangential in the five principles that make up the Pancasila. But although it is only a minor premise on the technical law side, it is a major one in politics. The problem for the proponents of syariah has been how to convert the latter into the former, in short, from God as tangential to syariah as primary. I do not wish to push the Western analogy too strongly. But the drafters of the Constitution were in fact heavily influenced by the Western secular tradition, and this has remained the position of Indonesian governments to the present day. God, in the form of the first principle of the Pancasila, was written into the Constitution 60 years ago, and He is therefore as much an object of that history as is any other provision. That is the objective point of view, but it is not one which is necessarily decisive in Indonesian Islamic thought. The ongoing debate over the words dropped from the final version of the Constitution is evidence of the continuation of this fundamental argument.

---

8   The five principles are: (1) belief in one God, (2) humanitarianism, (3) national unity, (4) democracy and (5) social justice.
9   For citations from the elucidation to the Constitution, see Hooker (2003a: 18–19).

With these cautions in mind, we can now turn to the debate, although in what follows there is space only for summary comment.[10] For the 30 years of the New Order regime (1966–98), Pancasila was the basis of Indonesian state ideology. In 1966 the People's Consultative Assembly (Majelis Permusyawaratan Rakyat; MPR) declared it to be 'the source of all legal principles of the Republic [and unchangeable]'. The 1970 Law on Judicial Powers (Law No. 14/1970, article 3(2)) stated that 'upholding the law is based on Pancasila'. Pancasila was routinely cited, or at least referred to, in the preamble to all laws promulgated, including the KHI (see below). In 1978 the Soeharto government went even further, publishing its Guidelines for Instilling and Practising Pancasila (*Pedoman Penghayatan dan Pengamalan Pancasila*)—the so-called P-4 (Ismail 2004: 127 ff.). It elaborated all five of the Pancasila principles by explaining the values and norms associated with each, and set guidelines for instruction classes, including compulsory classes for government servants and state education institutions (Ismail 2004: 134 ff.).

From the Muslim point of view, the P-4 material (quite vast in bulk) raised two difficulties. First, the sheer scale and intensity of the instruction process on norms and values seemed to indicate that the Pancasila had itself become sacrilized—that the 'Pancasila morality' was either a religion or an alternative to religion. There were strong objections to this from well-known Muslim authorities, including Mohammad Natsir and Abdul Qadir Djaelani, based on Q3:19 (Ismail 2004: 154–7).[11] For example, Ismail (2004: 155) cites Sjafruddin Prawinagara as saying:

> ... formerly there was no 'Pancasila Morality' because problems of morality were left up to the individual religions. Then a committee was established consisting of people regarded as 'smart'—not a single *ulama* of good standing in the Muslim community was included—and this committee of smart people drafted a kind of holy writ filled with moral prescriptions that had to be studied and practised by all citizens, yet not all these prescriptions could be swallowed by the Muslims, for many of them contained tenets in conflict with Islamic teachings.

The second objection was that some passages in the textbooks explaining the P-4 guidelines—collectively called Pancasila Morality Education (*Pendidikan Moral Pancasila*)—could be interpreted as directly contradicting some Islamic principles. For example, the textbooks asserted that all religions were equal, and permitted Muslims to attend non-Muslim rituals and pray for members of other religions. This was not acceptable to Muslims, for whom Islam is the final and superior revelation. The government response was to insist that Pancasila be accepted as the national ideology of Indonesia while asserting that this acceptance should not be seen as an attack on any religion. On the contrary, because

---

10 A good full account is given in Ismail (2004).
11 Q3:19 reads: '... True religion is Islam ... if anyone denies the revelations of God, God is swift to take account' [Haleem].

Pancasila was for the national benefit and not itself a religion, it could be compatible with all religions, including Islam. Recognizing that compatibility was the key to gaining acceptance of Pancasila, in 1982 the government, *through the Department of Religion*,[12] issued its Guide for Implementing P-4 for Muslims (Departemen Agama 1982).

The basic proposition of this text is that by performing their religious duties correctly and faithfully, individuals are fulfilling the values of Pancasila. The values expressed in Pancasila are in fact reflections of religious principles, here Islam. The text provides examples to show the truth of this proposition. To cite a few examples taken from Ismail (2004: 172 ff.), the first principle, belief in one God, reflects *tauhid*, the oneness of God; it is supported by verses from the Qur'ān and selections from Hadith—in this instance Q112:1 and Hadith from al-Bukharī. Again, religious tolerance in the Pancasila is an expression of Q3:64 and Q41:15. The Pancasila principle of human equality can be read compatibly with Q49:13, '... We have created you that you may know each other ...', and so on *ad infinitum*.

The device of selective citation is not new; all religions have been and still are subject to their texts being used in this way. The incidence of the practice seems to rise in times of crisis or perceived crisis, with Indonesian Islam being no exception in this respect.[13] This is not our direct concern here, but it is important to understand the problems caused by selective citation. First, a selective citation can always be met by a counter-citation. Commonly, no criteria are given for that which is selected, so that a citation is personal, always ahistorical in the area of Islam, and therefore insufficient to maintain an argument. Second, and if this were not enough, there is no *necessary* connection between the proposition and the citation which purportedly supports it. The putative connection is faith based, and faith as such is not a proof in the argument. Of course this is not a position which Islamists can accept.

The consequences of rejecting the arguments against selective citation are twofold. First, in practical terms no rational discussion between 'secularists' and 'believers' is possible, even with all the goodwill in the world. At best there is only a fog of mutual incomprehension. The only way of resolving the position is by coercion; Pancasila is an ideological example of this alternative. Second, because selective citation *is always for a purpose*, it is the purpose that becomes a 'good' in itself. The result may be a denial of science[14] and, indeed, of any

---

12 Also called the Ministry of Religious Affairs. I use Department of Religion in this book.
13 See the examples in Fealy and Hooker (2006: 167–75).
14 The example with which most of us are familiar is 'Bucaillism', named for the French surgeon Maurice Bucaille. Bucaillism proposes that the principles of modern science are stated in the Qur'ān (see Bucaille 1979). But this is to argue backwards—that is, based on selective citation, to read into contemporary science a passage from the Qur'ān which predicts the latest discoveries in physics, astronomy and so on, even

intellectual rigour. The consequences of this are political and social corruption in the widest sense. The idea that a religion and a state ideology are mutually reflective and/or compatible is certainly ahistorical, and the Islam–Pancasila nexus is no exception.

Nevertheless, even the reflective 'Islamic' values in the Pancasila did produce some positive results in New Order Indonesia, two such being the reform of the religious courts in 1989 and the introduction of the KHI in 1991. People may question the motives for these innovations but the fact remains that they did occur. One can say that the 'Islamic' heritage has been mined or manipulated, but there has been a positive syariah selection in these two instances. We can be sure that there are no certainties for syariah in the Constitution and Pancasila (and its P-4 guidelines). Whether or not the much talked about 'fading' (*pudar*) of Pancasila will have any further impact is a matter for future politics.[15] It should be noted, however, that post-New Order, the right to make selections and choices is much disputed, and no longer the preserve of the central state alone. The regions are making their own selections of syariah and values, expressed in regional regulations (see Chapter 6).

2   THE RELIGIOUS COURTS

As noted earlier, the Dutch selected syariah out on the ground that it was not received. To this they added (in the 1900s to 1930s) discussion of the theoretical issues in private international law (conflicts of law) which the French had been busy developing in Indochina.[16] The basic proposition, as understood by the Dutch, was that the rules of private international law could be made to apply, by analogy, to places like the Netherlands East Indies that had discrete legal universes. The Dutch pointed to the race-based categories in the colonial law groups which they had developed as discrete systems since the late nineteenth century. The problem was that the syariah determined obligation (and rights) on the basis of religious adherence, not nationality or domicile. The fact remained that the majority of Indonesians were Muslims, for whom race and culture were

though the Qur'ān is not predictive in the scientific sense of observation, hypothesis and experiment. Some Muslim scientists themselves make this point (see, for example, Hoodbhoy 1992: 68). Bucaillism is nevertheless quite popular. The reader might like to look at a video—The Book of Signs—produced in 1986 by the Malaysia-based Regional Islamic Council of Southeast Asia and the Pacific and approved by Al-Azhar and the Rabitah Al-Alam Al-Islami of Saudi Arabia. One can see its appeal for the scientifically illiterate. For an Ahmadiyya version of Bucaillism, see Ahmad (1998).

15 For the legal implications of the idea of fading, see Waddell (2005).

16 With disastrous effect; see Hooker (1978: 175 ff.). For French theory, see Solus (1927).

not categories in the definition of duty. There was therefore no possible meeting point between these two views of attributing obligation.

The Dutch solution was to create the inferior courts referred to earlier (the Priesteraad) with a severely limited jurisdiction and subject to the 'greater power', on analogy with private international law principles. The greater power was the secular court system, which could accept or reject a finding of the subordinate religious court and which was, in all cases, responsible for the implementation of procedure and decisions.[17] Money and property, including the transmission of property, were excluded from the consideration of the religious courts. The whole system was impractical and widely recognized as such (see Hisyam 2000: 100 ff.) but it was nevertheless maintained through to the end of the colonial regime and even beyond. The Dutch legacy was the creation of a discrete, separate and subordinate world of religious jurisdiction.

The essence of private international law is conflict; that is what its principles deal with. This way of thinking about syariah, syariah courts and the state was carried through into post-independence Indonesia, where the acceptance of discrete legal worlds continued. However, in the actual practice of the religious courts the judges took a different line. Perhaps because of the very restrictions under which they were supposed to work, the judges invented devices to avoid the discrete-world legacy, that is, the problem of limited jurisdiction. Two such devices, both instances of pure selection from classical *fiqh*, may serve as examples.[18] The first was the device of issuing a *fatwā*. This was quite out of place, as judges do not issue *fatāwā* in the classical jurisprudence. That is the function of the mufti, whose traditions and training are quite different (Hooker 2003a). What we have in fact is a new *use* of the *fatwā* form for a purpose (to avoid lack of jurisdiction) and in the context of a court. The second device was to convert the idea of mediation in marital disagreements (*shikak* or *syikak)* into a judicial discretion to allow women to petition for divorce. Strictly speaking this was a quite unwarranted extension of the original form, but again, it filled a deficiency in the existing jurisdiction of the court.

The fact that judges felt forced to adopt these devices is a clear indication of the day-to-day crises they faced. Their response was to make decisions that had no basis in existing law. One can understand the motive to do justice in the individual case, but at the same time this meant that there could be no nationally consistent response to common problems in divorce, maintenance and so on. All would depend on how the individual judge saw his own role. The later Law on Religious Justice (No. 7/1989) again left considerable room for judicial initiative. Our concern is not with the law itself, which has been described in detail by others (see Cammack 1997), but with two other issues. First, which is more important, justice in the individual case or consistency of system? And second,

---

17 For details and sources, see Hooker (1984: 249 ff.).
18 These were first brought to attention by Lev (1972b).

what is the source of law, God or the state? The Law on Religious Justice is so drafted that alternative answers to the same problems are possible and in fact occur.

The evidence for this variability is in the *yurisprudensi*, the decisions (of various levels) of the religious courts. Drawing on these decisions is not without risk. They rarely contain a comprehensive discussion of principle,[19] so can only be used as illustrations and, perhaps, as showing a trend in judicial thinking. With this caution I take some illustrative decisions on the subject of marriage, always a contested area in state–syariah relations.[20]

Decisions are made by a panel of judges who are likely to hold widely varying perceptions about what a judge does or should do.[21] To take a striking example, one judge from the first-level court in Sleman, just outside Yogyakarta, has said that he includes both written and unwritten laws in his definition of law.[22] The former exist in law texts (*undang*), regulations (*peraturan*) and the KHI. The latter may be *adat* (customs), but not necessarily in their written form. Instead, *adat* has a deeper meaning, found in the social values and norms of society. The individual has a naturally occurring feeling for these and they thus constitute justice for that person. The judge specifically referred to the views of the late Professor Moh. Koesnoe; active in the 1960s and 1970s, he was a strong advocate for the fundamental nature of *adat* values—a rather unfashionable view at the time (Koesnoe 1969, 1970). The judge locates the values, norms or feelings of justice in the judicial process itself; they can be found or identified by way of discussion in the court involving all the parties. A compromise based on a mutually accepted understanding of justice is thus possible. That compromise may or may not be consonant with the written law. If it is not, then the written law must give way or, at best, be interpreted so as to give priority to these values. While cases may be similar, they are never the same; therefore, consistency of judgment is not a value in itself. For this reason, consistency and certainty are

---

19 Indonesian law does not have a doctrine of precedent. Judicial policy on a particular point is set by the Supreme Court through circular letters to the lower courts. Very often judges in the provinces and regions find themselves unable to implement the instructions given in these letters. 'That is all very well in Jakarta, but we cannot do that here; it is not possible in our local conditions' is a typical and often heard comment.

20 Dating from 1991 to 2005, these decisions were collected by the author and Professor Timothy Lindsey between 2003 and 2005. The collection is now held in the Asian Law Centre, University of Melbourne. It includes originals from Aceh; these must be the only records from the religious court in Banda Aceh that survived the 2004 tsunami.

21 Based on interviews with judges in Surabaya, Yogyakarta, Jakarta, Padang and Banda Aceh conducted between 2003 and 2007.

22 Drs. H.A. Mukti Arto, head of the Religious Court, Sleman, 2004 (interviewed by the author and Timothy Lindsey).

best seen as relative. Certainty may be important and have a value of its own in some circumstances, for example in cases of title to land and property where it is necessary to comply with positive law. However, where a case is about balancing individual interests (such as the distribution of property on divorce), then recourse to positive law (the KHI) may be necessary but is not necessarily fully determinative. Here mediation and compromise are more likely to provide justice. The judge felt strongly that it was the duty of the court process to achieve a degree of harmony among the parties to a dispute.

This judicial view is characterized by a considerable degree of judicial initiative and a willingness to adjust the positive law, in this instance the KHI. The (Arabic) *fiqh* texts can be a valuable resource but in practice are rarely consulted. The texts are not a binding source because they are remote from the practicalities of daily life. At most they are a reference point.

One can contrast this position with that of a group of Islamic High Court judges in Jakarta.[23] Here the emphasis is on the KHI as the appropriate law. At this level, the first-appeal level, decisions are made on the basis of *documents*. The question is thus whether the required technicalities have been properly completed.[24] The judicial reasoning at the higher level is more concerned with bureaucratic technicalities than with the sources of syariah or the explanation of syariah norms as they actually affect society. The individual has become merely a point of reference, so the whole context is different.

Perhaps these general remarks can be put into context by focusing on a series of 10 decisions on polygyny (*poligami*) from Surabaya dating from 2003 to 2005, with a few examples from other places.[25] Men who wish to take a second wife must apply to the religious court for permission to do so. The Qur'ān (Q4:3, Q66:6) allows men to have up to four wives provided equal justice can be shown to each. The practice is controversial but, as the religious court statistics show, very uncommon.[26] The government, through the 1974 Marriage Law and more particularly the KHI, permits polygyny with the 'fundamental precondition ... that the husband must be capable of behaving justly towards all his wives

---

23 Interview, Jakarta, 2004 (interviewed by the author and Timothy Lindsey).

24 I should point out that the number of appeals from the first level to the High Court and Supreme Court is very small, a tiny percentage of the whole. The last year for which complete figures for the whole of Indonesia are available is 1998. They show that out of 160,645 first-instance decisions, only 1,804 went on appeal. Incomplete statistics for 1999 to the present confirm the ratio (statistics supplied by the Department of Religion).

25 Collected in July 2005 from the first and appeal-level religious courts. They are now held in the Asian Law Centre, University of Melbourne.

26 There were 802 applications throughout Indonesia in 1998. For some reason the figures for Surabaya and Semarang were the highest in the country: there were 226 applications in Surabaya and seven appeals in that year, with 215 applications and one appeal in Semarang (statistics supplied by the Department of Religion).

and children' (article 55(2–3)). The existing wife's consent must be obtained, although the court may dispense with this (articles 58(3), 59).

Contrary to what the reader might expect, there is no need to go through the Surabaya decisions individually, because they all conform to the same pattern and have the same result. The Surabaya court is in fact operating on a *pro forma* basis. It works as follows. After the formal identification of all parties, the written consent of the first wife is presented and validated. Then follows a set of what appear to be rote phrases. They read:

> The reason for the applicant wishing to marry again is because the [existing wife] is unable to serve the applicant in fulfilling her obligations as a wife .... [This inability can refer to illness, inflexibility or marital discord—all set out in the KHI.] In order to make certain the applicant can guarantee the livelihoods of his wives and their children, he has made a statement of his income [acceptable to the court given his station in life]. ... Having regard also to the applicant's signed statement that he is able to do justice to his wives. ... The prospective wife states her readiness to be a second wife, and accepts all the risks of being a second wife and is willing to be kind to [the first wife] ..., [and confirms] that there is no relationship between the first and second wives[27]... Therefore, so that the applicant is not tempted into committing acts outside religion [that is, unlawful sex] ... permission is granted.

This standard form is accompanied by references to the standard authorities: Q4:3, article 5(1) of the Marriage Law and article 59(1–2) of the KHI.

I do not wish to suggest that standardization is common practice; we just do not know. By way of contrast one can cite proceedings that commenced in Yogyakarta in 1987 and went all the way to the Supreme Court.[28] The decision (result) was the same at each level, but the reasoning certainly was not, and that is what gives the case its interest for us.[29]

The parties had been married for nine years without children. The husband applied for permission to take a second wife (at this time the operative law was the Marriage Law of 1974) on the ground of infertility of the existing wife. Her chances of a natural pregnancy were slight, as had been medically confirmed in London. The husband was prepared to continue trying, but he was already aged 47; he was also prepared to give 'priority' to his first wife. His income was sufficient to support a second wife: he was a senior bureaucrat, as was his existing wife. He would guarantee the safety of property that had been jointly acquired;

---

27 That is, they are not related by blood or (rather rarely in practice) suckling (*radā '*).

28 PA No. 6/1987 Yogyakarta, No. 17/1987 PTA Surakarta and No. 133/AG/1987 of the Supreme Court. Note that all of these judgments were delivered in the same year, within a matter of months. This is most unusual, and suggests that both parties were highly connected and wealthy.

29 The proceedings took place in 1987, before the Law on Religious Justice (1989) and the KHI (1991). There would seem to have been some jurisdictional problems—the operative law at the time was the Marriage Law of 1974—but these were blithely ignored at all levels. Yogyakarta has about 25 per cent the Surabaya rate of polygyny applications.

he would not divorce the present wife and would maintain her. As a civil servant he had the requisite permission from his superiors to marry again.[30] The wife replied that she could conceive—she had had a miscarriage and an ectopic pregnancy—and asked for time to obtain IVF treatment. The prospective second wife made the formal promise of respect for the first wife and undertook not to attempt to take any jointly acquired property.

The first-level religious court approved the application on the grounds of infertility and permission from the husband's superior having been obtained. It cited the standard verse, Q4:3, but quite unusually also included a Hadith from 'Bajuri',[31] namely: '… if a man has two wives and does not do justice between them, then on the Day of Judgment [punishments will follow]'.

The wife appealed this decision. It is significant that Q4:3 and the Hadith just cited were not considered at all by the appeal court; rather, the fact of infertility was taken, on its own, as sufficient reason to reject the appeal. The appeal court ignored the wife's offer to obtain IVF treatment, despite medical evidence that it could result in pregnancy. It also rejected a new, technical–bureaucratic argument put forward by the wife, that because her husband had been a member of the Indonesian armed forces at the time of the first decision (three months earlier), his permission to remarry should have come from the army rather than (as it did) the governor of Yogyakarta.[32] The Supreme Court concurred that there were no grounds for variation or rehearing: each level of the judicial hierarchy had been correct in its respective findings.

This decision shows that the syariah was not the determining law at the highest level. Instead, it was the validity of the technical arguments that was the crucial factor. This can be illustrated further by examining the vexed issue of inter-religious ('mixed') marriage, a topic on which there has been much comment and disagreement.[33] During the colonial period inter-religious marriage was considered undesirable because it disturbed the race-based boundaries of the separate legal universes; but it was also a fact of life, because people were inconsiderate enough (from the bureaucratic point of view) to wish to marry outside their own religion. The colonial answer was special legislation to regulate the capacity to marry and, more importantly, to deal with its byproducts (children and property).[34] From independence until 1974, the status of inter-religious marriages involving Muslims remained debatable, but unions did occur and

---

30 See generally Butt (1999: 126 ff.).

31 This is Bujayaimi's *Al-Hāshiya* derived from Rāfiī's *Muharrar*, a very unusual reference in Indonesian religious courts.

32 That is how the court read the applicable regulation. The court actually cited only an administrative decision of the chief of staff (army), a highly selective and probably insufficient reference. This practice is not unusual in Indonesian courts.

33 See Pompe (1988, 1991) for analysis and sources. See also Butt (1999).

34 See Pompe (1988) for the history.

were registered in the civil registry. However, with the proposal and eventual realization of a national marriage law for all Indonesian citizens, the issue again became highly charged politically (Katz and Katz 1975).

The issue came down to the interpretation of article 2(1–2) of the Marriage Law of 1974. It says:

> A marriage is legitimate if it has been performed according to the laws of the respective religions and beliefs of the parties concerned.

There is nothing in this sentence to either confirm or deny the possibility of inter-religious marriage. But the crucial part of article 2 is in subsection 2, a point often overlooked in the polemics. It says:

> Every marriage shall be registered according to the laws in force.

This is a crucial sentence for one very special and obvious reason: that without the appropriate document—a certificate of marriage—a person claiming to be married is not recognized as such. No certificate, no proof, and therefore no marriage. To overcome this difficulty, the Supreme Court issued circular letters in 1975 and 1979 instructing the civil registry to conclude and certify inter-religious marriages. However, in 1987 a joint decision by the Ministries of Justice, Religion and the Interior stopped the practice (Pompe 1991). The registry office for Muslim births, marriages, divorces and deaths—the Religious Affairs Office (Kantor Urusan Agama; KUA)—would only register Muslim marriages; there was thus a registration vacuum.

In 1989 the Supreme Court pronounced on this state of affairs when it decided on an application before it concerning a Muslim woman and a Protestant man whose marriage could not be formalized because no registry would issue a certificate and none of the lower courts would order any registry to do so. The Supreme Court came to a somewhat problematic answer. On the ground that the couple had applied to the civil registry, it said:

> Considering that, in submitting an application for the formalization of a marriage to the Chief Civil Registrar of Jakarta, this should be interpreted as *testifying to an intention of having the marriage formalized not in accordance with Muslim religious prescriptions*, this in turn should be interpreted as testifying that, in submitting the application, *the applicant no longer had any regard for the status of her religion* (in this case the Muslim religion), so that article 8, clause (f), of Law No. 1 of the Republic of Indonesia, of the year 1974, with respect to marriage, no longer constitutes an obstacle to the performance of the marriage as desired by them, and in this case/situation the Civil Registry Office is properly obliged, as the only authority qualified to formalize or help formalize marriages between *two candidates who do not both profess Islam*, to accept the applicants' application. [Emphasis in the translation] (Translation by Pompe 1991: 266–7, who also provides the Indonesian)

The assumption that an application to the civil registry by a Muslim means apostasy is a large one, the more so because the Supreme Court itself (during the 1970s and 1980s) explicitly forbade the application of the colonial law on mixed marriage.

The issue of mixed marriage, like that of polygyny, certainly has a basis in the *fiqh* texts (and in the Qur'ān and Sunnah), but as we have seen they do not resolve the issue. As I have said already, these texts may be *fundamental* but they are not *primary*. There are in fact three other, quite different, primary factors involved: first, obviously, the actual law (the KHI); second, the bureaucratic function (the civil registry and the KUA), over which the courts seem to have little effective control; and third, the important variations in how individual judges or groups of judges at various levels see their role in delivering decisions.

For now, we can be quite sure that there are more questions than answers about the religious courts, and about the judges who staff them. While we know that the majority of judges now come from the country's State Islamic Institutes (Institut Agama Islam Negeri; IAIN), we have yet to establish what this means for actual decision making. We know too that the KHI is the basic text of the religious courts, but this tells us little about the social consequences of their *yurisprudensi*. There are almost conclusive indications that the material on which judges make decisions is not *fiqh* but the secularized KHI. However, whether this is true for all Indonesia has yet to be shown. About the only thing we can be certain of is that the statistics[35] currently available confirm the view held from the 1970s that the religious courts are primarily divorce courts, with competence also in inheritance and various forms of charitable gifts.[36]

This would have been the correct view until May 2006 when the revised Law on Religious Justice (No. 3/2006) came into force.[37] It came as somewhat of a surprise: the Department of Religion issued a short position paper in February 2006 and the new law followed in May. The new law extends the jurisdiction of the religious courts to syariah economics (*ekonomi syariah*), in addition to its existing responsibilities of marriage, divorce and so on.[38] No explanation was given for this extension except that, because syariah is involved, the religious court is the appropriate place for *ekonomi syariah* to be adjudicated. The definition of *ekonomi syariah* is very wide and encompasses syariah banks, cooperatives, insurance, investment funds, letters of credit, securities, pawn broking and

---

35 See data in the Asian Law Centre, University of Melbourne (http://www.law.unimelb. edu.au/alc/bibliography).

36 The actual classes of matters that can be brought before the religious courts have not changed, but the definitions are now much more specific. See the elucidation to Law No. 3/2006, article 22(c–h).

37 National legal policy from the 1990s has been to place all courts under the administrative and financial control of the Supreme Court rather than particular ministries. The intention is to do away with competing jurisdictions and blurred lines of judicial authority. The religious courts were, I think, the last to come under the aegis of the Supreme Court, effective September 2004. The relevant laws are Law No. 35/1999 and Law No. 4/2004. Note that these references are tentative and may be insufficient.

38 The same extension applies to Aceh; see Law No. 3/2006, article 3A.

contracts in general. This extra jurisdiction certainly puts a heavy load on the religious courts.

Many of the so-called 'Islamic' contracts are (a) based on secular law principles and (b) provide for arbitration only in case of dispute. Are the religious court judges competent in (a), and if so, does the exclusion clause in (b) oust the jurisdiction of the religious courts? What is the appropriate forum to decide the question? There is another problem: while the religious courts now have jurisdiction in syariah economics, do they also have the authority to override private contractual agreements? There are no data, but it is likely that individual agreements will have to give way to system-wide consistency. This is already the practice; whatever elements of *fiqh* remain in religious court judgments are subject to positive law and for most practical purposes have been selected out.

3 THE COMPILATION OF ISLAMIC LAW (KHI)

In 1991 Indonesia joined a long list of states that have codes of 'Islamic law' or, more accurately, 'laws for Muslims'. It is important to make this distinction here, at the beginning of this section, to avoid much unnecessary and pointless discussion. 'Islamic law' means the syariah as this is expressed in the totality of the *fiqh* texts and the discussions surrounding them up to the present. There are literally millions of texts of this type. No modern code (that is, any of the codes issued in the past 200 years) contains all or even a fair representation of this material; 'Islamic' as a qualifier is nonsense. Even those who restrict what is 'Islamic' to the Qur'ān and Sunnah—the so-called modernists—face a mass of material that can never be codified. 'Laws for Muslims', on the other hand, means exactly what it says: it is a selection from *fiqh* put into code and statute form. That is what the KHI is, but of course it is only the latest in a long line of selections throughout the Muslim world. These have been happening over the past 200 years either as a direct result of imperialism or indirectly where Muslim states have voluntarily adopted Western forms. Indonesia is but the latest state to go down the voluntary adoption path, through the KHI. The characteristic ideas involved in voluntary adoption are renewal and the acceptance of change as a necessary and ongoing factor.

'Renewal' is a tricky word; while it means 'to make new', it can also mean a reworking, a reformulation, a redefinition or even a purification. The last three decades or so have seen a renewal of Islam in one or all of these senses, including in Indonesia. But for renewal in any sense to take place, there must be opportunity and political space. This was not the case in the Netherlands East Indies, nor in the Republic of Indonesia until the late 1980s. Indeed, the 'Islamic' position was defensive in the face of a hostile state. Circumstances became somewhat easier politically in the last years of the New Order, and certainly more open after the end of the Soeharto regime. Renewal in all the above senses became at least possible.

For the proponents of syariah, however, renewal meant something much less than the introduction of an 'Islamic state' (that is, one 'founded on' syariah); it meant, rather, the codification of the syariah in law. The outcome was the KHI—certainly not renewal, but a real achievement given the past 150 years or so of syariah displacement in the state. The KHI claims a *fiqh* respectability and, to be fair, it does have this to a minimal degree. It also show an enthusiastic acceptance of change. However, accusations of unwarranted innovation (*bidah*) and indiscriminate mixing of rules (*talfiq*) brood over anything new, that is, not done before. The primary reference points of both are the orthopraxy of ritual and the certainty of *fiqh*, a frame of thought that is against any new formulation of syariah. In short, the fact that the KHI was ever drafted and promulgated (as a presidential instruction) is a real achievement. The KHI is a redefinition; it is certainly not a purification of syariah, but at the same time it is more than a selection or reworking because it imposes a new way of thinking about syariah.

The code form used by the KHI is a characteristic feature of the modern state. Like other codes it is arranged in books, chapters and articles, all by subject matter: thus, 'Book I, Chapter 2, article 5: The Conditions for Marriage'. The fact that the text states conditions in this form has already taken the reader, the judge and the administrator (bureaucrat) away from any one source. It allows the legislator to choose, select and modify materials from one or more sources and put them into books, chapters, articles and so on. The purpose of a code such as the KHI is to set down a text that is useable in practice. That is the intention of the drafter; to do less would be to fail. Obviously, to succeed, the drafter must accommodate or place the text within the surrounding, relevant or appropriate laws. We need to know how this was done for the KHI.

Compatibility

The KHI was drafted with two other laws in view. The first was the Law on Religious Justice (No. 7/1989). The religious courts established by that law (and later amendments) are the courts that implement the KHI. The second was the Marriage Law (No. 1/1974). The KHI is primarily on family law, so it is natural that its provisions would refer specifically to the Marriage Law. The first few articles attempt to clarify the relationship between the KHI and the Marriage Law. They take into consideration the fact that the status of the two texts is quite different—the Marriage Law is far above the KHI in the hierarchy of public legal instruments in Indonesia.[39] Thus, the preamble to the KHI instructs all agencies charged with its implementation (mainly the Department of Religion) to 'apply the KHI in conjunction with other laws' and its articles provide guidance on how this should be done. For example, article 4 of the KHI states that the validity of a marriage rests on compliance with article 2(1) of the Marriage

---

39 Now regulated by Law No. 10/2004.

Law. Registration, which provides proof of marriage, is subject to the registration requirements of existing laws.[40] The rules on age of consent, permission to take a second wife and grounds for the prevention of marriage, nullification of marriage (by way of blood, marriage or foster relationship) and termination of marriage are set out in the Marriage Law and acknowledged in the KHI.

The definition of marriage in the two texts is similar but not the same. The Marriage Law (article 1) states that marriage is:

> ... a relationship of body and soul between a man and a woman ... with the purpose of establishing a harmonious and lasting family (household) founded on belief in God.

The KHI (articles 2–3) says that it is:

> ... a binding contract made in obedience to the command(s) of Allah, and its implementation is a religious duty. Its function is to achieve a harmonious domestic life.

In short, compatibility is fundamental to the KHI, both because of its inferior status in the hierarchy of laws and because it is only one text among a number of laws ordering personal relationships. The most important of these are the Marriage Law and the Law on Religious Justice. No one article in the KHI can be read or interpreted without finding some reference to these laws.

One might be tempted to conclude that compatibility was a primary value in the drafting of the KHI. Evidence for this is found in the widespread acceptance of the text in the religious courts and the consistency with which it is cited in regional *yurisprudensi*. But is this enough? We already know the dangers of an uncritical reliance on the *yurisprudensi*. The suggestion must be left open for the moment but should be kept in mind when reading the following subsection.

Drafting the KHI

We begin with a quotation:

> In drafting the present code we have now gone outside [the syariah]. Nevertheless, seeing that among the opinions of the most authoritative jurists some are less rigorous and better suited to modern requirements than others, it is these we have adopted.

This passage comes from the preface to the Ottoman Code of Law (Ottoman Mejelle) published in 1869 (cited in Wilson 1907: 45). Compare it to the following from M. Yahya Harahap, a member of the KHI drafting committee:

> It is probably not an overstatement to say that there has been confusion about the understanding and implementation [of Islamic law] in Indonesian Muslim society. This has not been limited to ordinary Muslims. It has extended to religious scholars, general education and higher Islamic education. All of them identify *fiqh* with sharia or 'Islamic law'.

---

40 Laws No. 22/1946 and No. 32/1954.

The identification of *fiqh* with Islamic law has given rise to serious errors of im-plementation. In preparing their decisions for cases in the jurisdiction of the Religious Court (Pengadilan Agama), the judges turn to *fiqh* books of the schools of law, which are their first points of reference. This results in disparities between the decisions emanating from the religious courts depending on which school of law is followed and favoured by individual judges. [...]

[...] Surveys have shown that judges with strong backgrounds in a particular school of law are authoritarian, doctrinaire and descriptive [rather than analytical in their judgements]. They will not move one inch from the opinion of the authority they favour. If the presiding judge is from a Muhammadiyah background, or does not follow a particular school of law, he will always refer to the Qur'an and Sunnah. His views are more flexible; he will use legal thinking based on the use of 'informed opinion' [Ar.: *ra'y*] and take the teachings of the schools of law as guidance.

This is the picture based on research into the history and decisions of the religious courts. There is disputation between the schools of law and the law becomes a sec-ondary issue. Judgements are not based on law but are based on the doctrines of the schools of law as set out in the *fiqh* texts. The disputation is most striking when cases are taken to appeal [where appeal judges from different schools of law give different opinions]. [...]

[...] [I]t is erroneous to identify Islamic law with *fiqh*. *Fiqh* is not positive law that has been formulated systematically and in a unified way. It is the content of teach-ings or the science of Islamic law. For this reason *fiqh* is referred to as the doctrine of Islamic law. Or more accurately, *fiqh* is the opinions and teachings of the leaders of the schools of law. The books of *fiqh* are not 'law books'; they are books containing the opinions and independent judgements (*ijtihad*) of those leaders. (Harahap 1992: 21–2, cited in Fealy and Hooker 2006: 147–8)

There is no real difference between these two passages; in the Indonesian version the phrase used to describe the purpose and method of drafting is *mem-positifkan abstraksi hukum Islam*—'positivizing abstract Islam law'. This was the central justification for formulating the KHI. The passage is not just about the distinction that needs to be made between syariah and *fiqh*, but about the meaning of syariah and *fiqh* themselves in the Indonesian context. For the draft-ers of the KHI, this meant viewing the *fiqh* texts as the historically and spatially conditioned views of the respective authors rather than as the totality of syariah. It also meant recognizing the deficiency of the primary sources—the Qur'ān and the Sunnah—as comprehensive sources of law for a modern state. The drafters would therefore have to abstract principles suitable for Indonesia, and put them in a form capable of administration as *public law*—Harahap emphasized this phrase—in the state. This looks like and can be described as pure 'modernism'.

The process of selection and the subsequent draft certainly bear this out. Mawardi (2003), who provides a very good and detailed account of the birth of the KHI, points out that the idea of making a compilation was not new, going back to the 1970s. The idea is in fact much older still: the Dutch produced a draft in 1937 which sank without trace, being rejected out of hand by Muslim interests (Hooker 1984: 253). In any case, two institutions became involved in the prepa-ration for drafting: the Supreme Court and the Department of Religion. Prepara-tion began with the collection of data (*fiqh* texts); interviews with a cross-section of *'ulamā'*; compilation of comparative material drawn from Egypt, Turkey and Morocco; and finally, intensive discussion to actually formulate the KHI.[41]

In the best tradition of Indonesian Islamic scholarship, we take the last first. The KHI has a substantive explanation at the end which seems to encapsulate the tenor of the intensive discussion.[42] It can be summarized as follows.

1 The nation and state is based on Pancasila and the 1945 Constitution. There must be a national law that reflects the legal conscience of the Indonesian people and that guarantees religious belief based on belief in one God (the first Pancasila principle).

2 Religious courts are part of the formal judicial structure of the Republic of Indonesia (under Law No. 14/1970 and Law No. 14/1985).

3 The substantive law of the religious courts is Islamic law in the fields of marriage, inheritance and donations for pious purposes (*wakaf*). This law is sourced from 13 Shafi'i *fiqh* texts.

4 Additional sources are other *mazhab*, the *yurisprudensi* of the religious courts, the *fatāwā* of the *'ulamā'* and material from other countries.

5 The KHI is a compilation of the sources in (3) and (4); it is a guide for religious court judges.

It is clear from this summary that the drafters of the KHI were looking towards an Indonesian *mazhab*. This is also the view expressed within Indonesian Muslim scholarly circles (Lubis 1997: 76). For example, Harahap (1992: 37) says that: 'Indonesia has created its own ... *mazhab*, different from that which existed in the past'. We can also read this as confirmation that Hazairin's 'localization' has come to pass, although in a way he did not fully anticipate (see Chapter 2).

The drafters of the KHI were quite self-conscious about their purpose, which was to formulate a new text for the religious courts reformed in 1989. This does not mean that the classical *fiqh* was ignored; 38 *fiqh* texts were consulted.[43] The majority were Shafi'i texts, although the other Sunni schools,[44] Zahiri (Ibn Hazm's *al-Muhalla*) and some comparative material were also consulted.[45] However, as is apparent from the text of the KHI, not all texts were given equal weight and even those that were used were only partly decisive for the final KHI. Of these, a basic group of seven or so texts represented the nineteenth and twentieth-century Indonesian scholastic tradition, thus providing an impor-

---

41 See Mawardi (2003: 128–31) for details.

42 For comment, see Abdurrahman (1995). There is an English translation in Salim and Azra (2003: 322 ff.) and a good short summary in Lubis (1997: 75–6).

43 See Mawardi (2003: 128–9) for a list.

44 Ibn Qudamah's *al-Mughni* (Hanbali), Mālik's *al-Muwatta* and the *Fatāwā al-Hindiyyah* (Hanafi).

45 Sayyid Sabiq's *Fiqh al-Sunnah*, which is a popular teaching text in all IAIN.

tant continuity. They included *Bughyat al-Mushtarshidin*, *Fath al-Muin*, *Fath al-Wahab*, *Mughni al-Muhtaj*, *Kanz al-Raghibin*, *Tuhfat al-Muhtaj* and *Ianat al-Talibin*. These texts also appear in Indonesian *fatāwā* from the 1970s; indeed, the *Ianat al-Talibin* appears in over half the *fatāwā* for the past 80 years. Since 1957 the same texts have appeared on the Department of Religion's list of recommended texts for use in the religious courts.[46]

Structure and Content

The KHI is quite simple in its divisions:

- Book I: Marriage and Divorce (19 chapters, 170 articles);
- Book II: Inheritance (7 chapters, 43 articles);
- Book III: *Wakaf* (5 chapters, 13 articles);
- Article 229: 'The judge must pay serious attention to the values of the community, so that the decision is just';
- Explanation;
- Elucidation (containing a clarification of particular articles).

Well over half the KHI is on marriage and divorce; indeed, one could say that the religious courts are essentially divorce courts. It is true that *wakaf* has a significant place, but it is subject to considerable regulation by secular laws, especially land law. For the present discussion, therefore, we consider a syariah limited to family law with *fiqh* elements. As we saw earlier, these elements are subject to bureaucratic forms which change the nature of that which is being administered. In addition, there are some provisions in the KHI that reveal a basic incompatibility between *fiqh* and national secular interests. Some examples follow.

Inter-religious Marriage

The KHI forbids inter-religious marriage (articles 40(c) and 44). This is a deviation from the *fiqh* in that the latter permits a Muslim man to marry a woman of the *ahl al-Kitab*, that is, a Jewess or Christian. While there were rules about the precise definitions of 'Jewess' and 'Christian', the possibility of inter-religious marriage was still present. This has now been removed, almost certainly because of the deep suspicion in Indonesian Muslim circles that permitting inter-religious marriage would be to permit a creeping Christianization or even secularization of society (Lubis 1997: 77 ff.). This was certainly the view of one of the major *fatwā*-giving bodies, the Indonesian Council of Ulama (Majelis Ulama Indonesia; MUI), which ruled against such marriages in 1980 for reasons of public interest (*masālah al-mursalah*) of the Muslim community in avoiding possible harm (*mafsadah*) to the religion of Islam (see Hooker 2003a: 76 ff.). The con-

---

46 Circular letter, February 1958; implemented through PP No. 45/1957.

text was the contemporary politics of religion rather than the *fiqh* rules alone; other *fatwā*-giving bodies have not taken the same position in the past (Hooker 2003a: 77).

Polygyny

Like the Qur'ān, the KHI permits polygyny in principle (articles 55–59), so in this respect it is not in direct conflict with Qur'ānic principle. Permission is made contingent on the man being able to prove that he is able to deal with all wives equally justly (as stated in Q4:3 of the Qur'ān). This is of course a considerable barrier, especially when combined with the other conditions on which the religious court must satisfy itself. A man wishing to take another wife must show that his existing wife is unable to perform her functions as a wife, is incurably ill or physically incapacitated, or is barren (article 57). But even where one of these can be shown, that is not the end of the matter. Article 58(1) takes us back to the man's ability to prove he is able to act justly towards all his wives, but now with reference to article 5 of the Marriage Law (No. 1/1974). The preceding article 4 of this law is the same as article 57 of the KHI; article 5(1) adds the condition (also found in article 58 of the KHI) that the approval of the existing wife or wives is necessary. It is open to the judge to dispense with this requirement if permission is not forthcoming or is impossible to obtain. Whatever one might think of the actual formulation of these principles, they do constitute an extra barrier to unrestrained polygyny. However, the actual working of this provision is by no means uniform or consistent throughout Indonesia. Having said this, it is only proper to add that the statistical data are difficult to interpret and incomplete (Jones 1994: 268–87).

Capacity to Marry

The KHI (and the 1974 Marriage Law) make considerable changes to the *fiqh* in the area of marriage. Puberty (*'aqil baligh*) is no longer the test of being of marriageable age; instead, a minimum age of 19 for males and 16 for females is set out in article 7(1). There is provision for the court to vary these ages, although the KHI does not specify the circumstances in which this might be done (article 7(2)). The consent of both parties is required for a marriage to take place (articles 6(1) and 16–17). A guardian for marriage (*wali nikah*) must also consent to the contract, although he or she may be replaced by order of the court if consent is unreasonably withheld or is impossible to obtain by reason of absence (articles 19–23). This does away with the power of certain *wali* (*wali mujbir*) to formalize a contract of marriage on behalf of a woman without her consent—a recognized form in the Shafi'i *mazhab* and a source of considerable concern over many years. In the 1930s and 1940s, Ahmad Hassan argued in favour of the requirement to obtain the woman's consent, and this is in fact a necessary condition in the Hanbali *mazhab*.

The introduction of a minimum age at marriage, the reduction in the power of the *wali* and the granting of court jurisdiction over unreasonable *wali* all parallel earlier reforms in the Middle East and in Malaysia and Singapore. The most important result of these reforms has been to increase the power of the courts and the Department of Religion bureaucracy. In the case of the issues just described, the KHI is almost wholly taken up with ensuring compliance with the appropriate forms and with general paperwork.

Divorce

Divorce is now essentially a matter of judicial process. Unrestricted divorce at the initiative of the husband (*talaq*) is now a thing of the past. While the KHI does retain the classical steps of repudiation (articles 118 ff.), these must be gone through in the religious court (after an attempt at reconciliation). The husband must provide reasons acceptable to the court to support his action for a divorce (article 131(2)). Grounds for divorce include adultery, crime, desertion, imprisonment, cruelty, incapacitating illness, disharmony (the most common ground), breach of a marriage agreement and change of religion, and are applicable to both parties (article 116). The emphasis throughout this part of the KHI is on judicial process (see especially articles 129–131). In short, the classical *talaq* is much restricted in practice.

The majority of divorces (70 per cent) are initiated by the wife.[47] Important among the reasons women give for divorce is *ta'liq talaq*—divorce on the ground of breaking a condition set out in the marriage contract (article 116(9)). The KHI permits and regulates marriage agreements, which usually deal with (a) marital property and (b) the conditions under which *ta'liq talaq* may occur (articles 45–46). These conditions, formalized and printed on or accompanying the certificate of marriage, include desertion, lack of financial support, neglect for at least six months or physical violence. Breach of any of these does not automatically lead to divorce—the wife must still obtain an order from the religious court. Also, it should be noted that marriage agreements are limited to the extent that they must not contradict religion, that is, syariah in some *fiqh* form. This limitation is phrased vaguely in the KHI. This is important, because it means that the courts can overturn marriage agreements that include a condition barring the husband from taking a second wife.

Joint Property and Inheritance

The KHI makes quite fundamental changes to the *fiqh* rules on property and inheritance. So far as property jointly acquired during marriage is concerned, half

---

47 Statistics supplied by the Department of Religion, 1999 (the last year for which complete data are available).

goes to the survivor on death (article 96) and is excluded from the inheritance rules set down in the Qur'ān and Hadith (the *farā'id*). This departure from tradition can be explained either as a recognition of the *adat* rules (*harta sepencarian/gono-gini*) or as a promotion of female property rights. More importantly, it resolves the longstanding question concerning the extent to which *farā'id* can work in Indonesian circumstances. So far as inheritance is concerned, the KHI mostly repeats the *farā'id* in simplified form, although it recommends that the fragmentation of land be avoided. Following the *farā'id*, the KHI says that a will may only be made in respect of one-third of the net estate. But in a departure from the *farā'id*, it provides that adopted children have rights to succession (article 209), that they are classed as heirs and that their share of an estate is determined as if they were natural children (articles 176–193). The extent to which this equivalence is actually upheld in practice is unclear.

In these five areas, the KHI has made considerable changes to the *fiqh*. Can these be said to be decisive? Indeed, is the KHI itself truly decisive in its own terms: compatibility, principles of drafting, textual sources, structure and content? It is certainly decisive as the text of first reference in the religious courts, although some judges are still prepared to use a *fiqh* textbook if they feel justified in doing so.

The Counter Legal Draft

The KHI is not an uncontested document. In October 2004 a working group from within the Department of Religion produced a Counter Legal Draft to the KHI.[48] It created considerable controversy and was withdrawn by the department within a matter of weeks. For anyone who has read its proposals, the withdrawal is wholly understandable. It is a surprising document which, taken as a whole, absolutely rejects the established principles of *fiqh* in favour of a purely secular scheme of family law.

In the first place, the Counter Legal Draft declares marriage to be purely secular ('a normal human social relation'), not, as at present, a religious obligation. It proposes doing away with the requirement for a guardian (*wali*). Registration would be the essential element of marriage rather than just an evidentiary requirement as at present. There would be mutual marriage gifts in place of gifts in accordance with local *adat* (*mahr*). Controversially, inter-religious marriage would be permitted, despite the many *fatāwā* consistently forbidding such unions. Polygamy/polygyny would be abolished. The prescribed period during which a person may not remarry after divorce or the death of a spouse (*iddah*)

---

48 The Gender Mainstreaming Team was headed by Siti Musdah Mulia, whose views on certain aspects of syariah, especially polygamy, are well known (see Mulia 2004). The Counter Legal Draft is discussed in Fealy and Hooker (2006: 148–9, 348–52).

would be imposed on both husband and wife, rather than just the wife. Similarly, disobedience/defiance (*nusyuz*) would be a fault of both husband and wife. Males and females would inherit equal shares of an estate and non-Muslim claimants would be allowed to inherit.

It is obvious that these suggestions, especially when taken as a package, went too far to be considered a practical option. This is a pity, because parts, for example the inheritance laws, were well worth considering. What was needed at the time was a careful and focused explanation of the issues.[49] Instead, the argument for and against the Counter Legal Draft became bogged down in issues of democracy, justice and human rights, in which the actual technical possibilities in the proposed changes became lost.[50] The document was subjected to claim and counterclaim as to justice, democracy and so on, all undefined except through rather exiguous readings of the Qur'ān and Sunnah and the occasional technical class on subjects such as the purpose of syariah (*maqasid al-syariah*). The result has been the re-enforcement of fixed positions rather than any useful dialogue. The Counter Legal Draft thus remains in abeyance, although work on revising the KHI continues.

I think it should be acknowledged here that for a text that is only 15 years old, and as an original attempt at codification, the KHI has been remarkably successful. It certainly passes the efficacy test: it is used in every case at the lowest level of the religious courts, and the Indonesia-wide appeal rate from religious court judgments is minuscule.

3   THE *FATĀWĀ*: BETWEEN PURITY AND PRACTICALITY

A *fatwā* is formal advice given by one or (more commonly in Indonesia) several qualified scholars in answer to a question. Strictly speaking it is not binding, for two reasons. First, in its classical formulations it has never had this status; the recipient may or may not accept the advice. Much depends on the authority of the *fatwā* giver and the circumstances in which the advice is sought. Second, *fatāwā* are not formally recognized in the Indonesian legal system, although, as we have seen, the KHI does refer to them as a source. Nevertheless they are not without effect; at the very least they are persuasive, primarily because they are based solely on classical reasoning. For this reason alone they are an important public face, because they connect the Muslim public directly to the classical jurisprudence without any intervening European intellectual imperialism. On the other hand, the classical (Arabic) *fiqh* is by no means accepted uncritically; hence, there appears to be a disjunction between purity and practicality.

---

49   To be fair, this did in fact occur to some extent (see Mudzhar 2003: 171–3).
50   For extracts and sources, see Fealy and Hooker (2006: 351–2).

Indonesia has four major *fatwā*-issuing bodies: Nahdlatul Ulama (NU), Muhammadiyah, Persatuan Islam (Persis) and the Indonesian Council of Ulama (Majelis Ulama Indonesia; MUI).[51] Each claims a specific method and source, and we distinguish the four on that basis.

Nahdlatul Ulama (NU)

Founded in 1926 to represent traditionalist Islamic interests, NU has historically had a long and intensive concern with method and source. This is evident in its published *fatāwā*;[52] indeed, the second *fatwā* NU ever issued (No. 2/1926) was concerned with this issue. In an arrangement that has given the NU *'ulamā'* their reputation for conservatism, it was decided that the appropriate method (exercised by committee) was to consult a set of named *fiqh* texts, arranged in the following hierarchy. First, the *'ulamā'* would consult Nawawi al-Bantani's *Minhaj* and al-Rafi'i's *Muharrar*. They would try to obtain a consensus of the two, but if this was not possible then the former would prevail. In the case of further failure to decide the issue at hand, then al-Mahalli's *Kanz al-Raghibin*, Ibn Hajar's *Tuhfh al-Muhtaj* and al-Ramli's *Nihayah al-Muhtaj* would be consulted, in that order. NU's *fatāwā* followed this scheme fairly consistently until 1992, when the whole question was re-examined. By then it was obvious to all that the issues of the day were more difficult and complex than in earlier decades. The circumstances of society, in particular peasant society in Java, were not those of earlier times. The whole issue of method had to be revisited.

This revisitation resulted in a long and complex *fatwā* (Hooker 2003a: 57–9) that did three things. First, it repeated, in some detail, the notion of a hierarchy of Shafi'i texts. Second, in a 'system of legal decision making', it re-emphasized the primacy of collective effort by the national conference of NU *'ulamā'*; this is the body which has arrogated to itself the authority to issue *fatāwā*. Third and perhaps most importantly, it stated that a *fatwā* must take into account political, social, economic and cultural factors. In a sense this merely recognized what the NU *'ulamā'* had already been doing, but made these factors the components of a stated principle. How far and to what extent this new principle will mesh with the hierarchy of restated sources has yet to be determined. The contemporary NU *fatāwā* are in a state of flux.

A final point: the primary source of scholarship for Indonesian *fatwā* givers remains the Arabic-language texts. Only a very few people, by virtue of having

---

51   I exclude provincial and personal *fatāwā* because there are no comprehensive data on these as yet. Some Middle Eastern (Egyptian, Lebanese) collections have been translated into Indonesian, but they do not appear to be referred to extensively in the Indonesian *fatāwā*. The *fatāwā* of Sayyid Tantawi have been translated into Indonesian as *Fatwa-Fatwa Populer* (Thanthawi 1998; Skovgaard-Petersen 1997), and some of those of Yusuf Qardhawi as *Fatwa-Fatwa Kontemporer* (Qardhawi 1995).

52   For details, see Hooker (2003a: 246–9).

received the appropriate education, have direct access to these. *Fatwā* issuance is an elite matter, and that elite claims authority by reason of its special education. It follows that criticism, however well founded, is always open to rejection on the ground that the critic does not have the appropriate qualifications; that person is not an equal and need not be taken seriously. This, the 'scholastic' argument, does have merit, and certainly the NU *'ulamā'* see themselves as guardians of the scholastic tradition. But that tradition is not static; on the contrary, the IAIN educational reforms have much enlarged the field of scholasticism to the extent that there may now be more than one source (other than the Arabic texts) (see Chapter 3).

Muhammadiyah

Muhammadiyah is a modernist Islamic organization founded in 1912. Its Council on Law-making and Development of Islamic Thought (Majlis Tarjih) has been responsible for issuing opinions since 1927.[53] These opinions are not binding on members, as the council makes clear. The Muhammadiyah method is based on two propositions: (a) that the syariah has a purpose (*maqasid al-syariah*) which can be identified; and (b) that the purpose of syariah is public interest/benefit (*maslahah*) in the widest sense. This seems to suppose something like the 'greatest good', a pure natural-law idea—but of course it is constrained by Revelation. The nexus between the purpose of syariah, public benefit and the revealed texts (the Qur'ān and Sunnah) is found in independent judgments (*ijtihad*) or the method of reaching independent judgments (*metode ijtihad*). This means a scheme of reasoning (in the Muhammadiyah version, exercised collectively) where *maslahah* is taken as the basic context. Argument therefore runs back from the identifiable benefit. Where this can be shown in the Qur'ān and Sunnah, there is no problem. However, where benefit cannot be identified in the primary sources, then argument must proceed as follows.

The primary recourse is to *qiyas*, that is, extending the principle in an original (*asli*) case to a new case on the basis that the effective cause (*'illa*) is the same. The difficulty is to identify the conditions that are common to both cases. There is a large body of classical commentary on this problem,[54] but the council does not actually address the issue of what a condition is in the sense of the underlying rationale (*hikmah*) for the original rule.

The second recourse is to juristic preference (*istihsan*), that is, finding the right principle by exercising reason. The assumptions are: (a) that rationality is appropriate; and (b) that it is correctly exercised by properly qualified people. These are large assumptions, and indeed, the council is frequently criticized on

---

53   These have been collected and published in four sets of opinions called *Tanya-Jawab Agama*, published between 1990 and 1998 (see Hooker 2003a: 249–50).

54   See Hallaq (1984, 1997) for a leading contemporary comment.

the ground that it does not have properly qualified experts. Whether or not this is true, the fact remains that *istihsan* has always been problematic as a method. There is no real mechanism for avoiding personal or political bias, let alone dealing with highly specific circumstances.

The third recourse is to *saad al-dhara'i*, that is, 'blocking the means' [to commit wrong acts]. This principle permits the prevention of evil (*mafsadah*) before it occurs by classifying actions as (a) those that definitely lead to evil, (b) those that are likely to lead to evil, (c) those that frequently but not inevitably lead to evil, and (d) those that may but rarely do lead to evil. One can easily see the problems in defining actions which must, by the nature of things, be highly circumstance specific. The principle also covers the case where something that is normally forbidden (*haram*) is permitted (*mubah*); that is, a lesser evil is tolerated in order to prevent a greater evil. This use of the principle is now common in Indonesian *fatāwā* in the field of medical ethics, to permit organ transplants, for example.

The *fatāwā* issued by the Muhammadiyah council can never be more than a guide to sources. This is because *ijtihad* requires the council to make choices, in the context of *maslahah* (itself an undefined class), about the implications of Qur'ānic prescriptions. This is not to say that the choice is unrestricted; on the contrary, it must be exercised within the known canons of *ijtihad*.

Persatuan Islam (Persis)

Yet another method of reaching decisions is demonstrated in the *fatāwā* of Persis, a reformist Islamic organization founded in 1923 (Hooker 2003a: 48 ff.). In this instance we find precise language analysis of Hadith to determine whether a proposed act is permitted or forbidden. This requires showing (a) the truth of a cited Hadith and (b) that the proposed act falls within the permissible as defined in the Hadith. For practical purposes, therefore, a Persis *fatwā* rests on an examination of Hadith; the *fiqh* texts favoured by NU do not, as such, have any prescriptive authority, and *ijtihad* is not a primary recourse as in the Muhammadiyah method. Even such a basic concept as *ijma'*—consensus of the learned—is in doubt. The founder of Persis, Ahmad Hassan, rejected *ijma'* as a necessary determinant, and the basic collection of Persis *fatāwā* itself says: 'Allah did not command us to follow *ijma'* made by a crowd of *'ulamā'*" (Hooker 2003a: 51–2). A softening of this position can be detected since the 1990s, however.

The result has been to give us a strict, even literalist, reading of the syariah. While having the virtues of consistency and certainty, it also has the major fault of expecting people to be better than they can be or wish to be. Essentially, Persis asks men and women to conform to an ideal. There is no sympathy for human frailty, and of course *ijtihad* in the Muhammadiyah sense is unacceptable. From a purely technical point of view, the logic and consistency of the Persis *fatāwā* are impressive. From a realistic or sociological point of view, they are inordinately difficult—but that is always the position of scripturalism in any of the three monotheisms.

Majelis Ulama Indonesia (MUI)

MUI was founded in 1975 under the auspices of the Department of Religion to provide authoritative *fatāwā* on issues of national importance. As well as the central body in Jakarta, MUI has provincial committees in most provinces. Various collections of MUI decisions have been published (Hooker 2003a: 253–5). The members of MUI are drawn from a wide spectrum of Muslim opinion, and this is reflected in its method—actually, 'method' might be too strong a word; perhaps 'eclecticism of sources' would be more accurate. In its Guide to the Procedure for Determining a Fatwā [*Himpunan Fatwā*], MUI recommends turning first to the Qur'ān, Sunnah, *ijma'* and *qiyas*; then consulting the *fiqh* texts; and then, if still in doubt, using *ijtihad*.

This formulation attempts to have the best of all worlds. In practice, the MUI's *fatāwā* rely primarily on the Qur'ān and Hadith with occasional reference to *fiqh* texts, invariably from the Shafi'i school. There are also a few references to Egyptian *fatāwā*. The result of this way of proceeding is a collection of *fatāwā* that satisfies no one: a 'scripturalist' will object to practically everything, a 'modernist' to the *fiqh* texts and a 'traditionalist' to *ijtihad*. More importantly, perhaps, many MUI *fatāwā* are incoherent and raise more difficulties than they purport to solve. This is the consequence of eclecticism of sources.

The Bureaucracy

Where religion impinges on the actions of the state, the ministries of government have set up committees to evaluate the implications of their decisions for syariah. The Ministry of Health, for example, is frequently required to produce 'rulings' on matters such as blood transfusions, autopsies, organ transplants and the like. The booklets or pamphlets produced under the auspices of the ministries are decisive: they permit medical procedures; they involve public funds; and they present an 'Islamic science' face to the educated public (a sensitive area for Muslims, who are aware of the perceived inability of their religion to cope with modern science). But they have nothing to say about the methods used to reach decisions. This is no surprise, as the evaluation committees are not theologically inclined and are mainly interested in gaining some sort of 'Islamic' imprimatur or seal of correctness for their decisions. In short, the bureaucracy's *fatāwā*, while important, owe little to classical legal reasoning.

We are left, therefore, with Hadith analysis, *ijtihad* and the *fiqh* texts. Are they decisive? Do they actually determine the thinking of Muslims on particular issues? The answer is not clear, but as a general principle we can say that the more publicly divisive an issue is, the less the recourse to classical reasoning. For example, the debates that took place in the 1980s and 1990s on deviant sects were couched in terms of the need to preserve public order and maintain the unity of the Muslim community. The difficult theological issues surrounding deviance were not really addressed from within dogma. On the other hand, public representations of Islam in film, on television, on radio and in books are much more likely to be discussed in a discourse that can be called 'classical'. The point is that the *fatāwā* are inconsistent; rather than certainty, all one finds is variation.

These comments return us to purity and practicality. The *fatāwā* represent an attempt to state pure principle. That principle does not necessarily translate into a practical program. But this is to ask too much; in Indonesia the *fatāwā* are important because they are central to public debate on controversial issues such as interfaith marriage or religious pluralism. I suggest that their practicality really resides in their ability to formalize the terms of an issue for public debate.

5   ISLAMIC MONEY: SYMBOLIC OR REAL?

In this section, I distinguish between what is symbolic and what is real in Islamic forms of money. The main forms of what I term 'Islamic money' are the wealth tax (*zakat*), *wakaf* and Islamic banking. The first two have a long history in classical Muslim scholarship, but they also have an uncertain presence in modern Indonesia. The payment of *zakat* is widely avoided; *wakaf* is commonly seen as a private rather than state matter; and Islamic banking is widely regarded as purely cosmetic. Hence my use of the terms 'symbolic' and 'real'. I hasten to add that contemporary Muslim scholarship, while not using my terminology, recognizes the uncertainties surrounding these forms of money, in essence asking whether or not they are real.

Apart from this issue of definition, there are two further complicating factors that are relevant for all states with significant or majority Muslim populations. The first is that their governments must demonstrate their 'Islamic credentials'. One way of doing this is through money,[55] of which *zakat*, *wakaf* and banking are obvious public forms. Whether or not they make any impact on the state budget is irrelevant; symbolic importance is everything. The second factor is corruption—a stark reminder of the contrast between how Muslims are supposed to behave (the symbolic) and how they actually do behave (the real). Indonesia is notoriously corrupt financially, at both the private and state levels.[56] The

---

55 The *hajj* is another; see Chapter 5.
56 For a short introduction to this subject with extensive references, see Lindsey (2000).

collection and distribution of *zakat* at the official level is seen as an open invitation to corruption and is resisted for that reason. To this we must add Indonesia's confused and inconsistent laws, regulations and instructions on all three forms of money. It is to these that we now turn.

Zakat

This particular form of money has considerable symbolic importance because it is one of the five pillars of Islam and thus an obligation on the individual to God.[57] It is also one of only two of the pillars directly involving money (the other is the *hajj*). *Zakat* is the annual payment due from individual Muslims (of sufficient means) to set classes of beneficiaries. The classes are set out in the Qur'ān (Q9:60) and are thus inviolate. They are: those in need (the relief of poverty); the agents (*amil*) who collect the payments; those 'whose hearts need winning over',[58] that is, those who have the intention of converting or are newly converted to Islam; slaves (in order to free them) and those who are in debt; those who act in 'God's cause'; and finally, travellers in need. These classes of beneficiaries are clearly specified and the duty is a personal one.

The latter two characteristics of *zakat* present problems for the contemporary nation-state. The individual Muslim is no longer just a Muslim; he or she is also a citizen, and therefore subject to the secular laws of the state. *Zakat* is a tax, and taxes are a state matter with their own laws.[59] Moreover, the classes of beneficiaries set out in Q9:60 are now seen, from the state point of view, as unnecessarily restrictive. Given that the purpose of *zakat* is to provide relief from disadvantage (financial or social), it follows that new ways of spending *zakat* income must be established.

The government of the Netherlands East Indies attempted very little in the area of *zakat*.[60] *Fatāwā* from the 1970s through to the present have always insisted that payment should be personal, and hence that the individual should be able to choose the amount and method of payment (Hooker 2003a: 111 ff.). *Zakat* has two components: *fitrah*, a small sum paid as part of one's religious obligations at Ramadan, and *zakat maal*, a larger sum based on one's disposable income. *Fitrah* was and is always paid (otherwise Ramadan is voided). The state

---

57   The five pillars of Islam are the five duties incumbent on every Muslim. They are: (1) profession of faith (*shahadah*); (2) performance of ritual prayers *(shalat)*; (3) fasting *(sawm)*; (4) payment of *zakat*; and (5) performance of the *hajj*.

58   See the comment in A. Yousuf Ali's (1934) translation of Q9:60.

59   This is clearly demonstrated in Malaysia, where *zakat* is treated as a tax and its assessment and payment are closely controlled (see Ghazali 1991).

60   See Juynboll (1930: 99 ff.) for a description of the minimal regulation in force at the time.

did not intervene seriously in the collection of *zakat maal* until 1999.[61] To be sure, there were (and are) non-state collection and payment agencies, and in the New Order period a blatantly political attempt was made to organize payments on a national basis. It came to nothing, however—there was simply no national machinery available (Salim 2003).

A national system was introduced in 1999 under the Zakat Management Law (No. 38/1999). It attempted to do two things: first, to institute an effective nation-wide system for the collection and distribution of *zakat*; and second, to reconcile the state and private systems through the provision of a common administrative framework. The law permits the collection of *zakat* by two sorts of agency: a national Zakat Collection Board (Badan Amil Zakat; BAZ) and private Zakat Collection Agencies (Lembaga Amil Zakat; LAZ). The latter include organiza-tions of varying sizes and capacities. There is no machinery to compel payment, although at the time of writing some district and city authorities were doing so in the case of civil servants. In theory, the amounts paid in *zakat* are deductible from income tax.[62]

The Zakat Management Law is wholly administrative. It sets out a hierarchy of management from national to provincial to regional agencies. It includes pro-visions on audits, although the details on how audits are to be conducted are not clear. The LAZ are recognized as legitimate collection agencies, provided they have a recognized legal entity, income from *zakat* and an approved work plan. As is usual in Indonesian legal drafting, the core administrative procedures are in the subordinate regulations. These are Ministerial Decision No. 581/1999 and, more importantly from a practical point of view, the Department of Religion's guide to *zakat*.[63]

This key text is divided into four sections. The first is on organization and the hierarchy of responsibilities. It states that the BAZ is to be made up of five general committees responsible respectively for planning, collection, utilization, administration and finance. The same functions are repeated at the provincial, district and village levels, with a requirement for reporting and auditing at each level (although the law does not say who the auditors are to be). At the village level—the most important level given that this is where payments of *zakat* are actually collected—the scheme is as follows. The local authority (a commu-nity or religious leader) is to establish a policy stating how the collection is to be made. In consultation with local religious leaders, scholars and prominent community figures, that person must then draw up a policy for disbursement within a budget, and account for the money spent. The Department of Religion's

---

61 The figures given by Taufik (1991) are instructive as illustrations, although they are confined to the Jakarta municipality. *Zakat* statistics are incomplete.

62 The *zakat* collection agencies are supposed to act in concert with the income tax authority.

63 Pedoman Teknis Pengelolaan Zakat No. D-291/2000.

guide goes into considerable detail on the mechanics of these activities at the respective levels. For instance, payees, amounts, receipts and places must all be recorded. The money that is collected must be deposited in a specified bank account reserved for *zakat*.

The second section, on development, is not all that clear. It talks about developing policies and implementing 'transparency' and 'professionalism' to achieve 'empowerment'—the language of modern managerialism. How this is to be done through the committees and subcommittees established[64] is not clear, except that an auditing process is considered crucial to the collection and distribution of *zakat*. There is no general account of audits available at the moment.

The third section, on management policy, contains much more specific statements on the functions of the BAZ and LAZ. It does two things: it settles the status of the LAZ as *zakat* collection units (*unit pengumpul zakat*), thus giving bureaucratic form to non-government collection agencies; and it sets out the policy on distribution. It repeats the classes of payee as set out in the Qur'ān, but emphasizes the priority of the poor. Food and money may be given monthly or on days of celebration. This section of the guide also prioritizes the need to eradicate poverty in rural areas, to provide education through scholarships and to 'empower' the local economy. In other words, it proposes two kinds of distribution, one for the short-term relief of poverty and the other to eradicate the causes of poverty over the long term. The official view is to give the former priority; indeed, the latter can only be undertaken with whatever surplus is available, and anecdotal evidence suggests that surpluses are uncommon. But the possibility of long-term measures for poverty eradication raises the issue of capitalization of *zakat* money. Only the state BAZ or a large-scale LAZ (such as those operated by NU or Muhammadiyah) would have the capacity to collect and invest such sums over the long term. But assuming that it were possible, there is a *fiqh* difficulty. Payment is a personal obligation—so can it be delegated to an organization for the purpose of accruing capital? There are *fatāwā* that reject that option (Hooker 2003a: 11 ff.).

The final section of the guide provides rates for calculation of the amounts of *zakat* to be paid. The *fitrah* is ignored because the sums involved are tiny and are, in any case, always paid at the end of Ramadan. The guide concentrates instead on *zakat maal*, the general calculation on disposable income.[65] The rates vary according to property type and source of income, providing an interesting example of how the *fiqh* classes can be revised to make them conform with the reality of a modern nation-state. Here, we have to bear in mind that the rural population of Indonesia constitutes about 65 per cent of the total population,[66] so that *zakat* payments have to make sense in that context. Similarly, the propor-

---

64 Ministerial Decision No. 1/2001.

65 Set out in table form as an attachment to D-291/2000.

66 According to the population census for 1990.

tions of wage earners and self-employed must be addressed in the guide tables. The tables do attempt to accommodate the entire constituency of *zakat* payers.

The tables have two parts. The first is made up of three general categories of income.[67] The first is income from agricultural production (rice, fruit, vegetables, animals). The rate is 5 per cent if the production does not involve inputs such as irrigation and fertilizer and 10 per cent if it does. The justification given for the higher rate is that inputs make a crop surplus—and thus extra income from sales—possible, but the table also sets out the varying opinions of the four Sunni *mazhab* on this matter. In the case of natural increases in livestock (goat, sheep, cattle), the table sets a rate of 2.5 per cent of the increase, or the donation of one or more live animals depending on number and type.

The second general category is income from the production of goods and services, including manufactured goods (cement, textiles and so on) as well as import and export activities. Such income is taxed at a rate of 2.5 per cent. The income earned by professionals, (consultants, medical practitioners and the like) is taxed at the same rate. This category is a modern one, and the rate seems to be set on analogy with income derived from gold and silver or, more generally, trading. In contrast to the other general categories, there is no reference in this category to the views of the various *mazhab* or to the associated *ijtihad*. Gold and silver is a separate general category, but the basic rules and rates are so well known they need not concern us here.

Finally, there is a category dealing with mining and the extraction and production of minerals. The recommended rate for such activities is 2.5 per cent, but the views of the four *mazhab* are given, along with the rates they recommend—which in some cases (for example, Hanafi) can be as high as 20 per cent.

The second, much shorter, part of the tables provides examples of how an individual who receives cash income from employment (for example, an office worker) should calculate the amount of *zakat* to be paid. The calculations are based on income, marriage status, number of children, income tax rate (which also depends on personal circumstances) and administrative costs. These are all taken into consideration before the 2.5 per cent *zakat* rate is applied.

There is nothing surprising in the tables and rates. Indeed they confirm the known *fatāwā* on *zakat* (Hooker 2003a: 115 ff.). The impression one gains from the guide is that the intention is to implement a standardized system nationwide. This is reinforced when we look at its distribution list; the recipients include the minister, secretary general, regional heads and staff of the Department of Religion, the minister of finance, the secretary general of parliament, the rectors of the IAIN and State Islamic Colleges (STAIN), and all district heads and mayors.

---

67 There are actually five categories, but I have collapsed them here to avoid lengthy repetition.

The formal structure I have just described is just that—a formal scheme. There is much we do not know about how the scheme actually operates across the country, although I give one (tentative) example for one province elsewhere in this book (see pp. 256–7, 275–6).

Wakaf

The best neutral translation of *wakaf* is 'gift for pious purposes'. In English such a gift is often called a 'charitable trust', and indeed, in countries such as Malaysia (with its colonial legal history) it is actually now treated as such. In Indonesia the term retains the element of pious purpose, although, as one might expect, it is formulated in local idioms that express a regional understanding of the relevant Qur'ānic injunction (Q107:17): ' ... to supply ... the needs of one's neighbours'. The institution of *wakaf* is of concern to all governments of Muslim countries because it almost invariably involves land dedicated for pious purposes (mosques and schools as well as productive agricultural lands). These dedications can and do involve large sums·of money.

Wakaf is the subject of Book III of the KHI (articles 215–229). The book begins with a short section on definition (article 215) that provides a concise overview of the relevant *fiqh* in this area. Thus, *wakaf* is a legal act by a person or legal entity institutionalizing assets for religious purposes or other public needs in accordance with the teachings of Islam. *Ikrar* is a declaration of intent to create a *wakaf*. The assets must be durable, of commercial value and unencumbered. The *ikrar* must be registered at a special office.[68] Article 215 does not specify the consequences of non-registration, but it is probable that a non-registered *wakaf* would be invalid.

The remainder of the articles in Book III provide a rather minimalist set of principles on the implementation and administration of *wakaf*. Articles 220–221 describe the duties of the *wakaf* supervisor (*nadzhir*), namely the implementation of the *wakaf* and the production of the required reports. Article 221 also sets out the rules for dismissal of a *nadzhir*, namely inability to act or committing a criminal offence. The authority for dismissal and subsequent replacement is vested in the KUA, *not* the donor's family or any beneficiary. This is a significant departure from the classical texts and common practice, which locate the right to dismiss and appoint in those closely associated with the *wakaf* property. This has always been a difficulty for secular systems of law, which reject the notion that donations or the charities themselves may somehow come back to benefit the original donor or that person's family. Article 221 comes down in favour of separation of control, although how this works in practice is not yet known.

---

68 These Offices for Implementing the Intention to Create Wakaf (Pejabat Pembuat Akta Ikrar Wakaf) are a division of the Department of Religion and exist at the provincial, regional and district levels.

In the articles dealing with rules and registration (articles 223–224), the bureaucratic forms become even more dominant. Registration is by the KUA and requires production of evidence of ownership. The remaining provisions repeat the administrative imperative. The purpose of a *wakaf* cannot be changed without permission from the KUA acting on the advice of the local council of *'ulamā'*. The grounds for change are that the original purpose is no longer possible or that considerations of public interest (not defined) require the change. Disputes are to be dealt with by the religious courts (article 226).

Throughout Book III, the instructions include phrases such as 'in accordance with existing/appropriate law' without stating what this actually means. We must therefore turn to the complex set of instructions and decisions defining how *wakaf* works in practical administrative terms. These derive from the enabling law on land, the Basic Agrarian Law (No. 5/1960). Two are especially important. Regulation No. 10/1961 sets out the procedures for registration of land, including *wakaf* land. It is concerned especially with accurate surveying of land area and the processes of registration. Regulation No. 38/1963 concerns institutional ownership—a common a feature of *wakaf* landholding—and sets out the appropriate registration procedures.

Until recently, the most important regulation specifically on *wakaf* was Regulation No. 28/1977 of the Department of Religion—the Wakaf Regulation (Peraturan Perwakafan).[69] Pre-dating the KHI, it consolidated the then-existing law on *wakaf* from the department's point of view. Far from interfering with the Basic Agrarian Law on registration matters, it emphasized the priority of this law and the earlier regulations in matters of registration.[70] Its purpose was to confine *wakaf* to donations of wholly owned land, so that it could be held in perpetuity without being subject to claims for other purposes. We should remember, however, that the regulation did not apply to private or family *wakaf*, where (presumably) this limitation did not apply. Registration, therefore, was the ultimate proof of public *wakaf*.

This trend towards absolute state control continues in the latest legislation, Law No. 41/2004, which establishes the Indonesian Wakaf Board (Badan Wakaf Indonesia). In other respects, it is essentially an updated and refined version of the earlier law.

Islamic Banking

Islamic banking is a new phenomenon dating from the last quarter of the twentieth century. Beginning in Egypt, it soon spread to the Gulf states. It first appeared in Southeast Asia in 1982 with the establishment of Bank Islam Malaysia Berhad

---

69 The latest version I have is the Department of Religion text of 1998.
70 See the elucidation and Chapter III, article 10.

in Malaysia.[71] This was rapidly followed by the opening of 'syariah windows' in Malaysian commercial banks.

The purpose of Islamic banking is to organize state and personal finance in a way that does not contravene *fiqh*. This means (a) that schemes of investment must not involve forbidden objects such as alcohol or gambling (the stock exchange is a problem here), and (b) that interest as a profit mechanism must be replaced by other forms of contract operating on joint venture principles (Saeed 1996). Despite initial scepticism, the Islamic banking model has proved relatively successful, if on a small scale—none of the Islamic banks in Southeast Asia have succeeding in raising their Islamic banking transactions to more than 3–4 per cent of total bank transactions.

One point should be clarified here. It is that an Islamic bank is not 'based on' syariah, but rather 'does not contravene' syariah in its operations. A moment's thought will show that these are substantially different things, even though they are often treated as if they were interchangeable. This can easily be shown *by reading the actual Islamic bank contracts.* While it is true that the contracts have Arabic names or are described as syariah contracts, the actual provisions binding the parties are either derived from or actually reproduce secular contract law. Muslim scholars in Southeast Asia certainly recognize this fact.[72] This is not to say, as some critics do, that Islamic banking is just a facade, a view that is both offensive and untrue. The Indonesian view, very well put by Rahardjo (1988: especially 159 ff.), is that Islamic banks perform the essential function of distributing accumulated funds to persons who would otherwise be unable to access credit, for public or social purposes. The particular focus is on benefiting the poorer classes, especially in rural areas and through cooperative movements. Of course the issue of how to deal with interest and administrative costs is of central concern, but there is at least room for debate about the meaning of interest (*riba*).[73]

Indonesia established its first Islamic bank, Bank Muamalat, in May 1992.[74] This was followed by the establishment of People's Syariah Credit Banks and the introduction of syariah windows in commercial banks. The most common forms of contract offered by these institutions are:

- in equity financing, *mudarabah* and *musharakah*;
- in trade financing, *murabahah*;
- in debt financing, *bai bithamam ajil* and *bai inah*; and
- in lease financing, *ijarah*.

---

71 See Richards (2003) and Man (1988).
72 References for Malaysia are given in Richards (2003). More generally, see Lubis (1996).
73 For recent discussion, see Antonio (2001: 37 ff.).
74 Laws No. 7/1992 and No. 10/1998.

Mudarabah (based on profit and loss sharing) is the most commonly used contract, and is especially suitable for small and medium-sized enterprises. In theory, under this form of contract money is advanced by the bank, the borrower contributes labour and skills, and profits are shared in an agreed ratio with any loss to be borne by the bank. In practice, however, the borrower is subject to strict financial controls, usually on a monthly audit basis, and the bank can terminate the contract at its own initiative. In addition, the bank may require guarantees from the borrower to cover negligence resulting in loss, where negligence is defined broadly or not at all. In short, risk is shifted away from the bank onto the borrower. The terms of a typical *mudarabah* contract are drawn from the existing civil laws on contract;[75] they are not 'syariah based'. The same is true for the other forms of contract listed above.

This brings us to the contradictions inherent in the Indonesian form of Islamic banking contracts. The assumption in 1992 was that the contracts were 'based on' syariah (although, as we have seen, this is not the case). It followed that there could be no recourse to the civil courts, for which syariah was off-limits. However, the religious courts also had no jurisdiction, because this was not specified in Law No. 7/1989. How then to resolve disagreements? The answer was to include an arbitration clause as standard in all the contract forms. Arbitration was to take place under the auspices of MUI, again on the ground that the contracts were based on syariah. Although this was apparently the practice until recently, I have no data on the process or the results.

The position changed in May 2006. Under the revised Law on Religious Justice, Law No. 3/2006, the religious courts acquired jurisdiction over *ekonomi Islam*, including Islamic banking contracts. The new law brought its own uncertainties. Do the arbitration provisions in existing contracts exclude the jurisdiction of the religious courts, and what of future contracts which persist with arbitration? What law(s) should the religious court judges apply, given that the substance of the contracts is secular law? More specifically, do the religious court judges have the requisite knowledge and competence in secular law?[76]

At first glance, this brief introduction to Islamic forms of money in Indonesia seems to show a marginalization of syariah, hence the symbolic nature of Islamic money. This is true enough if we confine our gaze to the bottom line, to the profit and loss accounts of state budgets and the organizing principles of accountancy that describe *zakat*, *wakaf* and Islamic banking. But to take such a narrow view of the issue and simply ask whether a certain form of money is Islamic or non-

---

75 The Civil Code (Kitab Undang-Undang Hukum Perdata; KUHP).

76 This is properly a subject for Chapter 3, but I will note here that Law No. 3/2006 seems to have given added impetus to the movement to review the IAIN curriculum so that it can cope with issues such as these. That is certainly the impression I gained from discussions in late 2006.

Islamic is to force a yes or no answer upon us. The reality is much more complex and cannot be reduced to such a simple dualism. A more useful approach, I believe, is to take the examples explained above as arrangements *informed by* Islam. This allows us to see the rather subtle nuances of Islamic forms of money. 'Symbol' and 'real' arise naturally out of *informed by*, by leaving space for something called 'syariah money' to develop. At present the Islamic contract is very much in embryo form,[77] and much remains to be understood about Islamic forms of money. Rather than asking the wrong question—Is transaction X Islamic?—an important starting point is to allow the actual contracts to illustrate the complexities for themselves.

6 CONCLUDING REMARKS: THE NEW *FIQH*

In its formal structures, the Indonesian national *mazhab* is quite young; the religious courts and the KHI are only 15 years or so old. Of course, the religious courts existed long before that, but with a severely restricted and dependent jurisdiction. The political debates are also of longer standing. But having said this, it is also true that an *effective*, *sustainable* system of syariah is a very recent creation.

Despite the considerable uncertainties and inconsistencies that remain, we have at least some answers to what the new *fiqh* means. It means what the state says it means. The new *fiqh* is found in the positive laws of the state. At this very basic level this is what syariah 'in the state' means. But the new *fiqh* is not wholly disassociated from the classical texts. For example, while it may be possible to understand and administer the KHI without any knowledge of these texts, it would certainly not be possible to comment sensibly on the difficulties of application that arise. The rules in the KHI are sourced from (various) *fiqh* texts, but they also require a new way of thinking because of the way they are expressed in the code. A boundary has been crossed and another, state-derived, legitimacy is in place, but this does not mean that the old legitimacy can be done away with. As a further illustration, one can point to *zakat* and *wakaf*. Here, the new *fiqh* is little more than the classical texts in rewritten form, but the new form (laws, ministerial decisions, Department of Religion guides, bureaucratic requirements for registration and so on) imposes extensions on the classical functions. Thus, one finds consideration of capitalization in the case of *zakat* and limits on continuing donor interests in the case of *wakaf*. Both examples go to the heart of the classical *fiqh*, either rejecting or severely modifying its rules.

Where is legitimacy now to be found? The resolution of this question lies with the judges of the religious courts, but the courts have their own difficulties. A major but often overlooked one is the very low level of finance and resources

---

77 See the essays in Archer and Karim (2007).

available to them (Hooker and Lindsey 2002: 272 ff.), which directly affects the efficiency and long-term development of a national *fiqh*. The new regional laws, particularly the Special Autonomy Law for Aceh, are already intensifying national differences in the approach to *fiqh* (see Chapter 6). The Supreme Court, under whose jurisdiction the religious courts now fall, has not as yet established anything like a uniform policy for the new *fiqh*.

As a definition of syariah, the new *fiqh*, even in its restricted positive-law form, leaves much to be desired. Nevertheless, despite its uncertainties and contradictions, it does have a minimal level of efficacy.

2 Syariah Philosophies: From God to Man and Back Again?

The 'philosophy of syariah' is an enigmatic phrase. It has been used to construct philosophies of law from very different premises: first, where the major premise is the Qur'ān and Sunnah; second, where it is historical *fiqh*; and third, where it is the actual facts of political, social and legal life in a particular time and place. I am not suggesting that these are the only possible premises, but they are necessary if not wholly sufficient for the present. If we choose to emphasize one premise over the others, then we introduce a weight that shifts the balance (of what is 'true', 'good', 'workable') in favour of that one. Thus, if we choose the first, we can come up with a system that justifies a caliphate, or can be made to seem to do so. The second gives us a philosophy rooted in scholasticism and the third may lead to the unrestrained use of independent judgment (*ijtihad*)—even, eventually, to Western social science and positive law.

These are the issues I explore in this chapter. For the sake of initial clarity, it is as well to emphasize again that Islam/syariah has a presence in public life—that is, in politics—as well as in public documents such as the Constitution (Pancasila) and laws. The time with which I am primarily concerned is the 1940s to the present. My purpose is to explore a variety of syariah philosophies that I believe define the syariah possibilities for a distinctly Indonesian school of legal thought (*mazhab*). I purposely use the plural, because Indonesia has not decided on 'a' syariah philosophy. The five philosophies I discuss in this chapter are acknowledged alternatives; although I deal with them separately, they are often conflated. Just as frequently the balance between and within them oscillates. Their respective boundaries can be indicated but have to be considered porous.

1   SYARIAH AS SUFFICIENT

This view holds that the syariah, 'properly understood', fulfils all the conditions necessary to constitute a true legal system or legal system 'properly so called'. The issue is quintessentially nineteenth–twentieth century and is found in Muslim scholarship responding to European dominance. For practical purposes the syariah was no longer a given (as in pre-modern times), and for it to regain its relevance required a return to the only source still available. This is the basis of the modernist movements that turned to the Qur'ān and the Sunnah. The syariah had to be reformulated from revelation and the divinely inspired examples in the Sunnah. This process, a reconstruction, still continues.

Moenawar Chalil

Our first example is found in the work of Moenawar Chalil (1908–61), whose long career was devoted to the task of reconstructing syariah in a form that was compatible with the fact of the secular state as the dominant political form in Indonesia.[1] However, in the two key issues—legal system and sufficient conditions—he was only partly successful.

Chalil never really provided a definition of what he meant by 'legal system'; indeed, he barely raises the issue. If by legal system we mean prescription that has efficacy, as we must, then the best answer by Chalil is that a reformed Muslim society is a pre-condition for an effective legal system to operate. That is, a proper application of religion (*din*), faith (*iman*) and choice (*ikhtiyar*) all lead to a syariah that has efficacy. Society must be made to change to make possible the performance of the duties the individual owes to God. It is not surprising to find Chalil take this position; for a long time he was a member of the purist movement Persis, and this is a pure Persis view. But efficacy cannot wait on social perfection or even social change; it must be operable in imperfect conditions. Conditions in Indonesia are not perfect: there was and is no Islamic state in Indonesia.

There is a second aspect to the legal system issue. This is the classical natural law dilemma that is particularly characteristic of revealed religions: how and by whom are the relations between positive (man-made) prescription, naturally derived (through the capacity to reason), to be understood with reference to the revealed text (here, the Qur'ān and the Sunnah)? Here Chalil is on more certain ground, with recourse to *ijtihad*, unquestioning acceptance of the religious rulings of a higher religious authority (*taqlid*), reason (*akal*) and exegesis (*tafsir*). These do provide methods, internally valid for syariah, for arriving at a 'system'. But the validation is only internal. The man-made prescriptions (for example, *fiqh*) that it describes do not carry an efficacy that is sufficient in the wider Indonesian society, as Chalil himself seemed to realize. This brings us to the conditions for establishing such an efficacy for syariah.

Most of Chalil's efforts were directed at establishing the sufficient conditions that would make an efficacy for syariah possible (Chalil 1970), although, as we have seen, he did not discuss this exhaustively in terms of a system. His discus-

---

1   See Hamim (1997) for an outline of Chalil's career and a guide to further reading.

sion rests on one proposition: the immutability and absolute rightness of syariah. This is a given—in its own way a perfect 'positive' law. Not surprisingly, then, he begins with the notion that 'pure' Islam in Indonesia has attracted accretions that diminish it and must be removed. Purity is to be found in the Qur'ān and Hadith (the inclusion of the latter being a purely Persis proposition). Purification of public Islam is therefore the first sufficient condition that must be established. Essentially, this derives from *iman*, faith in the oneness of God (Q12:17, Q9:62). One demonstrates *iman* at the personal and public levels through the right performance of religious obligation derived from the Sunnah. The will to action itself is thus defined in Hadith. The implications for syariah are obvious: if one establishes the right definition of duty on this basis, *taqlid* must be rejected and there will be no place for local tradition and practice.

His second condition is that the interactions in society governed by Islamic law (*mu'amalat*)—as distinct from the prescribed ritual duty to God (*ibadah*)—should be made consonant with syariah imperatives. In his view, this can be achieved through a process of choice, that is, 'right reason' (*ikhtiyar*) (Chalil 1970). His authority for this is Q2:141 '... They shall reap the fruit of what they did ...'. That is, local and other actions outside *ibadah* are temporal, whereas that which is prescribed (in Hadith) is valid for all times and all places. Thus, efficacy is attainable: God has said it; mankind is therefore duty bound to accomplish it. The 'it' being referred to here is to achieve a rightly reasoned syariah—extending also to *mu'amalat*. The efficacy condition will thus be fulfilled, and a truly 'Islamic' (syariah) system will come into being.

The reason this has not yet happened is that mankind has so far failed to learn enough about 'pure' syariah, and therefore to accept or understand the need for it. Like Ahmad Hassan, his Persis colleague, Chalil lamented this fact and devoted considerable energy to publishing instructions in the form of newspaper articles and small booklets to 'remedy ignorance' (Hooker 2003a).[2] He believed that correct understanding would lead to correct behaviour, and this in turn would lead to acceptance of syariah as the deciding law(s) for daily life. In short, because syariah is sufficient it *must* be the law. It is therefore the duty of the individual and the Islamic community (*ummah*) to make it so through individual and social reform. This begins with a proper understanding of the Qur'ān and the Sunnah.[3]

So far, the *ummah* has steadfastly refused to come up to the standards necessary to form the sufficient conditions for syariah acceptance. The sufficiency

---

2 From 1941 to 1961, Chalil was chair of the Indonesian Committee on Hadith (Ahli-Ahli Hadits Indonesia), which put out *Al-Fiqh al-Nabawy* through various publishers in monthly instalments. Read with the *Soal-Jawab* of Ahmad Hassan, it is a very valuable source for the period. I rely on it for this part of the chapter.

3 In developing this line of argument, Chalil quotes extensively from Muhammad Abduh (1849–1905) and Rashid Rida (1865–1935), with both of whom the reader will be familiar.

argument is therefore dependent on the *ummah* behaving in a manner consistent with a pure Islamic system. The underlying premise that it is possible to establish such a system may be false, but this does not mean that the situation cannot be remedied. It is no doubt difficult, as Chalil recognized, but it is a personal duty to try.

Whatever a purist like Chalil might hope for or claim, the duty is always contextual. For example, Mohammad Natsir (1908–93), a scholar with tremendous practical political experience,[4] eventually came to the view that religion (Islam) could be assimilated into, and indeed inform, the state ideology (Pancasila) through the idea of nobility of character (*akhlaq al-karimah* or *makarim al-akhlak*)—the idea that what Islam and Pancasila have in common is an appeal to the more noble side of human nature. This would fulfil the sufficient condition necessary for syariah, which would then take on a life of its own. As we know this did not happen and the secular position triumphed.[5] The issue did not go away, however.

We should pause here to notice that there are already two strands in the argument so far. While Chalil and Natsir agree on the primacy of the Qur'ān and the Sunnah, they are writing from fundamentally different viewpoints for fundamentally different audiences. Chalil was a scripturalist. In the Indonesian context of the time, this meant that his arguments were written for and confined to an intellectual audience. Natsir, on the other hand, was a practical politician concerned about the right distribution of power in an independent state and the proper basis on which that distribution should be made. His answer was 'Islam', but his use of the term was so broad and general that it became overly diffuse and, hence, dismissible in favour of the 'real' facts of life. In the end, what Indonesia was left with was scripturalism and the fact of the nation-state. Sufficiency has yet to be demonstrated as a practical proposition.

Front Pembela Islam (FPI) and Hizbut Tahrir Indonesia (HTI)

There are contemporary versions of the sufficiency argument that are continuations of the earlier argument but rather more complex in form. Such complexity is to be expected given the increasingly sophisticated material that has become available since the late 1970s, including especially contemporary Islamic thinking from the Middle East. From the huge range of material that is available, I have selected several recent examples.[6] They should be considered illustrative rather than determinative.

---

4   Almost always on the losing side! See Ihza (1995) for a brief biography.
5   See the Soekarno–Natsir debates in Noer (1973: 275 ff.).
6   For a comprehensive range of perspectives, see the extracts in Fealy and Hooker (2006: 207–71).

My first example is taken from a defence of the Jakarta Charter written by the co-founder and chair of the Islamic Defenders Front (Front Pembela Islam; FPI), Habib Rizieq Syihab (1965–). He states that Muslims have an obligation to 'enforce the syariah' and insist that it be made the law of the country (Syihab 2000: 13–39).[7] The argument is built on analogy with a commercial enterprise and runs as follows. If an individual succeeds in creating a successful economic enterprise, then he is entitled to make rules for his employees and require all employees to obey them. God created mankind, endowed human beings with senses and reason, and gave them the means to secure a livelihood. Therefore, He has the right to 'determine the limits and norms of human life which He has created'. Humans must 'obey the rules of the Creator'.

This is a wildly inappropriate analogy demonstrating a high degree of theological illiteracy. It shows a complete lack of comprehension of first cause. A company is created, goes in and out of existence and is subject to the laws of the state. God is not caused; He is, and He is without cause. As to the proposition that syariah must be imposed and enforced, there are the obvious objections as to what syariah means, entwined with the complexes of the free will versus individual responsibility and determinism debates. No proper explanation of these issues is given. Instead, we are presented with an essentially personal view without qualification or substance. All revealed religions are susceptible to this practice, one that is quite rightly condemned. I am not mounting a defence of the 'schoolmen' or, in this case, the *'ulamā'*, but simply pointing out that an 'authoritative hierarchy'[8] of scholarship is necessary to maintain doctrine. Because the syariah is in doctrine, failure to observe the canons of scholarship will ultimately destroy the efficacy of the law. Misunderstanding or, more usually, incomprehension of the doctrine of first cause is absolutely fatal to the case for sufficiency.

In my second example, I widen the focus to take necessity with sufficiency. I admit that it is not a wholly satisfactory way of proceeding because, generally, it confuses conditions with purpose, but this is so common in contemporary Indonesian discussion on syariah that it almost seems irrelevant.[9] In any case, I indicate some of the problems below.

The Liberation Party of Indonesia (Hizbut Tahrir Indonesia; HTI) was established on the model of Hizbut Tahrir, founded in 1953 in Jerusalem. Its central objective is to re-establish an Islamic caliphate (*khilafah Islamiya*) as an institution. HTI specifically rejects force or violence but it does take the primary Middle Eastern text, *Manhaj Hizbut Tahrir fi al-Taqhyir* [Method for Change of Hizbut Tahrir], as its basic policy program. Muhammad Ismail Yusanto (1962–)

---

7 An extract can be found in Fealy and Hooker (2006: 234–6).
8 The phrase is that of Hallaq (1997: 209). He is actually discussing judicial administration, but the point holds good in any case.
9 For the classical Islamic positions, see Hallaq (1997).

is the deputy chair and public face of the organization, and has written several papers outlining its thinking.[10]

HTI's 'method for change' has three connected parts. The first and basic proposition is that Islam, specifically syariah, is a gift from God to the whole of mankind. It will therefore bring good to all, Muslims and non-Muslims alike. This good includes civil society and access to the benefits of science and technology (Yusanto 2003). It is the special duty of Muslims to accept the totality of Islam (again, specifically syariah); indeed, God requires full acceptance (Q2:208, Q4:65). Those who deny this are in fact denying Islam rather than submitting to the will of God as is required (Q24:51). Muslims have no choice in this matter; to refuse to accept the will of God is a betrayal (Q33:36). This is an internal argument based on the premise that a Muslim has no choice but to accept syariah. However, syariah is not defined in this opening part.

The next proposition is that the syariah will provide a just society—that 'Indonesia will be saved by syariah' (Yusanto 2003: 137). Capitalist and socialist ideologies have failed to solve the massive economic, social and political problems facing Indonesia. The solution is syariah, which, by implementing the spirit of Islam as a manifestation of life's purpose, is the only method that can deal with the crises of modernity. Syariah is not anti-technology or anti-progress; on the contrary, by ensuring the implementation of Islamic values it can provide true guidance so as to avoid the ills of modern society. These ills are a consequence of permitting that which is forbidden by God and forbidding that which is obligatory under God. Here follow examples: financial and political corruption, violence, unlawful sex and so on. These serious social and individual defects will be removed by the application of syariah, which 'offers a system for human life that totally fulfils people's spiritual and physical needs' (Yusanto 2003: 168).

The third part sets out the process for implementing the method for change. The HTI position here is that the Muslim world is tragically disunited. Its fragmentation can be traced to the senseless abolition of the (Ottoman) caliphate in 1924, which was not only unnecessary but deeply damaging to the unity of the *ummah* (Yusanto 2004). We have here an interesting historical reference. The caliphate was the subject of intense debate in pre-independent Indonesia, where it aroused considerable discussion on the twin themes of nationalism and pan-Islamism.[11] Although nothing of practical importance came out of this discussion, pan-Islamism has never been wholly absent from Indonesian Muslim thought, and the contemporary HTI proposals can be seen in this light.

The actual argument begins with Q3:110: 'Believers, you are the best community ...', from which Yusanto makes the observation that Muslim commu-

---

10 See the extracts from Yusanto (2003, 2004) in Fealy and Hooker (2006: 163–5, 167–8 and 236–9).
11 See van Bruinessen (1995) for an incisive discussion.

nities are in fact in a state of 'regression' in all aspects of life (cited in Fealy and Hooker 2006: 237). The Western invasion ('Westoxication') has succeeded through intellectual means in destroying the authority of God's revelation.[12] This has happened because of Muslim disunity and can only be repaired by recreating the caliphate. There are three reasons why this is necessary. First, the existing international Muslim organizations—the Organization of Islamic Conference (OIC), the Arab League and so on—are ineffective and 'cannot stop the killing machines from taking Muslim casualties daily' (in Afghanistan and Iraq) (cited in Fealy and Hooker 2006: 239). Second, the Europeans and Americans are already in a state of advanced unification because of their participation in groups directed towards economic expansion, such as Asia-Pacific Economic Cooperation (APEC), the ASEAN Free Trade Agreement (AFTA) and the North American Free Trade Agreement (NAFTA). Muslim countries must unite under a new caliphate to resist this type of aggression. In an age of increasing globalization, there is no other alternative. Finally, Yusanto cites selectively from Ibn Katsir[13] to the effect that deviation (*fitnah*) is a transgression of syariah and must be rejected. It can be countered by following the Prophetic traditions that emerged during the Medina period, the most important element of which is the unified will that can only be achieved in or through a caliphate. The authority of the caliph is an essential foundation of the state, as was shown specifically in the golden age of the first four caliphs (632–661).[14]

The HTI arguments are eclectic in source. They are based on revelation; fourteenth-century scholarship and the history of the caliphate in the period immediately following the death of the Prophet; and the history of the Ottoman caliphate. From the point of view of sufficiency, the first two are appropriate given the primacy of revelation. However, the later historical references raise necessity to sufficiency, which is not a logical possibility. Additionally, of course, the caliphate, from whatever period, was not a unifying concept, and was successful only for short periods through the application of force. Indeed, it encouraged conflict among competing powers for the right to use the title as a legitimating label. Some modern Indonesian commentators actually see the caliphate as a form of totalitarian rule (Assyaukanie 2004).

What can we conclude from these examples of the sufficiency argument? We begin by referring to a well-known survey published in Indonesia's respected *Tempo* magazine (30 December 2001). A sample of 2,000 Indonesian Muslims

---

12 It is instructive to read exactly the same argument, but from a Western viewpoint, in Lewis (2002).

13 Imad al-Din ibn Umar Kathir (or Katsir) (1302–72) was a Syrian exegete and historian. See Encyclopedia of Islam (second edition): Ibn Kathir.

14 This is a totally misguided reading of that period. See Crone and Hinds (1986) for an explanation of the complexities.

from 16 provinces were asked to share their views on Islam in public life, specifically the role of syariah. Over 60 per cent said that they thought that the state should implement syariah. However, when *hudud* punishments such as stoning for unlawful sex were specified as part of syariah, this figure dropped to 42 per cent. It dropped even further to 29 per cent when amputation for theft was mentioned. These figures are significant in themselves, but more to the point, they indicate one consistent feature of the sufficiency arguments—that all of them refer to 'syariah' without defining what it would actually mean in practice. This is either disingenuous or dishonest. The appeal for the simple and uneducated Muslim is to emotions and feelings, or to perceptions of threat by the 'other' (the powerful, the state, foreigners, the Christian West and so on). The truth or falsity of this threat is not the issue here; rather, it is that the sufficiency argument can all too easily open the gate to irrational conduct. This seems to have been one of its practical consequences in Indonesia—although irrational public behaviour does not necessarily invalidate an argument.

There are two main problems with the syariah as sufficient argument in the Indonesian context. First, an argument based on history must be founded on an acceptable historiography, but this is totally lacking in the Indonesian case. The Indonesian argument is ahistorical; it may even be thought of as historical romanticism—always a potent force. Second, the Indonesian sufficiency argument does not tell us what the process of transition is to be when moving from contemporary state structures to a caliphate. Any transition needs to be explained. No doubt an appeal to an ideal can be made, but the practical must also be addressed. In philosophy of law we are well accustomed to considering questions of efficacy, and this is the issue here. Not to address it is intellectual avoidance of an imperative. It is dishonest, because it denies an existing, manifest condition, namely the existing Indonesian state institutions. It says they have no value when in fact they do, in the simple, boring, mundane matters of everyday life: buying a house, getting a loan, getting married and so on. Of course these things could be done better, and there is certainly plenty of room for Indonesia to improve. The syariah sufficiency case must provide a detailed program showing how this would be done. At least one example must be put forward. None has.

2   LOCALIZED SYARIAH

Localized syariah holds that, leaving aside prescribed ritual duty (*ibadah*), all other parts of the syariah may be adapted to suit local conditions.[15] So stated, the

---

15 But see, for example, Ramsay (2006: 32) on Cambodia's matrilineal Bani Cham, whose ritual is decidedly unorthodox. Although not directly relevant to the case of Indonesia, this does provide an example of deviant forms of *ibadah*. Are the Cham

proposition appears to be both simple and a matter of common sense. There are, however, two difficulties. First, the line between ritual duty and non-ritual duty is not always easy to draw; the method of payment for *zakat*, for example, is still contested in Indonesia. Second and perhaps more importantly, the last 200 years have seen the secular state (colonial and post-colonial) increasingly arrogate to itself the right to decide such issues. Adaptation to local conditions—localization, for short—has been and is a state matter. It is imposed by political policy, exercised through state bureaucracies and adjudicated in state courts. This form of localization is now standard throughout all states with Muslim populations, including the Southeast Asian states.[16]

Before turning to Indonesia, we should indicate the two problems Muslims face when they attempt to 'localize' syariah. The first is what to select out of syariah for localized treatment. The consistent response over the years has been to select family law and charitable trusts as the ambit of syariah, whether colonially imposed or freely adopted. In more recent years (the 1970s onwards), some forms of 'Islamic' finance have also been introduced. The point to note is that the selection is made from the point of view of *state interest* as to what syariah is. The second problem is to establish boundaries, within the selected material, between that which can be altered by the state institutions (courts, codes, bureaucracies) and that which cannot. The typical solution in the case of clear but controversial Qur'ānic injunctions (on, for example, polygamy) has been to permit or retain the principle while making it difficult or almost impossible to achieve in practice. These two problems face all states with Muslim populations and are endlessly debated.

Indonesia is something of an exception to some of the comments just made. There was no imposed localization of syariah in the Netherlands East Indies; instead, it was separated out and subordinated to customary law (*adat*). This was an exclusion rather than a localization, unless one stretches the definition of the latter. This meant, first, that a formal process of state-directed localization had to wait until after independence, and second, that there was no colonial heritage on which the newly independent Republic of Indonesia could draw as in the neighbouring British territories. The practical consequence of this absence of model was that the whole issue was approached by way of philosophy of law, itself a hotly debated issue in the 1940s and 1950s. Essentially Indonesia was trying to invent a new way of thinking about law that would simultaneously get rid of the colonial heritage, express the ideals of the new republic and be practical. It has not succeeded in any of these lofty aims except in the field of syariah.

Muslims, as they claim to be? Who is to decide, and what are the consequences of any decision? It should be noted that the Cham who make the *hajj* are not refused entry to the Haramain by the Saudi government.

16 For an outline see Hooker (1984). This work is still accurate for the colonial period but out of date for the years after 1979.

Hazairin

Indonesia's success in adapting the syariah to local conditions owes much to the thinking of one man, Hazairin (1905–75), the founder of localization theory.[17] This is all the more remarkable considering the lack of official interest in or even tolerance of the syariah during the 1950s to 1970s, the period in which he was most active. Hazairin's work made little practical impact at the time, although it did create intense debate within Muslim circles, especially among the more conservative *'ulamā'*. Hazairin's particular concern was to create a national syariah—a *mazhab nasional*, in his famous phrase. He was particularly interested in inheritance, especially as it affected female rights to property. As a Dutch-educated scholar of *adat*, he was very aware of the variety of inheritance principles (unilineal and bilateral) extant in Indonesian society. Although not formally trained in syariah, he was also well aware of the clear Qur'ānic rules on inheritance (the *farā'id* rules),[18] which did not fit at all easily with Indonesian practices. Nor for that matter did the inheritance rules as explained in the classical *fiqh* texts then in use in Indonesia. Many *'ulamā'* viewed Hazairin's attempts to identify and resolve these difficulties as a direct attack on their status as guardians of Islamic learning. This explains much of their hostility towards him.

Hazairin's premises are: (a) prescription can be sourced from both revelation and Indonesian social structures; and (b) these sources must be ranked, with revelation having precedence.[19] This means that the Qur'ān and the Sunnah are the prior sources. However, acceptance of this priority does not mean acceptance of the idiom (Arabic language and culture) in which revelation is expressed. So far as inheritance is concerned, Hazairin identifies the principles of patrilateral bias and/or patrilineal preference as Arabic idiom. He considers it not only possible but also necessary to replace these with the bilateral or parental idiom that is characteristic of Indonesian social structures. In this way efficacy of system may be achieved through a method not open to Chalil. The argument is superficially attractive but it runs up against the fact that the *farā'id* rules, expressed in patrilateral or patrilineal idiom, are clearly stated in the Qur'ān itself and so must be considered prior.[20]

Hazairin attempts to resolve this difficulty by suggesting a new definition for the classes of heirs to replace the basic classes used hitherto.[21] To arrive at this, he reinterprets the relevant verses in the Qur'ān, concentrating on the range of

---

17 On Hazairin, see Feener (2001) and Thalib (1976).

18 These are found in Q2:180, Q2:240, Q4:7–9, Q4:11–12, Q4:19, Q4:33, Q4:176 and Q5:109–111.

19 Hazairin's thinking is set out in a series of books; see Hazairin (1951, 1958, 1960, 1968) and many later reprints.

20 The *farā'id* rules are clear injunctions (*naṣṣ*).

21 These are male agnates (*'āsaba*) and non-*'āsaba*, though even this formulation has its own difficulties (see Coulson 1971).

meanings that the Arabic for 'heir(s)' (*mawla*, plural *mawali*) can bear. As Cammack (2002) has shown, an expanded definition of 'heir' can accommodate the idea of 'representation' so that females are not excluded *ab initio*. To this Hazairin adds the idea of 'priority' (based on Q4:11–12, Q4:176), which means that entitlement is based on membership of a class and that nearness of degree within a class is not, on its own, a condition for succession. Both males and females are included in class membership, from which it follows that females in a higher-priority class will have precedence over males in a lower-priority class.[22] The outcome is (a) an equal *entitlement* for males and females to succeed, but (b) the retention of an unequal 2:1 ratio in favour of males. Representation and priority between them certainly do advance the entitlements of women but the 2:1 ratio cannot be overcome. To this extent Hazairin's proposition is only partial and it has never been accepted in Indonesia. The reasons for this lie in his failure to debate the *fiqh* texts combined with the lack of acceptance of his expanded definition of heir(s).

But what about his theory of localization in the light of his comments—the idea of a ranked dual source? The answer is that it does not provide a satisfactory basis for a philosophy of syariah because it involves an inherent contradiction. I formulate this briefly as follows: to deny the validity of the Arabic idiom/context, but then to identify the essence of prescription (from the Qur'ān and Sunnah) as being suitable for one's own (twentieth-century) idiom/context is ahistorical and reduces the revealed texts to temporal relativity.

This is the classical modernist dilemma—whether to elevate contemporary concerns or purposes above the absoluteness of revelation or give the latter primacy. Of course a modernist would reply that true meaning is contingent on the time and circumstances in which one lives and that there is a duty to relate revelation to these factors. Given this duty, one is obliged only to avoid excessive relativity so as to preserve the 'essence' of revelation in a form that is suitable for local and temporal conditions.

A further and important result is that the authority of the *fiqh* texts is much diminished, because they are seen as creations of their times and thus captive to particular historical circumstances. In Hazairin's view, they should not be part of the new *mazhab nasional* to be created. More precisely, the doctrine expressed in *taqlid* is simply not appropriate. In this he was supported by some of his contemporaries, notably Hasbi Ash-Shiddieqy (1904–75), who recognized the existence of complex and localized versions of syariah as characteristic of the Muslim world (Ash-Shiddieqy 1966). Even Ahmad Hassan, perhaps the most literal of the Persis scripturalists, was occasionally prepared to accept some sort of prior status for culture and tradition—in one case on the issue of the necessity to obtain the consent of the female to marriage.[23]

---

22 For detailed argument, see Cammack (2002).
23 For details of his (unconvincing) *fatwā* on this issue, see Hooker (2003a: 139–40).

What then should we make of Hazairin's localization of syariah? Does it provide a method for arriving at a coherent and workable philosophy for syariah, as Hallaq (1997: 231) insists it must? From the strict viewpoint, as we have seen, the answer is that it does not, because Hazairin does not explain the necessary conditions for showing a link between his reinterpreted basic source (the Qur'ān and Sunnah) and Indonesian social structures. Is the link founded in dependence, and if so, which of the two is the dependent one? He would certainly have answered that revelation is prior; however, his understanding of revelation is itself formulated in terms derived from the whole Indonesian context for syariah—its 'social structures' of a time and place. This negates his order of priority because it is the latter that determine the order.

On the other hand—and this seems more likely—the link may be reflective. That is, because a link is necessary, *the action (which is also a duty) of searching itself constitutes the sufficient condition to show its rational possibility*. The fact that Hazairin failed in his attempt to reinterpret the Qur'ān does not affect the validity of the reflective search; it shows only that the search did not succeed in the terms formulated by him. Of course, it never could have succeeded in these terms, because Hazairin failed to deal with the implication of prioritizing revelation—that God is the cause. God as cause does not permit the acceptance or rejection of divine or divinely inspired prescription (identified in *qiyas/ijtihad*) on the basis of social science criteria. Hazairin's reinterpretation of the Qur'ān does not provide a solution.

At this point we must return to the idea of a reflective link. All this says is that the effort to show a link may be an effective condition. The effort itself is a possible definition of localization for syariah. As we have seen, Hazairin's attempt to reinterpret the Qur'ān was not successful and so must be rejected as a solution. However, this does not mean rejection of the *duty* to attempt the establishment of sufficient conditions. We now take two further examples of reflective effort.

H. Satria Effendi Zein

The first was developed by H. Satria Effendi Zein (1949–2000), a leading twentieth-century scholar who has exercised considerable influence despite the difficulty of his language (Zein 2004). He starts from the position that syariah and *fiqh* are open to the demands of time, circumstance and place. While he later distinguishes syariah from *fiqh*, he begins by examining how one should describe these basic categories. The usual starting point of most scholars is to adopt either a 'modernist' (*salafi*) or 'traditionalist' (*'ashrani*) approach. Drawing directly on the discussion of these two terms by Sa'id (1984: 91 ff.), Zein concurs with his view that the supposed differences or opposition between the two approaches are more apparent than real. According to Zein (2004: 127 ff.), the dyads have the following characteristics.

The *salafi* approach is to hold to a literal interpretation of the Qur'ān and Hadith, because these are expressions of the will of God. The facts of social life, that is, people's everyday difficulties and problems, must accommodate themselves to the primacy of revelation.[24] The Qur'ān is the key to revelation in that it contains prescription that cannot be questioned or reinterpreted (*qath'iy*). On the other hand, the prescription derived from scholarship (*dzanniy*), while authoritative, may be open to later interpretation. The *fiqh* texts are therefore relative or, in the language I have been using, reflective of circumstance. Zein concludes that, *in practice*, the *salafi* position allows a degree of latitude in interpretation—that the *qath'iy / dzanniy* boundary is in fact negotiable.

The *'ashrani* approach holds that a correct understanding of syariah must always consider the social and moral principles held by a society at a particular time and place. As principle, syariah is above circumstantial variation, but *fiqh* is socially dependent. Zein does not advocate ignoring the main *fiqh* texts, but simply recognizing that they are dependent on the social circumstances in which they were written.

Zein concludes that both the *salafi* and *'ashrani* approaches accept the circumstance of time and place. For him, this is not just a matter of emphasis in the mind of the scholar, but a real correspondence expressed in the *purposes* of syariah—the *maqasid al-syariah* (Zein 1991). Zein is referring here to the five aims of syariah as defined by al-Syathibi,[25] namely the preservation of life, the protection of property, certainty of lineage (descent), the protection of personal capacity and the defence/promotion of religion. For Zein, these are the key elements from which Muslim scholars must proceed when dealing with the challenges facing Islam in Indonesia.

What then of localization? The answer is that syariah values are revealed obligations (from the Qur'ān and Sunnah) and therefore prior by definition. Although they deserve the greatest respect, *fiqh* formulations are not prior in the same sense. The *maqasid al-syariah* encapsulates syariah values and therefore has priority over *fiqh*. This position is in fact very close to contemporary Islamic thinking outside Indonesia.[26]

The Compilation of Islamic Law (KHI)

How does this set of connected propositions translate in practice—to use the empiricist's question, does it work? This brings us to our second Indonesian example of localization, the Compilation of Islamic Law (Kompilasi Hukum

---

24 A 'pure', scripturalist version of this for Indonesia is found in the Persis *fatāwā*. See the *Soal-Jawab* by Ahmad Hassan and also Hooker (2003a).

25 The actual text is *al-Muwāfaqāt fī Uṣūl al-Ahkām* by Abū Isḥāq Ibrāhīm Shātibī (died 1388). For its importance in legal thought, see Hallaq (1997: 168 ff.).

26 See, for example, Rahman (1984).

Islam; KHI). The KHI was promulgated by presidential instruction in 1991 as a guide for the religious courts. Our interest here is in the thinking behind it, the view of syariah it presents, and why and how it was drafted in its present form. We are fortunate in having a first-hand account by a member of the drafting committee, M. Yahya Harahap. In an explanation published in 1992, Harahap provides a background to the KHI, which he describes as 'positivizing abstract Islamic law' (Harahap 1992).[27] This is the key to the KHI, which is now the basic reference text in the religious courts.[28]

What does 'positivizing' the syariah mean? The argument's basic premise is that it is incorrect to identify *fiqh* with syariah. The *fiqh* texts may have an authority from the past, but they actually represent 'the opinions and independent judgments (*ijtihad*)' of the leaders of the schools of law (Fealy and Hooker 2006: 148). In practical judicial administration, therefore, they are divisive and do not contribute to setting or maintaining a consistent standard of justice within the religious courts. For this reason they should not be a source of law and need to be replaced (by the KHI) in the interests of certainty and consistency. The argument is wholly utilitarian, but the separation of syariah and *fiqh* exactly parallels Zein's proposition. Each reached the same conclusion but by different reasoning: Zein through *maqasid al-syariah* and Harahap through the intention to avoid the fragmentation in decision making implicit in the variety of *fiqh* texts available. The absence of standardization is, in Harahap's view, directly against the public good (*masālah al-mursalah*). The introduction of the concept of public good does change the terms of the debate, moving it into a sphere where *fiqh* is judged by an outside, non-*fiqh*, criterion. This is a significant shift from the Zein proposition, in which the aims of syariah are set out from within Islamic legal thinking. Both Harahap and Zein concur, however, in their *fiqh* focus.

Thirteen *fiqh* texts were studied during the pre-drafting phase of the KHI, twelve of them Shafi'i texts.[29] But in the final draft these texts were massaged, smoothed out, almost defenestrated. The evidence for this is found in the provisions of the KHI itself. By its nature, the KHI is only a generalized statement of principles that do not offend any particular *fiqh* rule; it therefore manages to accommodate all *fiqh* texts without stress. The result is a standard text for the whole country that all religious court judges are required to observe. The following passage by Harahap encapsulates the fate of the *fiqh* texts and the reasons for it.

> Now, with the KHI, the values of the legal structure of Islam are clear and certain in the fields of marriage, gift giving (*hibah*), wills, donations (*wakaf*) and inheritance.

---

27 For an extract, see Fealy and Hooker (2006: 147–8).

28 Some judges do still refer to the *fiqh* texts, but they seem to be few in number. This is speculation, however, as no one has yet done the necessary religious court surveys.

29 Lubis (1997: 48) lists these texts. It is noteworthy that all appear in earlier lists (for Malaysia as well) used in the pre-KHI religious courts (Hooker 1984: 279–80).

The language and legal values decided in the religious courts ... will be applied in the same way by judges all over the archipelago.

The KHI is part of the whole Islamic legal structure and it can be upheld and its values enforced through the authority of the religious court. *The role of fiqh books in the application of law and justice will gradually fade and they will remain only as material for orientation and doctrinal study.* [Emphasis added]

... The legal guidelines and references to which the judges must adhere are to be the same all over Indonesia, that is, *the KHI is to be the only book of law that has legitimacy and authority.* [Emphasis added]

... They [litigants] can no longer present evidence from different schools of thought and force a judge to decide according to a particular opinion and *mazhab* doctrine. The [litigant] can no longer dispute the teachings of different *fiqh* books. (Harahap 1992: 22–3; translation by Virginia Hooker)

This passage seems clear enough. In this formulation and in the KHI itself, the *fiqh* texts are defenestrated. Or are they? Unless we examine actual practice in the religious courts themselves, we cannot be certain.[30]

Nevertheless, the KHI has been *fiqh* for Indonesia since 1991. Although the code has many critics,[31] the fact remains that the *fiqh* texts no longer represent standard legal values in Indonesia. They have been displaced by the KHI, which has been formulated 'in accordance with the needs of the Indonesian people' (Harahap 1992: 21–2) and defined as the public good (*masālah al-mursalah*). We must therefore conclude that the localization of syariah is (a) not *fiqh* but reflective of it, but (b) *maqasid al-syariah*, which is also reflective of *fiqh*. The KHI is actually rather minimalist in the latter sense. It can certainly be interpreted as directly and indirectly supporting the five aims of syariah as understood by Zein. If this is true (and I think it is), then the 'aims of syariah' and the 'public good' are collapsed categories—they have become indistinguishable. The result is that 'localization' means smoothed-out generalizations, or versions, of *fiqh*. There is absolutely no need to refer to the Qur'ān and Sunnah, as Hazairin thought in the 1950s and 1960s. The fact that the KHI exists is proof that this conclusion is right.

3 RATIONALIZED SYARIAH

The Counter Legal Draft to the KHI

The KHI is not necessarily inviolate. In 2004 the Department of Religion produced a revised version of the KHI focusing not on *fiqh* but on syariah. This brings us to the idea of syariah rationalized for the state.

---

30 During visits to Surabaya, Yogyakarta and Banda Aceh in 2004–06, I found some very preliminary evidence that the *fiqh* texts are still being used (see Chapter 1).

31 For an outline of pre- and post-KHI discussions, see Lubis (1997: 73 ff.).

The Counter Legal Draft to the KHI was produced in October 2004 by the Gender Mainstreaming Team of the Department of Religion.[32] In essence it does away with the *fiqh* entirely in the name of justice 'based on syariah'. Thus, for example, marriage is to be a social obligation whose validity rests on registration, a guardian (*wali*) is not required for marriage, interfaith marriage is to be permitted, polygamy is to be forbidden, the prescribed waiting period after divorce is to be the same for husband and wife, males and females are to inherit equally and so on. The document was quickly withdrawn in the face of predictable opposition.

Our interest here is in the arguments put forward by the authors to justify their rather extreme proposals. In their introduction to the Counter Legal Draft, they argue that there is a need for a new formulation of syariah that is 'in keeping with democratic life and reflecting the genuine character of Indonesian culture' (Fealy and Hooker 2006: 148). It is thus an alternative to 'total sharia implementation' on the one hand and the 'need to establish democracy' on the other. In this new formulation, all citizens have 'the same status and access to justice' and all are 'guaranteed equal rights'. The new syariah is founded on the 'basic aims of Sharia Islam (*maqashid al-syari'at*), that is, to establish values and principles of social justice, the welfare of the community of human beings, universal compassion and local wisdom' (Fealy and Hooker 2006: 149). The document has been 'prepared in Indonesian, *not Arabisms*, and can be understood by Indonesians' [emphasis added]. It draws on studies of legal history, the sociology and politics of law, and empirical evidence on how the present laws (that is, the KHI and the Marriage Law) actually work in practice.

As this illustration of rationalized syariah shows, 'rationalized' means (a) that the syariah is judged as suitable (or not) for state foundation in the light of (b) whether it can be mined for material that can be used to support some (higher) purpose or position of the moment, such as human rights, social welfare, civil society or good governance. The fundamental point is that syariah has a value only insofar as it is or can be made congruent with the purpose or position chosen. There has been a huge effort in Indonesian Islamic thinking over the past half-century to show a suitably high degree of congruence. A cynic might say that all this amounts to is the 'Islamization' of non-Islamic constructions. But many others would say that human rights and similar values are already inherent in Islam—particularly syariah—and that the current efforts merely draw out or make plain values that are already there. It is simply a matter of identifying them in a form suitable for contemporary Indonesia. These opposing emphases are unlikely to be resolved any time soon.

---

32 The head of the team was Siti Musdah Mulia, who has also argued for an overhaul of the polygamy laws (Mulia 2004). See Fealy and Hooker (2006: 148–9) for an extract from the introduction to the Counter Legal Draft and Fealy and Hooker (2006: 348–52) for a summary of its content and commentary.

Perhaps I should make it clear that I do not hold out the description of 'rationalized' just given as the only definition. I do claim, however, that the descriptive features indicated are in the material. All I can do here is present the material, to show just how diverse the debates have become over the past half-century.

If there is one common thread in the following pages, it is the longstanding and contentious debate over the Jakarta Charter and Pancasila. In 1945, Muslim and nationalist leaders could not agree on whether the new Republic of Indonesia should have an Islamic or secular basis. The committee drafting the Constitution eventually accepted Soekarno's five principles (Pancasila), the first of which—belief in one God—went some way towards persuading Muslim leaders that the new state would have a religious basis. However, they still felt the need for a specific clause that would oblige Muslims to implement syariah law. Contained in the Jakarta Charter, this clause consisted of seven words, which can be translated as: 'with the obligation to implement the syariah for adherents of Islam'. The Jakarta Charter was accepted in the draft constitution but dropped from the final version, a decision that created enduring bitterness among some Muslims. Implementation of syariah 'for adherents', or at least some minimal degree of implementation, had to wait until 1989 (the reformed religious courts) and 1991 (the KHI).[33]

Zainal Abidin Ahmad

The debate over how to achieve congruence between Islam and the state has remained remarkably consistent over the past half-century or more. The basic question is: What is 'Islam/ic'? The consistent answers are (a) 'syariah' (usually undefined) and (b) 'Islamic values', extending variously to human rights, freedom, democracy, social justice, good governance and so on. This whole revolves around an 'Islamic state', for which there are strong supporters and equally strong opponents. Some, such as Zainal Abidin Ahmad (1911–83), place the Islamic state idea in the context of the postwar creation of new states with Muslim populations (Ahmad 2001). The context is thus de-colonization, a time for renewal.

Ahmad starts with Q4:58–59:

> Render back your trusts to those to whom they are due; And when ye judge between man and man, ... judge with justice ... Obey God, and obey the Prophet and those charged with authority among you ...

From here he proceeds to the practice of the Prophet and the first four caliphs, to modern examples of the Islamic state, singling out Pakistan.[34] He finds that these

---

33 The intervening period, 1989–91, was confused and incoherent. See Lev (1972a) on sources of law and the jurisdiction of the religious courts.

34 With all due respect to Ahmad, and with the benefit of hindsight, this selection is a mistake. Pakistan has one of the most corrupt, incompetent and vicious versions of

sources, both singly and in combination, add up to a state that is both 'Islamic' and constituted by the *trias politica*, that is, the separation of legislative, executive and judicial powers—in fact, a constitutional system on modern lines. The difference is that in a truly Islamic system, ultimate authority rests with God. In practical terms this means that Muslims must form the majority of the population, that the head of state must be a Muslim, that laws must be consonant with Islamic principles and values, and that justice is essentially founded on the revealed Qur'ān and the divinely inspired Sunnah.

Nurcholish Madjid

In one form or another these have been the parameters of the last half-century of discussion of the appropriate place of Islam in the state. The emphasis on the respective elements has changed over time, with Pancasila being vehemently rejected at times[35] and the idea or political proposition of an Islamic state being just as emphatically rejected at others.[36] The reasons for rejecting an Islamic basis for the state are various, but one explanation that has attracted considerable interest in recent years is the contention by Nurcholish Madjid (1939–2005) that the call for an Islamic state is merely a form of *apologia*, indicating lack of confidence in oneself and one's religion, and therefore harmful and ultimately unnecessary (Madjid 1987: 253–5).[37] Madjid argues that the proposal for an Islamic state is a reaction to Western political and constitutional thought; it does not follow from any active premise in Islam's own history. To propose such a state is to surrender the agenda to the West. His second point is that the Islamic state–syariah nexus is purely legalistic in that it emphasizes a classical prescription (*fiqh*) that is largely culture and tradition bound, and unworkable for modern Indonesia. In this he is partly right and partly wrong: right in that the classical forms do not work at present, but wrong in that they can be (and in fact have been) adapted into a workable form in some areas of law (family law and even contracts). In the area of private law, these adaptations are generally known as 'syariah'. But this is not the 'syariah' of the political theorist, or of those who study and promote the 'proper' form of what a state populated by Muslims should be like (see further below, pp. 65 ff.).

---

so-called 'syariah' in practice today (Kennedy 1988). Pakistan's notorious Hudood Ordinance was repealed in December 2006. What effects this repeal will actually have, only time will show.

35 See Hamka, cited in Fealy and Hooker (2006: 218).

36 See the extracts in Fealy and Hooker (2006: 222–30) outlining contemporary argument.

37 See the extract in Fealy and Hooker (2006: 222–4).

Harun Nasution

We seem to be bedevilled by 'syariah', by its use to mean different things. So far we have: moral values, the public good, *fiqh*, the state (which is also 'democracy'), Pancasila, human rights and so on.[38] This is the philosopher's nightmare of the empty class. Until recently, the only consistent attempt over time to fill these classes was found in the work of Harun Nasution (1919–98). While his career spanned both the colonial and post-colonial periods, the eclecticism of his education was unusual by the standards of the times.[39] He attended a modernist Islamic secondary school in West Sumatra, Al-Azhar University (Faculty of Usūl al-Dīn) and the American University (education and social sciences) in Cairo, before entering the Indonesian Ministry of Foreign Affairs. He later undertook postgraduate studies at Canada's McGill University, gaining an MA in 1965 and a PhD in 1968. He taught at UIN Syarif Hidayatullah Jakarta, where he became rector. In educational circles he is remembered for his curriculum innovations in Islamic studies (see Chapter 3).

Nasution was more concerned with ethics, political philosophy and education than with the philosophy of law.[40] Nevertheless, he does provide important insights into contemporary syariah philosophy, especially in his *Islam Rasional* [Rational Islam] (Nasution 1995). Earlier in this section I said that, in Indonesian usage, 'rational(ized)' with reference to syariah means that syariah must be congruent with some non-syariah value. This appears to be the operative principle in *Islam Rasional*, but Nasution's use of *rasional* has given rise to considerable misunderstanding both inside and outside Indonesian law circles. He does not mean 'rational' in the sense of a cognitive process that is reliable, or at least not inconsistent, and therefore sufficient. Neither does he mean 'rationalism', that is, unaided reason that can dispense with the divine, although he has been accused of this (Rasjidi 1977). However, he does admit 'rationality' in the sense of a full acceptance of man's ability to reason so as to achieve some purpose (such as 'truth', 'right conduct' or the avoidance of destructive 'passion').

For example, Nasution holds that it is not possible to put one religion above another or to say that anyone has a monopoly on the truth, because all religions express or attempt to express the numinous (he does not use this term, but that is what he means). This has been widely misunderstood to mean or imply a denial of God's final revelation to the Prophet in the Qur'ān. In fact, Nasution was attempting to express the fact that an impulse towards the divine is common to all mankind (Nasution 1977: i–11 ff.). In no sense did he ever deny revelation or reject the finality of the Qur'ān. This is a good example of how the use of a loan word such as *rasional* can easily be misinterpreted. The lesson is that we

---

38 For other examples, see Fealy and Hooker (2006: 224 ff.).
39 For a biography of Nasution, see Muzani (1994).
40 See, among his many publications, especially Nasution (1977, 1986a, 1986b, 1987).

must distinguish all the varieties of rational/ity/ism. I have selected three papers from Nasution's work, trying to make them representative in the context of state and congruence, that is, as a practical program for the new state and, as Nasution hoped for, the state in the future.

The first is his 'Islamic Perspectives on Justice' (Nasution 1995: 61–77, originally published in 1978). Here, he locates the 'Islamic concept' of justice in the Qur'ān, the Sunnah and later commentary, providing examples by way of extensive citations. Nasution's point seems to be to demonstrate that there is a critical mass of citations that in spread and depth demonstrate a theory of justice.[41] He further proposes that the Islamic concept of justice can only be understood by providing a suitable method for putting that theory into practice. This he locates in the classical dyad of the Mu'tazilite and Asy'arite positions. In the former, the concept of justice supposes that God is bound to act within His own stated terms (that is, the Qur'ān); in the latter, the concept supposes that the power of God cannot be qualified. From this, it follows that man's soul can express justice through the exercise of reason. Justice can also be expressed within or by (Nasution is not clear as to which) Sufism (*tasawwuf*), which allows for purity of thought and deed in the social and environmental circumstances. 'Practical syariah' derives its character from these circumstances, and they are the basis for appropriate prescription.

While individuals may be equal in their entitlement to justice, the principle of equality is not unrestrained (as is apparent, for example, in the inheritance rules, Q17:82). One justification for this is the physical and sociological fact of natural discrepancies in human capacity. If one accepts this, then it follows that justice and prescription need not be absolutely conterminous, and that the former is prior (Q4:7–9, Q11:85, Q17:34–35 among others). A sense of justice is therefore essential to deal with human inequality, and prescription must be assessed on this basis. Thus, the rights of the individual and the general rights of the *ummah* must be balanced; the concept of public good (*maslahah*) likewise expresses a public sense of justice. Nasution's general conclusion is that one can find precedents, especially in Hadith, to show that justice rather than the textual norms of the Qur'ān is prior in the context of 'social reality', by which he means family matters and economic transactions. In short, he advocates a 'socialization' of Islam.

This argument is continued in a second paper on 'Islamic Law and Social Dynamics' (Nasution 1995: 195–200, originally published in 1980). Nasution's argument can be summarized briefly as follows. The Qur'ān and Hadith do not cover all possible circumstances in society, and prescription must therefore be developed through reason (*ijtihad*). The fact that there are four schools in

---

41 To take just two examples, Nasution cites Q82:7, Q6:152 and Q2:82 on 'straight', correct' or 'right'; and Q42:14, Q4:3, Q4:129, Q5:8 and Q7:81 among many others on 'just'.

the Sunni *mazhab* is evidence enough that creative reasoning is necessary, and indeed, the history of Islamic thought consistently demonstrates this. The syariah is therefore dynamic by its own nature. Since the early twentieth century, and especially since independence, the need for this type of reasoning has become even greater. In short, the syariah must be reformulated, based on 'the spirit and values of the country', to create an Indonesian school of syariah, that is, a '*mazhab syariah*' or '*mazhab nasional*'.

A third paper on 'Islam and Pancasila' continues this theme in more detail (Nasution 1995: 218–23, originally published in 1984). Essentially the essay attempts to show that Pancasila is perfectly compatible with Islam. Nasution's approach is to take each of the five Pancasila principles and demonstrate, through the use of Qur'ānic citations, that they are supported by the Qur'ān. Thus the first principle, belief in one God, is an affirmation of monotheism (*tauhid*). The second principle, humanitarianism, is defined in Q7:189, with the divisions among humans (pluralism) identified in Q10:19. The third principle, national unity or nationalism, is found in Q49:13 '... And made you into nations and tribes ...', which recognizes national groups and various cultural identities. The fourth, on government by negotiation or deliberation (democracy) takes us to deliberation (*shura*) as a method of government (Q3:159, Q42:38). Here Nasution also refers to the Sunnah of the Prophet and to the history of Muslim politics. The final social justice principle is supported by Q59:7, with *zakat* being interpreted as the redistribution of wealth for the purpose of creating social justice. In short, Islam and Pancasila are complementary formulations of principles held in common. The two are parallel, not contradictory. This is the most that can be asked for given that the Qur'ān and the Sunnah were never meant to formulate a theory of state. Nasution maintains that it is legitimate to abstract general principles from the sources just described to support Pancasila as the basis of the state. After all, Indonesia has a majority Muslim population and a Muslim head of state.

The three elements we find in these papers are, first, that justice and prescription both derive from the Qur'ān and Sunnah but can be distinguished; second, that prescription is contingent on social factors; and third, that the ideology of a state is acceptable if it is not contrary to Islam or if it can accommodate 'Islamic principles'. Nasution's position certainly can accommodate the idea of congruence. In more general terms, we find in his work an Islamic version of natural law theory which holds that there is an objective set of principles, knowable by reasoning, expressing God's will for mankind. The moral status of any prescription is to be judged by its congruence with divine will or intention. Divine will is expressed through the revealed or divinely inspired text(s), although, by definition, these are not fully intelligible. God did enact 'positive law' (examples being the laws on marriage, inheritance and interest in the Qur'ān) but He did not provide for a constitution or government. Nevertheless faith and reason are always compatible, because reason or rational conduct is part of faith. That being so, all temporal rule is an emanation of God's absolute power and must therefore be congruent with it.

Hamka

In Nasution's view, Pancasila is sufficiently congruent with Islam as the basis for the state. Others disagree. For example, in an address to the Constituent Assembly in 1957, Hamka (1908–81) made the following impassioned rejection of Pancasila:

> They [the secularists] do not want to accept Islam as the foundation of the state, when in fact it is the original background of the largest group in our country, which is deeply rooted and constitutes the Indonesian people's identity. Because they are scared of Islam, people are shameless enough to lie about history … Pancasila has no historical basis in Indonesia. (cited in Fealy and Hooker 2006: 218)

But despite such views, which are still current, the 'reasonable' congruence position remains the status quo.

Mohamad Roem

We have room for just one more example, this time from the work of Mohamad Roem (1908–83). He was a former head of Masyumi[42] and the deputy prime minister of Indonesia in the early 1950s. He writes as a historian and as a man experienced in the vagaries of power during the turbulent years of political change in Indonesia (the 1940s to 1980s).[43] His view of the Islamic state is that an organized polity certainly existed at the time of the Prophet, but in a special form because the Prophet was alive. After his death an Islamic state became a 'good aspiration' that would 'never be achieved, but rather only be approached as closely as possible' (Fealy and Hooker 2006: 227). That is, all one can do is try to live in accord with Islam. No defined and certain public form of the state (except possibly a republican form) is specified in revelation, tradition or history. Roem is referring here to the Qur'ānic recommendation for government by consultation—*shura*—which he extends to include representation and even democracy, a position also held by Nasution. However, whatever the form of the state, it must comply with the Qur'ān.

What, then, should we make of rationalized syariah? From the point of view of achieving or keeping open the possibility of political accommodations, it can be judged useful for a time and place. But as a coherent doctrine, the Indonesian version is not acceptable, because it does not provide a settled method for assessing the validity of congruence. It is open to anyone, however unqualified, to claim that such a congruence does or does not exist. In formal language, the

---

42 The Indonesian Muslim Consultative Council (Majlis Syuro Muslimin Indonesia; Masyumi) was formed in 1943. It became a political party in 1945 and was banned by Soekarno in 1960.

43 See Santoso (2004) and, for a summary of his ideas, the extract in Fealy and Hooker (2006: 226–8).

process of establishing congruence is comprised of free variables, none of which is true except in the belief of the chooser. The definition of a variable put forward by person A is no more valid than the definition put forward by person B, because there is no criterion common to both definitions. In this test, congruence can never be the answer to anything, let alone the definition of an Islamic state. However, as I have just said, congruence is useful, and as such is often called pragmatism. All this means here is that congruence is true if it works, that is, if it makes a belief real. The true test would be success in determining the basis of an Islamic state. So far, that has not happened.

4 HISTORICAL AND CONTEXTUAL SYARIAH

While Islamic history was an important if unstated datum for Chalil, Hazairin and Nasution, for Madjid it was primary—not as a source of prescription but as a demonstration that faith and knowledge are not the same, even if they are related. The nexus connecting them is found in the idea of context or contextualization. This can be explained as follows.

The Qur'ān is absolute and inviolate and the Sunnah is an exemplification of the absoluteness of revelation. Revelation does not regulate every last detail of life; hence the scholarly jurisprudence in the *fiqh* texts. The idiom of revelation is expressed in seventh-century Arabic language and culture. One must therefore isolate those principles in the Qur'ān that directly state social justice prescriptions, specify their seventh-century idiom and then state the contemporary context in which these principles are to be applied.

There are obvious similarities between the views of Madjid and those of Hazairin—especially in the importance both attach to Muslim history—but there are also substantial differences. Thus, while both hold that the Qur'ān is absolute, Madjid gives the Sunnah a less normative value in identifying prescription, thus opening the way for specifically Indonesian circumstances to become relevant. However, the consequences for formulating a system of prescription (*ahkam*) are not unrestrained, and any set of prescriptions identified on a contextual basis must be read with revelation. Thus, from a pure natural-law position, human authority is limited. Just as important is how 'context' is to be established. Is it to be established through philosophy, through the sociology of Indonesian Muslim society or through politics, and is the test to be efficacy? Both Madjid and Hazairin largely failed to answered these and other questions.

Returning briefly to history and the issue of seventh-century Arabic idiom, it is a huge assumption to think that one can identify an idiom dating from 1400 years ago with reasonable certainty. This assumes an objectivity for history, a subject that is bristling with difficulties in historiography (Oakeshott 1962: 137 ff.). From the point of view of that discipline, the criteria for identifying contexts and whether these can ever be found in 'pure' natural-law form are highly debatable. But should one even search for purity? Is not some criterion, even a flawed one, better than nothing? The answer depends, first, on the purpose of the inquiry. In this case, Madjid is searching not for objectivity as such but for a definition of social justice that can be used in the contemporary world. The answer also depends on the nature of the material, which ultimately derives from revelation. Again, for modern historiography, God (revelation) cannot be a historical cause, but that misses the point for Islam. For Muslims, God *is* the cause, and the methods developed by Muslim scholars over the last 1400 years are sufficient to show what that cause is and how it is to be worked out. In short, the argument has shifted from the canons of historiography to the canons of legitimacy appropriate to a revealed system of duties (which are 'to God').

Looked at this way, Madjid's propositions avoid both the ill-advised historical interpretations of Hazairin and the barrier of a historiographical tradition that refuses to accept the authority of revelation. He does provide a method, at least in embryo form. However, the real importance of this has been somewhat obscured in Indonesia by the unfortunate terminology used by Madjid. Much of the difficulty has revolved around the use of a term borrowed from English, *sekularisasi* (secularism or secularization)—showing once again how easily loan words can be misinterpreted. The point Madjid was trying to make is that faith and knowledge are not the same and must be approached by different means. This was comprehensively misunderstood by, among others, Nasution. However, to be fair to the latter, he does take the point, essential in Madjid, that tradition and dogma are not the same.[44] The former is not necessarily binding, although the boundaries of what *is* 'necessarily' binding are, at best, opaque.

These comments can best be understood by introducing the idea of a *sense of history*. All this means at this point is that historical explanation is essential to an understanding of syariah in the present. No one could seriously dispute this as a proposition, although one is continually surprised by the ahistoricism of much contemporary social science—and law for that matter. I should be careful to say that a sense of history in this very general sense does not necessarily mean historicism. I do not use it to mean that there is an inevitable process governed by its own law and thus immune to human choice. On the other hand, I should also point out that some extreme Muslim apologists in Indonesia and elsewhere do use it to mean this.[45] Having made clear what a sense of history is *not*, we can better see what it has come to mean in Indonesian Muslim thought.

There seem to be two separate but linked approaches to Islamic history: history as explanation and history as philosophy. Both are best represented by Nurcholish Madjid and Abdurrahman Wahid.

---

44 See Nasution (1995: 188–94, especially 193–4, originally published in 1973).
45 They are from the 'wilder shores' but nevertheless do have a following. The proponents of violent *jihad* in Indonesia are one example (see extracts in Fealy and Hooker 2006: 355–412).

History as Explanation

To understand and interpret the past is also to understand the present. This is the essence of historical explanation, which is always done for a motive or purpose (Collingwood 1946). In the present context, the reason Muslim scholars try to provide an explanation for past events is that this is crucial for historical syariah (undefined for the moment)—or just for the idea of 'syariah' as an historical artifact—because it has immediate practical consequences, now, in the contemporary Muslim world.

As matters of historical fact the historian is presented with the Qur'ān, the Sunnah, the historical personage of the Prophet and his successors, and the work of later generations of scholars and commentators. This is a huge mass of material. The problem for the historian is to restrain motive and clarify intention so as to do no violence to historical fact, while at the same time advancing a case or demonstrating one or more practical consequences for our own times. Nurcholish Madjid provides a striking example of how this might be done for Indonesian syariah.

I take first his views on 'reinvigorating religious understanding' (Madjid 1987: 239–56), where he directly discusses the Islamic state in the context of modern history. He begins by asking why people put the idea of an Islamic state forward. What is their motive?

His historical explanation is that the Islamic state idea is essentially an *apologia*, a reaction to Western ideas of state that have proved successful. While acknowledging that some Western versions of the state (such as fascism or communism) have failed, he maintains that the European state has nevertheless proved successful as a *system* (though he does not use this term). The secular, pluralist, democratic (whatever the adjective) state delivers social and economic benefits in the complete absence of religion. In contrast, Muslim states or those that call themselves Islamic states have failed to deliver such benefits. The response of Muslims, as apology, has been to call for an 'Islamic' system that can (a) catch up, (b) restore pride and (c) preserve culture. These are also contemporary arguments. Madjid observes quite simply that a recourse to Islam that is apologetic or desperate just does not work; it does not deliver. What, then, is the answer for the *ummah*? According to Madjid, it is to develop a proper sense of pride in Islam and, following from this, an openness to knowledge from non-religious sources. Openness is the key, because it is within the tradition of Muslim thought and can be demonstrated from modern history.

Madjid's explanation of the modern (immediate post-World War II) history of Islam is that it exhibits an unnecessary sense of inferiority that inhibits the ability of Muslims to learn and to create. It is in fact a denial of Islamic values. He goes on to say, with specific reference to the Islamic state idea, that *'fiqh-ism'*, that is, an undue emphasis on past scholarship, distorts any possibility of understanding the nature of the relationship between Islam and the state. He is prepared to admit that *fiqh* was fundamental to pre-modern Muslim politics but maintains that this is no longer the case. Moreover, to equate *fiqh* with syariah—as he accuses the modernists of doing—unnecessarily restricts the meaning of syariah by confining it to a very narrow sphere. *Fiqh* itself must be reformed to suit modern conditions.

The idea of inferiority as an explanation is superficially attractive, especially in its variant of 'defensiveness'. This had been suggested before, if only in passing.[46] I think one must be rather sceptical about this, because inferiority and defensiveness lead us to issues of motivation (including moral motivation)—of why people do the things that they do. The difficulty is to be able to state the empirical tests to show the link between intention and action. A further difficulty in the case of historical materials is that they allow too much room for later authors to introduce their own biases or preconceptions into the material. This gives us the historian as arbiter or, more generally, history as re-enactment (Collingwood 1946: 281 ff.). On the other hand, many Indonesian Muslim scholars certainly do support the inferiority argument, a fact that cannot be ignored.

Similar views, though rather more sceptical in form, are held by Abdurrahman Wahid (1983).[47] He asks whether Islam actually has a concept of 'state' and, by implication, whether 'Islam', 'concept' and 'state' can be proved to be historically congruent. Wahid himself is doubtful about this. If the Prophet had intended to found an 'Islamic state' (in quotes in Wahid), then he would have made provision for his own succession and for a method of succession. He did not do so. One might argue, as some now do in Indonesia and elsewhere, that Islam does provide a model for an Islamic state: the caliphate. However, this ignores the historical evidence that authority in God's law historically rests with the *'ulamā'*, not with a caliph, who can sustain his position only by force.[48] A caliphate was and is ephemeral.

Wahid briefly traverses the states that call themselves 'Islamic' (Iran, Saudi Arabia). He finds that they have nothing in common except the adjective 'Islamic', and that they lack the clear historical referents that would allow them to call themselves 'Islamic states'. The implication for contemporary Indonesia is that the claim to a formalized Islamic state (as in Khomeini's Iran) has no prior historical substance. Therefore, it can only be discussed indirectly in terms of the existing structures, the most important of which is Pancasila. If there is no unanimity of concept or practice in the Middle East (including Iran), with its much longer Islamic history, how can Indonesia, with its paucity of historical referents, be expected to develop a theory of the Islamic state?

Wahid is obviously driven by historical scepticism. This eventually and logically leads him to the dyad of religion (Islam) and place (Indonesia). Given that

---

46 See, for example, Hooker (2003a: 40 ff.) citing Wahid (1996: xiii).

47 A brief summary of his thinking on the concept of an Islamic state is given in Fealy and Hooker (2006: 230–2).

48 See Crone and Hinds (1986) on the caliphate in the first centuries of Islam.

Indonesia is a Muslim but not an Arabic country, the history of Indonesian Islam must become prior. 'Arabization is [not] appropriate for our needs', says Wahid (cited in Fealy and Hooker 2006: 417). Revelation, however, must be understood in its original context. It cannot be assimilated, because that would involve the loss of some original characteristic. The Qur'ān, for example, must always remain in Arabic. But in the wider sense, Islam can encompass local culture by allowing variation in the interpretation of the *fiqh*. Variation in such a controlled sense is not syncreticism (which leads to pantheism), a position to be avoided. In short, Indonesian Islam must be accepted for what it is and in the forms in which it manifests itself. The proviso, of course, is that deviation in dogma is not permitted. 'Indigenization' of Islam is a historically known process and must be accepted as such.

What Wahid has done here is to give us a succinct introduction to a philosophy of history. We turn to this now in the work of Nurcholish Madjid.

History as Philosophy

Some years ago I described a preliminary outline of Madjid's philosophy of history for Indonesian Islam (Hooker 2003a: 42 ff.). It seemed to me then, and even more so now, that Madjid provided a coherent method for constructing a workable system for syariah founded in the philosophy of history. The argument put forward then needs further explanation, not least because the language Madjid uses is not readily understood by a non-Muslim (secular) audience. Nevertheless he crossed an important boundary in making mutual comprehension possible. He was, of course, perfectly aware that he was attempting such an exercise; his language and references show this. He never fell into the trap of simulation—reliving the past as though he were there—a characteristic feature of the syariah as sufficient school. The past may be relevant to the present but it cannot be recreated as such; to suppose that it can is to deny history itself. Madjid comes down strongly in favour of what he calls 'readiness for change in a positive and constructive way', citing both classical sources and contemporary Western scholarship (Madjid 1994: 71). Definitions of the past have no mechanical application just because they exist, and this includes *fiqh* and *ijtihad* (Madjid 2004: 28–9). Past thought must be judged objectively. This is the key to his philosophy of history, which I read with emphasis on the difficulties that his views raise. This is not criticism for criticism's sake, but rather an acknowledgment of the complexity and sophistication of his thinking. I trust that this is clearly understood by the reader.

First, Madjid argues that revelation—that is, the Qur'ān—is prior. This is the founding premise of Islam and must be accepted as such by non-Muslims, including Western scholarship. Whether or not non-Muslims believe in God is beside the point. This premise, as a matter of historical and contemporary fact, is the position from which all other discussion then flows. The Sunnah, on the other hand, though divinely inspired, may have a normative value independent of direct revelation, particularly so far as prescription is concerned. This is a much more difficult position to defend. A strict Sunni response is to reject the idea. However, there is historical evidence to show a wide-ranging debate within Muslim scholarship concerned with establishing a method to validate actual prescription based on the Sunnah (Hallaq 2005: 102 ff.). For Madjid, this debate has contemporary relevance, because the question of where the binding force of prescription is located is a crucial one. The answer or answers to that question are directly influenced by the purpose for which the question is asked. Majid's own general purpose is to arrive at 'social justice'.

Second, Madjid argues that the *fiqh* texts have no necessary prior status. They are written by men and therefore belong to a time and place. The only criterion on which they can be judged is their suitability or usefulness. By definition, this criterion allows for a variety of judgments; variation of interpretation is thus a characteristic of the different schools of law. In short, the *fiqh* texts carry no necessary authority. This argument is attractive and can also be shown to be historically sustainable. For example, the KHI is in fact a selective rewriting of some *fiqh* texts for a limited purpose, thus demonstrating that the criterion of use for a time and place passes the efficacy test.

However, the argument tends to disguise or obscure a more fundamental point that Madjid addresses only indirectly. This is the issue of authority to state prescription in the Indonesian context. A substantial majority of Indonesian *'ulamā'* hold that the *fiqh* texts (the *kitab kuning*) are such a source of authority.[49] They justify this on historical grounds, arguing that, for practical purposes, 1400 years of text and commentary written under a strict discipline provide a distillation of the divine imperative. Modernists, of course, reject this view but there is no mechanism for resolving the different positions. Madjid's own answer to the authority issue is the indirect one of 'usefulness in context', that is, to use the *fiqh* texts to further a particular purpose (social justice) in the context of modern Indonesia.

Third, Madjid holds that prescription and morality cannot be separated; indeed, they must operate as a whole for purposes of social justice. This is a pure natural law position, within the constraints imposed by revelation. The issue for both syariah in its widest sense and classical Western formulations of morality of law (for example, Aquinas) is to establish the nature of these constraints. How and by whom are they identified? What is the nature of human authority (reason) in God's design for humanity? Madjid's answer is to say that prescription is knowable only by reference to its context and is therefore relative, whereas divine will is knowable through (God-given) reason and is absolute. Specifying

---

49   The *fiqh* texts are cited, for example, in the *fatāwā* of Nahdlatul Ulama (NU) and in the various religious forums (*bahtsul masail*) held to discuss theological and other issues.

the underlying principles necessary for correct reasoning is another matter, however. Social justice, despite its appeal, is a purpose, not an answer. A related issue is the proper identification of prescription. For Madjid, this is again a matter of context—respectively the Arabic idiom and contemporary imperatives. For the reasons set out earlier the former cannot be considered decisive and, indeed, must change; the method that should be used to achieve this is a 'more evolved *ijtihad*' (Madjid 2004: 29). What this means and how it is to work are yet to be fully explained.

Fourth, context is a key idea in both Wahid and Madjid, although it seems to be used in a number of different senses. At the risk of oversimplifying, contemporary Muslim culture in Indonesia provides one important reference point and the political manifestations of Islam another. Others are found in a variety of philosophies from the Middle East (from Muhammad Abduh to the present, including Syed Qutb, Hasan al-Banna and Yusuf Qardhawi). The debate about context is ongoing.

Madjid's philosophy of history and context is a real advance in developing a philosophy for syariah. He provides a multi-layered and internally consistent foundation on which a new *mazhab* might be constructed. His proposed relativity of *fiqh* has already been successfully demonstrated as practical. When linked with his purpose of social justice, the morality of Islam may yet result in a distinctive method for constructing a coherent philosophy for syariah.

5 SOME PRELIMINARY COMMENTARY

Each of the four philosophies outlined above is incomplete as a theory for syariah; they are often opaque, ambiguous or both. This is not surprising given that all the authors are engaged in building and justifying a new syariah. Not surprisingly, there is no agreement on basic principle (but neither is there in so-called 'developed' Western legal thought). This would be to ask the impossible; to demand a syariah in some positivist form would accomplish nothing and simply provide an opportunity for further misunderstanding. Uncertainty and contradiction must be accepted as facts of syariah life and thought. Commentators writing from within the Western tradition would do well to remember their own legal history, the debates then and the contemporary debates now.[50]

To narrow these generalities, we may say that opaqueness and ambiguity are characteristic of theories in the process of being built and of attempts to tease out prescription from revealed texts. Such prescription is always inconclusive but that does not mean it is always unworkable. However, it does indicate the complexity of the interplay between politics, practical administration and defini-

---

50 A remarkable work by Glenn (2000) provides an excellent comparative-law overview of the world's legal traditions, including syariah.

tions of 'justice'. Each of the four philosophies discussed above is an attempt to address the problem of revelation. Each author has identified a solution and attempts to explain it for practical purposes. The key to our understanding of these explanations is *how the problem is identified*, because this determines how the author handles the material of revelation and reaches the proposed solution.

Each of the four philosophies has its own view about the true nature of the problem. For the syariah as sufficient school, the problem is to identify the founding principles of the state, and thus to identify the conditions under which an Islamic state can come into being. For the localization school, the problem is the utilitarian one of determining the relevance of *fiqh* and defining how it should be used in practice. This means reducing the *fiqh* texts to sources and subjecting them to the test of usefulness. For the rationalized syariah school, the problem is to determine the place of reason and the extent to which it can be made compatible with revelation. And for the contextual syariah school, the problem is to develop a legal history or, better, a historiography of legal thought, for a purpose: social justice. This is the most complex of the four philosophies.

Stated in such brief and rather elliptical terms, it might appear that the four philosophies are separate, each inhabiting its own world. But this is not the case, for two reasons. First, in purely philosophical terms each is an example of either idealism or empiricism. For a syariah idealist, God is the sustaining cause who makes possible the attributes of humanity (reason). For a syariah empiricist, experience shows facts ('reality') that can only be accommodated by the use of reason for defined and specific purposes. Second, a full reading of the theorists cited so far would show that all are inconsistent and frequently change their positions—opaqueness and ambiguity once again. It is perfectly possible in all cases for any one individual to be simultaneously a syariah idealist and a syariah empiricist.

But this still leaves us with a further difficulty. May we criticize an author's choice of problem? Is not this a matter of individual preference, so long as the choice is made within the general parameters of the subject—that is, syariah in the contemporary Republic of Indonesia? If we decide that author X has chosen inappropriately, what are our criteria for doing so? One answer is to say that all authors must exhibit a certain degree of objectivity in choosing the precise problem to be addressed. The problem must, for example, be explainable in terms of the syariah materials; it must also be at least cognisant of the existing legal system. Within these parameters, there is room for individuality of choice in which the author's interests may legitimately determine the choice of problem.

6   OBJECTIFIED SYARIAH

Objectified syariah is now 200 years old. It is a direct result of orientalism and what we now call the globalization of law. The claim is to a European monopoly of method in describing and classifying all laws everywhere—the literature of comparative law and legal history.[51] This claim has not gone uncontested; indeed, it has been suggested that some parts of (English) common law derive from syariah.[52] But our interest here is in the Indonesian syariah experience. We have already seen something of this in the brief description of pre-modern texts in Chapter 1, and I return first to this material.

Law as Evolution

The syariah texts of the Indonesian and Malay archipelagos were initially described by nineteenth-century scholars who were also imperial administrators. Theirs was not a 'pure' scholarship, if such is indeed possible, but a scholarship directed towards the purposes of government. Without repeating analyses published elsewhere (Hooker 1986), it is clear that these purposes set the parameters for the colonial scholarly enterprises. Underlying them was the view that a law text had to be (a) clear and consistent, and (b) rational. These were believed to be essential characteristics of law at any time and in any place; where they were not present, there was no real law. The intellectual justification for this view was provided by Sir Henry Maine, whose *Ancient Law* (Maine 1861) was hugely influential among both British and Dutch administrators. He held that what he called 'status' laws were characteristic of closed and 'unprogressive' societies, and lower on the legal evolutionary scale than the contract-based laws of 'progressive' societies, that is, laws based on the mid-nineteenth-century ideal of freedom to contract. It followed that the texts of the less progressive societies were not rational, and not useful.

The mid-nineteenth-century imperial successes, based as they were on mercantilist efficiency and military dominance, seemed to prove such a thesis. European sovereignties were clearly superior. In the imperial possessions in Asia this superiority was expressed by rewriting and selecting from 'native' laws, including syariah texts.[53] Clearly the latter were not suitable for the new age. That view came to form an important part of internal Muslim resistance to European rule, first in Egypt, where syariah reform was seen as an essential step towards the renaissance of Islam, and later in the Netherlands East Indies.[54] The effects of this did not become apparent until well into the twentieth century, so that evolu-

---

51 For a recent example, see Glenn (2000).
52 See, for example, Makdisi (1981) and Makdisi (1985).
53 See, for example, the work of the late eighteenth-century orientalists in British India, whose revised texts are still the basic laws for Indian Muslims today. See Hooker (1975: 94 ff.) for sources.
54 Muhammad Abduh's theses were known and disseminated in Indonesia by the early decades of the twentieth century (Azra 1999a).

tionary law, combined with selections to serve the colonial regime's purposes, remained an important characteristic of the Indonesian legal system.

Religion, primarily Islam but also Hinduism in Bali, always retained its importance for the scholars and administrators. But again, the evolutionary idea or impulse was to move away from the 'classical' texts towards some new, revised selection which could be shown to be useful in practice. The 'classical' texts provided the initial difficulty. If this meant the *fiqh* texts, then it could be shown that *in fact* these were not operative and so the difficulty of accommodating them did not arise. If, on the other hand, it meant the indigenous body of Malay and Javanese manuscripts with demonstrably clear connections to syariah, then it was clear that they did not fit the evolutionary (status → contract) scheme of law either. The fact that they were in written form argued the achievement of sophisticated status in the development of legal history. But at the same time, they were of no practical use to the colonial state because they located the source of authority in Islam and in the Muslim ruler as God's representative on earth. That was not acceptable to the colonial regime because it denied its sovereignty.[55]

We can see how difficult it would have been for the colonial scholars and administrators to maintain the legal evolutionary line with any degree of internal consistency. Their response with respect to the Malay–Javanese manuscripts was to say that they were not part of, but rather a corruption of, a recognized classical tradition (that is, the Middle Eastern *fiqh* texts). Therefore they were aberrant, incorrect and, by reason of that fact, inferior to the originals. Because they were regressions, it would be wrong to give them credence. This did not prevent selective adaptations being made, although this was rare except, oddly enough, for Bali Hindu law (Hoadley and Hooker 1986). But this is to stray outside the bounds of the topic.

From the late nineteenth century, practical experience began to show that the syariah could not be dismissed as aberrant. However, the version of syariah that could not be dismissed was not the syariah of the law texts but the version of *fiqh* rules that ordinary people understood and adhered to.

Before coming to this, it is important to remember that the law as evolution theory does not hold up in practice. The premise that a later law—by the fact of being later in time—must somehow be an improvement and so 'better' is simply not true. The Malay–Javanese law texts are later in time than the classical *fiqh* methodology and they may be (and in fact are) technically inferior. This proves nothing except that, while the two sets of texts are related, they are not the same. On the contrary, the changes (so-called corruptions) in the later texts were purposeful for the times and places in which they were written. The law as evolution

---

55 The French, Dutch, British and Czarist regimes had exactly the same problem. They responded by restricting syariah to family law or, in the Czarist case, abolishing it altogether—to no effect, as we now know.

theory is inadequate to explain even this one case, but has nevertheless had the unfortunate effect of seriously distorting Islamic legal history in Indonesia as well as in the rest of Muslim Southeast Asia.

Perhaps more importantly, a Western theory of law that seemed so obviously right at the time that it was put into practice at the highest level proved to be wrong. Moreover, the nineteenth-century dismissal of the indigenous syariah manuscripts continues into the present day. They do not appear on the IAIN syllabus even though they are an integral part of Indonesian Islamic history and show a real originality of legal thought.

Legal Positivism and Legal Pluralism

By the third quarter of the nineteenth century, the law as evolution position had become untenable. However, it had achieved one thing: the syariah, however defined, with whatever meaning, was not to be the law for native Indonesians. In historical jurisprudence terms, it could be intellectually rejected as not representing the *volk*.

How was this rejection justified? The answer comes from the Netherlands East Indies Constitution of 1854, which formally established two principles. The first was that the law represented the commands of the sovereign; it emanated from and was a demonstration of state sovereignty. Second, the constitution allowed for a set of parallel legal universes—legal pluralism—through which each racial group would have its own laws. By the 1880s the system was well established, with separate regimes for natives (*adat* law), Europeans and persons assimilated to that status (Dutch civil law) and foreign orientals (the appropriate laws for Arabs and Chinese).[56]

Syariah was excluded from these regimes for two reasons. First, it seemed to the Dutch administrators that *adat* already provided the basic laws for indigenous peoples (*inlanders*). Of course, the increasingly bureaucratic colonial administration recognized the variations between *adat* regimes and even identified elements of syariah in many areas. However, by the early 1900s (and dates are crucial here) an established colonial bureaucracy was firmly entrenched and its primary aim was certainty of data for administration. From the 1880s on, data on *adat* laws were collected and compiled in a massive handbook—the *Adatrechtbundel*—that was updated year by year. It was the bible for *adat* law administration. Syariah was not in it, except as it was dependent on *adat*.

Second, syariah was excluded because it could not be made to fit into what was considered to be the proper legal theory for a colonial possession. The debates of the 1890s to 1920s came down in favour of a pluralism of sources for law, emphasizing in particular the central importance of *adat*. *Adat* was consid-

---

56 On legal pluralism, see Hooker (1975); on laws for foreign orientals, see Coppel (2002) and Burns (1988: 169–71).

ered to reflect justice as it was understood by the vast majority of Indonesians. The resulting colonial legal policy was built on this proposition, supported by the constantly updated data in the *Adatrechtbundel*. A happy exercise in bureaucratic convenience was thus combined with an intellectual and moral justification!

But there is more to the second answer. By the 1920s Dutch scholarly theory, following the French on colonial laws or legal systems,[57] had become enmeshed in the debates on private international law (conflicts of law). These debates were influential because they used language that, combined with the fact of separate law groups (that is, discrete legal universes), allowed a purely Euro-centric definition of colonial law. This was a disaster for the French in Indochina,[58] and not much less so for the Dutch in the Netherlands East Indies.[59] Briefly, private inter-racial law constituted its own discrete legal universe in the same way that nation-states possess their own legal universes. As a result, conflict-of-law principles had to be introduced to solve the inevitable difficulties arising from cases involving more than one system of law (such as inter-racial marriage or contracts for the sale or mortgage of land held under different laws). These conflict-of-law principles (private international law) proved unworkable; discrete legal groups within a territory are not analogous to the legal systems of nation-states. This was not understood until well into the 1930s, however. The syariah had no place in this scheme. Certainly a religious court (Priesteraad) had been established in 1882 for Java and Madura, but it was little more than an arbitration tribunal. It could not execute its own judgments but had to apply to the secular court authorities for this. In general it was incompetent and corrupt. By the late 1930s, reforms to the conflict-of-law problem and to the status of the religious courts were being proposed but they came to nothing (Hooker 2003b: 13–14). Then World War II intervened.

The syariah was effectively excluded from the colonial legal system because it did not constitute a discrete legal universe. Even if it had, it would have remained unworkable because it was not expressed as positive law. The classical *fiqh* had no mechanism or procedure for European-style conflict-of-law settlement. The respective bases by which an individual was attached to the legal system in Indonesia required different points of contact. In *fiqh*, this was defined by one's religious status (Muslim or non-Muslim); in European laws it was defined by one's nationality or, in the English law case, domicile. There was and is no possible meeting point between the two. When one adds to this the extra complexity introduced by racial classes, it is easy to see why no logical solution was available.

---

57 Solus (1927) was particularly important.
58 For sources, see Hooker (1978: 175 ff.).
59 See Kollewijn (1929) for a contemporary account of the mess the Dutch got themselves into over this issue.

What is the lesson of the supremacy of positive law? It is that one law, and only one law, can be dominant in the nation-state. A 'pure' syariah cannot accept a subordinate position, so compromises such as the KHI are all that is possible, and even these are endlessly debated. The idea of separate legal universes is not practical because the internal conflicts of law that arise are ultimately self-destructive (Hooker 1975: 257 ff.).

The Sociology of Law

Sometimes called 'sociological jurisprudence', the sociology of law denies that law (that is, positive law) is a closed system with its own sovereign value. Instead, it proposes that any value, if identifiable, is not self-contained or formalistic but rests upon practical reasoning that is open to divergent and competing political and social claims. Sociology of law comes in a myriad versions, ranging from socialism (in its strong and weak versions) to the 'social construction' of reality. Sceptics point out that there is no such thing as social 'science'—hence sociological jurisprudence—because what is written down by the jurist is merely a response to events occurring around that person and therefore unpredictable. It is not, in fact, true jurisprudence, but merely comment on passing ephemera—or, as someone once said, 'jargon-ridden reporting that the newspapers do better'! This sort of polemic is not particularly helpful but it does illustrate, in a coarse sort of way, that sociology of law is often on the defensive about its own philosophy. The same is true for comparative law as now practised; is it sociological jurisprudence (whatever that is) or merely a branch of legal history? This is not a rhetorical question for Indonesian Islam; nor is it wholly unconnected with the historical and positivist law positions outlined earlier. The latter are discussed and debated in texts, making it perfectly possible to remain in the text field and conduct a sensible and lucid argument. This is what legal historians do, and it is probably the reason why comparative law is essentially legal history.

However, that sort of discussion is only part of the syariah debate in Indonesia, and it does not tell us what Islam means for the individual Muslim. The purpose of the ethnography of law, as I understand it, is to fill that gap—to inform the sociology of law through the addition of ethnographic fact. But there is a further problem: what is ethnographic 'fact'? That is, how much of what we call fact is genuinely observed (if that is possible) and how much is explained or interpreted by the observer for that person's putative audience (essentially, the observer's colleagues) in the language of the discipline?[60] The same question can be asked of all the social sciences. As Ellen (1983: 90–1) said over 20 years ago:

---

60 What, then, is 'correct'? See Quine (1960) for a rather extreme view.

Changes in anthropological fashion have permitted new glimpses into the complex sociology of Muslim societies, but they have brought with them ideological and intellectual artifacts of their own making.

Syariah, considered sociologically, requires an understanding of the methodologies used. The information acquired over the past 40 years and published in thousands of papers and books reveals a huge variety of 'syariahs' at the local level. From a formal and textual position this is unsettling and disturbing, as are the accompanying notions of incoherence of doctrine and variation in practice. There is, naturally, considerable resistance to these data,[61] or at least doubts about their significance and value, although there should not be, because this is clearly one of the strengths of the sociological approach. It directly challenges the comfortable view that texts are conclusive when in practice they are not. A further benefit of the sociological approach has been to make available new theories on types. The most famous example is the late Professor Clifford Geertz's *abangan–santri–priyayi* typology of Javanese Muslims.[62] Views about the correctness, congruence with reality and usefulness of this model vary, with some wondering whether it has a predictive function. But whatever one might think, it cannot be denied that the model and its current 'ideological and intellectual artifacts'[63] have been part of the literature of Islam in Indonesia for a long time.

A more straightforward example of direct ethnographic reporting is found in Fox (2002), which draws attention to a variety of ethnographic methods in studies of subjects as wide ranging as 'Islamic resurgence', 'transformation of tradition' and 'tradition in the *pesantren*'.[64] Some of the case studies he describes have direct relevance for syariah, including matters of disputed doctrine. The material brought forward is 'syariah' in the understanding of those who believe in or practise it even though it may be doctrinally false. It is therefore both true and not true, and one must accept this state of affairs. However, if the ethnographer then takes a further step and claims, on the basis of his or her own methodology, that the ethnographic material is, *in reality*, the only true syariah—what then? The objection from the text scholarship side is that if such a position is accepted, then non-text reasoning and method must be accepted as prior. It follows that syariah will always be uncertain, because it will depend on the vagaries of social science fashion. One might point to the fashions encapsulated in terms such as 'traditionalist', 'radical', 'fundamental' and so on. An answer to this objection is that certainty has no superior value as such; in practice, it is neces-

---

61 Or there was until recently in, for example, the *pesantren* milieu. But this is changing; see, for example, Jabali and Jamhari (2003: 79–120) on *pesantren* and IAIN.

62 Geertz categorized Javanese Muslims as being nominal (*abangan*) Muslims (the majority of the population), pious (*santri*) Muslims or those belonging to a small cultural elite (*priyayi*).

63 See Bowen (1995b: 78 ff.) on these.

64 See also Muhaimin (1999).

sary only in limited and defined circumstances. The actual rules, drawn from text sources, are always contingent and negotiable. But as we saw earlier, the choice of circumstance and the issue to be investigated may pre-determine the method.

These comments sum up the real value of sociological jurisprudence. It asks difficult questions of those who claim that syariah/*fiqh* is only to be found in texts, a feature of 'real' scholarship involving Arabic and classical commentary. Bowen (1995b: 81–2) says that there is a general paucity of classical training among social scientists. If this is true, it does at least have the advantage of avoiding an arid or even constricting approach. The downside is that social scientists may lack a sense of history and the capacity to deal with the complex formal structures of syariah, in particular the normative classes and how they are used.[65] For example, under syariah, the procedure for resolving disputes is quite complex and involves extensive discussion of syariah technicalities.[66] But even if we understand the process through which decisions are arrived at, we still do not know what actually happens in practice, that is, whether and how these decisions are translated into action.

It is here that sociological jurisprudence makes its second important contribution to syariah study: the case study on dispute resolution, now long established as a method of sociological jurisprudence,[67] not just in Indonesia[68] but throughout the entire legal world. These closely observed accounts of dispute resolution show in detail: (a) how and by whom resolution is arrived at; (b) how and by whom the resolution is implemented; and (c) its relation (if any) to formal laws. Commonly the latter are not binding on the religious courts, although they may act as a point of reference. So far as syariah is concerned, 'formal' law consists of actual *fiqh* rules, the KHI and local understanding of syariah *vis-à-vis adat*. The references can therefore become quite complicated.

These case studies do not in any way set precedents in the Anglo-American common law sense,[69] although one may trace their genesis, in contemporary sociology of law, to the American Realist movement of the 1930s.[70] Law is 'law in action' through the decisions of some body—formal or informal.[71] The under-

---

65　Hallaq (1997: 207 ff.) provides a good contemporary treatment of the formal structures of syariah.

66　See Zahro (2004) on the NU process of dispute resolution in East Java.

67　In anthropology of law from the 1960s; see Moore (1978) and below.

68　For an Indonesian example, see von Benda-Beckman (1984).

69　Indonesia does not have a doctrine of precedent, which is not to say that the idea is wholly unfamiliar. Collections of case studies (*kumpulan putusan*) are available, but they are put forward only as examples of best practice. See Subekti and Tamara (1965) for an *adat* example.

70　See the classical position in Llewellyn (1940).

71　An interesting version of a semi-formal dispute resolution system dealing with issues involving syariah and *adat* was produced in British Malaya in the 1930s (see Taylor 1929, 1937).

lying belief is that the process will tell us what law *is* in real life; where 'is' means the resolution of a dispute, however convoluted or inconsistent the process of arriving at it has been.

The question then arises as to whether the dispute resolution mechanism is premised on something else: a sense of justice perhaps, or a higher order? The syariah is supposed to encompass these things, but the connection between them and the process of dispute resolution is not clear. The process may be driven by self-interest, altruism or base motives, for example, but nevertheless come to a conclusion that is based 'just' on the facts. 'Just' on the facts means that each person in the dispute gets (more or less) what he or she wants *and* that this can be validated ('justified') by reference to, say, a syariah or *adat* law or a formal state regulation or law.

These issues are addressed in some detail by Bowen through what he calls the 'anthropology of public reasoning': a discussion based on argumentation at various levels (within the family, in the courts, and in national syariah and policy formulations).[72] His major claim, directly of interest here, is that the Indonesian case 'challenges the analytical adequacy of Western political theory for the comparative study of political and legal reasoning' (Bowen 2003: 10–12). Western political theory is not, on its own, necessarily capable of providing a satisfactory explanation for the Indonesian case. He cites, for example, work with pretensions to application outside the West by some modern political–legal theorists from the Anglo-American tradition. He focuses in particular on the work of John Rawls (1921–2002), who has had an undoubted and positive influence in the field of political philosophy.[73] But as Bowen shows, Rawls's analyses of dispute settlement procedures are not directly extendable to an Indonesian Muslim society whose social premises are derived from revelation. As Bowen himself says about public reasoning, the anthropology shows 'the ways in which citizens take account of *their own* pluralism of values as they carry out their affairs' [emphasis added] (Bowen 2003: 12).

This does not mean that the work of Rawls and others must be dismissed as entirely inappropriate. It is true that it is not directly applicable as a model; its underlying assumptions drawn from liberal democracy do not translate outside that sphere. But reading Rawls and similar contemporary authors[74] forces us to state (or at least acknowledge) our own underlying assumptions as we try to explain syariah reasoning through, in this case, the anthropology of dispute settlement. In short, it provides us with a more refined method that does not necessarily give us 'the answer' but does make it possible to draw out the complexities

---

72 Bowen developed his concept of an anthropology of public reasoning based on data from Gayo, North Sumatra; see Bowen (1995a, 1999, 2003).

73 See in particular Rawls (1996).

74 See, for example, Raz (1970) on the legal system and Raz (1994) on political theory and pluralism.

of the material. How to arrive at and then make sense of these complexities is the great contribution of the sociology of law. Rather than providing answers, it tells us whether the questions we ask are useful or even real.

The fact that we move in a sea of ambiguity and uncertainty is a true reflection of reality. The 'certainties' of historical jurisprudence and legal positivism do not exist in fact.

7 CONCLUDING REMARKS

There are as many definitions of law as there are commentators, and the syariah in Indonesia is no exception in this respect. One thing is clear: there is no monolithic syariah. Instead we find ambiguity in reference, variety of source, positive laws of the state (in the KHI and the judicial process), political philosophy and description of the 'real' (in the anthropology of law). When we take these together we have uncertainty, perhaps to an excessive degree. In any case it is clear that the state does not have a monopoly on the definition of public law. In this sense and to this degree, public law fails the efficacy test. This leaves the field clear for the proponents of syariah to define syariah in a multitude of ways. Even such positive state expressions as the KHI or judicial decisions or bureaucratic forms are therefore open to debate and scepticism in actual practice.

The four philosophies or principles of syariah definition put forward in this chapter are not themselves certain about how to go about establishing and confirming their own premises. This is not surprising given the very few years in which the syariah has been debated as a system of law for the Indonesian state. None of these philosophies rests on secure foundations. To take, first, the syariah as sufficient view. If the model for this proposal is the period of the first four caliphs, then it rests on highly disputed historical evidence that is unlikely ever to be resolved conclusively. If the period chosen is the Ottoman caliphate, then the historical difficulties are still immense. The Ottoman caliphate lasted for 400 years and extended its reach over much of southeastern Europe and the Middle East. So which time and which geographical area should be the basis for the model, and how should it deal with the manifest corruption and eventual internal collapse of the caliphate?[75] There is the further difficulty of showing a progression from the period chosen to the circumstances of modern Indonesia, and of designing an actual program of work to achieve an efficacy for syariah. None of this has been done.

Localized syariah presents a different set of issues. The most striking feature of this model is that *fiqh* is not *a priori* but reduced to one reference point among others. The result of denying *fiqh* absolute authority is to permit either localized versions of *fiqh* or selections from it that suit the conditions and legal policies

---

75 See generally Lapidus (1988: 328–58).

of the time. In both cases, the choice of version or selection is based on non-*fiqh* criteria. In short, the *fiqh* is only one element in the whole national legal policy and is defined by that policy.

Rationalized syariah is the result. This means a syariah that is congruent with the state structure; it may contain references to the Qur'ān, but these are references only. Congruence is about political accommodation, about viewing *fiqh* as something that can and should be accommodated within limits. In this view, *fiqh* can never be more than a set of texts from which the state authority can choose, rephrase and apply a rule as it thinks fit. Localization and rationalization thus go together, and in this the Indonesian experience parallels that of other contemporary Muslim nations. It is worth emphasizing that both localization and rationalization have gained general support. But there are limits to this, and exercises that transgress *fiqh*—such as the Counter Legal Draft—are clearly not acceptable. In other words, there must be some demonstrable fidelity to *fiqh* and *fiqh* argument.

This is not the case with historical and contextual syariah, for the obvious reason that the Qur'ān and the Sunnah are its basic texts. Even to formulate the proposition in this way is to invite controversy: the Qur'ān and Sunnah are *not* texts in the same sense that *fiqh* is. For many Muslims, scholars and non-scholars alike, to treat all these writings in the same way is not just aberrant but blasphemy. It is of course problematic to take a passage from the Qur'ān, give it a reading, derive its fundamental purpose and then propose an application for that purpose in the present. The purpose itself (social justice, natural equity, democracy) may be equally controversial. I addressed these issues earlier through the writings of Nurcholish Madjid, a serious scholar who expressed his views in an entirely proper way. The criticisms I made of him were within the discipline of historiography. But there are other criticisms that have been levelled at Madjid of which all readers should be aware.

The first criticism, that he was not a true exegete (Johns and Saeed 2004), is easily answered. Madjid did not claim to be an exegete, holding that traditional exegesis had proved rather limited, if not a dead end, for Islam in Indonesia. This does not mean that he dismissed it or judged it to be of no account; on the contrary, he considered it to be fundamental scholarship of inestimable value.[76] Madjid's purpose was social justice and religious pluralism in Indonesia, and for that to be achieved, the Qur'ān had to be read historically and with regard to context. Neither history nor context derogate from divine revelation.

This is the point at which the second criticism or, more accurately, misunderstanding, arises. The historical and contextual view of syariah has come to be identified with orientalism and is therefore often viewed as an attack on the truth of the Prophethood of Muhammad. Is it permissible to read the Qur'ān as text? Of course exegesis (*tafsir*) is permissible, but hermeneutics is another

---

76 Personal conversation, Paradamina University, Jakarta, 1997.

matter. Hermeneutics is the critical study of text as text with the goal of establishing philological and historical certainties and thus explaining meaning. The text is therefore an object to be studied; it has no status of its own. This is not the internal Muslim position, and when applied to the Qur'ān, hermeneutics is often interpreted as an 'invasion' (Husaini 2005).[77] Although rather overemotive, this is not entirely unfair; after all, hermeneutics is always subjective and can often lead to excessive relativism. That is not an option in Islam.

Classical exegesis, on the other hand, has yet to deal with the issue of increasingly rapid and frenetic change. The exegete's fundamental position is that the changes we see around us are ephemera and that reality is found in God's revelation to the Prophet. This is a straight-out appeal to faith, not a program for coping with change—unless this can be achieved by returning to an imagined historical purity. The contrary position is found in the objectification of syariah, which describes change and adaptation using the methods of Western science. At the very least, the data brought forward by this approach force a new definition of syariah onto the stage, one that calls into question the very idea of certainty for syariah as a body of rules. We are back again into ambiguity and opacity, which at best give us only partial and fragmented perceptions.

This discussion is continued in the epilogue (see Chapter 7). I hold it in abeyance here because the material in the following chapters adds materially to the discussion of legal philosophies in this chapter.

---

77 Similar responses are found in respect of Burton's (1977) *The Collection of the Qur'an.*

3 Learning Syariah: The National and Regional Curricula

A law school curriculum is a fundamental exercise in all legal systems. It is intended to provide a professional, practical training while also, ideally, acting as a transmitter of wider social, political and ethical values. It has diverse functions, so the emphasis on one or another aspect of the curriculum obviously varies over time. Some of these changes in emphasis are a matter of fashion, and therefore ephemeral, but it is hard to recognize which are passing fads until long after the unfortunate student has graduated. Essentially a curriculum defines law for public administration and private law, and the graduate is bound by the definition(s) current for his or her time.

A curriculum is a way of setting out definitions. On paper it always appears systematic and certain—such and such a subject is stated, the rules are explained and the readings are set. In reality, however, all curricula are ambiguous, because what a student learns may or may not be useful in practice. At the tertiary or university level, competing dogmas (as distinct from rules) are commonly taught, so that the interpretation and significance of a rule often becomes a matter of debate. In fact the very notion of 'rule' is itself debatable.

These general comments apply fully to the syariah curricula in Indonesia.[1] To illustrate this I have chosen a rather narrow focus: first, the curriculum produced for national use by the Department of Religion; and second, the curricula used by Indonesia's State Islamic Universities (Universitas Islam Negeri; UIN), State Islamic Institutes (Institut Agama Islam Negeri; IAIN) and State Islamic Colleges (Sekolah Tinggi Agama Islam Negeri; STAIN),[2] which incorporate but also vary the national model. These curricula set out the material that future

---

1   We would do well to remember that curriculum development has a long history in Islam; indeed, so far as law is concerned, the Muslim model influenced medieval European practice in some respects (Makdisi 1981).

2   Indonesia has five UIN: one each in Jakarta, Yogyakarta, Malang, South Sulawesi and Riau. Each province has one IAIN. The STAIN are regional institutes, dependent on the provincial IAIN.

judges and civil servants must learn. There are, of course, other paths to instruction in syariah,[3] but the advantage of narrowing the scope is to see in some detail just what the contemporary issues are and how they are being addressed.

As yet there is no general history of Indonesia's UIN, IAIN and STAIN (henceforth IAIN, except where it is necessary to distinguish them), only self-reflections on their role and function in the Indonesian syariah world.[4] Two ideas predominate: first, that change is rapid and constant, and second, that there is no one syariah orthodoxy. In short, the definition of syariah is wide open, leaving considerable room for variations in treatment and topic.

Within the IAIN, the idea that syariah need not—indeed cannot—be expressed in some monolithic set form has given rise to many questions. What materials should be used to teach syariah? What is the appropriate balance between classical (Arabic) sources and modern (Arabic and Indonesian) commentary in the curriculum? What is the appropriate balance between Indonesia-wide and local components? What is the place of secular methods (social science) in syariah studies? Should the IAIN have other roles in addition to their teaching function? Do secular subjects have a legitimate place in the IAIN, and if so, what is the appropriate balance between them and the religious subjects? Should the IAIN be organized by the Department of Religion (as at present) or by the Ministry of Education?

As these questions indicate, the IAIN are in a state of intense flux. Two clear trends are discernible, however. First, some UIN are rapidly expanding their teaching and research activities outside religious subjects. For example, UIN Syarif Hidayatullah Jakarta recently established a medical school, while other UIN, IAIN and STAIN are beginning to offer a wider range of secular subjects, especially in the area of economics and business studies. Second, the Department of Religion is responding to the demands for change through its national policy on the IAIN curriculum. For example, in 2004 it introduced a 40:60 rule whereby the national content in the curriculum would fall from 70 per cent to 40 per cent, with local content to increase from 30 per cent to 60 per cent. This has given the IAIN scope for a much greater degree of local initiative than formerly, and all institutions have responded by drafting new courses that reflect local interests. We may be seeing the start of a fragmentation of the national curriculum, although it is too early to say so with certainty. What we *can* say is that the balance seems to be shifting towards non-religious subjects being taught in the IAIN, 'in an Islamic context' (see section 4).

---

3   These include the private Islamic universities operated, in particular, by Nahdlatul Ulama (NU) and Muhammadiyah, the Islamic boarding schools (*pesantren*) and, for a very basic level of instruction, the Islamic schools (*madrasah*). Much has been written about these institutions; for selective accounts, see, for example, Azra (1999b), Dhofier (1994), Rahardjo (1974) and Burhanudin and Afrianty (2006).

4   See, for example, Mudzhar (2003) and Jabali and Jamhari (2002).

It is important at the start to emphasize two factors. The first concerns dates. The material in this chapter dates from 1995 to 1998 in the case of the national curriculum and from 2001 to 2003 in the case of the UIN, IAIN and STAIN curricula. All these curricula are undergoing extensive revision: a new national curriculum is being prepared but is not yet available, while the UIN, IAIN and STAIN curricula change so quickly that it is impossible to keep up even on an annual time scale. I have had to choose a cut-off date, because without it any general overview or introduction would become impossible. This has some unfortunate aspects. For example, although I know that the IAIN are currently rewriting their curricula to provide a more comprehensive treatment of Islamic economics (*ekonomi Islam*) for the next generation of religious court judges, I do not know the content of the new courses and so cannot cover them in any detail here. This is just one example, but it does illustrate the uncertainties in the formal structure of the syariah curricula. This has to be accepted; after all, it is less than 40 years since Harun Nasution persuaded the IAIN to adopt a new curriculum in Islamic studies stressing understanding and analysis rather than rote learning of Islamic texts.[5]

The second factor to emphasize is that all curricula are directed by the state towards a standard set of courses and subjects. The UIN, IAIN and STAIN curricula are based on the national curriculum developed by the Department of Religion, and it in turn is directly modelled on the framework for the secular curricula set by the Ministry of Education. That is, the Islamic curricula replicate the formal structures established by the Ministry of Education, just as the religious courts replicate the formal structures of the secular courts (see Chapter 1). At the subject level, the Basic General Subjects (Mata Kuliah Dasar Umum; MKDU) taught in the IAIN are the same as those taught in secular tertiary institutions. In short, the Islamic institutions have the same formal structure as the secular institutions, even to the extent of having a common introductory syllabus.

The structure of the national syariah curriculum is shown in Table 3.1.[6] All of the UIN, IAIN and STAIN have five basic divisions (faculties): Civilization (Adab), Education (Tarbiyah), Principles of Theology/Philosophy (Usuluddin), Outreach (Dakwah) and Law (Syariah). All faculties share a common curriculum of Basic General Subjects. In addition, all students are required to take at least one course on law chosen from the Basic Skills Subjects (Mata Kuliah Dasar Keahlian; MKDK). The syariah faculty has four divisions: Civil Law (Ahwal al-Shakhsiyah), Contract Law (Mu'amalat), Comparative Law and Schools of Law

---

5   The new curriculum was introduced in 1973. In developing a curriculum for the IAIN, Nasution was strongly influenced by the Western approach to Islamic studies, which he experienced while studying at McGill University in Canada.

6   In the national curriculum, each of the courses shown in Table 3.1 is accompanied by both a list of topics and a list of required readings. For simplicity, these have been omitted, but the topics and readings are described in the rest of this chapter.

Table 3.1   Structure of the National Core Curriculum of 1998

No.	Code	Subject

Basic General Subjects (MKDU)
(taken by all UIN, IAIN and STAIN students)

1	INS 101	Pancasila
2	INS 102	Kewiraan (Military–Nationalist Studies)
3	INS 103	Bahasa Inggris (English Language)
4	INS 104	Bahasa Arab (Arabic Language)
5	INS 105	Bahasa Indonesia (Indonesian Language)
6	INS 106	Ilmu Alamiah Dasar (IAD), Ilmu Sosial Dasar (ISD) dan Ilmu Budaya Dasar (IBD) (Basic Natural Science, Basic Social Science and Basic Cultural Science)
7	INS 107	Metodologi Studi Islam (Methodology of Islamic Studies)

Basic Skills Subjects (MKDK)
(taken by all UIN, IAIN and STAIN students)

1	INS 201	Ushul Fiqh (Principles of Jurisprudence)
2	INS 202	Ulumul Hadits (Sciences of the Hadith)
3	INS 203	Ulumul Qur'ān (Sciences of the Qur'ān)
4	INS 204	Ilmu Kalam (Science of Dialectical Theology)
5	INS 205	Ilmu Tasawwuf (Science of Sufism)
6	INS 206	Filsafat Umum (General Philosophy)
7	INS 207	Metode Penelitian (Research Methods)
8	INS 301	Fiqh (Jurisprudence)
9	INS 302	Hadits (Hadith)
10	INS 303	Tafsir (Qur'ānic Exegesis)
11	INS 210	Sejarah dan Peradaban Islam (Islamic History and Civilization)

Specialist Skills Subjects (MKK)
(taken by Faculty of Syariah students)
Subjects taken by all Faculty of Syariah students

1	SYA 401	Ilmu Tafsir (Science of Qur'ānic Exegesis)
2	SYA 402	Tafsir Ahkam (Qur'ānic Exegesis of Legal Principles)
3	SYA 403	Hadits Ahkam (Legal Principles from Hadith)
4	SYA 404	Ushul Fiqh (Principles of Jurisprudence)
5	SYA 405	Ilmu Hukum (Science of Legal Studies)

Specialist subjects in the Faculty of Syariah
Ahwal al-Shakhsiyah (Civil Law/Non-*Fiqh* Law)

6	AHS 501	Hukum Perdata Islam di Indonesia (Islamic Civil Law in Indonesia)
7	AHS 502	Peradilan di Indonesia (The Courts in Indonesia)
8	AHS 503	Hukum Acara (Law of Procedure)
9	AHS 504	Metodologi Penelitian Hukum (Legal Research Methodology)

Table 3.1 (continued)

No.	Code	Subject
Mu'amalat (Contract Law)		
6	MUA 501	Fiqh Mu'amalat (Contract Law)
7	MUA 502	Ilmu Ekonomi dan Perbankan (Science of Economics and Banking)
8	MUA 503	Lembaga-Lembaga Perekonomian Ummat (Economic Institutions of the Islamic Community)
9	MUA 504	Metode Penelitian Mu'amalat (Mu'amalat Research Methods)
Perbandingan Hukum dan Mazhab (Comparative Law and Schools of Law)		
6	PMH 501	Perbandingan Hukum dan Perundang-Undangan (Comparison of Law and Legislation
7	PMH 502	Perbandingan Madzhab dalam Hukum Islam (Comparison of Schools of Islamic Law)
8	PMH 503	Fiqh Kontemporer (Contemporary Fiqh)
9	PMH 504	Metodologi Penelitian (Research Methodology)
Siyasah–Jinayah (Constitutional and Public Law)		
6	SWJ 501	Fiqh Siyasah (Constitutional Jurisprudence)
7	SWJ 502	Fiqh Jinayah (Criminal Jurisprudence)
8	SWJ 503	Al-Fatwa (The Legal Opinion)
9	SWJ 504	Metodologi Penelitian Siyasah (Siyasah Research Methodology)

Source: Department of Religion.

(Perbandingan Hukum dan Mazhab) and Constitutional and Public Law (Siyasah–Jinayah). Nine subjects are taught in each division. Five of them are common to all divisions and four are specialist courses specific to each division.

There is thus a high level of standardization in the curriculum for a basic undergraduate degree. This is now changing, however. Some IAIN are providing a greater number of specifically local courses, especially at the postgraduate level, to cater for the need for specialization. In addition, some of the better-funded UIN (especially UIN Syarif Hidayatullah Jakarta) are adding new faculties in the sciences and medicine, a trend that will undoubtedly change the balance of teaching and learning.

I reflect these factors in this chapter through an examination of the national and local curricula. I start by describing the national curriculum of 1998, and the more detailed curriculum of 1995 on which it is based (see section 1). This provides a basis for comparing the ways in which the various local curricula have adapted the national curriculum to their own purposes, especially in the area of syariah (see section 2). I then look at the types of texts that form the basis of the syariah curriculum, and how the national and regional curricula achieve a balance between them (see section 3). In the final section, I discuss the vexed issue of how to achieve a balance between the secular and religious elements of the syariah curriculum.

A final caution: as I observed earlier, all curricula are now undergoing extensive revision. Therefore, some of the detail that I provide may well be out of date by the time of publication. I nevertheless believe that the broader outline of the formal structures I describe should remain reasonably accurate, and that the issues of standardization, variety and syllabus reading will remain the most important issues for learning syariah.

1   THE NATIONAL CURRICULUM: BASIC STRUCTURES FOR SYARIAH EDUCATION

This section describes the key elements of the 1998 national core curriculum, and the more detailed 1995 curriculum on which it is based. Both were developed by the Department of Religion.

Basic General Subjects (MKDU)

The Basic General Subjects (MKDU) are taught in all religious and secular tertiary institutions, and may therefore be considered to form the foundation of a general tertiary degree in Indonesia. There are seven MKDU in the 1998 core curriculum (five in the 1995 version). Three are straightforward instructional courses on languages (Arabic, English and Indonesian). As we shall see later, the local curricula are quite innovative in the ways in which they link Islam and syariah to language instruction. The remaining four courses focus on specific aspects of Islamic studies. Even at this early stage of the students' education, it is clear that a certain view of Islam—of syariah in the secular republic—is being inculcated.

The first of the Basic General Subjects is Pancasila. The topics covered include the 1945 Constitution, the values embodied in the five Pancasila principles, elements of nationhood, the Old Order and New Order governments, and the current relationship between citizens and the state. The classical formulation of Pancasila over the past 40 years is found in the P-4 summaries and booklets, which are specifically directed towards supporting the ideology of the state (see Chapter 1). At the time of writing, the treatment of this subject was being rethought and considerably modified.

The second subject is Military–Nationalist Studies (Kewiraan), essentially covering the political and developmental history of Indonesia. Topics include the war of independence, defence of the nation, defence of the archipelago, defence and Pancasila, and national defence and development policy. In the post-New Order environment, Kewiraan is undergoing a fundamental shift in concept and purpose, from a military and nationalist orientation to an emphasis on civic education, including democracy, human rights and civil society. While we look at the localized versions of Kewiraan later, it should already be apparent that the notion of 'nationhood'—hence, of Islam within the nation—has acquired a quite new focus.

The third, fourth and fifth subjects are the language courses (Arabic, English and Indonesian).

The sixth is Basic Science (Ilmu Dasar), consisting of Basic Natural Science (Ilmu Alamiah Dasar), Basic Social Science (Ilmu Sosial Dasar) and Basic Cultural Science (Ilmu Budaya Dasar). The main topic covered in Basic Natural Science is evolution from the Western and Qur'ānic points of view; science and technology in modern life is also studied. The topics covered in Basic Social Science are development, poverty, family, population and social interaction. The main topics covered in Basic Cultural Science are literature, religion, philosophy (including Western philosophy) and primitive and agrarian cultures. The Islamic reference in all of the basic sciences is slight but discernible.

The final subject is Methodology of Islamic Studies (Metodologi Studi Islam). Its purpose is:

> To enable students to know and understand the methodology of studying Islam, approaches to Islamic and religious studies, and models and theoretical constructions for the study of religion, and to apply that knowledge when writing papers and research proposals.

It covers the following 21 topics.

1 *Introduction.* Islam and religious studies; importance of Islamic studies; origins and growth of Islamic studies in the Islamic world.
2 *Religious studies.* The position of religious studies among other fields of study; approaches to Islam in religion; construction of a theory of religious studies.
3 *Models of religious studies.* Religion as doctrine; religion as a product of culture; religion as a product of social interaction.
4 *Islam and culture.* Definition of cultural Islam; Islam and ancient (pre-Islamic) culture.
5 *Islam as religion.* The role of Islam in life; what Islam teaches the world.
6 *History of Islam.* Islam during the time of the Prophet and the first four caliphs; periods of progress and regression; centres of Islamic culture and the spread of Islam throughout the world.
7 *Regional studies.* Islam in East Africa; Islam in Southeast Asia; Islam in Central Asia; Islam in China and Africa.
8 *Islam and Indonesian culture.* Islam and Malay culture; Islam and Javanese culture; Islam and other cultures in the archipelago.
9 *Islam at present.* Islam in Europe; Islam in the Middle East; Islam in Southeast Asia; Islam in Central Asia; Islam in China and Africa.

10 *Schools of Islamic thought and their history.* Schools of law (*mazhab*); schools of dialectical theology (*kalam*); schools of metaphysics and gnosis; schools of philosophy and theosophy.

11 *The Qur'ān as a source of Islam.* The role and function of the Qur'ān; approaches to understanding the Qur'ān; the Qur'ān as the literal word of God; the contribution of the Qur'ān to understanding other scriptures; the sciences of the Qur'ān; and Qur'ānic exegesis.

12 *The Sunnah as a source of Islam.* The Prophet as the source of the Sunnah; the position of the Sunnah and its codification; approaches to understanding the Sunnah.

13 *Independent reasoning (ijtihad) as a source of Islam.* Definition; *ijtihad* as a source of dynamism; the formation of Islamic culture.

14 *Doctrine of belief in Islam.* God, Revelation, the Prophets and mankind; the universe; eschatology.

15 *Dimensions of Islam.* Islamic law (syariah); esoteric paths of Islam (*tariqah*); Sufism; submission (*islam*), faith (*iman*) and virtuous acts (*ihsan*).

16 *Rituals and institutions in Islam.* Perspectives and theories; systems; elements; analysis.

17 *Islam and humanity.* The position of humanity among God's creatures; man's duties, man as vicegerent (*khalifatullah*) on earth.

18 *Islam and morality.* The purpose of the appointment of the Prophet Muhammad as Messenger, virtue according to Islam.

19 *Islam, the family and society.* The family as the foundation of society; group consensus and mutual assistance; intracommunity relations.

20 *Islam and the contemporary world.* Islam and current traditions; millennarianism; revivalism; fundamentalism; modernist tendencies.

21. *Islam and other religions.* Metaphysical and theological views on other religions; Islam's contribution to humanity in this day and age.

This is the only course among the MKDU that is directly on Islam. The range of topics covered is huge, and for this reason alone its authors cannot have intended it to be more than a general introduction to the subject. It also seems likely that they intended it to function as a sort of checklist of desirable subjects from which individual faculties might choose a selection of topics.

Essentially, the MKDU show us the general context within which syariah will be studied. This context encompasses both ideology and science. The coverage of the latter may be minimal, but it is nevertheless significant that it is covered at all.

Basic Skills Subjects (MKDK)

The 1998 core curriculum contains 11 Basic Skills Subjects (MKDK), reduced from 15 in the 1995 curriculum. They are: (1) Principles of Jurisprudence (Ushul Fiqh), (2) Sciences of the Hadith (Ulumul Hadits), (3) Sciences of the Qur'ān

(Ulumul Qur'ān), (4) Science of Dialectical Theology (Ilmu Kalam), (5) Science of Sufism (Ilmu Tasawwuf), (6) General Philosophy (Filsafat Umum), (7) Research Methods (Metode Penelitian), (8) Jurisprudence (Fiqh), (9) Hadith (Hadits), (10) Qur'ānic Exegesis (Tafsir) and (11) Islamic History and Civilization (Sejarah dan Peradaban Islam). Only one of these—General Philosophy (Filsafat Umum), covering philosophy from the time of the Greeks through to the modern period—is not purely Islamic. The remaining subjects represent the basic syariah subjects in the curriculum.

Specialist Skills Subjects (MKK)

This more complex block of subjects for students specializing in syariah is divided into four sections in both the 1995 and 1998 curricula: Civil Law (Ahwal al-Shakhsiyah), Contract Law (Mu'amalat), Comparative Law and Schools of Law (Perbandingan Hukum dan Mazhab) and Constitutional and Public Law (Siyasah–Jinayah). The same arrangement is followed in all IAIN curricula, providing a formal structure in the sense of a standardized or uniform set of courses throughout Indonesia.

Nine subjects are taught in each of the four divisions: five prerequisites that are common to all divisions and four specialist courses that are specific to each division. The five prerequisites are Science of Qur'ānic Exegesis (Ilmu Tafsir), Qur'ānic Exegesis of Legal Principles (Tafsir Ahkam), Legal Principles from Hadith (Hadits Ahkam), Principles of Jurisprudence (Ushul Fiqh) and Science of Legal Studies (Ilmu Hukum). The first four of these are versions of the classical Arabic *fiqh* subjects. The fifth, Science of Legal Studies, covers such topics as the nature and function of law, sources of law, types of law, judicial decisions and the role of the judiciary, and law in society. This course would not be out of place in any Western law faculty. As a theoretical underpinning for the study of law, it is a decisive break from the classical syariah tradition.

Civil Law (Ahwal al-Shakhsiyah)

Literally, Ahwal al-Shakhsiyah means 'private matters', a translation that is not particularly helpful without some additional context. Different IAIN define the term differently, but the best general paraphrase I have been able to come up with is 'matters affecting Muslims' or 'civil laws for Muslims'. I am the first to admit that these are not entirely satisfactory translations either.

The first subject taken by students specializing in civil law is Islamic Civil Law in Indonesia (Hukum Perdata Islam di Indonesia). It covers family law, trusts, gifts and wills, but with reference to legislation and bureaucratic regulations—in short, the classical subjects in modern form. The second subject, Courts in Indonesia (Peradilan di Indonesia), provides a survey of the entire judicial system in Indonesia. It is heavily descriptive with no analytical elements at all. The same is true of the third and fourth subjects, Law of Procedure (Hukum Acara) and Legal Research Methodology (Metodologi Penelitian Hukum).

Contract Law (Mu'amalat)

It is hard to find an acceptable simple definition for Mu'amalat. In Indonesian usage it describes, first, the legal transactions (most often in contract form) between individuals. These may be adapted or changed according to circumstances, in contrast to the prescriptions in ritual (*ibadah*) where change is not possible. A secondary meaning, and the one that is relevant here, is commercial or contractual transactions—obviously a more specific version of the first meaning.

In this division, the five preliminary subjects are followed by four specifically on commerce and economics. The first, Contract Law (Fiqh Mu'amalat), is concerned with property, trade, loans, mortgages, partnerships and interest. These topics are all treated with reference to the classical *fiqh* rules. The second, Science of Economics and Banking (Ilmu Ekonomi dan Perbankan), is also drafted in terms of the classical jurisprudence; even the 'Islamic bank' is described solely in these terms. The third, Economic Institutions of the Islamic Community (Lembaga-Lembaga Perekonomian Ummat), deals with Islamic banks, Islamic insurance (*takaful*), cooperatives and the wealth tax (*zakat*). These topics are again discussed in (almost) wholly classical terms. The final subject is Mu'amalat Research Methods (Metode Penelitian Mu'amalat).

Comparative Law and Schools of Law (Perbandingan Hukum dan Mazhab)

Comparing the rules of the four Sunni *mazhab* has been an integral part of syariah since the schools were established in the second to eighth centuries. There is therefore a complex jurisprudence on this subject (see generally Hallaq 2005: 150–77). The idea of comparative thinking about law is, therefore, not new; indeed, Islamic law has the longest history on this subject of all legal traditions.

The four additional subjects in this section of the curriculum are as follows. The first, Comparison of Law and Legislation (Perbandingan Hukum dan Perundang-Undangan), defines the objects of study and then deals with the civil law system, customary (*adat*) law and some elements of syariah. The topics covered are marriage, inheritance and contracts. Essentially, there is little reference to classical *fiqh*. The second subject, Comparison of Schools of Islamic Law (Perbandingan Mazhab dalam Hukum Islam), is a wholly classically oriented course on *mazhab*, including the Zahiri *mazhab* and the Imami and Zaidi *mazhab* of the Shi'a sect. The third subject, Contemporary Fiqh (Fiqh Kontemporer), is described as enabling 'students to understand problems of *fiqh* that have emerged in the life of society in recent times and which require a resolution based on Islamic law'. It is about the use of *ijtihad* to resolve controversial issues such as abortion, in-vitro fertilization, family planning, women in politics, credit and credit cards, and gambling. The required reading consists of modern Indonesian texts and, to a lesser extent, modern Arabic books such as Ali Fikri's *Mu'amalat* [Contract Law] and al-Khafif's *Asbab al-Ikhtilaf al-Fuqaha* [Reasons for Differences among the Jurists]. The final subject in this part of the curriculum is Research Methodology (Metodologi Penelitian).

Constitutional and Public Law (Siyasah–Jinayah)

This is a combination of *siyasah* meaning 'politics' or 'policy' and *jinayah* meaning 'criminal matters'. It can be translated as 'public law' in the civil law sense. It comprises criminal law and state legal policy as well as administrative and constitutional law.

The first of the four additional subjects in this section of the curriculum is Constitutional Jurisprudence (Fiqh Siyasah), which deals with the relationship between the law and the state. The topics covered are state administration from the eighth century CE to the present, the modern state and Islam, finance and administration, and international treaties in Islam. The second subject, Criminal Jurisprudence (Fiqh Jinayah), takes its treatment of the subject from the classical *fiqh* texts. The third, The Legal Opinion (Al-Fatwa), expounds classical theories of the *fatwā* while also incorporating modern Egyptian and Indonesian *fatāwā* from a variety of sources. This course is more concerned with the theory of *fatwā* than with examining specific *fatāwā* themselves. The final subject in this part of the curriculum is Siyasah Research Methodology (Metodologi Penelitian Siyasah).

Islamic versus Secular Law: The Search for Balance

This overview of the four basic divisions of the Specialist Skills Subjects (MKK) shows that each has a common classical core. In addition, we can see that there are five secular subjects in the first division; that all of the subjects in the second division are classical; that secular subjects predominate in the third division; and that the classical component predominates in the fourth division (although there is a secular component). Turning to the overall balance of subjects in the national curriculum as a whole, we find languages and ideology in the Basic General Subjects (MKDU), classical *fiqh* in the Basic Skills Subjects (MKDK), and a mix of classical and modern secular subjects (and, hence, approaches) in the Specialist Skills Subjects (MKK).

This overview suggests that the core curriculum is neither simplistically Islamic nor predominantly secular in its approach. It is 'a little Islamic', 'totally Islamic', 'partly Islamic' and 'Islamic in an Indonesian context'. The terms themselves demonstrate the danger of relying on labels; none of them makes sense except at a very superficial level. One might, for example, argue for (or against) the core curriculum on the grounds that its 'classical' and 'secular' components are roughly equivalent, as indeed they are in a count of subjects. Certainly it would be wrong not to consider the possibility that the proportion of subjects has real significance, but what does a simple equivalence of subjects actually mean? The debates of the 1960s and 1970s were concerned with precisely this issue: how much of the curriculum had to be 'Islamic' and how much could be 'secular'. The 'had'–'could' opposition was crucial for those holding that the syariah was indivisible—that the only true and proper syariah was that which was given (by God) and known through the *fiqh* texts. In contrast, the 'could' position held that the syariah was not native to Indonesia and needed to be adapted to Indonesian legal reality. That reality included *adat* law, the colonial inheritance and the imperative of creating a national law for the new Republic of Indonesia. In short, the classical *fiqh* was not primary, but one relevant source of law among others.

It is here that purpose and balance become significant, as exemplified in the Nasution reforms of the 1970s.[7] The purpose of the reforms was to make syariah compatible with existing Indonesian circumstances, not the other way round, which was (and continues to be) impractical. A workable Indonesian syariah could only be achieved by striking the correct balance between all the elements in the curriculum. While not sufficient on its own, this focus on balance does direct the curriculum towards compatibility and integration. A successful curriculum must be made up of compatible elements that are successfully integrated into a workable whole. We have already seen how this was achieved in the 1998 core curriculum, but what about the more detailed 1995 curriculum? What is its approach to the issue of compatibility and integration?

In its simplest sense, compatibility means that elements drawn from disparate sources must be made to match. The 15 Basic Skills Subjects in the 1995 curriculum can be characterized, in a single word, as representing a 'transition' from a purely Islamic to a more secular way of thinking about law. By this I mean that the subjects move progressively from the basics (the Qur'ān, Hadith and so on) through comparative syariah (Islamic law in the Middle East and Southeast Asia, a comparative account of the four Sunni schools) to the philosophy of syariah, the science of law (the function, politics and classification of law) and, finally, Indonesian public law (civil, criminal, agrarian, administrative, procedural and so on). But although the transition is clear, does it actually achieve compatibility between secular and Islamic legal thinking?

---

7   Nasution (1977, 1986a) advocated a 'rational' Islamic theology emphasizing the need to understand the history and philosophies of Islam as well as the sociological and political realities of present-day Indonesia (see Chapter 2, this volume). This required a special emphasis on research methods and pedagogy, both of which are now standard features of the IAIN curricula. For further details on the Nasution reforms, see Halim (2001), Muzani (1994), Jabali and Jamhari (2003: viii–ix, 37–9, 124–5) and Subhan (1999).

To take an example, two courses in the 1995 curriculum, General Philosophy II (Filsafat Umum II) and Legal Principles from Hadith II (Hadits Ahkam II), deal with the same subjects—family, marriage and gifts for pious purposes (*wakaf*)—in the same way. That is, they cover exactly the same topics, using the same method of instruction and the same analytical approach. The difference between the two courses lies in the required readings, which are Indonesian and English texts in the former case and Arabic texts in the latter case. The respective literatures are quite dissimilar, leading to different ways of thinking about the topics under study, even though the course framework and the topics themselves are the same. Nevertheless, these ways of acquiring knowledge are certainly not incompatible.

To take a broader example: about half of the Specialist Skills Subjects in the national curriculum are classical subjects. Their treatment (unlike that of the preceding Basic Skills Subjects) is not heavily descriptive but rather directed specifically towards Indonesian circumstances. The whole of Contract Law (Fiqh Mu'amalat), for example, is about the integration of Islamic principles into the formal legal structures of the Indonesian state.

The key words in thinking about the level of integration between the Islamic and secular components of the curriculum, therefore, are 'compatibility' and 'transition'. However, integration does not mean the loss of syariah identity but its retention *in an Indonesian context*. Moreover, it needs to be remembered that transition is an ongoing process in which different degrees of integration are accepted as normal. The drafters of the national curriculum clearly had this in mind, as I show in a final example.

In the 1980s, the Department of Religion (through its research department) issued a book jointly written by teachers from two IAIN (now the Jakarta and Yogyakarta UIN) for use in the national curriculum as an integrated teaching text. *Islam Fiqh* [Islamic Law] is in three parts, the first part dating from 1982, the second from 1984–85 and the third from 1986. It is about 270,000 words in length—long in any terms. The first part describes the five pillars of Islam and their correct ritual performance with reference to the relevant Qur'ānic verses and Hadith as well as the classical Arabic *fiqh*. The second part is much broader in scope and intention. It contains chapters on the nature of society, the nature of womankind, and general principles of marriage and family, again with reference to the Qur'ān and Hadith as well as the *fiqh* texts. Part 3 describes the national legal system.

Islam Fiqh provides a short, simplified and standardized coverage of the material that students would expect to study in a *pesantren*. But while the content may be the same, the method of learning is not: students do not need to be able to read Arabic to access the information, which is conveyed in Indonesian, although still with the appropriate references to the standard Arabic texts. What we have, then, is an integration of classical content into a national state curriculum designed and promoted by an agency of the state. This sort of penetration a particular way of thinking about Islam into what is conventionally considered the preserve of the *pesantren* is likely to have severe long-term consequences for the latter's educational autonomy. The push by the *pesantren* to increase their enrolments and influence by promoting the development of *madrasah* suggests that they are aware of this threat. But what happens to *madrasah* graduates? They go on to study at IAIN. The point is that the common national curriculum has become pervasive at the tertiary level, so there is no escaping its influence.

2   VARIETIES OF LOCAL CURRICULA

Because of the all-pervasive nature of the common national curriculum, the thousands of law students who graduate each year have a common understanding of what syariah is in Indonesia. But the uniformity of structure imposed by the state could also be restrictive, tending to stifle any local, let alone personal, initiative. It is therefore to the great credit of the Department of Religion that local variations in the curriculum are permitted. Under the 40:60 rule introduced in 2004, the scope of these was much enlarged, although the cynical observer might say that the Department of Religion had little or no choice given the strength of the alternative courses of law offered by NU and Muhammadiyah in the regions. I prefer to believe, however, that there is a general understanding that variation is in itself a good thing, as well as being practical—Islam 'is', after all, pluralism.

All Muslims knows the passage:

> Whatever it be wherein
> Ye differ, the decision
> Thereof is with God ... (Q42:10)

This is the principle on which the IAIN have built their respective curricula, thus demonstrating a real *ijtihad*, expressed in the past by Nasution (1995: 211 ff.) and continued into the present by committed IAIN scholars throughout Indonesia. The Department of Religion has interpreted this principle in a letter of instruction that sets out a working plan for the localization of syariah studies (SK No. 383/1997). The first section of this two-part plan calls for the core subjects (public law) to be rethought at the local level, while the second section states that new courses suited to the needs of particular localities (provinces, districts) can and should be made available. If we take Q42:10 and SK No. 383/1997 together—and how strangely appropriate such a pairing becomes—we find that both are 'local', but in different senses of the word.

Regional Rewritings of the Core Curriculum

Basic General Subjects (MKDU)

We begin with a totally unexpected subject from a totally unexpected source: a compulsory course in basic English language offered by STAIN Batusangkar in West Sumatra. The following is a comprehension passage (English as in the original):

There is no God but Allah.

A. Human being believes in God. He is created by God and will return to God. He does everything to please his God. He worships his God heartfully and asks Him the right path. Some believe in one God. They are called monotheism. Others believe in more than one God: they are called polytheism. Still others do not believe in God at all. They are known as atheism.

Unfortunately, what man may regard as God is not really the true God. Rama, according to Hindu's follower is his God. Christian believes that Jesus is his God. And Shinto follower believes that the sun is God. Jewish believes that Judaism can bring them to God.

Muslim believes that true God is Allah. He shows us His existance through His creations. He creates the universe. He creates the heaven, the earth and whatever inside between them. Even, what is believed as God by non-believer is also Allah's creation. Allah sends us a guidance to come to Him. Whoever accepts His guidance will live in peace. Whoever rejects it will live in severe. The guidance is called Islam which means peace and the follor [*sic*] is called Muslim. It prescribes the Muslim to bear that there is no God but Allah.

B. Using the Prefix–root–suffix method, try to grasp the meaning of your underlining words.

C. Comprehension Question
Does human being believe in one God?
Do all human being believe in one God?
Do you belong to monotheism or polytheism?
Who is your God?
How do you know the existance of God?
What does Allah send to us as a guidance?
What does it mean Islam in English?
What is the key to convert Islam?

The interesting point about this passage, and its accompanying instructions, is the overt use of religion to teach what is essentially a non-religious subject— English. The grammar the student is learning is focused on Islam as a body of knowledge and takes place in a religious context. There is thus a dual discourse: English grammar and the truth of Islam.

IAIN Raden Fatah Palembang also bases its English-language course on a text with a religious theme—'Prophet Muhammad'—with the topic headings clearly drawn from the Qur'ān. Thus, the topics for English Language I are Allah the God, Faith in Islam, Books of Allah, The Angels, Life after Death, The Dawn of Islam, The Day of Peace, Praying during Travel, Fasting in Islam, The Pilgrimage, Culture in Islam, and Equality in Islam; and the topics for English Language II are Culture Shock, The Role of Women in the United States, Energy Crises, and Living a Long Life. The required reading is *English for Islamic Study* by Djamalludin Darwis, which I have not been able to trace.

The English-language course offered by IAIN Imam Bonjol (Padang) could not be in greater contrast. It is a straight grammar course covering nouns, articles, verbs, pronouns, tenses, adverbs, clauses and so on. The required readings are the texts typically used to teach grammar to non-native speakers.

UIN Syarif Hidayatullah Jakarta occupies a middle ground between these two extremes. Its English-language course teaches formal grammar and basic skills such as sentence construction, 'recognizing paragraph patterns' and 'recognizing the author's intention, attitude and bias'. In addition to five standard grammar texts, the course requires students to read the Qur'ān (Yusuf Ali's translation) and textbooks by Esposito (1991) and Lapidus (1988) on Islamic society and history.

The MKDU on which one would naturally concentrate here are Pancasila and Military–Nationalist Studies (Kewiraan), both courses in ideology. Almost without exception, the local institutions have scaled down their Pancasila courses in the post-New Order period—often to just one semester—although there is very little evidence of any local variation in content. There have, however, been fundamental changes in Kewiraan, in both name and content. The popular new names for this course are Civil Society (Masyarakat Madani) and Citizenship (Kewarganegaraan). This subject is currently undergoing extensive reformulation in all IAIN, making data hard to come by. But there are two preliminary versions showing what such a course might look like, both from UIN Syarif Hidayatullah Jakarta.

The first is a (2001) course called Education in Citizenship (Pendidikan Kewarganegaraan). It is based on the following core topics: nation, identity, national identity, state, ideology, the Constitution, religion and the state, human rights and democracy, the state and civil society, decentralization and regional autonomy, and the structure of the districts under regional autonomy, including their financial structure.

The second is found in a collection of essays by academics from UIN Syarif Hidayatullah Jakarta on how the new citizenship program might be formulated (Ubaidillah et al. 2000). It suggests that such a program might consist of the following eight parts.

1 National identity (ideology, especially the ideology of Pancasila, national integration, the nation).
2 The state and citizenship (definition of 'state', laws of the state, democracy and citizenship).
3 The Constitution of 1945.
4 The civil and the military in the state.
5 Religion and the state (the politics of religion, religion and society).
6 Civil society (characteristic features, how democratization might proceed).
7 Democracy (characteristics, religion and democracy).
8 Human rights (including the Medina Charter).

These suggestions are not as revolutionary as one might suppose. It is certainly innovative to include autonomy and human rights as formal components in the curriculum, but the other topics are clearly in the pre-democracy tradition. The MKDU are subject to local variation, but they continue to stress correct ideological thought and the correct basis for arriving at that thought.

The Basic Skills Subjects (MKDK)

As we saw earlier, the core Basic Skills Subjects are wholly Islamic, and one would therefore expect little or no change at the local level. This expectation is only partly supported by the evidence, however. For example, while there is little or no evidence of localization in this subject area in IAIN Sunan Ampel Surabaya, IAIN Ar-Raniry (Banda Aceh) or IAIN Imam Bonjol (Padang), UIN Syarif Hidayatullah Jakarta does provide an example of localization.

Its course on Science of Qur'ānic Exegesis (Ilmu Tafsir) goes beyond the usual treatment of this subject to discuss an analytical methodology for exegesis. In contrast, the Department of Religion's course mainly consists of a listing of Qur'ānic verses accompanied by a very minimal and quite traditional set of topics for discussion. The contrast is therefore between an emphasis on function and purpose on the one hand and the repetition of known classes on the other. This contrast carries through into the required readings, which are much more extensive in the UIN syllabus.

However, the same cannot be said of the university's course on Science of Dialectical Theology (Ilmu Kalam), which is much the same as the Department of Religion's course. The courses are organized differently, and the UIN course has some additional elements and a more extensive modern Arabic reading list, but apart from this there is a high degree of similarity between the two. The essential similarity of the UIN Syarif Hidayatullah Jakarta and Department of Religion curricula can also be demonstrated by comparing their versions of another Basic Skills Subject, Islamic History and Civilization (Sejarah dan Peradaban Islam) (see Table 3.2).

Of course, it may be objected that this is hardly a core subject in the *pesantren* sense,[8] and this objection is certainly sustainable. The real test must be how the core of the curriculum—*fiqh*—is handled. The *fiqh* courses in the national and IAIN curricula are much the same; as one would expect, they cover the Qur'ān, the Sunnah, reasoning by analogy (*qiyas*), consensus among experts on points of law (*ijma'*), juristic preference (*istihsan*), the public good (*maslahah*) and so on. However, we must be a little careful here, for two reasons. First, at least one IAIN, Sunan Ampel Surabaya, has its own 'local' version of Systems of Jurisprudence (Kaidah-Kaidah Fiqhiyah) at the MKDK level—although on its own this may not mean too much because of the very general nature of this

---

8   There is no space in this essay for a survey of the *pesantren* curriculum, but see van Bruinessen (1990) on the texts used in the *pesantren*, and Jabali and Jamhari (2003: 79–120) on *pesantren* reform.

Table 3.2   Islamic History and Civilization: Two Versions

UIN Syarif Hidayatullah Jakarta	Department of Religion
1 Philosophy and method of historical analysis	1 Introduction to historical method and Islamic cultures
2 Arabs before Islam	2 Islam in Arabic culture at the time of the Prophet and its influence in the West
3 Development of Islam at the time of the Prophet	3 Islam in the culture of Persia/Iran
4 Development of Islam at the time of the first four caliphs	4 Islam in Turkish culture
5 Islam in the time of the Umayyad	5 Islam in African cultures
6 Islam in the time of the Abbasid	6 Islam in India
7 The Mongol war and invasion	7 Islamic influence in Malay–Indonesian cultures
8 Islam at the time of the Mamelukes in Egypt	8 Development of Islamic social principles
9 Islam in Ottoman Turkey	9 Development of Islamic thought
10 Islam in Safafid Persia	10 Development of Islamic arts and architecture
11 Islam in Mughal India	11 Development of science and its contribution to world civilization
12 Nationalist movements in the Muslim world	12 Mystical organizations (*tasawwuf* and *tarikat*)
13 Islam in Spain	13 Islam and the West: conflict and accommodation
14 Islam in Indonesia, Malaysia, Thailand and the Philippines	

Source: UIN Syarif Hidayatullah Jakarta; Department of Religion.

subject. Second, all IAIN use the MKDK section of the curriculum as a lead-in or introduction to the MKK. They do this by transiting from *fiqh* to contemporary *fiqh* (*fiqh kontemporer*). The latter is *fiqh* in the state, as administered by the institutions of state. (It also often refers to *fatāwā*).

To summarize, then, the purpose of the Basic Skills Subjects is to instruct students in the basics of classical *fiqh*. The national curriculum is decisive in this area; while there is some local input, there is no evidence of localization in this section of the curriculum more generally.

The Specialist Skills Subjects (MKK)

We should remind ourselves at this point that it is important to examine the detail of the national and local curricula because it reveals the extent to which local institutions have altered the nationally prescribed forms. The preceding discussion suggests that there has been only limited local initiative in the MKDU and MKDK sections of the curriculum, although whether this is qualitatively decisive is another matter. Here, in the MKK section of the curriculum, we should be able to obtain a clearer idea of the qualitative importance of local variations, judged by the only practical test available: congruence or compatibility with the imperatives of the national legal system. After all, that is the purpose of the MKK section of the curriculum. This section of the curriculum is also meant to encourage specialization, including local innovation.

The Specialist Skills Subjects make up the largest and most comprehensive section of the national and local curricula. As discussed above, students can specialize in one of four areas: Civil Law; Contract Law; Comparative Law and Schools of Law; or Constitutional and Public Law. Each of the divisions offers a common core of four *fiqh* courses. They are:

1 Qur'ānic Exegesis of Legal Principles (Tafsir Ahkam);
2 Legal Principles from Hadith (Hadits Ahkam);
3 Principles of Jurisprudence (Ushul Fiqh); and
4 Philosophy of Islamic Law (Filsafat Hukum Islam) at an advanced level.

In addition, all IAIN students study a set of five non-*fiqh* courses on the institutions of state. They are:

1 Islamic Law in Indonesia (Hukum Islam di Indonesia);
2 Religious Courts of Indonesia (Peradilan Agama di Indonesia);
3 Religious Court Procedure (Hukum Acara Peradilan Agama);
4 Civil Law (Hukum Perdata); and
5 Civil Law Procedure (Hukum Acara Perdata).

I take the former group first.

Qur'ānic Exegesis of Legal Principles (Tafsir Ahkam). The regional curricula for this subject follow the national curriculum very closely. Some IAIN, such as Sunan Ampel Surabaya, claim to have localized their courses, but all this means is that the selection and order of Qur'ānic verses vary somewhat from the national model. On the other hand, one can see something of a local originality in the balance between classical *fiqh* and modern Arabic commentary in the IAIN reading lists. The modern texts appear more frequently in local curricula than in the national curriculum. However, it is not possible to read too much into this, especially given the extensive changes to the national and regional curricula now being drafted.

Legal Principles from Hadith (Hadits Ahkam). The same general comments apply. There has been little or no significant localization in this area.

Principles of Jurisprudence (Ushul Fiqh). It is difficult to make generalizations here, because of the range of responses. IAIN Ar-Raniry (Banda Aceh), for example, follows the national curriculum, as does IAIN Imam Bonjol (Padang). But UIN Syarif Hidayatullah Jakarta, IAIN Sunan Ampel Surabaya and UIN Sunan Kalijaga Yogyakarta provide a far more elaborate treatment of particular topics (especially marriage and *zakat*), with a greater emphasis on modern Arabic commentary.

Philosophy of Islamic Law (Filsafat Hukum Islam). The treatment of this subject in the national curriculum varies depending on the faculty division. This variation is reflected in regional curricula, as one would expect from a course on philosophy. So, for example, the topics in the course offered by IAIN Raden Fatah Palembang include the development and method of philosophy of Islamic law; trends and assumptions; law and divine authority; principles and essentials; ethics and aesthetics; and law, society and the state. IAIN Imam Bonjol (Padang) offers a very similar course. The corresponding course in the national curriculum concentrates primarily on family law, however, as does that of IAIN Sunan Ampel Surabaya, despite its claim of localization.

Perhaps the most elaborate course in Philosophy of Islamic Law is that offered by UIN Syarif Hidayatullah Jakarta. Its course has 11 sections, each with detailed subdivisions. The first, understandings (*pengertian*), contains subsections on the language of philosophy, the language of Islamic law, the development and elaboration of that philosophy, method(s), the relationship of Islamic legal philosophy to other sciences, basic assumptions of Islamic law, and the philosophy of Islamic law in the context of other legal philosophies. The second, philosophical thought (*pemikiran filosofi*), contains subsections on ontology, epistemology and the study of values (*aksiologi*). The third, the judge (*hakim*), consists of two parts, the first containing subsections on the essence and existence of God, arguments for God, and the implications of the existence of God for law or legal thinking (hence the authority of God); and the second covering exactly the same topics, but this time with reference to the Prophet. The fourth section concerns the implementation of law in society (*pelaksanaan hukum (manusia)*), or how mankind can fulfil the divine imperative in society. Subsections include the essence and existence of man, reason and unreason (emotion) in mankind, the awareness or instinct of man towards law, and man and Islamic law. The fifth section, on Islamic law, contains subsections on the principles and foundations of Islamic law, the characteristics of Islamic law, ethics and aesthetics in Islamic law, and the process of forming and developing Islamic law. The final six sections, all entitled 'considerations' (*tinjuan*), relate the foregoing sections to specific topics. These are: Islamic law generally, personal laws, *ibadah*, contracts and commercial laws, and crime/public order.

This is such a huge course that it is difficult to see how it could possibly be covered, even as an introductory treatment spread over two semesters. In the absence of classroom data on actual teaching and supervision, it is probably safe to assume that selections rather than the whole course are taught.

It would certainly be characteristic of Indonesian Islam if selection were the key to the syllabus. For example, one book that commonly appears as required reading for Philosophy of Islamic Law courses is *Philosophy of Islamic Law and the Orientalists* by Muhammad Muslehuddin (1977). The first five chapters provide an overview of legal philosophy based on Western jurisprudence; they cover the Greek philosophers, Bentham, natural law, nineteenth-century positive law and ideals of justice. The descriptions are basic, not to say naive; modern legal theory from the 1960s onwards is not mentioned at all. The next 12 chapters give a potted history of syariah and the schools of legal reasoning. They are based on a narrow range of sources; significant Muslim and non-Muslim authors from the 1950s through 1970s are not considered or even cited. The remaining five chapters are on comparative law and the families of law (civil, common, socialist and so on).

The section of the book that is of most interest to us here is two chapters critiquing Coulson's *Conflict and Tensions in Islamic Jurisprudence* (Coulson 1969) and Kerr's *Islamic Reform* (Kerr 1966), both classics in their field. The author is strongly polemical, even extreme, in his views. For example, in his introductory remarks on Coulson, Kerr and other 'orientalists', Muslehuddin says:

> Orientalists are unaware of their own laws, let alone the sharia law, whose language they have not mastered (Muslehuddin 1977: xv)

and

> Orientalists have launched a campaign to subvert Islam by their unfair criticism of Islamic law. (Muslehuddin, 1977: xv)

To direct remarks such as these against Coulson and Kerr is breathtaking effrontery. On the other hand, they can perhaps be explained as being due to fundamental differences in the Islamic and Western conceptions of the definition, role and functions of law. Thus, whereas Coulson acknowledges change and inconsistency ('conflict', 'tensions') in the contemporary legal world of Islam, and asserts that there is nothing new in this, Muslehuddin rejects this, preferring instead to emphasize the certainty of revelation (which, for him, is the Qur'ān) and the concomitant fallibility of jurists both ancient and modern. This is an extreme form of the 'argument from within', but that is not to say that it is not a respectable position. The problem, however, is that it does not allow for an accommodation of the changes that are actually occurring in the legal world, so promoting an essentialism which denies any function for human reason. Thus, we find Muslehuddin asking: 'Is he [Coulson] justified in suggesting to Divine Law free use of human reason which is fallible and deficient?' (p. 205). The answer, of course, is 'no'. This is the essentialist or syariah as sufficient position described in Chapter 2. While fairly common in Indonesia (see Husaini 2006 and below), it suffers from the defect that it does not actually reflect reality. It proposes an ideal state of affairs without establishing any method for bridging the gap between new developments and the ideal. One can understand why the IAIN syllabuses would wish to reflect the ideal; why they have chosen a less than scholarly exposition as a vehicle to do so is more difficult to understand. There are no criteria stated for a selection such as this, and in the absence of detailed understanding of curriculum development, one can only accept the choice.

Having said this, I should point to the role of such mundane factors as library resources and funding. The Jakarta and Yogyakarta UIN have respectable libraries and the money to support them. But other major centres, such as Medan, Surabaya and Aceh (even before the tsunami), are very badly off. The same is true for Padang and Malang. This means that books, especially in the English language (now a major language for Islamic studies), are just not available. My own notes show just how frustrating this is for teachers in the IAIN.

Of the core subjects in the MKK section of the curriculum, we can conclude the following. First, in Qur'ānic Exegesis of Legal Principles, Legal Principles from Hadith and Principles of Jurisprudence, there is little or no variation between the national curriculum and local curricula. These are basic classical courses, so this is to be expected. Second, in Philosophy of Islamic Law, there is room for greater freedom of interpretation and, thus, local emphases. A variety of materials presenting a variety of different views are being used to teach this subject. The choice of material may simply reflect the personal preferences of the teaching staff of individual institutions at any one time. On the other hand, it may show, in embryo form, the beginning of a longer-term trend towards the development of regional variants. In the light of the syariah varieties discussed in the next subsection, this seems a distinct possibility. After all, philosophy of law is supposed to be the subject that presents and explains choices to the student.

In addition to the four core *fiqh* courses, five non-*fiqh* courses on the institutions of state appear in all IAIN programs of study throughout Indonesia.

Islamic Law in Indonesia (Hukum Islam di Indonesia). Taught in three stages, the national curriculum's coverage of this subject is essentially a summary of the Compilation of Islamic Law (Kompilasi Hukum Islam; KHI). The first section concerns the capacity to marry and the formalities of marriage, including polygamy; in addition to the KHI, it refers to the Marriage Law of 1974. The second section concerns divorce, again closely following the main headings set out in the KHI. The third section, which is also based on the KHI, covers such subjects as guardians (*waris*), reimbursement (*radd*) and *wakaf.*

IAIN Ar-Raniry (Banda Aceh), IAIN Sunan Ampel Surabaya, IAIN Imam Bonjol (Padang) and UIN Syarif Hidayatullah Jakarta all follow the national curriculum. In 2003, UIN Sunan Kalijaga Yogyakarta was drafting a new curriculum. Details were not available at the time of writing, but it appeared that its course on Islamic Civil Law in Indonesia (Hukum Perdata Islam di Indonesia) had been retained, and to this extent at least, the national curriculum was being followed. IAIN Raden Fatah Palembang covers the same topics as are in the national curriculum, but in separate courses. These include Inheritance Law (Fiqh Mewaris) and Islamic Civil Law in Indonesia (Hukum Perdata Islam di

Indonesia), something of a composite course on inheritance, wills, *wakaf* and *wakaf* property, and divorce. There is nothing original of note here except, perhaps, an emphasis on family without overly dividing the law into separate categories as the national curriculum does.

This close correspondence with the national curriculum is repeated in the remaining four non-*fiqh* subjects: Religious Courts of Indonesia (Peradilan Agama di Indonesia), which is a summary of the Law on Religious Justice (No. 7/1989); Religious Court Procedure (Hukum Acara Peradilan Agama); Civil Law (Hukum Perdata); and Civil Law Procedure (Hukum Acara Perdata).

To summarize: at the MKDU level, we find local variation in the English-language and ideology courses, but at the MKDK and MKK levels there is little evidence of local innovation. It appears that the national curriculum has successfully imposed itself as the standard curriculum. This means that there is an Indonesia-wide acceptance of what the syariah is so far as the state (that is, the Department of Religion) is concerned. But of course this is not the end of the matter. There are in fact significant variations in the regional curricula, and it is to these that we now turn.

Syariah in Practice: Regional Initiatives in the Law Curriculum

What is 'syariah in practice'? Even to ask this question is to infer that the *fiqh* is no longer decisive. Students are still required to know what the *fiqh* is, and it is still part of the national and local curricula, but it is now mediated through a new element—syariah in Indonesia. In other words, 'Islamic' law is more than just the *fiqh*. Here, we look at syariah in practice through the medium of regional initiatives in the curriculum. The regions have always had a degree of initiative in syariah education, but this has increased with the passage of the 1999 Regional Autonomy Laws, which allow a formal recognition of regional and local interests, and with the adoption of the 40:60 rule.

The question of interest to us here is whether the regional IAIN curricula reflect local concerns *bearing in mind the standard core national curriculum*. We attempt to answer this question within the standard national framework of the four syariah divisions: Civil Law, Contract Law, Comparative Law and Schools of Law, and Constitutional and Public Law. The advantage of doing it this way—not that there is much choice—is that the material from all IAIN can be examined within a common study program.

Civil Law (Ahwal al-Shakhsiyah)

UIN Syarif Hidayatullah Jakarta. We begin with the curriculum developed by Syarif Hidayatullah. The first course of interest to us here is International Private Law (Hukum Perdata Internasional). This is an extremely difficult subject in any legal system. Very few law students in any country take it, because it requires competence in both a foreign language and comparative law. Why, then, is it such an important part of the curriculum in modern Indonesia? The answer goes back to the colonial period, where inter-racial private law (*inter-gentiel recht*) was an important and compulsory segment of the legal curriculum given the separate legal systems for Europeans and 'natives'.[9]

The course on International Private Law offered by Syarif Hidayatullah treats syariah as just one among several valid approaches to the subject. It covers domicile, choice of law and even *renvoi* ('return'), a pure (Dutch) civil law category. In short, the student is being introduced to a framework within which syariah is merely a variable. This is a long way from the concepts of law in the two groups of core subjects just described. Obviously, from the point of view of syariah itself, the *fiqh* can never be a variable; it is primary and decisive. How Syarif Hidayatullah explains this inconsistency, or even potential conflict, is not known. So far as I know, no one has researched this rigorously by undertaking the requisite classroom and examination paper surveys.

UIN Syarif Hidayatullah Jakarta also offers an interesting variation on the national curriculum's treatment of marriage and the family. The subject is approached by way of a comparative course called Administration of the Islamic State (Administrasi Negara Islam) based on data from the Middle Eastern states of Egypt, Sudan and Saudi Arabia on the one hand and the Southeast Asian states of Malaysia, Singapore and Brunei on the other. But many of the texts set for the last three states are out of date and the all-important subject of English law precedent is not covered. The Indonesian student is not well served in this subject.

Fortunately this is not the case for Contemporary Islamic Law (Hukum Islam Kontemporer). Based mainly on modern Arabic[10] and Indonesian *fatāwā*, the course covers such topics as the fast, the *hajj*, family planning, Islamic insurance, bank interest and *zakat*. At first sight this may appear to be a rather random set of topics, but in fact they have all been chosen because they represent 'edge' issues, that is, highly disputed issues in contemporary syariah. Contemporary Islamic Law is taught in all IAIN and has become code for the modernization of, or new ways of thinking about, *fiqh* rules. It is therefore an important subject in its own right. Although the *fatwā* form is not binding, leaving room for a variety of opinions, it is a known form with its own rules. Using this form to canvass difficult issues in this way is a modern Indonesian innovation, and is widespread among the IAIN.

UIN Syarif Hidayatullah Jakarta also has a solid block of courses on the formal secularized *fiqh*, beginning with Science of Laws (Ilmu Undang-Undangan), a preliminary course on Indonesian sources of law (the Constitution of 1945 and

---

9   See Burns (1988) for an extensive discussion.
10 Yusuf Qardhawi is the usual source.

MPRS XX/1966[11]), and on the meaning and drafting of laws. This course is cur-
rently undergoing considerable amendment. It is followed by Islamic Laws of
Indonesia (Undang-Undang Islam di Indonesia), a straightforward exposition of
the Marriage Law of 1974, the KHI and the role of the religious courts, and Civil
Laws of Islam (Hukum Perdata Islam) on marriage, wills and gifts. Land Law
(Hukum Agraria) traces land laws from the time of the Dutch East India Company (Verenigde Oostindische Compagnie; VOC) through to the 1960 Basic
Agrarian Law, and also examines issues of land reform. Islamic Law Policies in
Indonesia (Politik Hukum Islam di Indonesia) also takes a historical approach to
its subject, covering such topics as the religious courts, Pancasila, the law theo-
ries of Hazairin, and *reformasi*, democracy and civil society.

I have spent some time on UIN Syarif Hidayatullah Jakarta because of its status as a flagship institution. It is lavishly funded (by Indonesian standards), has
extensive international links, and publishes (in Arabic, Indonesian and English)
Studia Islamika, Indonesia's leading journal of Islamic studies. It is the model
that all other institutions, especially the IAIN, attempt to emulate. However, this
does not extend to emulation of all its courses, eschewing regional variation.

IAIN Sunan Ampel Surabaya. In the case of Sunan Ampel, it is easy to identify regional variants designed to suit the special local conditions of its catch-
ment area, East Java. A good example is its range of courses on *adat* law. *Adat*
has always been important in rural Indonesia, and even the Basic Agrarian Law
of 1960 paid it the compliment of calling it the basic principle on which land
tenure is founded (article 5). That was, of course, merely a rhetorical flourish
inspired by the political ideology of Guided Democracy, and certainly had no
substance in the laws and regulations of the next 40-odd years. However, *adat*
has made a considerable comeback in recent years, especially since the end of
the New Order and subsequent enactment of the Regional Autonomy Laws. The
new *adat* is not the *adat* of the Dutch era; instead, it is being reinvented to support land claims or, more accurately, security of occupation on disputed land,
particularly land that has been reoccupied by dispossessed peasants. This reinvented *adat* is politically potent in the districts where the newly autonomous district governments have the unenviable task of sorting out the competing claims
to land (Lucas and Warren 2003: 99 ff.).

IAIN Sunan Ampel Surabaya has three courses designed to instruct students
in the realities of *adat* and its implications for syariah. The first is a general
course called Adat Law (Hukum Adat). It traverses reception theory, the structures and forms of *adat* (bilateral, matrilineal, patrilineal) and the functions of
adat in rural communities. The basic text is Ter Haar (1948), which continues to
exercise considerable influence in *adat* studies despite being written at the very

---

11 Interim People's Consultative Assembly (MPRS) Decree XX/1966, dated 5 July
1966, formally established the 1945 Constitution as the supreme source of written
law in Indonesia.

end of the Dutch period. Ter Haar's main legacy is the acceptance of his view that judicial decisions make concrete the principles 'drawn from a multitude of less precise living patterns, from concepts and values cherished in the community'. This view was especially influential in the 1960s (see Subekti and Tamara 1965) and continues to influence the religious courts. The second course, Marriage Law and Adat Inheritance Law (Hukum Perkawinan dan Hukum Waris Adat), explores *adat* conceptions of marriage and inheritance. The third course, Land Law (Hukum Pertanahan), concludes Sunan Ampel's coverage of *adat* laws by examining the *adat* approach to land sales, credit and land reform.

In addition, the Sunan Ampel syllabus treats contemporary and controversial topics in Islam from a sociological perspective. For example, Problems (Masalah-Masalah) deals with such matters as HIV-AIDS and cloning in the context of philosophy and sociology. The sociological perspective is generally very apparent in this IAIN; for example, Sociology of Law (Sosiologi Hukum) is a required course at all levels.

UIN Sunan Kalijaga Yogyakarta. In many ways the curriculum of Sunan Kalijaga is comparable with that of UIN Syarif Hidayatullah Jakarta. This is not surprising given that both began to develop their curricula at around the same time (in the 1990s) with mutual knowledge of each other's programs plus considerable financial aid from abroad. Each also has a teaching staff that includes a quite high proportion of foreign-trained teachers. The result is a much more clearly bifurcated curriculum arrangement in which we find standard Arabic and/or Indonesian texts on the one hand, and English-language materials on the other. The inclusion of English-language texts can be seen as innovative in the sense that they are required reading even in basic subjects such as family law.

IAIN Ar-Raniry (Banda Aceh). The curriculum of Ar-Raniry is currently being revised to take account of the introduction of a code of syariah law—the Aceh Qanun—in the province. Much of the material required to understand and teach the Aceh Qanun is already present in both the national and existing curricula on the basic *fiqh*, so this revision may not be as extensive as some might suppose. The best example of regional initiative in the current Ar-Raniry curriculum is found in Contemporary Fiqh (Fiqh Kontemporer), where students study the *fatāwā* in the collection issued by the province's Consultative Council of Ulama (Majlis Permusyawaratan Ulama; MPU) (Komisi Fatwa 2000). A knowledge of these *fatāwā* is essential to understanding syariah in Aceh, because they reveal the issues of most concern to the region. Uniquely in Indonesia, the question of deviance or deviant sects is prominent in the province: *fatāwā* on deviance make up about 13 per cent of *fatāwā* in Aceh compared with a national average of 1 per cent. We do not yet understand the reasons for this comparatively high figure, but the Ar-Raniry course provides a valuable introduction to the topic.

Other IAIN. The courses offered by IAIN Raden Fatah Palembang generally follow the national curriculum quite closely, as do those of IAIN Imam Bonjol (Padang) and IAIN Sumatera Utara (Medan). At most, one might say that there is an extra emphasis in these IAIN on finance and management courses, such as Islamic insurance, banking, loans and money transactions generally.

Comparative Law and Schools of Law (Perbandingan Hukum dan Mazhab)

All IAIN offer introductory courses on the *mazhab*. These follow a fairly standard pattern. They begin with the biographies of the four Sunni *imam* (Abū Hanīfa, Mālik, Shāfi'ī and Ibn Hanbal), concentrating on how and why the authority of each in law and doctrine was established. This is followed by a description of each school's method of legal reasoning, the geographic diffusion of the schools, and the major and minor points of difference between them. The courses explain important jurisprudential concepts such as *istihsan, ijtihad* and *ikhtilāf* (scholarly disagreement). These terms, and the methodologies attached to them, have always been the subject of ongoing debate,[12] but this has reached a new pitch of urgency in the face of the state takeover of syariah in contemporary Muslim states, including Indonesia.

The current position in Indonesia is as follows. The Dutch legacy of plural laws has been to force Indonesian law makers to compare the merits of a number of different legal systems, including syariah. With the establishment of the religious courts in 1989 and the introduction of the KHI in 1991, syariah became a formally recognized element of the Indonesian legal system, although with limited jurisdiction. As a result, the classical jurisprudence could no longer be considered sufficient on its own. The IAIN responded by devising new courses that both retained the classical jurisprudence (that is, demonstrated an 'Islamic' or *fiqh* element) while also being practical, usable and workable in a state context. In short, they developed courses that accommodated the needs of the secular state.

UIN Syarif Hidayatullah Jakarta. Syarif Hidayatullah offers two complementary courses in comparative law: Method of Comparative Law (Metode Perbandingan Hukum) and Comparative International Law (Perbandingan Hukum Internasional). Both are method-oriented courses focusing on legal system structures. Method of Comparative Law compares Islamic law with English common law and civil law (using the example of the German civil code), to highlight the processes of and lessons from comparative law. Comparative International Law is concerned with world legal systems and the place of Islamic law in the greater family of laws. The theoretical component of the latter course focuses on contemporary issues, using Huntington's *Clash of Civilizations and the Remaking of World Order* (Huntington 1996) as a reference text. Although this is a distinctly surprising choice, it is perhaps less so if one accepts that the intention is to differentiate syariah from other legal systems as a special and unique system of law.

---

12 For example, writing in the fourteenth century, al-Shātibī specifically warned against combining 'convenient opinions' (Hallaq 1997: 202).

Further evidence for this proposition is found in other courses as well, in both this and other divisions. For example Islamic International Law (Hukum Internasional Islam) defines international law wholly within the classical categories of syariah, that is, the Qur'ān, Hadith and *fiqh*. It places considerable emphasis on the non-Muslim world (*dar ul-harb*) and non-Muslims protected by law (*dhimmi*) under Islam, as well as actual practice towards non-Muslims under the first four caliphs and the Ottomans. An accompanying course, Politics and Ethics in Islam and the West (Etika Politik dalam Islam dan Barat), also emphasizes points of difference, despite discussing such concepts as democracy, accountability and the rule of law. The same is true of related courses on civil, criminal, administrative and land laws. To take one final example: Islamic Criminal Law in the World (Hukum Pidana Islam di Dunia) examines the status of syariah criminal law in two groups of countries: those that have formally adopted syariah in criminal matters (Saudi Arabia, Pakistan, Sudan), and those that have not despite having majority Muslim populations (Egypt, Indonesia, Malaysia, Brunei). While it is true that this course is based on comparative data, it does not establish a methodology for understanding the differences between the two groups of countries. This absence of method is in marked contrast to the methodology developed by the classical *fiqh* texts to study the differences between the Sunni *mazhab*.

In a curious way this returns us to Huntington. By assuming that the purpose of comparative study is to confirm difference, these courses actually bear out Huntington's claims for a clash between civilizations. Despite the weakness of his analysis of Islam (especially his failure to recognize variation in the expression and forms of law), he nevertheless seems to have struck a chord in Indonesia. Many Muslim scholars accept his views as confirmation of their own views.

IAIN Sunan Ampel Surabaya. Sunan Ampel follows the standard national curriculum on comparative law at the MKDK level but offers an additional course of great interest. This is Orientalism in Islamic Law (Orientalisme dalam Hukum Islam), where orientalism is used as a connecting device to study the characteristics of Islamic law and Western law. This is a true comparative law course in the sense that a method is being proposed. The purpose is to assess the value of orientalism for syariah study in general and Indonesia in particular. The topics include the history of orientalism, prominent orientalists, the orientalist with specific reference to Islam and syariah, continuity and change in syariah, differences between syariah and Western law, and renewal of syariah in the Middle East and Southeast Asia. The required readings include Said (1978), Coulson (1969) and Hallaq (1997), all quite complex texts.

IAIN Raden Fatah Palembang. Raden Fatah has an extensive complex of courses on comparative law covering a wide range of subjects. As well as the standard national courses, it offers a number of interesting additions. Two merit particular attention. The first, Comparative Political Theory (Perbandingan Mazhab tentang Siyasah), covers the caliphate, the imamate, Fatamid practice, modern Iran, contemporary 'idealistic trends' (Rashid Rida, Hasan al-Banna, Syed Qutb, Maududi, Taha Hussein), nationalism, feudalism, socialism and democracy. The second, Comparative Political Streams in Islam (Perbandingan Aliran Politik dalam Islam), covers the history of Sunni and Shi'a political thought as well as international Islamic organizations, Western political theory, Islam in the contemporary world and Pancasila.

I do not have space for further examples but those given here would seem to indicate two conclusions. First, true comparison, in the sense of establishing a method of comparison, is confined to the classical courses on Comparative *Fiqh* Principles (Ushul Fiqh Perbandingan) offered by all IAIN. But although the method is well established, the classical *fiqh* itself is no longer sufficient on its own. The last 200 years have seen the Western state—an invasive form for syariah—become firmly established. In Indonesia, the legacy of Dutch legal pluralism has been to place the syariah in a subordinate position. It is that legacy and its elaboration over the past 50 years that defines the current legal system. The IAIN courses certainly acknowledge this fact, but although they explain and elaborate the differences between legal systems, they do not establish a satisfactory method for comparing them. Part of the difficulty is that Indonesian syariah is a hybrid, and neither *fiqh* nor modern (Western) comparative law is able to cope with hybrid sytems.[13] The IAIN courses on orientalism are a useful starting point for developing a methodology for comparative law, but that is all they are at the moment.

Constitutional and Public Law (Siyasah–Jinayah)

All the IAIN offer a broadly similar range of courses in Constitutional and Public Law (Siyasah–Jinayah). The following courses illustrate the range of topics covered.

UIN Syarif Hidayatullah Jakarta. The Siyasah–Jinayah courses provided by Syarif Hidayatullah follow the national curriculum in structure and content, although with some elaboration. In the area of criminal law (*jinayah*), the university offers two sets of classes that are run in parallel: the first an entirely *fiqh*-based course on criminal jurisprudence (*fiqh jinayah*), and the second a course on the contemporary criminal law (*hukum pidana*) of Indonesia. The former is a two-part course based on the Qur'ān and Hadith. The first part covers general principles and the second part covers specific topics such as sexual misconduct, the consumption of alcohol, apostasy and the classical punishments,

---

13 Modern comparative law has its own difficulties; for a start, it cannot make up its mind whether it is sociology of law or a branch of legal history (see, for example, Mattei 1997). It is wholly unsuitable for Southeast Asian law, especially the various forms of syariah in the region.

namely monetary compensation (*diyat*) and the prescribed punishments for certain offences (*hudud*). The latter course covers definitions of and punishments for criminal conduct (murder, assault, rape and so on) as these are dealt with in the secular courts. Islamic Criminal Law in the Muslim World (Hukum Pidana Islam di Dunia Islam) has a comparative aspect. On the theory side, Criminology (Kriminologi) is a purely secular course on modern Western theory of criminal conduct, with the courses all based on English-language materials.

In the area of politics (*siyasah*)—comprising policy of law, constitutional law and law administration—the delineation between the classical and modern traditions is less strict. Constitutional Jurisprudence (Fiqh Siyasah) is a historically based course taking students from the Umayyad to the present via national socialism, communism, democracy and civil society. It is based on Arabic and contemporary Western sources. Legal Policy (Hukum Politik), on the other hand, is wholly concerned with Indonesia. It covers the period from the Netherlands East Indies to the present. The topics include Pancasila and an introduction to the theories of Hazairin. (Classical) Constitutional Jurisprudence (Fiqh Siyasah (Klasik)) is a large, two-part, historically based course. The first part begins with the Qur'ān and Sunnah and ends with contemporary nationalism, secularism and civil society. The references are to both classical *fiqh* and modern sources. The second part, Islamic Political Thought (Pemikiran Politik Islam), covers contemporary theorists such as Hasan al-Banna, Hasan al-Turābī and Ruhollah Khomeini.

Finally, UIN Syarif Hidayatullah Jakarta offers a set of courses dealing with the relationship between law and state. Between them, Law and the State (Hukum Tata Negara) and The State in Islamic History (Praktek Kenegaraan dalam Sejarah Islam) provide an extensive survey of the subject, from the seventh century CE to the present. The student is introduced to Plato (*The Republic*), Jellinek (1900), Kelsen (1989), Rosenthal (1965), Watt (1988) and Sjadzali (1991), among others. This is a huge load for teachers and an extremely difficult reading course for Indonesian students.

The range and complexity of these courses bring us to the issue of assessment. How does one weight and evaluate the integrated and parallel courses just described? The answer adopted by Syarif Hidayatullah has been to introduce a competency-based curriculum (*kurikulum berbasis kompetensi*) based on three sets of courses: 'main' courses on *fiqh* and Indonesian secular law (worth 60 credits); 'supporting' specialist courses on the same subjects (90 credits); and a miscellaneous grouping of 'other' courses (10 credits).[14] The effect of this is to confirm a generalist emphasis, because 75 per cent of the credits for a full undergraduate degree are still allocated to subjects common to all students in all faculties. With specialist courses limited to the remaining 25 per cent of credits,

---

14 See Azra (2005: 16 ff.). I am grateful to the author for allowing me to use this unpublished paper.

real specialization begins only at the postgraduate level. One consequence of this is that, at present, students who are not in the Faculty of Syariah are not seriously disadvantaged for later employment in syariah posts, thus collapsing the distinction between the faculties. However, we must be a little careful here; to my knowledge there are no published data on the nexus between syariah specialization and later employment in a syariah specialist position. But whatever such data might show, the *kompetensi* scheme represents a considerable departure from the original Department of Religion assumptions on specialization in the national curriculum. Other UIN and IAIN appear to be following or preparing to follow the same model, with all realizing that success in turning out competent syariah scholars will require strong postgraduate programs.

IAIN Sunan Ampel Surabaya. Sunan Ampel offers a number of interesting local Siyasah–Jinayah courses. I have chosen the following because they claim a 'relevance to modern needs and conditions' (*relevan dengan sistem kenegaraan dan pemerintahan kontemporer*). Political Thought (Pemikiran Politik) consists of 15 selected political themes from thinkers such as Plato, Aquinas, Hobbes, Locke, Mill and Marx and politicians such as Lenin, Stalin, Roosevelt and Attlee. All except one of the reading texts (Noer 1997) are in English. While we come back to the issue of readings in due course, it is worth noting here that this is an extremely difficult course that requires a high level of competency in English. All IAIN offer similar courses that satisfy a felt need to understand Western thought on politics and the state. This is not surprising given that the curriculum is itself a Western construction. However, these courses do not stand alone; they are invariably followed by courses in Islamic Political Thought (Pemikiran Politik Islam). While they are similar in structure, they feature a wide range of Muslim thinkers, from Ibn Taymiyah, al-Ghazali and Ibn Khaldun to al-Afghani, Maududi, Husayn Haikal, Yusuf Qardhawi and Ruhollah Khomeini. Some IAIN also include more radical thinkers such as Hasan al-Banna and Syed Qutb.

Sunan Ampel also offers two dedicated reading courses on Siyasah–Jinayah, one in Arabic and the other in English. Essentially they consist of a list of texts accompanied by an abstract of topics. Students in the Arabic course read al-Mawardi's *al-Ahkam al Sulthaniyah*, concentrating on *fi'aqd al-imamah*; then al-Zuhaili's *al-Fiqh al-Islam wa 'Adillatuh*, concentrating on the *imam* and discretionary punishments (*ta'zir*); and finally 'Abd al-Qadir' 'Awdah's *al-Tasyri' al-Jina; al-Islami*, concentrating on *siyasah–jinayah* more generally. The companion English course essentially focuses on criminal justice, and is quite modern in focus. However, it does include an extensive discussion of *siyasah–jinayah* in pre-modern Iran drawn from Anne Lambton's *State, Government and Medieval Islam* (Lambton 1962). The specific topics covered include religion and the state, religion and politics, society and religion, and the imamate.

UIN Sunan Kalijaga Yogyakarta. Sunan Kalijaga offers a long and complex set of courses on Law and the State (Hukum Tata Negara). Its 14 sections range over the whole spectrum of politics of law from 1945. The first section begins by defining law and state, separately and in relation to each other. It also covers the sources of law, the functions of law, and types and categories of law. The second section, on sources of state law, specifies the sources of law considered appropriate in Indonesia. These are the Constitution, laws (*undang*), regulations (*peraturan*), judicial decisions (*yurisprudensi*) and doctrine of law (*doktrin hukum*). The third and fourth sections provide a political history of the Indonesian state from the war against the Dutch in 1945–49 to the establishment of the Federal State in 1949 and the period of liberal parliamentary democracy in 1950–59. The reintroduction of the 1945 Constitution in 1959 is then considered with special reference to the authority of the President. The sixth section considers the nature of the law-based state—the *Rechtsstaat* or *hukum negara*—described by way of fundamental concepts (*dasar-dasar konseptual*). This leads into the seventh section, on the institutions of state under the 1945 Constitution, with particular reference to the People's Consultative Assembly (Majelis Permusyawaratan Rakyat; MPR), the People's Representative Council (Dewan Perwakilan Rakyat; DPR), the executive powers of the president, and the relationship between the president and the legislature. This section of the course is currently being revised. The eighth section deals with the devolution of powers to the regions following decentralization. It examines the concepts of democracy and decentralization, the duties of the district head and the theory behind the development of local regulations. Finally, there is a set of complementary sections dealing with human rights and civil society, and the duties of citizens, under the 1945 Constitution and the post-*reformasi* amendments to it.[15]

The interesting feature about this set of courses (and its equivalents in other institutions) is that the required readings are entirely in Indonesian.[16] I believe this indicates just how sophisticated the discussion of *siyasah–jinayah* has become in contemporary Indonesia. This is significant, because it provides evidence of the development of a specifically local, Indonesian constitutional-law doctrine within the context of an Islamic tertiary education program.

---

15 See Lindsey (1999) for a comprehensive summary.

16 The reading list is as follows: Arbi Sanit, *Perwakilan Politik di Indonesia* [Political Representation in Indonesia]; Bintan R. Saragih, *Sistem Pemerintahan dan Lembaga Perwakilan di Indonesia* [System of Government and Representation in Indonesia]; Ismail Suny, *Pergeseran Kekuasaan Eksekutif* [Alteration in Executive Powers]; Joeniarto, *Negara Hukum* [The Law State]; Moh. Tolehah Mansoer, *Pembahasan Beberapa Aspek Kekuasaan-kekuasaan Eksekutif dan Legislatif di Indonesia* [Discussion of Aspects of Executive and Legislative Power in Indonesia]; Moh. Mahfud MD, *Perkembangan Politik Hukum* [Development of Political Law]; Moh. Mahfud MD, *Dasar dan Struktur Ketatanegaraan Indonesia* [Foundation and Structure of the Indonesian Legal System]; Muhammad Yamin, *Naskah Persiapan Undang-Undang Desar 1945, 3 jilid* [Draft of the 1945 Constitution, 3 volumes]; Sri Soemantri M, *Prosedur dan Sistem Perubahan Konstitusi* [Procedure and System for Constitutional Amendment]; Sri Soemantri M, *Lembaga-Lembaga Negara menurut UUD 1945* [State Organs according to the 1945 Constitution].

Contract Law *(Mu'amalat)*

Contract Law (Mu'amalat), the largest and most complex of the curriculum classes, generally covers non-*fiqh* matters. Some of the older Indonesian dictionaries describe it as a 'science' and the current *Kamus Besar* defines it as the 'science of knowledge' (*ilmu pengetahuan*). In both the 1995 and 1998 national curricula, and in the IAIN curricula, it essentially means money matters—the whole range of contracts, including those related to land, the national economy, banks, insurance and so on. The key to understanding the material is its inclusion in the 'syariah' curriculum. Syariah not only influences but is integral to *mu'amalat*, as I demonstrate below. Local variation is the norm in this subject area, but I start with the national curriculum. I focus on three of the four courses in the MKK section of the core curriculum; the fourth—Research Methods (Metode Penelitian)—is covered separately below.

The purpose of the first of these courses, Contract Law (Fiqh Mu'amalat), is 'to enable students to understand ... property according to Islamic law as a guide to the resolution of problems'. These problems are wholly commercial in nature and include forms of property, contract, trade, hire, loans, mortgages, partnerships, cooperatives and interest. The actual prescriptions relating to these are from *fiqh* and the references are to Arabic *fiqh* texts. The second course, Science of Economics and Banking (Ilmu Ekonomi dan Perbankan), covers basic economics in the nation-state. Topics include the definition of economics, financial institutions, the central bank and public banks. The references are solely to modern Indonesian and English economic texts; there is no reference to *fiqh*. The third course, Economic Institutions of the Islamic Community (Lembaga-Lembaga Perekonomian Ummat), covers the syariah classes: *zakat*; spending (to help others) (*infaq*); interest (*riba*); *zakat* administration through a centralized institution (the Baitulmal); and *wakaf*. The references are to Arabic, Indonesian and English texts. Taken together, these three courses attempt to cover both *fiqh* economics as well as modern economics by placing the former in the context of the latter. The question of interest to us here is whether this means that the latter is likely to overwhelm the former. As we shall see, the answer is not clear-cut.

UIN Syarif Hidayatullah Jakarta. In its 2000 syllabus, Syarif Hidayatullah offers a complex set of MKK courses that, taken together, effect a reconciliation between *fiqh* and modern economics. Contract Law I (Fiqh Mu'amalat I) is similar to the same course in the national core curriculum. Legal Principles from Hadith (Hadits Ahkam II) sets out the classical Arabic *fiqh* positions on interest, partnerships, associations for trade and profit. Islamic Economics (Islam Ekonomi) gives a straightforward exposition of Western economic theory but, usefully, in the context of regional autonomy. Its companion course, Basic Islamic Economics (Dasar-dasar Ekonomi Islam), deals with the same subjects but stresses the relationship between Islamic and conventional economics. Islamic Bank Management (Manajemen Bank Islam) concentrates on interest, investment and liquidity, while Management of Finance (Manajemen Keuangan) focuses on asset management and profitability. Of course, there is considerable overlap between the latter two courses. They are followed by two courses on accounting principles and cost accounting. There is nothing of particular interest here, except that these courses exist! One might conclude that modern economics is triumphant, to the total exclusion of syariah. But this would be premature, as we shall now see.

The courses in the microeconomics section of the syllabus are sufficient to show this. They start with the history of Islamic economic systems, under the early caliphs, the Abbasids and then the Ottomans, and in the later Muslim world. This is followed by an explanation of each *mazhab*'s theories on consumption, including interest, inflation and investment. The nature of property, including forbidden (*haram*) goods and taxation, are also described based on *fiqh* sources. Classical Western economic theory (supply curves, marginal costs and so on) is covered, but again with reference to *fiqh*. For example, there is a long and complex discussion of 'unfair markets from an Islamic perspective'. Comparative material (capitalist, socialist and Islamic) is also considered in detail. Some representative courses include Islamic Microeconomics (Mikro Ekonomi Islam) on investment and consumption, Management and Marketing (Manajemen Pemasaran) and a group of statistical courses on Islamic banking and Islamic insurance (*takaful*).

Syarif Hidayatullah's MKK program on *takaful*—Islamic Insurance (Asuransi Islam)—consists of 21 courses, including those just mentioned. The balance is about half secular law, half *fiqh*-based law. The secular courses cover the technical aspects of banking, finance, statistics, accounting, trade and property. The *fiqh*-based courses teach the principles of contract and money contracts drawn from *fiqh*, but also refer to conventional financing. For example, a major topic in the 'operational problems' section of Management of Islamic Insurance (Manajemen Takaful) is the concept and philosophy of conventional insurance as these are relevant to *takaful*; the course makes comparative reference to Malaysia's Takaful Act of 1984, which is essentially an 'Islamized' version of conventional insurance law. Takaful Products (Produk Takaful) describes insurance in terms of 'endowment', a purely Western concept. The accompanying courses, Takaful Investment (Investasi Takaful) and System of Takaful Amortization (Sistem Pelunasan Takaful), draw heavily on the concepts of profit sharing and risk minimization, in principle and in practice.

These courses are certainly much more elaborate than those in the national curriculum. Nevertheless, the same principle prevails, of compatibility with rather than giving way to Western commercial law.

IAIN Sunan Ampel Surabaya. The 20 MKK courses in Contract Law (Mu'amalat) offered by Sunan Ampel have the same general structure as those offered by Syarif Hidayatullah, but are given in less detail. Western economic theory is covered in Contract Law (Fiqh Mu'amalat), and Islamic economics in an accompanying but separate course. The *fiqh* and Western approaches to insurance and banking are also dealt with in separate but parallel courses, as are management, accounting, Islamic banks and business. Perhaps we can hazard a generalization here and say that there is less focus on integrating the Western and *fiqh* approaches to *mu'amalat* in IAIN Sunan Ampel Surabaya than there is in UIN Syarif Hidayatullah Jakarta.

UIN Sunan Kalijaga Yogyakarta. Banking and economics with reference to Islam is the topic chosen for a Sunan Kalijaga course called Reading English Texts (Membaca Teks Inggris). The main focus is interest, especially interest-free banking, and only English-language materials are used. Islamic Insurance (Asuransi Islam) covers the various forms of insurance, including life insurance, social insurance and *takaful*, as well as appropriate ways of investing the proceeds from insurance, based on Arabic, English and Indonesian texts. Contract Law II (Fiqh Mu'amalat II) deals with banks, leases, contracts, money contracts and monopolies, mainly based on Arabic references. Islamic Economics and Banking (Islam Ekonomi dan Perbankan) covers the functions of the central bank, private banks and money, based on Indonesian references. Economic Institutions of the Islamic Community (Lembaga-Lembaga Perekonomian Ummat) covers *zakat*, Islamic banks, interest, the Islamic Development Bank, the State Treasury (Baitulmal), conventional insurance and *takaful*, based on Indonesian, Arabic and English texts.

IAIN Raden Fatah Palembang. Raden Fatah offers an interesting *mu'amalat* curriculum in two parts. The first part consists of six subjects that we now recognize as fairly standard. For example, Contract Law (Fiqh Mu'amalat) examines the nature and types of property, interest, banking, commercial associations and intellectual property, based on Arabic readings. Science of Economics and Banking (Ilmu Ekonomi dan Perbankan) focuses on the Indonesian economy, including national economic policy, Islamic banks and the role of the People's Credit Bank (Bank Perkreditan Rakyat). Economic Institutions of the Islamic Community (Lembaga-Lembaga Perekonomian Ummat) deals with *zakat* (including comparative material from outside Indonesia), interest, Islamic banking and Islamic insurance, with reference to Arabic works. System of Islamic Economics (Sistem Ekonomi Islam) discusses general principles of Islamic economics, banks, business ethics, interest, cooperatives, and the concepts of *halal* and *haram* and their implications for Islamic economies. It contains extensive references to English-language sources.

The second part of the MKK curriculum focuses on banking. It consists of 34 courses: eight on Islamic banking of the type already described, and the remainder conventional Western economics courses on banking, statistics, accounting, management and computer studies.

IAIN Imam Bonjol (Padang). Fourteen of Imam Bonjol's 19 local courses on *mu'amalat* deal with the secular laws of Indonesia. The remaining five are Islamic courses that conform fairly closely with the national curriculum courses on Contemporary Contract Law (Fiqh Mu'amalat Kontemporer). This part of the syllabus reveals a concern to show that the classical *fiqh* can be adapted or modified to deal with such complexities as multi-level marketing, agribusiness and value-added transactions. The readings are all in Arabic.

Summary

The preceding discussion leads to two preliminary comments. First, the treatment of the two groups of core MKK subjects does not vary greatly between the national and regional curricula. There is one exception: the range of readings set by the IAIN is much greater than that in the national core curriculum, and includes a much greater proportion of contemporary English-language material. This suggests that we may be seeing an internationalization of the IAIN syllabus. Second, turning to the faculty divisions, the initiatives in the local syariah curricula are generally consistent across Indonesia, especially in *mu'amalat*. The treatment of Islamic economics is the obvious example, but to a lesser extent this is also true of family law and criminal law.

These comments are necessarily somewhat speculative, because all curricula are now undergoing extensive change under the 40:60 rule. In addition, the greater freedom now perceived to be available under the new regional autonomy arrangements will inevitably affect the curricula. What we do know, even from this limited survey, is that syariah learning has some unexpected expressions. For example, the Aceh curriculum does not place undue emphasis on 'local' as opposed to 'national' elements of the syariah curriculum, even though the province is often accused of having an 'excessively Islamic' approach. On the contrary, there is extensive recourse to Western sources in the required readings, and although the classical Arabic inheritance is fully maintained, it is embedded in the wider national model. How this will be affected by recent developments in Aceh, in particular the adoption of the Aceh Qanun, is unknown, but at present the Aceh curriculum cannot be said to be 'excessively Islamic'.

It is important to recognize that when one talks about a curriculum being local (*lokal*), it may mean that it reflects local interests, in which case it may vary considerably from the national curriculum, or just that it has been *drafted* locally, in which case there may be little or no variation from the national core curriculum. The latter reflects a difference of expression rather than substance, as is apparent in the case of the IAIN Sunan Ampel Surabaya curriculum. UIN Sunan Kalijaga Yogyakarta, on the other hand, does provide true variation in some subjects. *Lokal* may also mean that the institution in question offers undergraduate or postgraduate courses *in addition* to those in the national curriculum. IAIN Raden Fatah Palembang, for example, offers postgraduate courses on money contracts and banking. UIN Syarif Hidayatullah Jakarta also offers an extensive selection of additional courses on syariah, at both the undergraduate and postgraduate levels. In short, it is becoming increasingly difficult to make clear distinctions between curricula on the basis of their degree of 'localization'.

This difficulty is likely to increase under the twin impulses of the 40:60 rule and decentralization.

3   READING THE SYLLABUS AND SYLLABUS READING

In this section we approach the curriculum by way of syllabus readings. A syllabus is made up of sets of topics, with each set having an attached list of readings. The topics and the readings together tell us: (a) what each institution considers important; (b) what subjects are generally considered important; and (c) the reasoning behind the whole curriculum. To some extent these issues are explained in the introductions to each course, but they are typically short and rather vague. We therefore need to look at the topics and readings together to get a better understanding of the syllabus.

Research Methods

Research Methods (Metode Penelitian) is found in all syllabuses, though with varying degrees of emphasis. In the national core curriculum of 1998, it appears at all levels and is an integral part of the study programs of all four divisions in the Faculty of Syariah (see Table 3.1). This is an advance on the full 1995 curriculum, where it appears only once. Taught at the MKDK level, the 1995 course is essentially about the qualitative social science research method of data collection and analysis. In contrast, the 1998 curriculum places far more emphasis on Islam as an appropriate object of study, analysis and theory. Islam may be a given in society and politics, but it should not be accepted uncritically for that reason alone. Nevertheless, the degree of critical analysis does seem to vary according to subject; 'method' is value laden depending on the subject, as the following examples show.

The national curriculum on methodology consists of three essential basic courses: Methodology of Islamic Studies (Metodologi Studi Islam), Legal Research Methodology (Metodologi Penelitian Hukum) and Research Methods (Metode Penelitian). Methodology of Islamic Studies is a straightforward introduction to the sciences of Qur'ānic exegesis (*tafsir*), Hadith, *fiqh* and dialectical theology (*kalam*), and Islamic history and culture (see section 1). It is a purely didactic course that lies wholly within the classical Islamic tradition. Its purpose is clearly to serve as an introduction to the classical sources. Legal Research Methods could not be in greater contrast; it does not contain any *fiqh* at all. This course covers secular Indonesian law as well as Western-derived approaches to history-of-law typologies (normative, positive, sociological), ethics and various legal doctrines (the state, justice). Research Methods introduces students to epistemology: approaches to theory, hypothesis, research design, data collection, quantitative analysis, data collection and so on.

Although all the UIN and IAIN follow this pattern very closely, one does find some regional variation. A few examples follow.

UIN Sunan Kalijaga Yogyakarta. Sunan Kalijaga's MKDU-level course in Methodology of Islamic Studies (Metodologi Studi Islam) certainly contains a local element. The readings for the course include selections from the local (Central Java) literature. A section on inscriptions (*prasasti*), for instance, directs students to issues in philology while also including Islamic material. Other readings include works on 'post-modernism and Islam'. The course goes well beyond the national curriculum, not just because of the Central Java reference, but also because the critical or philological method used is such a departure from the traditional approach. Indeed, Sunan Kalijaga's MKDK-level course in Research Methodology (Metodologi Penelitian) even includes critical study of *pesantren* and *madrasah* methodologies.

IAIN Raden Fatah Palembang. While it includes survey methods and content analysis, the main focus of Raden Fatah's course on Research Methodology (Metodologi Penelitian) is translation techniques from a comparative perspective. Students are required to study highly technical works on translation methods, usually in English, and translate passages from Arabic-language law texts. The course on Methodology of Islamic Studies (Metodologi Studi Islam) follows the national curriculum quite closely, but also includes local innovations in the areas of secularism and secularization, modern science and education.

IAIN Imam Bonjol (Padang). Imam Bonjol has produced a striking example of local innovation in its course on Legal Research Methods (Metode Penelitian Hukum). The course focuses on family law, contracts and criminal law. It begins with a brief introduction to the concept and functions of methodology, types of study and types of data. It then sets out a typology of legal studies, presented in tabular form (see Table 3.3). This is followed by a list of topics elaborating and explaining the content of each division in the table. They include setting up a hypothesis; setting standards of proof depending on the nature of the data (data analysis); clarifying the purpose of research and selecting the appropriate research method; identifying and correctly describing problems/issues; and writing papers and reports.

This very brief survey of research methods shows just how wide a range of approaches is to be found in the contemporary curriculum. The national curriculum has imposed a high degree of standardization, but not to the extent of stifling local innovation. This is apparent in the choice of issues at the local level and the weighting of methods to suit these choices. At the general, Indonesia-wide level, the research methods syllabus reflects the peculiar nature of syariah education. In some respects, the syariah curriculum is wider than academic or professional study of law as understood in the West. In particular, it requires students to study the history of syariah as an essential component of the curriculum. Syariah is simultaneously historical and contemporary; therefore, the research methods utilized by the IAIN need to be complex and multi-faceted to cope with the dif-

Table 3.3   Typology of Legal Studies at IAIN Imam Bonjol (Padang)

Concept of Law	Type of Study	Research Method	Orientation
Law, justice, universal principles	Philosophy of law	Deduction from normative premise, self-evident principle	Philosophy
Positive norms of national/state law	Law as written in the text	Law as doctrine, positive law	Positivism
Law as judicial decision, law as concrete decision	American sociological jurisprudence	Court behaviour	Behavioural sociology
Law as derived from empirical social study	Law in society	Non-doctrinal, macro-quantitative survey	Structural
Law as manifested in human action, interaction	Sociology and anthropology of law	Non-doctrinal, qualitative micro-analysis	Symbolic, interactional

Source: IAIN Imam Bonjol (Padang) curriculum.

fering demands of historical syariah, syariah in contemporary social science and syariah in contemporary state law. The underlying premise of syariah is that the centrality of God's message and the duty owed to Him can only be maintained through the correct transmission of syariah, and this in turn requires the appropriate study method. But in fact there is no one method that can be applied to all texts; instead, the method must vary according to the text being transmitted. The danger is in not realizing this fact. It is to the great credit of the curriculum drafters, both national and local, that this danger has largely been avoided.

These comments bring us to the actual syllabus readings. Are they appropriate to the topic? Do they support the syllabus or is the syllabus constructed around what is available in the library? This is a very real issue in a country where, with one or two exceptions (Jakarta, Yogyakarta), IAIN library resources are quite limited. Finally, are texts given different weightings or values depending on how 'authoritative' they are? These questions can only be answered by accepting that the written material—the text—differs in type and authority.

The Readings

The written texts on which the study of syariah is based differ in type and authority. The main types of syariah texts are: the Qur'ān, which is divinely revealed and absolute; the Sunnah, which is divinely inspired; the historically authoritative *fiqh* texts; the analytical modern Arabic and Indonesian commentary; and Western commentary. The method of ascribing value or relative value to each of these sources is crucial. In some cases, the method is not in dispute; the classical *tafsir* literature uses an established method with respect to the Qur'ān and Hadith, for example. But syariah necessarily demands other types of texts as well, and the relative degree of authority and proper place of each is not so clear-cut. Scholars occupy different positions on this subject, depending on their conceptions of what a legal education is *for*. Their positions are reflected in each IAIN's choice of readings.

The Qur'ān and the Sunnah

The Qur'ān and Sunnah are fundamental to all syariah study. They form the core in the transmission of syariah across Islamic legal history. Both the national and IAIN curricula treat them with the same formal consistency. They are studied with reference to the standard classical Arabic literature, although, as we have seen with the methodology courses, issues of selection and emphasis always arise. These in turn are dictated by the purpose of the course, and this purpose further depends on the scholar's understanding of the texts. With 'understanding the word of God' (*kalam*) a matter of scholarly interpretation, it is not surprising to find that Science of Dialectical Theology (Ilmu Kalam) is a compulsory core course in all curricula.

The national curriculum course on *kalam* states its objective as being 'to enable students to become religious scholars who can recognize and understand *kalam* method'. The first section of the course gives an introduction to the Arabic acceptance and redefinition of Greek philosophy. This leads into an examination of the relationship between *kalam*, philosophy (*filsafat*) and mysticism (*tasawwuf*), through a survey of the classical *kalam* thinkers and schools of thought. It is given in dyadic form: Khawarij and Murjiah; Jabariyah and Qadariyah; Mu'tazilah and Shi'a. This is followed by a list of issues that are common to all theologies dealing with the fundamentals of belief. They include the nature of faith and belief (and unbelief); the nature of sin; the nature of God so far as it can be known given the limited nature of human capacity to understand divine will; and the concept of the caliphate (*khilafah*] as a manifestation of faith. A critical study of each of the *kalam* schools of thought follows. The final section is on modern (twentieth-century) scholars of *kalam*, including Muhammad Abduh, Muhammad Iqbal, Hasan Hanafi, Ismail al-Faruqi, HM Rasjidi and Harun Nasution. The reading list consists almost entirely of modern Arabic textbooks, with just one Indonesian work (Nasution 1986a) included.

Although their courses in dialectical theology are structured like the national curriculum course, the IAIN vary quite widely in their choice of the contemporary *kalam* scholars to be studied. Figures like Hasan al-Banna, Ali Syari'ati, Haji Agus Salim, Ahmad Hassan and Hamka appear on some regional curricula.

One might speculate that the IAIN are tending to give greater prominence to Indonesian scholars than was formerly the case. If so, then this would be further evidence that an Indonesian *mazhab* is in the making.

The purpose of *kalam* is to provide theological literacy. For this reason it is one of the most vital courses in the curriculum. It implicitly denies the more extreme forms of modernism that say that the individual—theologically illiterate though he or she may be—has the right to interpret divine texts. This is not the Islamic position, which demands at least a modicum of theological literacy.

The Fiqh Texts

The historical authority of the *fiqh* texts is no longer as clear-cut as it once was. They are still considered authoritative by the Indonesian *pesantren*, but they are no longer authoritative in the religious courts, where they have been replaced by the KHI. They retain their authority in the national and IAIN curricula, most obviously in the core syariah courses. But are they still the texts of first recourse? The answer in the case of the national curriculum is that they are not. Even a brief reading of that curriculum (either the long or the short version) shows that the compulsory texts tend to be Indonesian-language introductions to *fiqh*, or translations of contemporary Arabic introductions to *fiqh*. The best that can be said is that this is classical *fiqh* at one remove, filtered through a secondary voice. The same is true even for such basic Islamic texts as Hadith, the Qur'ān, *kalam* and so on. This is not to say that the classical Arabic texts are entirely absent; al-'Asqalānī's *Fath al-Bārī*, al-Malībārī's *Fath al-Muīn*, and one or two other *fiqh* texts still have a place in the national curriculum. Nevertheless, in terms of frequency and weight of authority, the classical texts are much diminished.

It is difficult to know whether the same is true across the whole range of IAIN curricula; this should become clearer once current revisions take effect. However, it does seem likely that the classical texts will continue to be important in some subjects, such as the study of *fatāwā*. Again, *fiqh* texts as well as modern Arabic commentary are prominent in some parts of *mu'amalat*—specifically banking, Islamic insurance, money management and cooperatives. In these instances, the *fiqh* texts do not constitute prescription as such, but instead set the limits or boundaries beyond which a modern form of contract may not go. What seems to be happening is that the IAIN are recognizing the increasing importance of *ekonomi Islam* in the curriculum by adding new English and Indonesian texts to their required reading lists. The *fiqh* texts remain important as a point of reference but they do not set the agenda for any syllabus in this subject area.

Modern Commentary

The readings for all curricula are now overwhelmingly in Indonesian and English. Nearly all of them are commentary, that is, explanation grounded in a particular time and place. These standard law, history and social science textbooks all address syariah and, indeed, define it for their own particular purposes. They are nothing like the classical Arabic texts in form or content. Instead, they are written to show 'the place of syariah', 'syariah in the state', 'syariah and social development', 'women/feminism and syariah', 'syariah economics' and so on. These sorts of books are not concerned with the transmission of prescription so much as with stating a position from which the appropriateness of syariah can be judged. All such books maintain that they are 'relevant' to the modern world.

A common technique in these texts is to take a point of syariah and investigate its meaning both historically and for contemporary Indonesian Islam. The meaning arrived at comes out of the dialogue between then and now. Of course there is huge variation in the quality of the explanation, and therefore in the usefulness of any one example. These texts also differ depending on whether they are written from an internal (Muslim) perspective or from an 'orientalist' viewpoint. However, the national and regional curricula make no distinction by type of author; although criticism of orientalism has a place in some syllabuses, Muslim and non-Muslim authors appear without overt distinction in just about the whole range of courses.

4   THE IMMANENCE OF SECULARISM?

Is religion being swamped by secularism? This is an obvious question, and one that every observer of Islam (within and outside Muslim circles) asks. I think it is the wrong—or at least a misdirected—question, because 'secularism' is so vague a word as to be practically meaningless. Moreover, discussion of the opposition between religion and secularism is almost always pejorative, making it unlikely to be helpful in any strict sense. Nevertheless I address the issue here because of its common currency.

In the context of Indonesian Islam and the syariah curriculum, this chapter has shown there are at least three ways of considering the relationship between religion and secularism. First, in the Indonesian context, syariah needs to be managed as part of the wider secular curriculum. The national syariah curriculum has succeeded in imposing a standard curriculum nationwide. Standardization means (a) that certain basic courses are taught in all UIN, IAIN and STAIN, and (b) that these are framed and written in a common form. The readings for some courses may differ between institutions, but only in the case of non-*fiqh* courses. This framework allows a standard form of syariah to be integrated into the national system of legal education insofar as this affects religious justice. This means that the syariah (from the given and authoritative texts) must be managed *within* the Indonesian context. Making the *fiqh* texts compatible with the national secular system, without succumbing to secular (that is, non-*fiqh*) reasoning, is an ongoing process.

Second, the innovations that are occurring in regional curricula should not be seen as a threat to *fiqh*. The data in this chapter show that there is local variation in syariah curricula. In a formal sense the national curriculum may be decisive, but at the same time the syariah content in regional curricula does vary. This is especially true in Comparative Law (Perbandingan Hukum), Contract Law (Mu'umalat) and Islamic Studies (Studi Islam), including orientalism. But these variations do not amount to the demise of *fiqh*. Instead, there is a consistent and conscious effort towards compatibility of sources.

And third, the syariah curriculum has shown that it can accommodate more than one form of legal reasoning. There are two forms of legal reasoning in IAIN curricula, one drawn from classical Muslim sources and the other from the Western tradition. The IAIN curricula are now 40 years old. How would the founding father of curriculum development, Harun Nasution, view the material described in this chapter from the point of view of balance, local variation and compatibility? His intention in reforming the Islamic studies curriculum was to bring about a renaissance in Islamic education and, thus, *of Islamic thinking for Indonesia*. This last is crucial; Indonesian conditions and needs are the key to the structure of the syariah curriculum. We can be somewhat optimistic that Nasution would be reasonably satisfied with the level of compatibility and balance in the present curriculum. On the other hand, he would probably argue that the compatibility between the two forms of legal reasoning is achieved only with considerable effort. A large part of this effort must take account of the heavy load on staff and students in learning three languages and three ways of thinking about law. On top of this, the curriculum must meet the demand for a well-functioning legal system in Indonesia. This forces the issue to one question: Does any one text or set of texts have greater authority than any other? This question is often phrased, somewhat dramatically, as 'orientalism' or 'Westernization' versus 'the truth'.

Although the authority of texts is a crucial issue, the either/or opposition does not accurately reflect the complexity of the current debate over the IAIN curricula. To take one example, Husaini (2006) argues that there is a 'hegemony of Christian and Western thought in higher Islamic education'—that Islamic studies in the IAIN are essentially orientalist in nature. He believes that this is a consequence of foreign funding,[17] which allows staff to be trained overseas (by 'Jews and orientalists') and encourages the introduction of general or liberal subjects into the curriculum to the detriment of 'correct' Islamic studies. Even worse, Western methodology is used to deconstruct the authenticity of the Qur'ān and Hadith. He cites as examples two courses offered by UIN Syarif Hidayatullah Jakarta—Orientalist Studies of the Qur'ān and Hadith, and Hermeneutics and Semiotics—both of which rely primarily on Western sources.

It is true that neither of these courses owes anything to classical Islamic scholarship, but that is not, in itself, a reason for them to be dismissed. Both

---

17 For example, from the Ford Foundation or The Asia Foundation.

are in fact important, given that the discourse of Islam has not been confined to classical sources for the past 200 years. It is essential that graduates understand this fact and are equipped to discuss Islam in terms of current methodology. The definitions of syariah offered in such courses may not be the traditional ones, but this only confirms that *fiqh* is a work in progress indeed. The real issue for critics like Husaini is not Western scholarship as such but its underlying philosophy (or theology). This scholarship has undoubtedly advanced the study of syariah, and even contemporary critics have much to learn from this work. But is it possible to separate the work from its underlying premises? Probably not; it is a package which must be taken as a whole. Of course some elements of Western scholarship are more sensitive than others, critical text-based study of the Qur'ān being the most obvious example. But is there any real necessity for such a stand-off? Educational institutions are supposed to engage with scholarship, both past and present. The IAIN do this through their curricula, and these curricula should be discussed on their scholarly merits alone. To define merit as excluding scholarship from a particular (that is, orientalist) source is not a sufficient argument (see Chapters 2 and 6).

There is a further issue that is only now receiving attention. This is the effect of IAIN graduates in transmitting the 'new' syariah to the regions. A recent study has shown that these graduates now form a major cohort among *pesantren* teachers (30 per cent or more in some cases), and they are equally important in the *madrasah* (Jabali and Jamhari 2003: 96 ff.). However, the same research shows that local and regional pedagogical traditions still persist in quite some strength (Jabali and Jamhari 2003: 44 ff.).

The national and IAIN curricula have not, therefore, achieved full standardization in practice. Ongoing studies confirm a variety of local responses, accommodations and variations.

4 The Public Transmission of Syariah: The Friday Sermon

The reader might well ask why one would give space to the Friday sermon—the *khutbah*—in a book on syariah. The answer is that the *khutbah* is the main vehicle through which the 'ordinary' Muslim is instructed in his or her duty to God; it is how that person knows the syariah. The syariah encapsulates theology in the form of prescription. That is what we mean when we say that Islam does not recognize distinctions between law, ethics, morality, the syariah and the totality of these. Any comparison with the contemporary Christian sermon is not sustainable because 'God's laws', expressed theologically, are no longer primary in Western society. The law, one's personal and social duty, is found elsewhere, in codes and statutes.

The instructional functions of *khutbah* are crucial to individual and social duty and they are, thus, syariah texts. In this sense they are the most public of the faces of syariah in all Muslim countries. Indonesia is no exception in this regard, and has its own vibrant *khutbah* publishing industry.[1]

The function of the *khutbah* is purely didactic: to instruct the faithful in religion. This means instructing the Muslim in his or her individual duty to God as this is understood in a particular place, at a certain time. *Khutbah* are, therefore, specific and local. This may seem obvious, but it was in fact the subject of intense debate in Indonesia in the 1920s through 1950s. The central issue concerned language: should the *khutbah* be delivered in Indonesian or Arabic? In the 1920s, Nahdlatul Ulama (NU) recommended Arabic accompanied by an Indonesian summary, on the basis that the *khutbah* is integral to the prescribed ritual prayers (*shalat*), for which Arabic is required.[2] Although the use of Indonesian has been standard since the 1930s, the same issue occasionally surfaces even now. As Ahmad Hassan, the founder of Persis, said as far back as the 1930s:

---

1 For the published texts used in this chapter, see Appendix A4.1. Citations from the Qur'ān are from A. Yousuf Ali's (1934) translation.
2 See Hooker (2003a: 104–5) for *fatāwā* references on this subject.

[T]he sermon cannot offer advice if it is not understood … [I]f it is obligatory for the sermon to be in Arabic, then it would be obligatory for all Muslims to know Arabic, which we know it is not … [I]f you deliver a sermon in a language that people understand, you are following the Prophet's purpose, that is, to give advice. (Cited in Hooker 2003a: 105)

In short, the *khutbah* is a public exposition of syariah each week, and that is why we examine it here.

The Indonesian *khutbah* has a standard form. It consists of two parts—recitation of a passage from the Qur'ān (in Arabic), and a translation and explanation directed towards some issue which the person delivering the sermon (the *khatib*) considers important. The *khutbah* may be as simple as an exhortation to behave better and fulfil one's duty to God, or it may be a more complex comment on social problems, government policy or the politics of the day. Traditionally the syariah set the agenda for the *khutbah*, but this is no longer the case. Certainly the syariah *informs* the text of the *khutbah*, but it is the *issue* that now sets the agenda. This may seem like a significant shift, but evidence from the Middle East suggests that radio *khutbah* have often taken a proactive stance on issues of concern to Muslims (Antoun 1989). That is, syariah appears to be moving into the realm of public discourse, some of it sophisticated and some of it less so.

As these comments indicate, the *khutbah* is an indirect rather than direct way of looking at the syariah; that is, the message of the syariah is mediated through the medium of the *khutbah*. This is a very different thing from the scholarship of law books, text books and other learned commentary, none of which is read by ordinary Muslims.

There are two main modes of *khutbah* delivery. The first can be called the 'performance' medium. By this is meant the actual delivery of the *khutbah* in the mosque and, in the contemporary version of this, on television and radio. Tone, language and intonation are important components of these performances, through which much can be implied and understood as well as said. This is the *khutbah* as drama and theatre. The second mode of delivery is the printed and published collection of *khutbah*, designed to be read, discussed and used as a model. This is the material that is examined in this chapter.

The Printed *Khutbah* as Model

Most, though not all, of the printed collections aspire to model status. That is, the authors hope that both the content of their *khutbah* and the way they are arranged will be emulated by other authors and that their *khutbah* will be used in the mosque by the *khatib*. Many of them claim to have delivered *khutbah* in mosques throughout Indonesia or even overseas, and to have received requests from listeners to publish their sermons in more permanent form for wider circulation. The combination of a wide geographic area of circulation and an appreciative response from listeners seems to persuade authors that they are creating model texts. This is evident in the extent of reworking and improvement undertaken by the authors of the more complex texts, as I show below.

The Text as Literary Composition

The collections also differ in their literary aspirations. On this dimension, they can be divided into two main types: the 'little' books and the 'literary' books. The little books are small, short and written in simple idiomatic Indonesian. They read rather like verbatim versions of the lecture notes that an *imam* might keep as an *aide-mémoire* for his *khutbah*. They are unpretentious and are directed towards an equally unpretentious local audience. However, it would be arrogant indeed to suppose them to be without merit or influence. Their greatest claim to merit is that they convey syariah, reasonably accurately, as a set of simply stated duties; that is, they demonstrate certainty of conduct for the ordinary person. Indeed, they can be read as practical manuals whose aim is to reassure readers that if they follow the text then they will be fulfilling their religious obligations. Certainty is not to be underestimated; one has only to think of the extreme anxiety (*was-was*) in the performance of religious duty to appreciate this function.[3]

The literary books are larger and provide more complex treatments of the material. While described as *khutbah*, the sermons in these books are much more elaborate in argument and detail than those that would ever be delivered in a mosque. Many of these books now appear in multiple editions, with each edition elaborating and improving on the last.

In short, the *khutbah* genre has moved from the reproduction of speech (in the little books) to written expositions (in the literary books) to ever more elaborate written commentary (in subsequent editions of the literary texts).

The Audience

The *khutbah* collections are meant to be read, studied and absorbed by the reader, either alone or as a member of a group. In this milieu the *khutbah* retains its didactic character but has a somewhat broader function. It is now partner in a dialogue between itself and the reader. The text assumes a reasonable degree of literacy and, in the case of the more complex *khutbah*, some knowledge of syariah and its principles. That is, the reader is now an active discussant. This is a long way from the mosque where the spoken *khutbah* is delivered each Friday. In the latter case the vitality with which the message is delivered, and the sacred space itself, is an important part of what is a purely temporal experience.[4]

---

3   It is worth noting that one can read some contemporary *fatāwā* in the same way; see Hooker (2003a: 101–3) on prayer.
4   For *fatāwā* on 'appropriate space', see Hooker (2003a: 92, 127).

The Published Form

The *khutbah* in the published collections follow a standard form. All begin with a citation from the Qur'ān, often accompanied by one or more Hadith. This is followed by an explanation or comment, often with specific reference to contemporary events. The literary texts are more likely to refer to contemporary events, the little books less so. Common to both is the failure to adequately identify citations from the Qur'ān and Hadith. This is not such a problem with the Qur'ān, but it can be with Hadith, especially where, as sometimes occurs, the passage in the text is inaccurately reported.

Topics

The topics covered by the published collections of *khutbah* are generally of three types: (1) worship (*ibadah*); (2) the conduct required of good practising Muslims; and (3) 'edge' issues (contemporary social and political issues). It is rare for the little books to deal with edge issues; as suggested above, their main function seems to be to provide reassurance in the conduct of one's personal religious duty. In contrast, the more sophisticated texts devote considerable space to edge issues, so confirming their dialectic function.

The *'Ulamā'*

The *'ulamā'* (singular, *'alim*) are a crucial part of any discussion of syariah and *khutbah* because it is they who write and deliver the *khutbah*. Literally meaning 'the learned', the usual translation of *'ulamā'* is 'religious scholars'.[5] The term encompasses a number of groups, the most important ones for our purposes being religious experts and heads of *pesantren* (*kyai*); mosque prayer leaders (*imam*); mosque preachers (*khatib*); teachers, male (*ustadz*) or female (*ustadzah*); and itinerant or lay preachers, male (*muballigh*) or female (*muballighah*).

All of the published collections of *khutbah* devote considerable space (about 18–20 per cent on average) to asserting the authority of the *'ulamā'* and the respect and deference which must be shown both to them as a class and to the individual *'alim*. Leaving aside an undoubted element of self-interest, this emphasis does raise the fundamental issue of authority.

The first point to note here is that the *'ulamā'* are a self-appointed and self-perpetuating class by virtue of their education, and thus members of a known scholarly tradition. Until recently this meant being a graduate of a *pesantren* owned and run by a *kyai* whose position likewise depended on his scholarly descent. More recently it has become possible to attain *'ulamā'* status through other avenues, for example by graduating from a State Islamic Institute (Insti-

---

5   See Encyclopaedia of Islam (second edition): *'Ulamā'* (in Southeast Asia).

tut Agama Islam Negeri; IAIN), although *'ulamā'* from the *pesantren* tradition often dispute this. The point is that there is a self-recognizing class which claims authority to explain and teach religion, including syariah, by reason of scholarly attainment.

The second point to note is that this self-appointed status does in fact command wide acceptance across all social classes. This acceptance rests not only on the *'alim*'s scholarly attainment (in whatever form this is defined) but also on his wider popular appeal, as measured by television and radio appearances and sales of audiotapes.[6] However, the degree of acceptance within social classes varies and is not so easy to pin down, as anthropologists working on Indonesian Islam have long known.[7] In a study of *muballighah* in West Java and Jakarta, Marcoes (1992) shows that the authority of the individual is derived from her relationship to an authoritative male (husband, father) as well as from her ability to hold and entertain an audience. *Ustadzah* who do not have a familial link must rely more on their personal authority and theological competence. In a more detailed examination of *'ulamā'* in Madura, Mansurnoor (1990) again finds that authority is essentially established through kinship links, reinforced by personal links deriving from a common educational background and the day-to-day profession of running a *pesantren* or *madrasah*.[8] At the same time, individual *kyai* do stand out as being more learned, more competent or more progressive than others.

1   CALENDAR AND TOPIC-BASED COLLECTIONS

Before turning to the texts, it is as well for us to remember that the *khutbah* has a known form that is 1400 years old.[9] When delivering the sermon, the *khatib* must be in a state of ritual purity and remain standing. There must be *shalat* for the Prophet, prayer on behalf of the faithful, recitation of a Qur'ānic passage in the first *khutbah* and so on. Although the form is fixed, there is some variation in the order of prayers on special occasions such as Idul Fitri and Idul Adha.[10] All the texts we consider below go to considerable lengths to follow the correct ritual procedure, including following the classical admonition to keep the *khutbah* short (in practice, about 10–15 minutes). The only deviation, if one can call

---

6   Audiotapes of *khutbah* are hugely popular. Because authors commonly publish their texts in both written and cassette form, the cassettes both compete with and complement the written texts.

7   See, for example, the seminal paper by Geertz (1960) on *kyai*. See also Keeler (1998) on authority deriving from the style of delivery of *khutbah* in Java.

8   See Mansurnoor (1990), especially Chapters 9, 10 and 12.

9   Encyclopaedia of Islam (second edition): *Khutbah* (*khaṭaba, khatib*).

10   Idul Fitri is the Islamic holiday on the first day of the month of Shawwal marking the end of Ramadan. Idul Adha is a festival celebrated during the *hajj* in the month of Dzulhijjah. It commemorates Abraham's willingness to sacrifice his son for God.

it that, is in language, where either Indonesian or a regional language such as Javanese or Acehnese might be used.

The Indonesian texts discussed in this chapter are arranged in two ways: (1) according to the Muslim calendar, with each month generally having four *khutbah*; and (2) by topic. The topics commonly relate to special days in the secular Indonesian calendar, such as Indonesian Independence Day or Pancasila Day. The intention seems to be to provide an Islamic reference for such days, to make them resonate with the audience or to give them a religious duty connotation.

Calendar-based Collections

The Muslim (Hijiri) calendar consists of 12 lunar months: Muharram, Shafar, Rabi'ul Awwal, Rabi'ul Thani, Jumadal Ula, Jumada Thaniyah, Rajab, Sya'ban, Ramadan, Shawwal, Dhu al-Qa'dah and Dzulhijjah. The obvious question in the case of calendar-based collections is whether each month has a distinct character that determines the topic to be discussed in the four weeks of that month. To put it another way, is each month so distinct from the others that it is appropriate to discuss just that topic? In the Hijiri calendar, four months have particular religious significance: Muharram, Rabi'ul Awwal, Ramadan and Dzulhijjah. During Muharram, Muslims commemorate New Year; it is unlawful to fight during this month. During Rabi'ul Awwal, Muslims celebrate the anniversary of the birth of the Prophet. Ramadan is the fasting month, the most holy month of the year. Dzulhijjah is the month in which the *hajj* pilgrimage takes place. The other months have varying degrees of religious significance.

The first collection examined here is an Indonesian translation of *khutbah* written in Arabic by an Indonesian *'alim*, Nawawi al-Bantani (1813–97) (No. 12 in Appendix A4.1).[11] The editor and translator is Ahmad Sunarto. Nawawi's *khutbah* for Muharram, Ramadan and Dzulhijjah focus closely on the obvious religious reference for each of those months while also introducing an extra element in each case: one's duty to orphans in the case of Muharram; the opportunity to improve one's character in the case of Ramadan; and the importance of the *hajj* and spending *zakat* wisely in the case of Dzulhijjah. In the case of the other months, however, there seems to be little in the way of direct connection between the month and the *khutbah*. For example, although the Night Journey and Ascension of the Prophet (Isra' and Mi'raj)[12] is celebrated during the month of Rajab, only one of the *khutbah* for Rajab directly concerns this theme; oth-

---

11 Described by van Bruinessen (1990: 236) as a 'popularizer', Nawawi wrote widely on a number of subjects. Although his works are now over a century old, they are still consulted extensively. The Indonesian text examined here is a heavily edited version of the original collection.
12 See Encyclopaedia of Islam (second edition): *Mikraj*.

ers are on good conduct in society and the characteristics of a hypocrite. Again, although the fifteenth night of Sya'ban (Nisfu Sya'ban) is a time for concentrated prayer to achieve one's destiny as a chosen one of God, only one of the *khutbah* mentions this; the accompanying *khutbah* deal with the importance of charity and ways of avoiding spite and revenge. Of course one could make a connection between the acts to be carried out or avoided and the month itself, but that would involve a fair amount of speculation. Finally, one would expect the *khutbah* for the month of Shawwal to take up the theme of Idul Fitri, but in fact there is no obvious connection.

In other examples of calendar-based collections as well, the choice of subject matter often appears to be rather idiosyncratic. For example, Rathomy (No. 3 in Appendix A4.1) covers the usual subjects for Muharram but, in addition, provides a *khutbah* on sexual relations between men and women. The subjects for Shafar are faith, the education of children and the consequences of one's deeds for life after death. Those for the month of Rabi'ul Awwal concern the birth of the Prophet and the importance of this event for the Islamic community (*ummah*). The *khutbah* for Jumadal Ula concern the Muslim's obligations towards the Prophet, the duties of the individual towards other Muslims and the importance of the Friday prayer. The topics for Jumada Thaniyah include the spiritual needs of humanity, the signs that Judgment Day is near, and Islam and the enemies of Islam. The latter two months are of relatively less religious significance. The *khutbah* for the following month, Rajab, commemorate the birth of the Prophet. In preparation for Ramadan, the emphasis in the *khutbah* for Sya'ban is on humility and the relief of poverty—especially through alms giving—and Islam as it exists in contemporary Indonesia. There is also a strong connection between month and subject matter in the *khutbah* for Ramadan and Dzulhijjah, with the exception of one sermon for the latter month on Indonesian independence.

Our third example, by M.A. Fuadi Sya'ban (No. 4 in Appendix A4.1), is a relatively short collection consisting of only 28 *khutbah*—two for each month—most of them quite aggressively didactic. The two *khutbah* for Muharram are respectively on worship (*ibadah*) and implementing syariah for national development. The two for Shafar are both on education. The *khutbah* for Rabi'ul Awwal are respectively on modern society as a new state of ignorance and the Prophet as a bringer of mercy and promoter of development. Those for Jumada Thaniyah are on '"Socializing" the Qur'ān and "Qur'ānizing" Society'—essentially the cultivation of the physical and mental capabilities of young Muslims. The *khutbah* for Rajab interpret Isra' and Mi'raj for medical science and discuss the connection between spirituality and faith in God. Those for Ramadan are on fasting as a method of developing social and individual tolerance. The *khutbah* for Shawwal focus on fraternity and respect for one's parents. The topics for the month of Dzulhijjah are quite straightforward and directly comparable with those in the first two collections. However, this is certainly not the case for the bulk of this collection, where the author is clearly inserting issues based on his own view of their importance rather than any connection with the month. There is nothing wrong with this as such, but it is clearly a very different approach to that taken by Nawawi and Rathomy. In Sya'ban, the month certainly does not dictate the content.

Our fourth example is a collection by HM Hasan Abdul Qahar (No. 9 in Appendix A4.1). At least one of the *khutbah* for each month is directly related to the theme of that month, and the obvious topics are chosen for Ramadan and Muharram. Apart from this, the topics seem to be chosen as the compiler sees fit. In other words, the collection follows the calendar format but its references do not do so with any consistency.

Abd. Hamid Zahwan (No. 11 in Appendix A4.1) provides an interesting variation on the preceding examples in that the collection is based partly on the calendar system and partly on the topic system. The first four *khutbah* and possibly four others are calendar based and the remainder are topic based *but with a reference to the calendar system*. This short text is divided into three parts. The *khutbah* in the first part cover the two most significant months in the Islamic calendar, Muharram and Ramadan, as well as important duties such as the payment of the wealth tax (*zakat*) and the performance of the *hajj*. Another *khutbah* in this section deals with the subject of eclipses. The second part contains *khutbah* on important days in the secular nation-state, such as Indonesian Independence Day and National Education Day. The focus here is on the significance of these events for Islam and the contribution Islam makes to each. The third part is on broad Islamic themes such as prayer, children and religion, and faith. Taken as a whole, this collection admits a new definition of calendar-based *khutbah*, where both secular and religious references are permitted.

A collection edited by Mustofa W. Hasyim (No. 13 in Appendix A4.1) adopts a similar approach. The *khutbah* in Part I cover important Islamic and secular days. Those in Part II discuss the fundamental principles of Islam. Part III consists of prayers. In his introduction, Hasyim emphasizes the importance of transforming the oral *khutbah* tradition into a written form as 'one part of the development of media communication'. The editor is making the point that the new form involves new ways of organizing the *khutbah*.

Our final example, a collection by Ustadz Labib Mz. (No. 23 in Appendix A4.1), returns us to the calendar month system but provides 10 *khutbah* for each month. An interesting if minor feature is that the prayer days are listed according to the Javanese calendar (*wage, legi* and so on). In only a few of the months is there a direct link between the subject of the *khutbah* and the religious significance of that month. Although the author claims that the topics are 'the most important for the designated times and events', this seems to be very much a matter of his own personal choice.

From this brief outline we can draw several preliminary conclusions. The first and most obvious one is that the calendar month system based on religious events is no longer the sole reference for what is appropriate for *khutbah*, making Nawawi look rather old-fashioned. The 'new' collections include *khutbah* on secular days that can be made to seem 'Islamic' to a greater or lesser degree. The distinction between Islamic and non-Islamic days has therefore become blurred. Second, each author, editor or compiler is now the arbiter of what is appropriate for the time and the audience. Each of them claims coherence for their selection, either directly in terms of Islam or indirectly in terms of 'the problems of our time' and 'the era of globalization', where Islam is claimed to have 'the answers'. Finally, there is an increasing recognition of the permanency that the print media brings. All of the authors examined above recognize that they are writing for a literate, Indonesia-wide audience rather than just the members of the local mosque. Important calendar days have thus become negotiable across time and place. Although the oral *khutbah* is still the norm, the new written collections are one of the foundations for 'Islam today', because they are part of the new media and reflect the improved levels of literacy in the Muslim community.

Topic-based Collections

As we have seen, the boundary between the calendar and topic-based collections has become blurred. However, we are still justified in treating the latter separately: much of the material is topic focused, and some authors seem to specialize in this form.

Our first example is by Ahmad Sunarto (No. 1 in Appendix A4.1), also the translator and editor of the Nawawi collection referred to earlier. In a short preface he claims that his collection is simply an aid to understanding religion. By this he means moral virtue rather than theology or doctrine. Thus, the topics include patience and gratitude, virtuous works, immorality, happiness, hypocrisy and so on, with the only direct references to religion being two *khutbah* on Idul Fitri and Idul Adha. He continues the same approach in a later collection (No. 2 in Appendix A4.1), except that this time he combines the general *khutbah* on morality with special *khutbah* on important Islamic as well as secular days. Baidlowi Syamsuri (No. 5 in Appendix A4.1) also follows more or less the same pattern.

There are, however, more complex examples of topic selection. One of these is Effendi Zarkasi's collection of *khutbah* (No. 6 in Appendix A4.1). The introduction states that Islam is the only religion to encompass all aspects of life, human and natural, for all times and places. It follows from this claim to universality that Muslims are obligated to interpret social and natural phenomena from an Islamic point of view. The purpose of this collection, then, is to act as a guide to dealing with natural and social phenomena in an all-inclusive way.

The collection has five chapters. The first is purportedly on theology (*aqidah*) but in fact contains *khutbah* on such topics as deviant or misleading spiritual practices, the horoscope and the causes of calamities. One could of course claim that these issues are at the outer edge of correct doctrine and therefore do constitute *aqidah*. This is a perfectly supportable argument but it loses its force somewhat if we look at the second chapter on education and character. It contains two *khutbah* on the Qur'ān and another 22 on such diverse topics as sports, women, the authority of teachers, alcohol, gambling, immorality, honesty, revenge, the simple life, mothers and television. The third chapter consists of a *khutbah* on the Islamic family written for Idul Fitri and one on independence written for Idul Adha. In the fourth chapter, the focus changes from the individual Muslim to the context of Islam. One such context is the public character of Islam, including Islam and extremism, Islam from the perspective of the infidel and the contribution of Islam to Indonesian culture. Another context is the use to which religion should be put in the social and political life of the country. Here there are *khutbah* on the challenges faced by contemporary Muslims, the need for vigilance, social disparities, the qualities of a good leader, Islam and technology, and legal injustice. This outline takes us back to Effendi Zarkasi's initial premise, the idea that the actual conditions of time and place are to be understood and judged from the perspective of religion. The *khatib* is urged to undertake an extensive personal *ijtihad*—'to contribute his own inspiration'.

That this is not an extreme or isolated view is shown by the collection published by Syahminan Zaini (No. 7 in Appendix A4.1). It contains *khutbah* on humanitarianism, fasting as a way of restoring man's natural character, and the scientific authenticity of the creation of the human body and the existence of the spirit. One of the most interesting *khutbah* discusses the role of worship (*ibadah*) in maintaining Pancasila and the nation. It is described in greater detail later in the chapter.

The collection referred to earlier by Mustofa W. Hasyim (No. 13 in Appendix A4.1) provides a related version of context through its treatment of fundamental Islamic values and contemporary issues. The context here is cultural change, as exemplified by *khutbah* on such subjects as environmental awareness (by Dede Zakiyudin), relationships with non-Muslims (by H. Mulyadi), education in an era of globalization (by Mahfud An) and the socialization of the Qur'ān (by Abu Imam Nurhidayat Cupo). These *khutbah* are written in sophisticated language and are directed towards an educated audience.

We might put forward the hypothesis that the practice of arranging *khutbah* by topic encourages or even demands that religion be treated in context. One implication of this might be that the emphasis on context could actually reduce the standing of religion and, hence, syariah. The standing of the syariah is, after all, determined by context, form, use and purpose, rather than being the determinant of these things. I return to these issues in the last section of this chapter.

To continue with the topic-based collections, Drs. Moh. Amin (No. 18 in Appendix A4.1) specifically claims to write for Muslims of different backgrounds: the educated and the non-educated, civil servants and traders. The collection is quite short, containing only 12 *khutbah*; the topics are very general and the language simple. In trying to appeal to such a wide range of people, the author is trying to do too much. Nevertheless, I look at two examples of his work later in the chapter.

The *khutbah* in the collection by Kafrawi Hamzah (No. 20 in Appendix A4.1) are overtly ideological. In his introduction, the author claims that most *khatib* serve the interests of government rather than religion, and that they blur or confuse the truths of Islam by using unclear and ambiguous laguage. His intention is to correct these defects by promoting Islamic outreach (*dakwah*) activities. Hamzah is able to draw on his experience as a *khatib* in Australia, where the collection originated. While he does not describe his audience, it must have consisted mainly of Indonesian and Malaysian students.

In a related vein, Ghufron Maba (No. 15 in Appendix A4.1) claims in his introduction that technology and globalization lead to materialism and secularism, a lowering of moral standards and an increase in crime and poverty. The purpose of the collection is therefore to defend the values of religion in society. Thus, it contains a *khutbah* for Isra' and Mi'raj on morality and good conduct; one on the Qur'ān as a philosophy and guide for humanity; one on independence as a basic right for all nations; and two on the congruence of Islamic values and Pancasila.

In the introduction to their collection, Drs. Sholihin Syaqiq and Drs. Sufyana Bakri (No. 22 in Appendix A4.1) say that a *khatib* must be aware of the differing needs of different people and tailor his *khutbah* accordingly. Their solution is to provide a large number of potential models (39 in all) to aid the *khatib* in his task. Like some other collections (for example, No. 17 in Appendix A4.1), the *khutbah* in this collection have no unifying principle—no common rationale or arrangement.

I began this section by saying that most of the published collections of *khutbah* aspire to be models or templates for other authors and the *khatib*. At the most basic level of format, there are two types of collection: calendar based and topic based. The calendar format does not stand up to the test of providing a real link between month and subject matter, with the exception, perhaps, of more traditional collections derived from Nawawi. It does, however, highlight the importance of certain religious events or days of special significance in the religious year—and even of important national days, which are imbued by the authors with religious significance. The secular founders of the Republic of Indonesia would certainly not have anticipated that the secular calendar would be Islamized in this way. But it is equally arguable that this Islamizing of the secular may be little more than symbolic, reflecting the day-to-day fluctuations in the relationship between Islam and politics over the years. The ambivalent attitude of Muslim authorities towards Pancasila over several decades is an obvious example of this.

The usefulness of topic-based collections as a template for authors is also unclear. However, some general comments can be made. First, all authors and editors recognize that topic-based *khutbah* are at least an important addition to the calendar method, because they allow room for discussion of contemporary subjects. Indeed, since the 1990s subjects such as globalization, the function of Islam in the state, government, women, humanitarianism and social issues have come to dominate a significant number of collections. Second, the topic-based collections show that their authors clearly understand the opportunities created by the development of new media for *khutbah*, such as books and audiotapes. Finally, the new literary form makes it possible for authors to write for particular, selected audiences. As a result, collections now vary in language and sophistication of argument, from the simple to the complex. Today's authors can tailor their collections to particular audiences. The new media for the delivery of *khutbah* allow them to explore a huge range of contexts and styles of exposition, selecting among them rather than being limited to just one.

'Selection': here it is again. As we saw in Chapter 1, this is a crucial word for understanding Indonesian syariah, and this will not be its last appearance.

In sections 2–4 of this chapter, I discuss the treatment of edge issues in the *khutbah* texts. This is not to deny the importance and relevance of the other subjects covered by the collections. However, the treatment of edge issues is of particular interest because it takes us into areas where the classical jurisprudence has difficulty providing appropriate solutions for contemporary Indonesian problems. The topics I have chosen appear in all the collections in Appendix A4.1. This makes it possible to gain a reasonable preliminary understanding of the full range of responses from authors, whether they write in a calendar or topic-based format.

2   LEADERSHIP

This section deals with the contentious issue of leadership. I begin with the core issue of the authority of the *'ulamā'* to make pronouncements not only on religious matters, but also on matters that some might consider the preserve of the secular state. I then discuss specific aspects of the interface between Islam and the secular state: government, Pancasila and the secular national days.

The *'Ulamā'*

The *'ulamā'* are the guardians and transmitters of syariah. Earlier I identified several groups of *'ulamā'*, including the authors of the spoken and written *khutbah*. Here I focus on their perceptions of their own status as leaders, based on the unique internal viewpoint offered by the *khutbah*. One might of course argue that the *khatib*, being members of the *'ulamā'* class, have a vested interest in promoting an exalted view of the *'ulamā'*. This is certainly too cynical a view, although readers of Nawawi could be excused for believing it.

Ahmad Sunarto's heavily edited translation of Nawawi (No. 12 in Appendix A4.1) presents an idealized picture of the *'ulamā'* founded on Q35:28:

> And so amongst men, ...
> Those truly fear God,
> Among his servants,
> Who have knowledge: ...

This verse is not usually taken literally, although the author of this *khutbah* claims that it should be. Through a number of Hadith (for which sources are not given), the *khutbah* makes the essential point that the *'ulamā'* are wise and thus deserving of respect and honour. The *'ulamā'* play a vital role in society because they are the inheritors of the Prophet's message and therefore directly responsible to God. They must show no fear of government, regardless of the consequences, because they are obliged to encourage good and forbid evil. If the *'ulamā'* neglect their duty, society and religion will decline. The *ummah* can demand that the *'ulamā'* fulfil their responsibilities properly. If they do, then they are fully entitled to respect and obedience. The *'ulamā'* are as essential to the state as a just ruler.

Sunarto provides a simplified version of this *khutbah* in a collection of his own (No. 1 in Appendix A4.1). In it he makes two additional points: first, that the *'ulamā'* are deserving of their high status in society because of their function as teachers and fearless speakers of the truth; and second, that those who do not show the appropriate respect to the *'ulamā'* will be punished by God, by dying without faith, by being subjected to tyranny or by experiencing failure in life.

A much more critical view of the *'ulamā'* is found in an elaborate *khutbah* by Kafrawi Hamzah (No. 20 in Appendix A4.1). It is important to note at the outset the difference in date and provenance. The version of Nawawi later compilers rely on is a heavily edited translation of a *khutbah* collection written in Mecca in the late nineteenth century when the Dutch were at the height of their imperial enterprise. But Hamzah was writing in the independent Republic of Indonesia in the mid-1990s, an era when the country was experiencing rapid globalization. The difference in context is reflected in Hamzah's approach to 'the *'ulamā'* problem', as he calls it. His initial proposition is that the nation depends on both the *'ulamā'* and the presence of a just ruler. The duty of the *'ulamā'* is to tell the truth and, if necessary, criticize the government, because they are 'the inheritors of the Prophet's message'. The *'ulamā'* must not only judge and speak out about social conduct, but also propagate the truths of Islam. If they neglect this duty then Islamic civilization will decline. The current decline in individual and social morality is caused by the *'ulamā'* putting their own personal interests before those of the *ummah*. They have destroyed the reputation of Islam by failing to supervise government. By remaining silent when they should have spoken out, they have permitted governments throughout the Islamic world to depart from religious principles and laws.

In reality, man-made laws and constitutions have been implemented to change Divine laws. Unfortunately, our *'ulamā'* do not take any action to prevent this. Prostitution and other forms of immorality are widespread ... The *'ulamā'* require Muslims to send their children to Islamic schools but they send their own children to public and secular schools. They order women to wear the veil but they let their daughters walk in public unveiled. (Hamzah 1994: 60)

Hamzah conludes these harsh criticisms by quoting from Q11:10, which warns the *'ulamā'* against falling into 'exultation and pride'. A damning comment indeed, and one that leads us into the dangers of excessive pride in leadership.

Government

There is a fine line between 'leadership' and 'government'; governments are supposed to demonstrate leadership but they do not always do so. The *khutbah* distinguish between the two terms, which are not conterminous in Islam. As we shall see, the *khutbah* quote from the Qur'ān and Hadith to draw a distinction between leader and state. This is perfectly understandable; the citations date from a period when the 'state' in the modern sense was not part of syariah, and there was no theory of state as such.[13] Today, however, the *'ulamā'* must carry out their duties, including the duty to lead, within a formal state structure in which it is the state that makes and administers the law—including laws on religion—and it is the courts and bureaucracy that implement them. An obvious question might be: is it still appropriate for the *'ulamā'* to cite the Qur'ān and Hadith on issues of leadership given that the form of the state has changed? But a more practical approach is simply to look at what the *khutbah* have to say about government, leadership and the role of the *'ulamā'* in the modern nation-state.

We begin with Kafrawi Hamzah, whose bitter criticisms of the *'ulamā'* have just been cited. He compares the righteous conduct of Caliph Umar bin Khattab[14] with that of modern leaders who neglect their duty, are totally self-interested and are often corrupt. These defects result from 'weak faith' and will be punished.[15]

In Ahmad Sunarto (No. 1 in Appendix A4.1), we find a blurring of the line between leader and government. The *khutbah* begins with the obvious reference:

> Obey God, and obey the Prophet
> And those charged
> With authority among you ... (Q4:59)

---

13 Some modern apologists have attempted to reinterpret the Charter of Medina as constructing a theory of state, but this is an ahistorical and essentially pointless exercise.
14 See Encyclopaedia of Islam (second edition): *Umar Khattāb*, second caliph of Islam.
15 This *khutbah* ends with what appears to be a reference to Q96:13–19, although I am open to correction on this point.

This means that one must obey, for example, the head of the household, one's employer, the president, the king, the judge and so on. In other words, the author is thinking in terms of a personalized government where there is a person in charge who is directly answerable to God. Sunarto cites the Qur'ān (Q11:113, Q42:42, Q14:42, Q28:59) to support this view, and to condemn all those in authority who act unjustly. In reality, as we know, there is no longer any one person 'in charge'; the state has its own momentum. But this is not the view expressed in the Qur'ān and the syariah, where the duties of the leader, and by extension the leadership of the state, are still regarded as personal.

In a *khutbah* entitled 'Implementing Justice in Leadership: Maintaining the Divine Mandate', M.A. Fuadi Sya'ban (No. 4 in Appendix A4.1) takes up exactly this point. He proceeds from the premise that a leader of Muslims is mandated by God to act justly and wisely and uphold the syariah. The leader is the servant of the people, not a self-interested master. The public interest must be his overriding concern, as befits

> Those who faithfully observe
> Their trusts and covenants (Q23:8–10)

This passage is usually interpreted as referring to individual (commercial) contracts, but as the present usage shows, it can also be made to apply to the duty of a leader as mandated by God. This brings us to the difficult question of the *form* of God's mandate for leadership in contemporary Indonesia. The answer of first recourse is, of course, the Pancasila.

Pancasila

The five Pancasila principles are very general, and therefore open to a variety of interpretations. The *khutbah* exploit this by using selections from the Qur'ān to give the principles an Islamic interpretation. These selections can be used to construct an ideology of leadership.

A good example is a *khutbah* on the fifth principle of Pancasila—the social justice principle—by Ghufron Maba (No. 15 in Appendix A4.1). He describes the Pancasila principles as having both spiritual and material dimensions; if these are understood correctly, then abuse of power by leaders will not occur. A leader has a responsibility to implement social justice because this is an aspect of just government. The supporting citation is Q4:58:

> God commands you
> To render back your trusts
> To those to whom they are due;
> And when you judge
> Between man and man
> Judge with justice …

All those in positions of authority must adhere to this principle, which is found in both Pancasila and the Qur'ān. The citation at this point is Q4:135:

> Stand out firmly
> For justice, as witnesses
> To God, even as against
> Yourselves, or your parents,
> Or your kin ...

Through these two citations, Maba provides a definition of social justice expressed in terms of the Islamic concept of leadership. They are reinforced by a Hadith that reports the Prophet as saying: 'Justice must be implemented by the ruler'.[16] In this way Maba effects a neat reconciliation between Pancasila and Islam in which the former is simply an expression of the latter.

In a *khutbah* on the first principle of Pancasila, belief in God,[17] the same author turns his attention to competing ideologies. Any ideology that denies the existence of God as a founding principle of government is by definition unconstitutional as well as being irreligious. The example put forward is Marxism, which, as is usual in Indonesian Islamic circles, is defined as denying the existence of God. The citation this time is Q2:217:

> But graver is it
> In the sight of God
> To prevent access
> To the path of God,
> To deny Him ...
> They [will] turn you back
> From your faith ...

Maba explains the success of the Indonesian Communist Party (Partai Kommunis Indonesia: PKI) in becoming a mass party in the 1950s and early 1960s as being due to the influence of unbelievers:

> Unbelievers spend their wealth
> To hinder men from the path
> Of God, and so will they
> Continue to spend ... (Q8:36)

In these two *khutbah*, we see Maba grappling with Qur'ānic definitions of leadership and the essential principles on which it should be based. Whether these are appropriate or practical is not the point. What they reveal is a view of leadership through the prism of Islam—a distorted vision, perhaps, but one that is nevertheless real.

A closely related *khutbah* by Abdul Muin in Mustofa W. Hasyim (No. 13 in Appendix A4.1) discusses the 'national tragedy' of September 1965, that is, the attempted PKI coup and ensuing loss of life (Schwarz 2004: 19–22). The author begins by citing Q4:59:

---

16 The reference is unclear but may be *Sahih al-Bukhari*, Vol. IX: 260–2.
17 As formulated in any one of the five scriptures formally recognized by the Indonesian state: Islam, Catholicism, Protestantism, Buddhism and Hinduism.

> Obey God, and obey the Prophet
> And those charged
> With authority among you ...

One must obey the lawful leader (the government) provided it is legitimate, that is, does not run counter to the principles of Islam. While acknowledging that Indonesia is not a theocracy, Abdul Muin argues that Pancasila is in fact an expression of Islam—indeed, the gift of unity and integration from Muslims. Therefore, any attack on Pancasila is an attack on Islam and the Muslim population, and the events of September 1965 must be assessed in that light. The leaders of the state at that time acted properly (Q4:59); it is the duty of today's leaders to continue to counter any latent threat of communism. It is also the duty of government to improve the economic status of the poor. Here the author cites Q59:7, the well-known verse saying that wealth is at God's disposal:

> What God has bestowed ... belongs
> To God and His Prophet,
> And to kindred and orphans,
> The needy and the traveller;
> In order that it may not circulate [only]
> Between the wealthy amongst you ...

A similar conflating of Islam, Pancasila and national development as collectively defining the basic duties of leadership is found in a complex *khutbah* by Syahminan Zaini (No. 7 in Appendix A4.1). This collection was written at the height of the New Order government's P-4 program of Pancasila indoctrination and must be read with that in mind. Essentially the author argues that the five principles of Pancasila are a secular expression of the five pillars of Islam: profession of faith (*shahadah*); performance of ritual prayers (*shalat*); fasting (*sawm*); payment of *zakat*; and performance of the *hajj*.

Zaini begins by saying that God created man to inherit the earth and fulfil His commands (Q30:72; Q51:56; Q11:61). Man's duty to God and his proper use of the things of this world are alike commanded by God. To carry out these commands, the individual Muslim must cultivate his essential nature to be strong and pure in mind. Although God has provided the means for man to carry out his duties, there are obstacles in the way; these include selfishness (Q12:53–54), Satan (Q12:5), unbelievers (Q2:217; Q8:3) and hypocrisy (Q2:9). These obstacles can be overcome by adherence to prayer, payment of *zakat*, performing the *hajj* and observing the fasting month. Each of these duties has direct consequences for society and national development: prayer prevents wrongdoing; paying *zakat* contributes to economic development; performing the *hajj* creates a sense of fraternity and unity; and observing the fast cultivates patience and tolerance. The author concludes that the actions demanded of a Muslim are the same as those required by Pancasila, the purpose of both being to develop the potential of mankind. One of the consequences of the equivalence of religious duty and adherence to Pancasila is that the leader (government) must provide freedom of speech to promote the teaching of Islam in society, facilities and services for the *'ulamā'*, most of whom 'live in poverty', and appropriate services and buildings to make Islamic education possible. That is, it is the duty of government to provide for the *'ulamā'* so that they may carry out their function as teachers and leaders.

Through the medium of the state ideology, Pancasila, both this *khutbah* and the preceding one by Abdul Muin claim a role for the *'ulamā'* as leaders, and stake out a territory for Islam in the secular state. But with the *'ulamā'* and the secular leadership both claiming authority in the secular state, there have always been varying degrees of cooption and cooperation between them. The treatment of national days in the *khutbah* provides a clear example of this.

The National Days

The subject of national days accounts for about 18–20 per cent of all *khutbah* in our sample. Even a very preliminary reading of these *khutbah* shows an insertion of syariah into what are essentially state celebrations.

Indonesian Independence Day

Our first example is a collection of *khutbah* by Ustadz Labib Mz. (No. 23 in Appendix A4.1), many of them on days of Islamic or national significance.[18] In a *khutbah* commemorating Indonesian Independence Day (17 August), Labib asks his audience to remember the heroes of the fight for independence and calls on the country's present leaders to continue to struggle for the goals of the independence fighters:

> And those who strive
> In Our cause—We will
> Certainly guide them
> To Our paths
> For God
> Is with those
> Who do right (Q29:69)

This verse is usually understood to refer to the individual's struggle to attain God's purposes for man. However, its insertion here is understandable given that the struggle for independence was against oppression by non-Muslims.

Drs. Imron Abu Amar (No. 14 in Appendix A4.1) also imputes motives of exploitation to the colonial power in a *khutbah* on Indonesian Independence Day. He points out that Muslims took a leading role in the fight against the Dutch. Those who lost their lives during the struggle died as martyrs. It is therefore the duty of Indonesian Muslims to repay those sacrifices by striving for national development and progress:

---

18 See Foulcher (2000) for other examples.

> It is He Who shows you
> The lightning, by way
> Both of fear and of hope:
> It is He Who raises up
> The clouds, heavy
> With rain (Q13:12)

A similar view, but this time framed in terms of human rights, is expressed in Ghufron Maba's *khutbah* commemorating Indonesian Independence Day (No. 15 in Appendix A4.1). He argues that it is justified to struggle against an aggressor because freedom is a basic human right. Like Labib, he cites Q29:69:

> And those who strive
> In Our cause, we will
> Certainly guide them ...

Love of country is also part of one's faith:

> Truth has now
> Arrived, and falsehood perished ...

Having achieved independence, the *ummah* is obligated to pursue cultivation and prosperity, as mandated by God:

> ... It is He Who has produced you
> From the earth and settled you
> Therein ... (Q11:61)

In doing so, Muslims must struggle against the dangers of corruption, collusion and nepotism, which arise from the impulse of the individual towards evil (Q12:53) and are a threat to civilization (Q23:71) emanating from Satan (Q24:21; Q4:60).

The God-given mandate privileges mankind alone among God's creations with freedom and independence:

> We have honoured the sons
> Of Adam; ...
> Given them for sustenance things
> Good and pure; and conferred
> On them special favours,
> Above a great part
> Of Our creation (Q17:70).

Freedom means, first, that the government or leader must guarantee the security of its citizens:

> Nor take life—which God
> Has made sacred—except
> For just cause ... (Q17:33)

> ... Eat not up your property
> Among yourselves in vanities ...
> Nor kill or destroy
> Yourselves ... (Q4:29)

It also means the freedom to work and support one's family. Corruption, theft and so on are a direct attack on this right and diminish the rights of people in general. At the same time, the rights of the individual must be balanced against the rights of others in the community:

> ... [Do not] eat up wrongfully and knowingly
> Some of other people's property (Q2:188)

Another view of human rights is given by Abd. Hamid Zahwan (No. 11 in Appendix A4.1), who brings a historical perspective to the subject. In 'Human Rights', he says that the concept of human rights was understood in pre-modern India, Egypt and Greece, with Islam also making its own particular contribution. In a narrow sense this meant respecting the rights of one's neighbours; the author cites a Hadith from al-Bukhari in support of this proposition.[19] In a wider sense it meant both leaders and citizens taking responsibility for the conduct of society and the nation, where there is a mutual balance of rights and responsibilities:

> He that works
> A righteous deed—whether
> Man or woman—and is
> A Believer—such will enter
> The Garden [of Paradise] ... (Q40:40)

> Then shall any person who
> Has done an atom's weight
> Of good, see it
> And any person who
> Has done an atom's weight
> Of evil, shall see it (Q99:7–8)

The Indonesian Constitution guarantees basic human rights and freedom of religion. These are major achievements. On the other hand, the author is not so sure that the true meaning of revelation is understood as it should be:

> Let there arise out of you
> A group of people
> Inviting to all that is good,
> Enjoining what is right,
> And forbidding what is wrong ... (Q3:104)

In a rather long *khutbah* on Indonesian Independence Day, the same author emphasizes the role of God in achieving Indonesian independence and the necessity for Muslims to continue to persevere in the struggle for advancement. Through the Will of God and with His blessing, the Constitution of 1945 was bestowed on Indonesia and Indonesians were granted success in their armed struggle against the Dutch. The first principle of Pancasila—belief in God—rec-

---

19 The reference is not clear but seems to be a version of part of Book 49 of *Sahih al-Bukhari* (on reconciliation).

ognizes the hand of God in national affairs. As well as thanking God for blessing these endeavours, Muslims must remember that the aim of independence is the betterment of all:

> So eat of the sustenance
> Which God has provided
> For you, lawful and good;
> And be grateful for the favours
> Of God ... (Q16:114)

Baidlowi Syamsuri (No. 5 in Appendix A4.1) also stresses the need to thank God for Indonesian independence, which is a gift of God and a mark of His generosity to mankind:

> And who is grateful
> Does so to the profit
> Of his own soul; ... (Q31:12)

Those who are ungrateful will, of course, suffer the consequences (Q34:16).

Armed Forces Day, Heroes Day and Sanctity of Pancasila Day

In a *khutbah* on Heroes Day and another on Sanctity of Pancasila Day, Ustadz Labib Mz. (No. 23 in Appendix A4.1) focuses on the defeat of the PKI in 1965. He begins by thanking God for protecting the country from 'Satan' [communists], citing Q7:96:

> ... But they rejected the truth
> And We brought them
> To book for their misdeeds

Once again we see the equation of Pancasila with Islam; this is a consistent feature of *khutbah* from the 1980s onwards. But which is internalizing which? At the very least we can say that in *khutbah* such as these, it appears that Islam is being treated as an ideology rather than a religion.

The same author provides a *khutbah* on Armed Forces Day (No. 23 in Appendix A4.1). After making the obligatory call for development, he stresses the primacy of obedience to God and the ruler, citing the well-known verse Q4:59:

> Obey God, and obey the Prophet
> And those charged
> With authority among you ...

Duty and loyalty are the basic responsibilities of a Muslim (here 'a Muslim citizen') provided no unlawful conduct is being demanded. 'Unlawful' means unlawful in Islam. In short, obedience to the ruler is an essential element in Islamic thought.

In a *khutbah* on Heroes Day, Baidlowi Syamsuri (No. 5 in Appendix A4.1) relies entirely on Hadith to pay tribute to the heroes ('the best people') who died during the fight for Indonesian independence. They served God and country at the cost of their own lives, and are therefore martyrs for the faith (*syahid*). Usually, *syahid* refers to those who die in a holy war. Syamsuri's extension of the meaning to refer to those who died in the struggle for independence brings about a new equation between wars of independence and holy wars. The author goes on to say that Indonesia's victory was a gift from God. The heroes of 1945–50 are a model for succeeding generations. Their struggle was an act of worship akin to prayer, fasting and pilgrimage from which we can draw lessons for our own times. The development of the state and the progress of its peoples are equally a struggle, ultimately undertaken for the sake of God. All must engage in this struggle (including government officers and other workers), just as all must engage in worship through prayer, fasting and pilgrimage. This is an unusually long and complex *khutbah* for this author.

In a *khutbah* on Sanctity of Pancasila Day, Abd. Hamid Zahwan (No. 11 in Appendix A4.1) begins by saying that Pancasila should remind Muslims of the brutality of communism. The killing and torturing of Muslim members of the Indonesian army by members of the PKI was totally against the values of Pancasila, which are also Islamic values:

> Shame is thrown over them
> ... because they rejected
> The signs of God, and slew
> The Prophets in defiance of right
> This because they rebelled
> And transgressed beyond bounds (Q3:112)

The author then takes each of the five principles of Pancasila in turn, showing how they equate to fundamental Islamic principles. The first (belief in God), he interprets as the 'Oneness of God', a clear reference to the doctrine of the unity of God (*tauhid*). This first principle can be equated with the Islamic injunction towards faith and obedience:

> For, Believers are those
> Who, when God is mentioned,
> Feel a tremor in their hearts,
> And when they hear his signs ...
> ... Put all their trust in God (Q8:2)

Zahwan interprets the second principle (humanitarianism) to mean the equality of all human beings regardless of ethnicity, age and social status. This is supported by an unidentified Hadith. The third principle, national unity, is matched with Q2:213:

> Mankind is one single nation ...

This means that the individual must put the interests of the nation before his own interests. The fourth principle, that consultation and consensus are essential to good government, is interpreted through two verses:

> ... And consult them in affairs ... (Q3:159)

> ... Who conduct their affairs by mutual consultation ...
> (Q42:38)

If the difficulty remains unresolved, then the nation must turn to the Qur'ān:

> As to those who turn
> [to God],
> His Apostle ...
> The fellowship of God,
> That must certainly triumph (Q5:59)

The author interprets the final social justice principle as meaning a general responsibility to donate part of one's wealth to others. He cites Q5:58:

> ... Those who
> Establish regular prayers
> And regular charity ...

Islam is opposed to communism because it advocates atheism. But communism is more than just the denial of God; it is itself a new faith (a valid point given that a true—that is, unreconstructed—Marxist will always admit that dogma requires faith). This cannot be allowed, because Islam is the only true religion:

> If anyone desires
> A religion other than
> Islam
> It will never be accepted
> Of him ... (Q3:85)

There is no place for communism in Islam or Pancasila. However, the author admits that in reality socialism still has many adherents. The only defence is in strong faith:

> Remember how the Unbelievers
> Plotted against you, to keep
> You in bonds, or slay you
> Or get you out of your home,
> They plot ...
> And God, too, plans
> And the best of planners
> Is God (Q8:30)

Similar citations are added to reinforce this position (Q8:45; Q13:42).

Youth Pledge Day

On 28 October 1928, a number of young Indonesians met to pledge their commitment to 'one homeland, one nation, one language'.[20] This day is now com-

---

20 See Foulcher (2000) for further details.

memorated as Youth Pledge Day. According to Ustadz Labib Mz. (No. 19 in Appendix A4.1), Youth Pledge Day is important because it encourages not only the physical and mental development of the young, but also mutual understanding and tolerance among people (Muslims) from different villages and regions. In support he cites Q49:13:

> ... We created
> You from a single pair
> Of a male and a female,
> And made you into
> Nations and tribes, that
> You may know each other
> Not that you may despise
> Each other ...

He compares the *ummah* with a body, each part of which helps and supports the other parts. The author then cites Q42:23:

> ... No reward do I
> Ask of you for this
> Except the love
> Of those near of kin ...

'Near of kin' is commonly extended to mean love of humanity, but here it simply means Indonesian Muslims.

For Drs. Sholihin Syaqiq and Drs. Ii Sufyana M. Bakri (No. 22 in Appendix A4.1), Youth Pledge Day signifies the importance of youthful idealism as a factor in attaining Indonesian independence. The authors draw a parallel between the faith of the young Indonesians commemorated on Youth Pledge Day and that of the Companions of the Cave whose story is recounted in Q18. They were a group of youths who took refuge in a cave to escape the persecution of idolaters (Q18:14–16) and maintain the purity of their faith in God. As a reward for their faith, God looked after them while they slept in the cave for several years, although to them it seemed just one day.

Abd. Hamid Zahwan (No. 11 in Appendix A4.1) approaches the subject of Youth Pledge Day through the concepts of nationality (*kebangsaan*) and nationalism (*nasionalisme*). By 'nationality' he means race or racial group; by nationalism he means a nation free from oppression. The significance of Youth Pledge Day is that it combines the two, resulting in a unified, integrated society based on One God and One Prophet. With the spirit of Islam as its foundation, the integrity of the *ummah* is paramount. It is therefore the duty of Muslims to overcome internal divisions. Muslims are fortunate, because God has given clear instructions on both prayer and ethical social conduct. These two things are complementary; one without the other is not sufficient:

> And when prayer
> Is finished, then may you
> Disperse through the land,

> And seek of the Bounty
> Of God ... (Q62:10)

But the former should never be used to disguide a deficiency in the latter:

> Woe to the worshippers
> Who are neglectful
> Of their prayers
> Those who want
> To be seen
> But refuse [to supply]
> The needs of one's neighbour (Q107:4–7)

3 WOMEN AND THE FAMILY

Kartini Day

Kartini Day commemorates the birth of Raden Adjeng Kartini (1879–1904) on 21 April 1879. She was an early proponent of education for women and is celebrated as a role model for female emancipation.

Two *khutbah* written for Kartini Day give an insight into Islam's equivocal approach to women's issues. First, Baidlowi Syamsuri (No. 5 in Appendix A4.1) acknowledges that the New Order government provided educational opportunities for females that greatly enhanced the status of women. As a pioneer of women's participation in education, Kartini can take much of the credit for this. Islam too supports women's right to an education, because respect for and participation in education is an essential element in Islamic thought and Muslim tradition. Education is a basic human right for all human beings, including women.

However, there are limits to the emancipation of women from an Islamic perspective. A woman may hold a high position in society but she must not neglect or ignore the essential femaleness of her nature. It is the nature of the male to be dominant in certain respects. The author's authority for this is Q2:228, especially the last sentence, which is often cited as demonstrating the equality of men and women:

> ... And women shall have rights
> Similar to the rights against them,
> According to what is equitable;
> But men have a degree
> Of advantage over them

Although the male is the head of the family, this does not prevent women from holding positions of reponsibility:

> Whoever works righteousness,
> Man or Woman, and has Faith,
> Verily ... will We give,
> A new life ...

We will bestow on such their reward
According to the best
Of their actions (Q16:97)

Neverthless, this does not overcome the issue of the essential difference between men and women. In particular, the Western concept of feminism disregards the status of women in Islam and is a betrayal of Indonesian women. Accepting it is to accept the possibility of renewed foreign dominance and the destruction of national morality. (By this time Kartini has got rather lost.)

The second *khutbah* discussed here is by Abd. Hamid Zahwan (No. 11 in Appendix A4.1). He portrays Kartini as a humble and thoughtful woman who dedicated her life to nurturing the spirit of nationalism among Indonesian women. She was also pious; because she did not understand Arabic herself, she persuaded 'Kyai Shalih from Semarang' to translate the Qur'ān into Javanese, and immediately circulated the translation for the general benefit. Her real impulse, therefore, was to advance religious education, especially among women. At this point, the author inserts a small portion of Q58:11:

[God will] ... Raise up ... those of you
Who believe and have
Been granted knowledge

Moving on to the question of the equality of men and women, the author says that men and women can be partners but are not equal as such:

Men are the protectors
And maintainers of women
Because God has given
The one more strength
Than the other ... (Q4:34)

The author observes that, as part of revelation, this passage is immutable; it in no way humiliates women. Both men and women are equally entitled to knowledge (Q58:11), but women have gone too far in pursuing emancipation, by demanding equality in male activities such as football, weight lifting and body building. These activities violate a woman's feminine nature, as do those of career women who compete with men and neglect their families.[21] In many cases, men end up doing jobs normally done by women, a reversal of the natural order.

Women in Society

At the same time, Abd. Hamid Zahwan (No. 11 in Appendix A4.1) is well aware of the forces of social change, the subject of his *khutbah* on 'The Emancipation of Women' and 'Mothers Day'. The author accepts social change as a fact of life

---

21 Women who work are a constant source of anxiety for Muslim orthodoxy. See Hooker (2003a: 127–8) on *fatāwā* that demonstrate this point.

and, indeed, says that Islam welcomes it. However, the pressures it imposes on the emotional nature of the female are such that they may threaten her ability to cope with day-to-day life. By observing the Qur'ānic injunctions, women can protect themselves against the uncertainties and difficulties of modern life. These difficulties are compounded when a wife and mother works outside the home. While there is historical precedent for working mothers in early Islam, and the practice can therefore be justified, this does not mean that it is automatically justified for women to pursue a career. Necessity, not personal pleasure, is a justification for having a career, but even here the agreement of the husband is necessary. In addition, while working outside the home, the wife and mother still has a duty to maintain her personal and moral integrity (Q4:34).

One way in which a Muslim woman can do this is to wear a headscarf (*jilbab*).[22] According to a *khutbah* on the *jilbab* by Hidayatul Muin in Mustofa W. Hasyim (No. 13 in Appendix A4.1), to avoid sexual exploitation—one of the consequences of modernity—it is more than ever necessary that a woman wear a headscarf. However, women who dress properly (Islamically) are often subject to harassment. For example, young women applying for admission to university are required to have their photograph taken without a headscarf. This denies them the right to carry out their religious obligation to dress modestly:

> ... They [wives and daughters] should cast
> Their outer garments over
> Their persons (when abroad): ... (Q33:59)

On a similar theme, in 'The Impact of Free Sex' Effendi Zarkasi (No. 6 in Appendix A4.1) claims that women are routinely mistreated and abused (including sexually). He gives three reasons for this. First, women are considered sexual commodities. While the sex drive is natural, it must be exercised subject to the strictures of religion. This means that sexual relations should take take place within marriage, which protects the lineage of the family (Q3:14, though this seems an inappropriate reference).

Second, women themselves must bear some responsibility for the way in which they are treated because they wear provocative clothing and aspire to have careers. Indeed, to be successful, women are required ('by the boss') to dress provocatively; women who dress modestly may lose their jobs and the possibility of advancement. Nevertheless, modesty is required for both males and females:

> Say to the believing men
> That they should lower their gaze and guard
> Their modesty ...
> And say to the believing women

---

22 On the *jilbab* and the headscarf debate, see Hooker (2003b: 126–7, 130–3, 258–9) and Fealy and Hooker (2006: 326–31).

> That they should lower their gaze and guard
> Their modesty ... (Q24:30–31)

Third, many parents do not supervise their daughters properly, permitting them to go out with young men. Daughters need supervision because 'they follow their desires rather than their reason'. As females, they are easily tempted. It is here that the mother is so vital to family and society. It is the duty of a Muslim to respect, honour and obey his or her mother because:

> ... In pain did his mother
> Bear him, and in pain
> Did she give him birth ... (Q46:15)

It is through obedience to one's mother that the individual's goodness and general morals take shape, and with them the person's chances of entering Paradise. The consequences for the individual in both this life and the next are therefore enormous. At the same time, the mother must be a 'good' mother, paying attention to the psychological development of her children.

But what does it mean to be a 'good' woman? The *khutbah* surveyed in this chapter commonly give two answers to this. The first is that the 'good' woman fulfils her religious obligations as a Muslim. Thus Ghufron Maba (No. 15 in Appendix A4.1) (selectively) cites Q2:228,

> ... And women shall have rights ...,

to show that Islam provides for the equality of men and women, and Q16:97 to show that men and women will equally enjoy the rewards due to all humankind:

> We will bestow on such their reward
> According to the best
> Of their actions

As well as fulfilling her religious duties, the 'good' woman fulfils her duties to society and the state. In a *khutbah* on the role of women in development, for example, Drs. Sholihin Syaqiq and Drs. Sufyana M. Bakri (No. 22 in Appendix A4.1) argue that Q2:228 gives women a role outside the home where they can actively participate in the development process. However, women's role in development is limited by her function as a wife and mother. At most she can be complementary to the male, although this should not be taken as denigrating the importance of her contribution. Here the authors cite Q16:97 (above) and Q30:21:

> ... He created
> For you mates from among
> Yourselves, that you may
> Dwell in tranquillity with them,
> And He has put love
> And mercy between you ...

In short, the good woman builds a moral family and participates in the betterment of society, subject to the needs of her family and the consent of her husband.

Another approach to the question of the role of women in society is to show the deficiencies of competing religions and ideologies and, hence, the superiority of the Islamic position. In a *khutbah* called 'Building a Faith-based Household', for example, Syahminan Zaini (No. 7 in Appendix A4.1) claims that only the syariah provides a suitable framework for women's rights. Hindu women have a low or servile status, no property rights and may even be required to perform *sati*, as used to happen in Bali. Confucian women had their feet bound to confine them to the home. Christian women are also subjugated to men: 'neither was the man created for the woman, but the woman for the man' (I Corinthians 11:9). The main part of the *khutbah* is devoted to the Women's Liberation movement in the United States in the 1970s. The author says that this was necessary because the status of American women was so low. There is no such movement in Indonesia because the progressiveness of Islam on women's issues renders it pointless and unnecessary. For example, polygamy (with due safeguards) is rational and progressive because it prevents illicit sex, prostitution and social moral degradation. The 2:1 rule in favour of the male in inheritance matters is equally progressive because of the greater responsibilities borne by men (Q4:11). In summary, Islam provides a practical and moral superiority in ordinary life that has been ordained by God.

Sex, Marriage and the Family

Three *khutbah* on sexual relations outside marriage all agree that this is sinful as well as having socially undesirable consequences. In 'The Prohibition on the Free Mixing of the Sexes', Ahmad Sunarto (No. 2 in Appendix A4.1) paints a picture of dereliction of parental responsibility in allowing the sexes to mix freely. Both parents are at fault but the main weight of blame falls on the mother, especially in respect of her daughters. In 'The Prohibition against Free Sex between Men and Women', Moh. Abdai Rathomy (No. 3 in Appendix A4.1) takes a more theological line, arguing that believers must accept the whole of the Islamic religion, not pick and choose those parts that suit their preferences. This applies just as much to sexual relations as to any other part of Islamic teachings. Muslims must therefore adhere to the syariah; not to do so is to diminish the primacy of revelation. Finally, in a *khutbah* on 'Unlawful Sex', Ustadz Labib Mz. (No. 23 in Appendix A4.1) emphasizes the consequences of sin in this life: poverty and social disaster.

It is interesting to note the diversity of these three responses to sexual relations outside marriage, despite their use of the same Qur'ānic citations to sustain their arguments (Q17:32; Q9:72; Q66:6; Q24:30). These citations can be shown to be appropriate in each case, and have in common an emphasis on responsibility, primarily to God and secondarily to humankind. But is this always true;

cannot the latter sometimes take precedence? To answer this question, I look at *khutbah* specifically on marriage and the family, an area in which it is particularly difficult to translate revelation into workable rules for the whole of society.

Baidlowi Syamsuri (No. 5 in Appendix A4.1) places the responsibility for creating a good marriage on the woman. She does this by showing obedience to her husband in all matters, from sex to finance to not leaving the house without permission. There is only one Qur'ānic reference (Q4:34) in this simply expressed *khutbah*.

A more complex *khutbah* on the harmonious family by Drs. Moh. Amin (No. 18 in Appendix A4.1) begins with the well-known and often cited Q30:21:

> ... He created
> For you mates from among
> Yourselves that you may
> Dwell in tranquillity with them ...

That is, the individual should control his or her sexual desires and have only known (legitimate) offspring. But in real life much may go wrong, perhaps through one's own fault or perhaps because it is the will of God. One must bear the good along with the bad:

> ... But it is possible
> That you dislike a thing
> Which is good for you
> And that you desire a thing
> Which is bad for you ... (Q2:216)

The author interprets this verse as meaning that a marriage must be a harmonious affair. The husband does his duty (as provider) and the wife hers (by being obedient). From these rather trite comments, the author goes on to list the specific characteristics of a harmonious family: that all members of the family understand and perform their religious duties; that they develop good psychological relationships with each other; that they are competent financially; and that they restrain or control their emotions and submit to God (Q24:36).

In the *khutbah* on parental responsibility that follows, the author sets out a number of recommendations for couples. The first is to carry out the appropriate ablutions and prayers before intercourse, so that God will bless the couple with children. The parents of a child have four duties. The first is to educate the child in religion while demonstrating a consistently high standard of behaviour, because children learn through word and deed. This is a serious duty with serious consequences:

> Save yourselves and your
> Families from fire ... (Q66:6)

Second, parents must themselves carry out their religious duties (prayer, fasting, acting with honesty and tolerance and so on). Third, parents must act as a 'human resource' for their children, the next generation. In building the character of their children, they must be aware that psychology, ecology and environment all play an important role in the development of a proper religious consciousness. Finally, parents should understand the psychological phases of child development so that religious instruction can be given in a suitable form at the appropriate time.

Marriage is based on agreement and entered into by contract. However, as Drs. H. Ahmad Yani (No. 17 in Appendix A4.1) points out in 'Building an Islamic Family', it is by no means easy to fulfil the terms of that contract. There must be mutual love and affection between a husband and a wife, not for its own sake but to achieve a happy and harmonious family (Q30:21 above, the standard citation). Marital problems must be kept within the family and not broadcast publicly:

> ... that
> They may learn self-restraint (Q2:187)

Excessive individualism is to be avoided. The same principles are stated by Moh. Syamsi Hasan and Achmad Ma'ruf Asrori (No. 8 in Appendix A4.1) in their *khutbah* on the Muslim family; it contains the usual citations (Q2:228; Q4:34–35).

What, then, can we make of this material? It is clear that family values and personal morality are of primary importance for all the authors of the *khutbah*. The only certainty in the modern world is that political and economic circumstances will continue to change. Returning to the basics of religion is the obvious answer to these dilemmas. But it would be remiss to leave it at that—the material we have summarized here is rather more subtle than this.

Because of their centrality, issues related to women and the family clearly invite, indeed demand, responses that are not necessarily consistent with, but mirror the tensions in, syariah values. As one might expect, the *khutbah* portray women as stereotypes and there is heavy emphasis on orthopraxy (clothing, maternal duty). The authors are also very selective in their Qur'ānic citations, usually to justify their own points of view. But there is also equivocation in selection, especially in the case of Hadith. The same citations are given different emphases or, less commonly, different interpretations. This suggests that the syariah values being espoused are themselves uncertain, and in a state of flux.

4   ISLAM (SYARIAH) IN SOCIETY

The *khutbah* examined in this section show the extraordinary breadth of the subjects covered in the material. Taken together, they illustrate how formidable the *khutbah* genre can be in social and political matters. The sheer range of topics is important, because it situates the Qur'ān at the centre of Indonesian life, politically, socially and personally.

Charity

Charity is a popular subject among the *khutbah* collections, where it is viewed as a duty to God as well as a way of helping those in need. All Muslims have a duty to pay *zakat*—the annual tax for charitable purposes—although many avoid this obligation. The rate by convention in Indonesia (and Malaysia) is 2.5 per cent of annual disposable income. The method of payment raises difficulties, because the Qur'ān is quite specific about the times of payment and the classes of donor (Q2:177). In Indonesia, the government has attempted to standardize and control *zakat* payments, with only moderate success.

It was Nawawi al-Bantani who, in the nineteenth century, set the agenda for the payment of *zakat* in Indonesia today. In 'The Value of Charity' (No. 12 in Appendix A4.1) he maintains that *zakat* has three functions, all stemming from Q3:180:

> And let not those
> Who selfishly withhold
> Of the gifts which God
> Has given them of His Grace
> Think that it is good for them;
> No, it will be the worse
> For them ...

The first and most important function is to purify the individual donor by eliminating greed and egoism. Paying *zakat* encourages a sense of personal responsibility and will be rewarded in the afterlife by God. The second function is to help the poor, and the third is to contribute to social harmony. Nawawi pays particular attention to the first function, emphasizing the benefits to the individual of carrying out the duty to pay *zakat*. State intervention disrupts this process, a view reiterated by contemporary *fatāwā* (Hooker 2003a: 80 ff.).

The same argument can be found in a *khutbah* on 'Social Disparity' by Effendi Zarkasi (No. 6 in Appendix A4.1). He says that non-payment of *zakat* is an indication of greed and moral impropriety, and will be judged as such by God (Q3:139). Muslims are commanded by God to practise charity:

> And they have been commanded ...
> To practise regular charity ... (Q98:5)

Ustadz Labib Mz. (No. 23 in Appendix A4.1) agrees that the believer is someone who:

> ... [Is] active in deeds
> Of charity ... (Q23:4)

Like Nawawi, he emphasizes the rewards from God for proper performance of one's duty to pay *zakat*, both in the hereafter (Q2:274) and in this world (Q34:39; Q2:261).

In a more scholarly rendition of the same point, Drs. H. Ahmad Yani (No. 17 in Appendix A4.1) begins by pointing out that *zakat* is one of the five pillars of Islam, along with prayer (Q98:5). Muslims who do not pay *zakat* are not true Muslims:

> But (even so), if they repent,
> Establish regular prayers
> And practise regular charity,
> They are your brethren in faith ... (Q9:11)

The purpose of *zakat* is to reduce greed, a characteristic of mankind that interposes itself between man and God. It is this barrier which must be removed:

> Truly, man was created
> Impatient,
> Fretful when evil
> Touches him
> And ungenerous when
> Good comes to him (Q70:19–21)

Those who do not carry out their duty to pay *zakat* will be punished (Q9:34–35) and the *zakat* debt owing at death will certainly be questioned by God (Q63:11). The author is clear about the social consequences of greed, which diminishes humanity:

> ... But that which you lay out
> For charity, seeking
> The countenance of God
> Will increase ... (Q30:39)

But the main benefit of *zakat* is that it provides a path towards piety:

> ... Those who spend their substance
> In the way of God
> [to them] God gives manifold increase
> To whom He pleases ... (Q2:261)

The payment of *zakat* is thus an exercise in faith so that one may approach God (Q91:9–10).

The social aspects of *zakat* emphasized by Nawawi in the nineteenth century are a major concern of later *khutbah* collections as well. In '*Zakat*', for example, Abd. Hamid Zahwan (No. 11 in Appendix A4.1) emphasizes that the purpose of *zakat* is not only to relieve poverty, but also to create a sense of social solidarity and promote social justice. Muslims should not think of *zakat* as simply giving money away, as would one give a present to a child, but rather as a way of achieving social welfare:

> But truly the Lord is
> Full of Grace to mankind:
> Yet most of them are ungrateful (Q27:73)

God requires all believers to attend to those who are disadvantaged; no one should live in luxury while others live in poverty (Q104:1–4; Q102:1–2).

The same point is made by Moh. Syamsi Hasan and Achmad Ma'ruf Asrori (No. 8 in Appendix A4.1), who say that one of the defining aspects of Islam is that it embraces social issues such as poverty. *Zakat* plays a fundamental role in this respect (Q19:103). Taxable income is income from any source, except improper sources such as alcohol and gambling. The authors support the introduction of some sort of professional administration for *zakat* so that a general benefit can be derived. (In fact this already exists, although its efficacy remains in doubt.)

Finally, Ahmad Sunarto (No. 2 in Appendix A4.1) sees *zakat* as a way of helping to bridge the gap between rich and poor, that is, as a method of redistribution.

Orphans are the object of charity most commonly mentioned in the *khutbah* collections. I have space for just a few examples. First, Ustadz Labib Mz. (No. 19 in Appendix A4.1) gives a straightforward account of the need to preserve an orphan's assets (Q6:152) and prevent abuse or corruption in the management of those assets (Q4:10). In both 'Helping Orphans and Preventing Abuse of Their Assets' (No. 1 in Appendix A4.1) and 'The Unfortunate (Disadvantaged) in the Community' (No. 16 in Appendix A4.1), Ahmad Sunarto emphasizes the need to protect and nurture orphans as a specific class of the poor and disadvantaged. The main emphasis in the earlier *khutbah* is on the need for continuing supervision to help the orphaned child grow to a proper maturity; the need to preserve the property of the orphan is also mentioned (Q4:2; Q4:10; Q6:122, Q6:152). The second *khutbah* emphasizes the social benefits of caring for the poor in general and orphans in particular, namely the promotion of peace, tolerance and harmony (Q70:24–25).

Relationships with Other Muslims and with Non-Muslims

In the wider social sphere, the *khutbah* collections concentrate on two types of relationships: those with neighbours (especially fellow Muslims) and those with non-Muslims. I take each in turn.

Relations with Muslims

All *khutbah* stress the need for harmonious relations with one's neighbours. This is a basic principle for Nawawi al-Bantani (No. 12 in Appendix A4.1), who cites Q49:10:

> The Believers are but
> A singe Brotherhood
> So make peace and
> Reconciliation ...

It is the duty of a good neighbour to be well mannered and offer practical help when necessary:

... And do good ...
[To] neighbours who are near,
Neighbours who are strangers ... (Q4:36)

In 'Maintaining and Strengthening the Islamic Fraternity', H.M. Hasan Abdul Qahar (No. 9 in Appendix A4.1) provides two theoretical underpinnings for this argument. First, Islam is inclusive; Muslims use 'we' and not 'I' when at prayer (Q1:5–7), for instance. And second, because of this, the function of syariah is to regulate the activities of people from different ethnic groups for the mutual benefit of society (Q22:77).[23]

In a *khutbah* called 'Interaction between Muslims', Abdullah Rasyid (No. 21 in Appendix A4.1) also emphasizes the importance of maintaining good neighbourly relations:

You who believe
... Spy not on each other
Nor speak ill of each other
Behind their backs ... (Q49:12)

In 'A Profile of Islamic Society', Drs. H. Ahmad Yani (No. 17 in Appendix A4.1) delves more deeply into the factors that characterize an Islamic society, whether it be the family, the immediate community or the nation. An Islamic society is defined as one in which Islam is implemented in all aspects of life, temporal and spiritual. Given that this is the purpose of the syariah, when syariah is implemented, an Islamic society exists (Q45:18). In such a society, syariah is the basic law (Q9:40); the values of its citizens are derived from the Qur'ān and the Sunnah; social ills like sexual relations outside marriage and pornography are forbidden; and, most importantly, the citizens follow the word of God (Q24:55). The result will be the creation of an alternative to secular society with all its ills.

M.A. Fuadi Sya'ban (No. 4 in Appendix A4.1) makes a similar point—in a rather unusual way—in a *khutbah* called '"Socializing" the Qur'ān and "Qur'ānizing" Society'. The author claims that a number of surveys conducted in 1982 by the Indonesian Institute of Sciences (Lembaga Ilmu Pengetahuan Indonesia; LIPI) show that those surveyed spent 75 per cent of their time working or sleeping, about 20 per cent of their time relaxing and only 4.4 per cent engaged in religious activities including prayer. Moreover, while 46 per cent of teenagers took religion seriously, 35 per cent did not and 19 per cent were ambivalent. On the basis of these findings (which were recent when the collection was published in 1985), the author predicts the impending collapse of Islamic society in Indonesia. The remedy is to make the Qur'ān and Qur'ānic study central to daily life in households, schools and public institutions, in short to 'Qur'ānize' society across the nation.

---

23 This reference seems inappropriate; he may mean Q22:78.

The logical progression is to call for the whole community of Muslims (*ukhuwah Islamiyah*) to pull together—to demonstrate intrafaith solidarity. Some *khutbah* go no further than this, simply recommending intrafaith solidarity as part of one's duty to God. But there are also more thoughtful accounts, and it is with these that we are concerned here. In a series of *khutbah*—'The Islamic Fraternity', 'The Muslim as an Example for Other Muslims' and 'The Characteristics of a Muslim'—Drs. Sholihin Syaqiq and Drs. Ii Sufyana M. Bakri (No. 22 in Appendix A4.1) comment that the concept of intrafaith solidarity is often discussed but rarely implemented in practice. In politics, for example, conflict is rife among Muslims. This has been a feature of Islamic history, and continues today at both the local and national levels. The solution is to return to the Qur'ān. Muslims must reject unjustified suspicions of the motives of others (Q49:12). They must also put aside their feelings of superiority over other Muslims (Q49:11), particularly where these spill over into intra-Muslim politics. Divisions such as those between 'traditionalists' and 'modernists' only do harm to Muslims. Equally, differences in ritual practice should be tolerated and not labelled deviance.

Relations with Non-Muslims

Although Muslims have a clear duty towards other Muslims, their attitudes towards non-Muslims are much more complex. This is apparent in the strength with which *khutbah* authors express their views on the non-Muslim world.

In a *khutbah* called 'Islam from the Perspective of the Infidel', K.H. Effendi Zarkasi (No. 6 in Appendix A4.1) accuses non-Muslims of ignorance and prejudice. Their equation of Islam with poverty, violence and conflict is based partly on historical memory (the Muslim expansion in Europe) and partly on the chaotic politics of the contemporary era. But terror and violence are not inherently part of Islam; they are found in all societies. The arrogance of the West originated with the Jews, who rejected the authenticity of Muhammad's Prophethood on spurious grounds and have been attacking Islam ever since:

> Never will the Jews
> Or the Christians be satisfied
> ... unless you follow
> Their form of religion ... (Q2:120)

It is the duty of Muslims not only to resist such attacks, including military attacks, but also to educate non-Muslims in the truth.

Moh. Abdai Rathomy (No. 3 in Appendix A4.1) expresses the relationship between good Muslims and 'others' in terms of struggle (*jihad*): an external *jihad* against non-Muslims (Q2:120), and an internal *jihad* against Muslims who deny their faith, neglect orphans, do not show charity and so on (Q106:1–4). At the same time, a degree of tolerance towards Jews and Christians in particular is possible.

Given the heterogeneous nature of Indonesian society, in a *khutbah* called 'Relations with Non-Muslims' H. Mulyadi (No. 13 in Appendix A4.1) counsels tolerance towards non-Muslims:

> Revile not
> Those whom they call upon
> Besides God ... (Q6:108)

But although it is important for Muslims to develop harmonious relations with non-Muslims, they must also remain true to Islam. This means observing certain rules of conduct, including dietary rules. Most importantly, Muslims should not participate in non-Muslim rituals such as prayers, funerals or festivals (Q109:1–4). The author mentions, but does not cite, *fatāwā* from the Indonesian Council of Ulama (Majelis Ulama Indonesia; MUI) and Muhammadiyah on this point.[24]

Ustadz Labib Mz. (No. 19 in Appendix A4.1) also counsels tolerance and good manners. In a *khutbah* called 'The Neighbourhood', he recommends avoiding religious debate as one way of maintaining good relations with non-Muslims:

> And dispute you not
> With the people of the Book ... (Q39:46)

Doctrine, Modernity and Science

One of the major contemporary questions for Muslims is the relationship between rationality (or science) and revelation. For one view of the nature of reason, we can look to Syahminan Zaini (No. 7 in Appendix A4.1), who provides a complex explanation of science, body and spirit. He begins 'Scientific Authentication of the Creation of the Body and the Existence of the Spirit' by asserting that God has endowed man with the capacity to reason. The exercise of reason is therefore a duty for the educated. For the uneducated, it is sufficient to have a simple faith, even if this leads to folk Islam. Although such distortions must be discouraged, variation is a natural part of life:

> ... God sends down rain
> From the sky [...] With it
> We then bring out produce
> Of various colours.
> And in the mountains
> Are traces of white and red
> Of various shades of colour ... (Q35:27)

This verse is usually interpreted as showing the beneficence of God in man's agricultural endeavours and in forming the natural beauty of the landscape.

---

24 See Hooker (2003a: 157) for *fatāwā* on Muslim participation in non-Muslim ritual.

Here, however, it is used metaphorically to show that the flowering of reason is a gift from God. This is reinforced by Q58:11:

> ... Make room ...
> God will raise up to suitable ranks
> Those of you who believe and who have
> Been granted knowledge ...

The author explicitly rejects the contrary view, that Muslims must unquestioningly accept the pronouncements (*taqlid*) made by previous scholars, on the basis of several citations. He begins by citing part of the well-known verse Q31:21:

> ... No, we shall follow
> The ways that we found
> Our fathers following ...

This is followed by Q21:53–54 in which God praises the conduct of Abraham:

> They said: 'We found
> Our fathers worshipping them'
> He said: 'Indeed you
> Have been in manifest
> Error' ...

and Q8:22:

> For the worst of beasts
> In the sight of God
> Are the deaf and dumb,
> Those who understand not

It is therefore the duty of the *'ulamā'* to pursue knowledge so as to be able to understand the truths of Islam. *Taqlid* is not an answer that suits the needs of our times.

At this point the *khutbah* takes an unexpected turn, with the author claiming that Western science *proves* the truth of revelation. He introduces an eclectic selection of discoveries made by (mainly obscure) Western scientists to support his case.[25] This is a dangerous road to take because it subjects revelation to the test of proof—even though God is not provable and revelation does not need proof in this sense. At the same time, it is easy to see why the author would be tempted to follow this line of argument, especially given the prevalence of secularism in the contemporary world. For the author, the secular world, with its emphasis on the material and its lack of (revealed) morality, demonstrates the need to bring moral values to the search for knowledge; one must seek knowl-

---

25 I have been able to identify only one of the scientists cited: Alexis Carrell (1873–1944), who was awarded the Nobel Prize in 1912 for his invention of a method of joining blood vessels. He is credited by our author with proving that man was created from a clod of earth, obviously a reference to Q15:28–29.

edge but the search can never be value-free. Science and revelation are therefore complementary, not opponents.

In 'Religion as a Remedy for Psychological Disorders' (No. 13 in Appendix A4.1), Aries Muthohar cites Western authorities to show that there is a high rate of psychiatric disorders in Western society. He says this is caused by the absence of religion. Religion is essential:

> I only created
> Jinns and men, that
> They may serve me (Q51:56)

Reason is dependent on faith, which alone provides the certainty and serenity necessary to ensure entry to Paradise (Q89:28–30).

Drs. H. Ahmad Yani (No. 17 in Appendix A4.1) makes a similar point about the high rates of mental illness in Western society and the role of faith in avoiding such illnesses, but cites different verses (Q13:28; 2:214; 3:126). He also cautions against 'pseudo-spiritualities', although he does not specify what these are.

K.H. Effendi Zarkasi (No. 6 in Appendix A4.1) provides two *khutbah* on what could be called the pseudo-spiritualities of sorcery (*perdukunan*) and astrology: 'Back to God's Path' and 'The Spiritual Practitioner'. The first stresses that the practice of sorcery is forbidden. The author says that he understands the motives driving people to consult these practitioners—fear and insecurity—but it is nevertheless forbidden:

> And we pried into
> The secrets of heaven;
> But we found it filled
> With ... flaming fires.
> ... Who listens now
> Will find a flaming fire
> Watching him ... (Q72:8)

The author comes to a similar conclusion about people who consult horoscopes. It is not only unscientific but also a denial of revelation (Q13:11) to think that one's time of birth can be a guide to one's character and the future.

5   THE CENTRALITY OF THE QUR'ĀN

There is no disputing the centrality of the Qur'ān in the *khutbah*. But what does this actually mean? One answer is that it means that most of the topics covered in the *khutbah* are sourced from the Qur'ān—but that is to state the obvious. If it means, in addition, that the Qur'ān determines prescription, then this is clearly not true for the authors of the *khutbah* or, for that matter, those who issue *fatāwā*. The *khutbah* surveyed in this chapter demonstrate, rather, that the Qur'ān has been sidelined in favour of an all-pervasive 'state Islam' (see Chapter 1)—although I believe that this sidelining is more apparent than real. The *khutbah* have a wide circulation and must be taken seriously; they are no longer confined to the mosque.[26] It is in this context of shifting interpretations of the Qur'ān, then, that the Qur'ān is central.

This is not a new observation; in his classic study of sermons in Jordan, Antoun (1989: 243) speaks of interpretations of the Qur'ān as using 'terms that can be construed as relating to degrees of religious commitment, indicating the movement from peripheral to central ...'. This is certainly true of the material surveyed in this chapter.

Importantly, all the *khutbah* collections aim to be *literary* models while also being usable in oral form. The ideal of a literary model (introduced at the beginning of this chapter) has come to dominate the genre. This model has two interconnected aspects. First, the fact that a *khutbah* is written changes the way in which information is imparted. This is apparent in a certain degree of standardization among the *khutbah*, in the verses from the Qur'ān that are cited, for example. Of course, some verses (especially from Q2) are so basic that they will always be cited, but this is by no means the whole explanation. In addition, a degree of mutual consultation and cross-referencing seems to be going on. The permanency imparted by publication adds an extra dimension to this. The texts may be useful as models for the *khatib*, but they are also bought by individuals and study groups as reference books and for private study. The mosque is no longer the only context for the *khutbah*. This is significant, because it is possible that the increased availability of published collections will accelerate the process of standardization.

The second aspect is the background of the authors of the *khutbah*. Who are the *khatib* or, more broadly, the *'ulamā'* who write the *khutbah*?[27] Even a brief glance at the material in this chapter shows that the majority of the authors have a tertiary education in Islamic studies. Many are graduates of the country's IAIN. They commonly buttress their Qur'ānic citations with material taken from outside sources, including science and Western commentary and analysis. The fact that the *khutbah* collections do not confine themselves wholly to the discourse of religion has the advantage of imparting vigour, but it also has the possible drawback of reducing the Qur'ān to just a reference text. This is a real danger; some of the topic-based collections examined above demonstrate this.

We pursue these two issues through an examination of *Beragama di Abad Dua Satu: Serial Khutbah Kontemporer I* [Religiosity in the Twenty-first Century: Contemporary *Khutbah* Series I] (No. 24 in Appendix A4.1). Edited by H.A. Syafi'i Mufid and Munawar Fuad Noeh, its 15 model *khutbah*—all by graduates

---

26 The bulk of the material is published in Surabaya and Jakarta but copies are available in Muslim bookshops throughout Indonesia.

27 The background of the scholars who issue *fatāwā* is described by Hooker (2003a: 245).

of IAIN or Western universities—encapsulate the question of Qur'ānic central-ity.[28] In their introduction, the editors say that the oral *khutbah* delivered in the mosque generally fail to address the important issues of the day; often descend into platitudes and extremism; and tend to be predictable, uninformative and overly legalistic. These are serious criticisms, but are they justified? Well, yes, up to a point. Most of the *khutbah* on women and the family are indeed platitu-dinous, and some of those on Muslim–non-Muslim relations are extreme. The *khutbah* also demonstrate a high degree of predictability, although this is not necessarily a fault. After all, the *khutbah* are meant to provide reassurance, to proclaim certainty in a changing world. But there are also plenty of exceptions to these generalizations, as indicated in the body of this chapter.

The editors go on to make a further point: that the main function of the *khutbah* should be education in social issues. This is not new, and many of the authors surveyed in this chapter already do this. For example, while many *khutbah* predictably preach the value of giving children an education in Islam (doctrine and so on), some also include the necessity for competence in secular subjects (within the framework of Islam). A noteworthy contribution is a *khut-bah* called 'Islam and the Challenge of the Changing World' by Drs. Imron Abu Amar (No. 14 in Appendix A4.1). The author identifies an education in Islam as vital in helping Muslims cope with the challenges posed by modern technology, because it provides an essential moral foundation. He quotes a 'famous' (uniden-tified) *'alim* as saying:

Islam neither follows nor opposes change, but supervises it.

In other words, Islam provides a basic reference point for Muslims experiencing the difficulties of change—but note that in this case the author does not support this proposition with citations from the Qur'ān.

The question is what the *khutbah* must do to be 'transformed and reformed' as the *Beragama* editors say it should. To address this, they propose a series of textbooks on various themes to serve as model *khutbah*. This may appear to be similar to the approach of the topic-based collections, but there is one signifi-cant difference—that the editors consciously propose a method to bridge the gap between Islam and its expression in society. This method consists of (a) adher-ence to the principles and values of religion, (b) in a form suitable for respond-ing to social issues in contemporary Indonesian Islam. Difficult issues are to be approached by way of social science data (that is, what is actually happening), assessed and valued through the truths of the Qur'ān and the Sunnah. The latter must be read in its historical context. In short, the method is based on revelation, the history of Islam, and the social and political sciences. The result will be an objective and complete response to any given issue, not the emotional, partial or

---

28 Rosidi (2003) provides a similar collection of model *khutbah* on civil society and governance.

subjective one of the existing texts. The driving motive is to state prescription from the Qur'ān (and Sunnah) in a modern form.

We have to be a little careful here about what we mean by 'modern'. The Qur'ān is not modern; it is timeless—quite another state. Human understanding of the Qur'ān, however, does exist in historical time (Madjid 1979, 1987, 1997). It is therefore necessary to distinguish between 'modern' and 'modernization'. As Antoun (1989: 128) points out in his discussion of the Jordan *khutbah*, today's *khatib* are often in favour of 'modernization' without being in favour of all that is modern, including the trend towards secularization. As I understand it, his view is that most *khatib* understand the circumstances of modern (contemporary) life and express this understanding in their *khutbah*. In them, they acknowledge the value of a secular education alongside the value of a knowledge of Islam. While both are necessary, an overemphasis on the former can lead to excess, and damage the social fabric. Both sets of data essentially depend on the Qur'ān, which is the ultimate source in each case; discussion of both is therefore accompanied by multiple citations from the Qur'ān. This is certainly true of the Indonesian material, and no doubt of material elsewhere as well.

The first *khutbah* in the *Beragama* collection is by Nurcholish Madjid, a leading theoretician of Islam in Indonesia. His subject is the role of Islam in building a strong civil society (*masyarakat madani*) in Indonesia. He opens with an abridged version of Q12:39–41:

> To those against whom
> War is made, permission
> Is given to fight, because
> They are wronged ...
> In defiance of right ...
> ... Did not God
> Oppose one set of people
> By means of another,
> There would have been
> Destroyed monasteries, churches
> Synagogues and mosques in which
> The name of God is commemorated ...
> [Those] who
> If we establish them
> In the land, make
> Regular prayer and
> Give charity, enjoin
> The right and forbid wrong ...

Again, to the same effect:

> ... And did not God
> Check one set of people
> By means of another
> The earth would indeed
> Be full of mischief ... (Q2:251)

A civil society is therefore one in which pluralism is accepted as the norm and right conduct is founded in Islam (Q41:33). This leads to justice and benefits for mankind (Q57:25; Q23:51). But those who fail to live up to their responsibilities in this area will suffer the consequences:

> After them came
> An evil generation; they
> Inherited the Book but
> They chose ...
> The vanities of this world ...

This *khutbah* sets the tone for the 14 that follow. At the risk of overgeneralization, one might say that what they have in common is an emphasis on the Qur'ān as constituting a personal moral philosophy for contemporary life. 'Liberal' (that is, secular) society has failed to uphold or promote personal moral values. Only Islam can do this, because revelation alone is the universal source of all moral values. However, cultivating moral values in society requires a degree of purpose and self-awareness.

In practice this is achieved in three interconnected ways. First, pluralism (and, thus, tolerance) is essential. In 'The Universal Islamic Mission in Developing a Religious Society', Drs. Abul Basit picks up the theme of the differences between, and need for tolerance among, people of different faiths:[29]

> Never will the Jews
> Or the Christians be satisfied
> ... unless you follow
> Their form of religion ... (Q2:120)

> And in the books
> Given to Moses, Jesus
> And the Prophets
> From their Lord:
> We make no distinction
> Between one and another
> Among them ... (Q3:85)

> ... 'People of the Book come
> To common terms
> As between us and you ...' (Q3:64)

Pluralism in religion is a fact of life and need not be negative; indeed, it can be positive both for the individual and for society. The same theme of tolerance and harmony is continued by Akhmad Roziqin, who cites Q6:108 and especially Q22:40 (a popular choice of other authors as well):

---

29 On the same point, there is an interesting discussion in Glenn (2000: 41–5) on 'commensurability' and 'communicable traditions', citing a range of modern Western jurisprudence.

> ... Did not God
> Check one set of people
> By means of another ...

Second, and following on from this, the 'other' (people, nations) also poses dangers. Urban society in particular is vulnerable to outside, including foreign, influences, not all of which are morally desirable. This is the theme of a *khutbah* by Mastuki on 'The Religious Orientation of the Urban Class'. The argument is partly based on Q49:13:

> ... And made you into
> Nations and tribes, that
> You may know each other ...

Other references are to Q3:112 and Q17:44. Difference is to be accepted, but theological difference is another matter. Secularism, which flourishes in the urban environment and in the West, is the main danger.

The final element in living a moral life is work: the capacity to work and succeed in the modern world. M. Samsul Hady, Zaenudin BK and Abdul Rozak take up this theme in *khutbah* on leadership, managing one's career and the work ethic. The Qur'ānic citations are the ones we would expect (Q2:213; Q3:131; Q4:128–9), and most have in fact already appeared earlier in this chapter.

The cumulative effect of the collection is to show that Islamic social ethics and personal morals are not inconsistent with modernity. That is, the Qur'ān is central to modern issues, defined in this collection to include pluralism, (non-Muslim) ethics and work.

Does this approach represent the new method claimed by the editors? If by 'new' we mean a sharp break with the collections described earlier in this chapter, then the answer is 'no'. The Qur'ān remains central and the authors continue to cite non-Muslim authorities to a significant degree. All we can say at the moment is that this collection of model *khutbah* is rather more self-conscious about the concept of modernity than others. But even this must be qualified: the idea of organizing collections by topic is certainly not new.

One final question remains (and must remain unanswered until the necessary research has been done): what effect do the *khutbah* have on those who hear them and, now, read them? Do they actually influence daily conduct? At the very least, the *khutbah* provide instruction in religion and the Qur'ān and insist on the primacy of revelation. However, a fair degree of contextualization is also going on. The centrality of the Qur'ān now seems to be negotiable, at least to some degree.

We might call the *khutbah* genre 'soft' or 'informal' syariah. From a strictly formal (*fiqh*) point of view, it may appear to have little significance. However, to adopt this position is to ignore the fact that syariah values are transmitted to millions of people on a regular basis through the *khutbah*; this is how ordinary Muslims find out about their duty to God and their fellow Muslims.

The topics covered by the collections in Appendix A4.1 illustrate the public nature of duty. In them we can see two patterns of orthopraxy: overwhelmingly they focus on proper public behaviour and the indications or markers of a 'good' Muslim. These constitute a nexus between syariah and the values of daily public life. The *khutbah* also show a capacity to respond to the issues raised by the 'new' institution of the state. Thus, there is a common emphasis throughout the collections on national days that are not in the classical canon but are now given equal space alongside the religious days. In short, the *khatib* are responding in creative ways to the challenges posed by the secular Indonesian state, by turning secular points of reference into 'Islamic' references validated by the Qur'ān.

The *khatib* have also managed to preserve a fair degree of independence. Most of the texts in Appendix A4.1 were produced during the New Order period but they show little evidence of any slavish reproduction of the somewhat primitive state ideology of that time. On the contrary, the *khatib* continued to consider it part of their duty to criticize the state and its functionaries. For this reason, they have managed to retain a high degree of public confidence. Indonesia is often criticized for being a bureaucratic state, and so it is at some levels, but this should not be allowed to obscure the fact that it has never suppressed *fatāwā* or attempted to impose a standard form of *khutbah* in the mosques.[30]

The *khutbah* is given in the mosque, which is a sacred space for prayer.[31] The mosque is also a place for the dissemination of information on Islam, including argumentation.[32] What is not so widely realized, however, is that the mosque is also a business enterprise. Mosque management (*manajeman masjid*) is consciously discussed and debated in the most up-to-date terms.[33] Similarly, the authors of the written *khutbah* texts are in the Islamic publishing business. While their stated motive is to explain and advance Islam, a possible financial motivation, of which we are wholly ignorant, has to be borne in mind. The importance of commercial motives and commercial viability should never be underestimated.

---

30 Its near neighbour, Brunei, does exactly this, providing a set government text for each Friday sermon.
31 See Headley (1989) for Java.
32 Much of it in the form of pamphlets; see Fealy and Hooker (2006: 126, 147) for examples.
33 See, for example, Rifa'i and Fakhruroji (2005).

APPENDIX A4.1   THE *KHUTBAH* COLLECTIONS

In this appendix I give details of the sources used in the chapter. In each case, I provide a brief summary of the author's purpose in publishing the collection, followed by the table of contents.

No. 1
Ahmad Sunarto (1987), *Mutiara Khutbah* [*Khutbah* Pearls], Surabaya: Karyma Utama, 184 pp. [22 *khutbah*]

In a short preface, the author presents his collection as an aid to understanding Islam and begs the forgiveness of God for any errors.

Contents
The Strong Believer
Patience and Gratitude
Helping Orphans and Preventing Abuse of Their Assets
Increasing Virtuous Works
Adherence to Government and Leader
Engaging in the Worship of God
The Advantages of Exchanging Greetings
Avoiding Immoral Acts
Avoiding Arrogance
Real Happiness
The Characteristics of Hypocrisy
The Wickedness of Carnal Desire
The Advantages of Prayer (*Shalat*)
The Nobleness of the *'Ulamā'*
Fasting and Its Benefits
Khutbah for Idul Fitri
Khutbah for Idul Adha
Second Half of Every Friday Prayer *Khutbah* A
Second Half of Every Friday Prayer *Khutbah* B
Second Half of the *Khutbah* for Idul Fitri and Idul Adha

No. 2
Ahmad Sunarto (1992), *Himpunan Khutbah Jam'at dan Dua Hari Raya* [Collection of Friday *Khutbah* and Two Great Days], Jakarta: Pustaka Amani, 126 pp. [22 *khutbah*]

This collection is unusual in being divided into general *khutbah* and special *khutbah*. The aim of the collection is to 'develop a new style of speech', as reflected in the Table of Contents.

Contents

Part I: Delivering the *Khutbah*
a   Directives for Speaking
b   Requirements
c   Additional Directives

Part II: General *Khutbah*
a   Belief in God
b   Being Committed [to Islam] until Death
c   The Obligation to Work
d   The Prohibition on the Free Mixing of the Sexes
e   Daily Prayer
f   Collective Prayer
g   The Obligation to Give Alms

Part III: Special *Khutbah*
a   National Education Day, 2 May
b   National Awakening Day, 20 May
c   Sanctity of Pancasila Day, 1 October
d   Fasting and Its Benefits
e   Prayer at Night in Ramadan and Lailatul Qadar in Ramadan[34]
f   Nuzulul Qur'ān[35]
g   Welcoming Idul Fitri

Part IV: Second *Khutbah*
a   *Khutbah* for the Friday Prayer

Part V: *Khutbah* for Two Great Days
a   *Khutbah* for Idul Fitri
b   Second Half of the *Khutbah* for Idul Fitri
c   *Khutbah* for Idul Adha
d   Second Half of the *Khutbah* for Idul Adha

No. 3
Moh. Abdai Rathomy (1998), *Penuntun Khutbah Komplit* [Complete *Khutbah* Manual], Surabaya: Ahmad Nabhan, 326 pp. [57 *khutbah*]

The emphasis in this collection is on ritual and ethics rather than social issues as such. It is written in 'simple Indonesian, as a guide for the *khatib* and to make it easy to understand'. The collection contains 50 texts for the Friday prayer, two for Indonesian Independence Day and Heroes Day, two for the second part of the Friday prayer, and three for Idul Adha and Idul Fitri.

Contents
1   Muharram Friday I: The Historical Background of the Muslim Calendar New Year in Islam
2   Muharram Friday II: Ash-shura Is the Day of Victory
3   Muharram Friday III: Mahsyar[36] on Judgment Day

---

34 Falling during the last 10 days of Ramadan, the Night of Power (Lailatul Qadar) is the most blessed night of the year. On this night a Muslim's prayers have particular strength.
35 Commemorates the day on which the Qur'ān was first revealed to the Prophet (the 17th day of Ramadan).
36 The place where the souls of the dead will be gathered on Judgment Day.

43 Dhu al-Qa'dah Friday I: A Good Deed May Serve as a Solution for Hardship
44 Dhu al-Qa'dah Friday II: Majority in Numbers Does Not Mean Victory for
    Muslims
45 Dhu al-Qa'dah Friday III: Surrendering to God after Doing the Best One Can
46 Dhu al-Qa'dah Friday IV: Future Events after Judgment Day
47 Dzulhijjah Friday I: Welcoming Idul Adha
48 Dzulhijjah Friday II: Performing the *Hajj*
49 Dzulhijjah Friday III: Our Possessions Are Due to the Divine Mandate of God
50 Dzulhijjah Friday IV: Self-introspection in the World before the Coming of the
    Hereafter
51 *Khutbah* on Welcoming Indonesia's Independence: Do Not Ignore the
    Guidance of God and Neglect His Blessing
52 *Khutbah* on Welcoming Heroes Day: Struggle (*Jihad*) for the Sake of Allah to
    Glorify His Works
53 Second Part of *Khutbah* (A)
54 Second Part of *Khutbah* (B)
55 *Khutbah* for Idul Fitri: Idul Fitri and Improving Obedience to God
56 *Khutbah* for Idul Adha: The History of Sacrifice (*Qurban*) and Its Essence
57 Second Part of the *Khutbah* for Idul Fitri and Idul Adha

No. 4
M.A. Fuadi Sya'ban (1985), *Khotbah Masa Kini [Khutbah* for Now], Kudus: Menara
Kudus, 208 pp. [28 *khutbah*]

This is a notable collection because it leans towards giving opinions on the difficult
'edge' issues affecting society. In his introduction, the author states that his purpose
is to provide the *khatib* with materials to use for the better understanding and dissemination of Islam.

Contents

Muharram
I   Celebrating Islamic New Year by Strengthening Prescribed Ritual Duty
    (*Ibadah*)
II Implementation of Syariah for National Development

Shafar
I   The Contribution of Islamic Education to Human Security in the World and the
    Hereafter
II The Importance of 'Character Education' in Life

Rabi'ul Awwal
I   Social Conditions in the Modern State of Ignorance (*Jahiliyah*)
II Muhammad as the Prophet of Development and Compassion for the Whole
    Universe

Rabi'ul Thani
I   Trust in God, an Escape from Frustration and Laziness
II Implementing Justice in Leadership: Maintaining the Divine Mandate

Jumadal Ula
I   Patience as the Source of Happiness
II   Acts of Devotion to God as the Main Duty of Man

Jumada Thaniyah
I   'Socializing' the Qur'ān and 'Qur'ānizing' Society
II   Cultivating the Bodies and Minds of Young Muslims

Rajab
I   The Significance of Isra' and Mi'raj for Medical Science
II   Cultivating Spirituality to Strengthen Faith in God

Sya'ban
I   Faith and Devotion as Bases for Human Life
II   Healthy Spirituality as Balance for a Healthy Physical Body

Ramadan
I   Fasting Leading to Tolerance
II   Ramadan with Double Rewards for Good Conduct

Shawwal
I   The Ties of Kinship (*Silat al-Rahm*) as the Ties of Human Fraternity
II   Respecting One's Parents Leads to Eternal Prosperity

Dhu al-Qa'dah
I   Being Mindful of Death Encourages the Spirit of Struggle and Good Deeds

Dzulhijjah
I   Struggle (*Jihad*) Requires Sacrifice
II   The *Hajj* as a Sacred Duty to God

Khutbah for Idul Fitri
Khutbah for Idul Adha
Khutbah on the Prayer at an Eclipse of the Sun/Moon
Khutbah on the Prayer for Rain (Istisqa')
Khutbah for the Second Part of the Friday Prayer

No. 5
Baidlowi Syamsuri (n.d.), *Himpunan Khutbah Jum'at (2)* [Collection of Friday *Khutbah* (2)], Surabaya: Apollo, 181 pp. [16 *khutbah*]

This is a physically small book and the second in what is obviously a series. Written in simple language, its purpose is both to help the *khatib* prepare the *khutbah* and to inform the common people. The author gives the *khatib* permission to adapt the material to suit the audience. He also welcomes criticism and suggestions for improvement.

Contents
1   The Importance of Patience
2   The Importance of Perseverance
3   The Importance of Reading the Qur'ān
4   Remembering God

No. 6

Effendi Zarkasi (1999), *Khutbah Jumat Aktual* [Actual Friday *Khutbah*], Jakarta: Gema Insani Press, 312 pp. [54 *khutbah*]

The author states that 'Islam is the only universal religion to encompass all aspects of human life for all contexts of place and time'. None of these aspects, social or natural, is outside Islam. Muslims must therefore acquire the capacity to observe and apprehend social and natural phenomena from an Islamic perspective. In so doing, they must make Islam the spirit for themselves so that they can live within the framework of Islamic teachings. Many Muslims are still unable to bring an Islamic perspective to bear on the problems of society. This book is therefore devoted to helping them do this. The author says that he deliberately does not include a preface for each *khutbah*, because the *khatib* is assumed to have learned the *khutbah* by heart. Nevertheless, at the end of the book he does provide some examples of prefaces for the first and second *khutbah* as well as some examples of closing prayers for the second *khutbah*. Particularly for Idul Fitri and Idul Adha prayers, the opening *khutbah* is always preceded by 'God is great' (*takbir*), recited nine times. For the closing prayers for Idul Fitri and Idul Adha, the *khatib* is invited to contribute his own inspiration in line with the existing conditions of time and place.

Contents

Chapter I: Theology (*Aqidah*)
Praying Only to God
Back to God's Path
The Spiritual Practitioner
The Horoscope
Man and Religion
The Qur'ān as the Path for Life
Why Do Calamities Happen?
Islam, a Religion of Peace

Chapter II: Education and Character
Understanding and Implementing the Qur'ān
The Qur'ān and the Life of the *Ummah*
The Teacher's Authority

Short-course *Pesantren*
Advantages and Disadvantages of Advertisements
Sports
Women
The Impact of Free Sex
The Impact of Alcoholic Drinks and Narcotics
The Impact of Gambling
Immoral Acts
Children with Deviant Behaviour
Careful Speech
Honesty
Children's Morals
Three Sorts of Love
Facing the Future (for the Family)
Revenge
Affection
A Simple Life
Humanitarianism
Hypocrisy
The Honourable Mother
Advantages and Disadvantages of Watching TV

Chapter III: *Khutbah* for the Two Idul
Building an Islamic Family (*Khutbah* for Idul Fitri)
Idul Adha and Independence (*Khutbah* for Idul Adha)

Chapter IV: Selected Writings
Islam Is Not an Extremist Religion
Challenges for Contemporary Muslims
Vigilance of Muslims
Woman's Role
The Hijiri Calendar from a Muslim Perspective
The Solar Calendar (Masihiyah)
Water as God's Gift
Social Disparity
Home Sweet Home
Islam from the Perspective of the Infidel
Criteria for a Good Leader
Subversion
Technological Advances
Contribution of Islam to Indonesian Culture
Legal Injustice
Balance in Life

Chapter V: Examples of Opening *Khutbah*
Opening *Khutbah* for Friday Prayers
Opening of the Second Part of the *Khutbah* and the Closing Prayer
Opening *Khutbah* for Idul Fitri Prayers
Opening *Khutbah* for Idul Adha Prayers

No. 7
Syahminan Zaini (1981), *Kumpulan Khutbah Jum'at* [Collection of Friday *Khutbah*], Surabaya: Al Ikhlas, 270 pp. [31 *khutbah*]

The author provides a brief introduction to the book, as follows:

> These writings were initially the texts for *khutbah* and other works delivered in several mosques and other places in Malang and the surrounding cities. Some were even delivered in West Sumatra and East Kalimantan. Many others have been mimeographed for mosques, Muslim organizations and discussion groups in Malang, Surabaya, Probolinggo and other cities. Also, some of them have been published in the Malang-based journal *Mutiara Khadijah* [Pearl of Khadijah]. Some young preachers (*muballigh*) and members of the community of followers (*jama'ah*) of several mosques in Malang urged me to compile these *khutbah* texts and publish them as a book. It is in this context that this book was written, in response to those requests. However, the texts in this book have been improved from their original drafts to a more suitable format, for the sake of the perfection of the book.

Contents
1   Building a Faith-based Household (Family)
2   Path for a Happy Life
3   The Purity of Man
4   The Role of Spiritual Maintenance in Human Life
5   The Function of Man
6   The Means of Obtaining Divine Blessings
7   Fasting Returns Man to His Natural Character
8   The Responsible Man
9   The Good Man from a Qur'ānic Perspective
10   Man's Impact on Humanitarianism
11   Why Does Islam Regulate Man's Behaviour?
12   Scientific Authentication of the Creation of the Body and the Existence of the Spirit
13   The Character of Man
14   Perspectives on Fasting
15   Everything Is Identified through Its Signs
16   The Urgency of Worship (*Ibadah*) in Maintaining Pancasila—and the National Struggle
17   Prayer (*Shalat*) as a Characteristic of the Believer
18   Human Beings and God's Law
19   Searching for the Identity of the Believer
20   Lessons from Prophet Abraham in Searching for and Enforcing the Truth
21   The Essential Meaning of Prayer (*Shalat*)
22   Philosophy of Idul Fitri
23   Woman's Role in the Qur'ān
24   The *Hajj*
25   What's Next after Worship (*Ibadah*)?
26   The Qur'ān as a Guide for Humanity
27   Spiritual Disease
28   The Divine Contract

29 The Dignity of Man
30 The Path for a Happy Life from Qur'ānic Teachings
31 Second Half of the *Khutbah*

No. 8
Moh. Syamsi Hasan and Achmad Ma'ruf Asrori (2002), *Khotbah Jam'at Sepanjang Masa* [Friday *Khutbah* for all Times], Surabaya: Karya Agung, 528 pp. [58 *khutbah*]

The intention of this lengthy collection is to provide *khutbah* for all 52 weeks of the year. In their introduction the authors emphasize that the *khutbah* is a special form of speech, separate from any other. This is because its primary purpose is to explain the syariah. The *khutbah* must therefore be well prepared and planned with this purpose in mind.

Contents
1   Gratitude to God
2   Maintaining Faith in God
3   Becoming a True Believer
4   Doing Good and Rejecting Evil
5   Understanding the Importance of Worship
6   Celebrating the Islamic New Year
7   The Majesty of Faith
8   On *Jihad* (the Importance of Struggle in God's Path)
9   Knowledge
10 The Virtues of the *'Ulamā'*
11 Work
12 Balance in Life
13 A Modest and Generous Life
14 The Good Things in Life, Beware Luxury
15 Celebrating the Prophet's Birthday
16 Respecting the Prophet
17 The Prophet and Social Change
18 Imitating the Prophet's Struggle
19 Relying on Islam
20 Cooperation and Mutual Help
21 *Zakat*: Its Contribution to Society
22 Promoting Piety
23 Developing an Ethics-based Life
24 Protecting Oneself and One's Family against Evil/Hell
25 Using Money with God's Purpose in Mind
26 The Muslim Family: Achieving a Harmonious and Happy Family
27 Educating One's Descendants in Islam
28 Islamic Education (Children)
29 Obeying Parents
30 Isra' and Mi'raj
31 Prayers to Prevent Evil Deeds
32 Humility
33 Overcoming Poverty

34 The Dangers of Males and Females Mixing Freely
35 Honesty, a Path to Heaven
36 The Dangers of Alcohol and Gambling
37 Remembering Death
38 Hypocrisy
39 Sya'ban
40 The Importance of Controlling One's Speech
41 Orphans
42 Fortitude and Patience
43 Welcoming Ramadan, Its Importance
44 The Qur'ān, Celebrating Its Revelation
45 Lailatul Qadar
46 Struggle (*Jihad*) against Sin and Evil
47 Lessons from the *Hajj*
48 Sacrifice
49 Marriage, Advice for the Groom
50 The Prayer for Rain (Istisqa')
51 Eclipse of the Sun/Moon
52 *Khutbah* for Idul Fitri
53 *Khutbah* for Idhul Adha

No. 9

H.M. Hasan Abdul Qahar (2003), *Himpunan Khotbah Jam'at: I Tahun* [Collection of *Khutbah* for 1 Year], Yogyakarta: Absolut, 477 pp. [52 *khutbah*]

The *khutbah* in this rather long book are arranged by calendar month. Each block contains at least one *khutbah* explaining the significance of that month. The author recommends that the *khatib* modify the text in accordance with local needs and asks for God's forgiveness for any mistakes.

Contents

Muharram
1 A New Spirit and Intention in the New Year
2 Hijrah
3 Days of the Prophet
4 The New Year (1st January): Gratitude

Shafar
5 Gratitude for a Long Life
6 Remembering [God] (*Dzikir*)
7 Obedience to Government
8 Hope and Fear
9 Unity among Us

Rabi'ul Awwal
10 The Prophet as an Example
11 Developing Motivation in Adolescents
12 The Prophet's Birthday
13 Obedience to God

Rabi'ul Thani
14 Good Deeds
15 Developing Empathy
16 Repentance
17 Daily Prayers

Jumadal Ula
18 Arrogance
19 The Inner Power Possessed by Believers
20 When the Prophetic Tradition Is Abused
21 Overconsumption

Jumada Thaniyah
22 The Strong Believer
23 God's Shelter on Judgment Day
24 Mutual Support
25 Cooperation

Rajab
26 The Importance of Rajab
27 Celebrating the Ascension of the Prophet
28 Hypocrisy
29 Achieving Spirituality

Sya'ban
30 The Importance of Sya'ban
31 Charity
32 Revenge and Hatred, Spiritual Diseases
33 The Divine Mandate
34 Love, without Forgetting Five Important Things

Ramadan
35 The Importance of Fasting
36 The Fast Contributes to Becoming an Admirable Individual
37 Welcoming Nuzulul Qur'ān
38 Reading and Implementing the Qur'ān
39 Teaching Islam

Shawwal
40 Maintaining and Strengthening the Islamic Fraternity
41 The Importance of Modesty
42 Purification of the Heart
43 Sincerity

Dhu al-Qa'dah
44 Arrogance
45 Respecting the *'Ulamā'*
46 Sincerity, Will, Immorality
47 Moral Society, Implementing Ethics

Dzulhijjah
48 The *Hajj*
49 Preparing Oneself to Face Change
50 Good Deeds Will Eliminate Evil Ones
51 Misdemeanour in the Muslim Community
52 Egoism

No. 10
Ahmad Sunarto (1991), *Khutbah Pedoman Muslim* [*Khutbah* for the Guidance of Muslims], Jakarta: Pustaka Amani, 171 pp. [26 *khutbah*]

This collection by a prolific author is still widely available. The author hopes that the *khatib* will find it useful as a guide and says that he welcomes criticisms and suggestions.

Contents
1   The Islamic New Year
2   The Evils of Desire
3   The Family
4   Disobedience (to God)
5   The Muslim Community (Neighbourhood)
6   Patience and Gratitude
7   Doing Good and Avoiding Evil
8   The Nobleness of the *'Ulamā'*
9   Modesty and Faith
10 The Fraternity of Muslims
11 The Divine Mandate and Responsibility
12 The Importance of Ethics in Islam
13 Remembrance of God
14 Good Deeds
15 True Happiness
16 Orphans
17 Obedience
18 The Prophet's Birthday
19 Indonesian Independence Day
20 Heroes Day
21 Idul Fitri
22 Welcoming Idul Adha
23 Second Part of the *Khutbah* for Idul Fitri and Idul Adha
24 Second Part of the *Khutbah* for Friday Prayers (I)
25 Second Part of the *Khutbah* for Friday Prayers (II)
26 Second Part of the *Khutbah* for Friday Prayers (III)

No. 11
Abd. Hamid Zahwan (1997), *Cakrawala Khutbah dalam Era Globalisasi* [Constellation of *Khutbah* in an Era of Globalization], Solo: CV Aneka, 185 pp. [36 *khutbah*]

This is a relatively short book given its rather ambitious title. However, the author does recognize the changes taking place in the wider world, and the role of the *khutbah* publishing industry in helping to raise awareness about these changes. His particular contribution is to persuade Muslims of the need to understand change. Because of this, I have chosen to discuss a higher than usual proportion of this author's *khutbah* in the text.

Contents

Part I: Essential Islamic Days
1   Welcoming the 1st Day of Muharram
2   The Prophet's Birthday
3   Isra' and Mi'raj: The Virtues of the Prophet's Ascension
4   The Coming of Ramadan
5   Nuzulul Qur'ān
6   Lailatul Qadar
7   *Zakat*
8   Idul Fitri
9   *Zakat Maal*
10 The *Hajj*
11 Idul Adha as a Way of Uniting Muslim Society
12 *Khutbah* on the Prayer for Rain (Istisqa')
13 *Khutbah* on the Prayer at an Eclipse of the Sun/Moon

Part II: National Days
14 Welcoming New Year
15 National Awakening Day
16 Kartini Day
17 National Education Day
18 Indonesian Independence Day
19 The Latent Dangers of Communism
20 Sanctity of Pancasila Day
21 Armed Forces Day
22 Youth Pledge Day
23 Heroes Day
24 Human Rights
25 The Emancipation of Women
26 Mothers Day
27 Non-smoking Day

Part III: The Islamic Mission
28 The Benefits of Prayer
29 Developing an Interest in Children to Read the Qur'ān
30 Islamic Fraternity
31 Faith as the Foundation of Life in Society
32 The Environment according to Islamic Teaching
33 Humanity
34 Therapy for Juvenile Delinquents
35 Second Half of the *Khutbah* for Friday Prayers I
36 Second Half of the *Khutbah* for Friday Prayers II

No. 12
Muhammad b. 'Umar al-Nawawi al-Bantani (trans. 1988), *Kumpulan Khutbah Jum'ah* [Collection of Friday *Khutbah*], translated and edited by Ahmad Sunarto, Surabaya: Amanah, 414 pp. [52 *khutbah*]

Nawawi al-Bantani (1813–97) was one of the most prolific authors in Indonesian Islam. His works still appear on the *pesantren* syllabus (see van Bruinessen 1990 for many references) and continue to be reprinted. For example, the latest version of Nawawi's *'Uquud al-Lujjayn* was published, with commentary, by the Forum for the Study of Kitab Kuning (Forum Kajian Kitab Kuning; FK3) as recently as 2001 (see FK3 2003 and the extract in Fealy and Hooker 2006: 307–8). This collection is of interest not only because of Nawawi's continuing influence, but also because of the way in which the text as a whole is set out (see table of contents). A comparison of this and contemporary collections shows that the later collections are modelled on Nawawi's original, in a clear case of transmission. Some reproduce Nawawi's *khutbah* without acknowledgement; the translator of the present collection, Ahmad Sunarto, does at least acknowledge his debt.

I bought my edition of this book in Banda Aceh in December 1998, 10 years after it was first published in Surabaya. The shop owner claimed at the time that there was no local publishing house on Islam or Islamic studies. Of course, Aceh's IAIN Ar-Raniry and Universitas Syah Kuala as well as the Department of Religion would have disputed this assertion.

Contents

Khutbah **for Muharram**
I   Celebrating Islamic New Year
II   10 Muharram, the Day of the Prophet's Victory
III Helping Orphans
IV   Being Grateful for God's Blessing

Khutbah **for Shafar**
I   Bad Conduct as a Characteristic of Feeble Faith
II   Unity and Integrity
III The Essence of Being Obedient to Government and Leader
IV   Honouring the *'Ulamā'* and Not Dishonouring Them
V   Belief in the Hereafter

Khutbah **for Rabi'ul Awwal**
I   Prophet Muhammad as a Model
II   Celebrating the Birthday of Prophet Muhammad
III Complying with the Prophet's Commands and Avoiding His Prohibitions
IV   Maintaining Cleanliness, Beauty and Health

Khutbah **for Rabi'ul Thani**
I   Performing the Five Prayers
II   Goodness as Being Able to Wipe Away Wickedness
III Faith (*Iman*), Ethics (*Akhlaq*), Actions (*'Amal*) and Worship (*Ibadah*)
IV   Repentance (*Tawbah*)

Khutbah for Jumadal Ula
I   It Will Happen that the 'Prophet's Sunnah Becomes Ruined'
II   Living Economically and with Dignity
III The Essence of Arrogance
IV Commanding Good Conduct and Prohibiting Evil Conduct

Khutbah for Jumada Thaniyah
I   Becoming a Devoted and Strong Believer
II   Remembering [God] (*Dzikir*)
III People under the Shield of God on Judgment Day
IV Slander (*Fitnah*) among the Believers

Khutbah for Rajab
I   The Excellence of Rajab
II   The Characteristics of a Hypocrite
III Implementing Good Ethics in Society
IV Celebrating Isra' and Mi'raj

Khutbah for Sya'ban
I   The Excellence of Sya'ban and Nisfu Sya'ban
II   The Value of Charity (*Sadaqah*) and Contributions (*Infaq*)
III Avoiding Spite and Revenge
IV Trusteeship and Responsibility
V   'There May Be People Who Love Five Matters and Ignore Five Matters as Well'

Khutbah for Ramadan
I   Fasting at Ramadan
II   The Role of Ramadan in Shaping Good Character
III Celebrating Nuzulul Qur'ān
IV The Virtues of Reading and Implementing the Qur'ān

Khutbah for Shawwal
I   Maintaining Fraternity
II   The Essence of Shame
III Sincerity
IV 'There May Be Selfish People'

Khutbah for Dhu al-Qa'dah
I   Being Generous
II   Trust in God (*Tawakkal*)
III Excessive Pride
IV The Islamic Perspective on Being a Neighbour

Khutbah for Dzulhijjah
I   Patience
II   The *Hajj*: *Khutbah* for Idul Adha
III Education
IV Spending *Zakat* Moneys

Khutbah for Second Half of Idul Fitri and Idul Adha Prayers
Khutbah for Second Half of Every Friday Prayer

No. 13
Mustofa W. Hasyim (ed.) (2003), *Khotbah Jum'at Praktis* [Convenient Friday *Khutbah*], Yogyakarta: Pustaka Pelajar, 228 pp. [35 *khutbah*]

Publisher's introduction:

This book is published in response to the increasing demand for written texts resulting from an expansion in the number of mosques being built. In addition, the text attempts to satisfy the demand caused by the increasing literacy of the Islamic community. The previous oral *khutbah* tradition has been transformed into a written tradition that requires publication. The written form is an effective method for transmitting the message of God. In addition, new or inexperienced *khatib* require written material for [*khutbah*] preparation. The *khutbah* included in the collection are taken from material previously published in *Suara Muhammadiyah*.

Editor's introduction:

The purpose of this book is to increase knowledge of religion. The book is in three parts and is organized by topic. Part I is on special days/events in Islam and also includes special (secular) days in Indonesia (for example, National Education Day). Part II is on fundamental values and current topics relating to contemporary issues. Part III provides prayers (*doa*) required for the Friday ritual. It is intended that the new *khatib* will find the book easy to use. ... [T]he cultural transformation of the oral tradition into a written tradition is one part of the development of media communication. The written document is important for [*khutbah*] preparation.

Contents

---

37 Day during Idul Adha on which animals are sacrificed to commemorate Abraham's willingness to sacrifice his son for God.

Part II: Fundamental Principles of Islam
18 Good Intentions
19 Religion as a Remedy for Psychological Disorders [by Aries Muthohar]
20 The Message of 'The Opening' (al-Fatihah)
21 Welfare according to the Qur'ān
22 Preventing Human Suffering
23 Islamic Discipline
24 That which Destroys Our Good Deeds
25 Confronting the Dubious
26 Mosque Activities for the Betterment of the Community
27 Rich and Poor
28 Encouraging Donations
29 Obstacles to Achieving God's Grace
30 Five Types of Misdemeanours
31 Searching for God's Will
32 The Importance of Environmental Awareness [by Dede Zakiyudin]
33 Cooperation, Deliberation
34 The Happy Family and the Trend towards Living Alone
35 The Head Covering for Women [by Hidayatul Muin]

Part III: Prayers

No. 14
Drs. Imron Abu Amar (1984), *Khutbah Jum'ah Populer* [Understandable *Khutbah*], Jakarta: Pustaka Amani, 109 pp. [15 *khutbah*]

This book is written in simple, understandable Indonesian to reach both a wide range of readers and the Friday prayer audience. The author hopes that the book will strengthen the audience's spiritual beliefs. More importantly, it is intended to contribute to the socialization of Islamic teaching and increase understanding of Islamic principles.

Contents

Part I
Guidance on Delivering the Friday *Khutbah*
1 Performing the Friday Prayer
2 *Jum'at Khutbah*
3 Recommendations for the *Khatib*

General *Khutbah*
1 Belief in God
2 Thanking God for His Mercy
3 Becoming a Good Muslim
4 Sincerity in Human Conduct
5 Islam and the Challenge of the Changing World
6 The Islamic Community and the Development Gap
7 Promoting Good and Happiness

Specific *Khutbah*
1   Commemorating the Prophet Muhammad's Birthday
2   Celebrating Isra' and Mi'raj
3   Commemorating Indonesian Independence Day
4   Celebrating the Islamic New Year
5   The Holy Month of Ramadan
6   The Commencement of the Qur'ān

Second *Khutbah* for Friday Prayers
Khutbah for Idul Adha and Idul Fitri

No. 15
Ghufron Maba (1998), *Kumpulan Khutbah Jum'at* [Collection of Friday *Khutbah*], Jombang: Lintas Media, 176 pp. [26 *khutbah*]

In his introductory remarks, the author says:

> This book is a compilation of selected *khutbah* given previously in my residency, Blimbing Lamongan, with some revisions for publication. The selection is based on the necessity for the Islamic community to cope with current issues, such as increased technology, modernization and globalization, which cause people to become materialistic, individualistic and secularistic. The decrease in morality and trust among people and the increase in crime and poverty are evidence of changing human thought and values associated with an increasingly secular lifestyle. This publication is therefore expected to contribute to the development of Muslims as the majority of the Indonesian people.

Contents
1   Islamic New Year
2   The First Month of the Islamic Calendar: Spiritual Values for 10 Muharram
3   Lessons to Commemorate the Prophet's Birthday
4   Isra' and Mi'raj, Morality and Good Conduct, Lessons for Society
5   Ramadan: Developing Good Ethics in the Month of Ramadan
6   Ramadan: Welcoming Ramadan
7   The Qur'ān: Commemorating Nuzulul Qur'ān
8   The Qur'ān: Philosophy and Guidance for Human Life
9   Indonesian Independence Day
10 Mothers Day
11 Independence Is a Basic Right for All Nations
12 Women in Islam: Kartini Day
13 The Importance of Education
14 Knowledge
15 Donations in Society
16 The Fifth Principle of Pancasila
17 The Function of Intellect
18 Careful Speech
19 Gambling and Alcohol
20 Prayer in Social Life
21 God's Purpose in Creating Mankind

22 War according to Islam
23 Misdemeanours and Untrustworthiness (Slander)
24 The Duties of Mankind as a Creation of God
25 The Religious Mission
26 The First Principle of Pancasila

No. 16
Ahmad Sunarto (2000), *Khutbah Jum'at Pilihan* [A Selection of Friday *Khutbah*], Surabaya: Amanah, 287 pp. [27 *khutbah*]

This book is written in simple, easy-to-understand Indonesian. The author thanks God for permitting him to complete the book and welcomes criticism.

Contents
1   The Unfortunate (Disadvantaged) in the Community
2   Good Manners
3   Those Who Reject the Traditions of the Prophet
4   The End of the World: Three Precious Things at that Time
5   Promoting Goodness
6   Variations in Faith
7   Islam May Only Be a Name and the Qur'ān Just a Book
8   Human Rights
9   Making a Living from Immorality
10 Hypocrisy
11 Money and How to Use It
12 Disobedience
13 Two Groups Who Will Be in Hell
14 Those Who Ignore What Is Permitted and Forbidden
15 Remembrance of God
16 Patience
17 Justice
18 Reading the Qur'ān
19 Struggle in the Path of God
20 Sin and Its Consequences
21 Envy
22 Selfishness
23 The Mercy of God
24 *Khutbah* for Idul Fitri
25 *Kutbah* for Idul Adha
26 Second *Khutbah* for Idul Fitri and Idul Adha
27 Second *Khutbah* for the Friday Prayer

No. 17
Drs. H. Ahmad Yani (2003), *52 Materi Khutbah* [52 *Khutbah* Materials], fourth edition, Jakarta: Cahaya Press, 320 pp. [52 *khutbah*]

Through the publication of this book, the author aims to remedy the serious shortage of simple, systematic *khutbah* for the Friday prayer, which is essential to Muslims.

Contents

47   The Negative Impact of Arrogance
48   Striving to Get Rid of Arrogance
49   Work is Piety (Pious Actions)
50   Pious Deeds (I)
51   Pious Deeds (II)
52   The Mosque and Politics
[Examples of prayers]

No. 18

Drs. Moh. Amin (1996), *Mutiara Khutbah Jum'at* [*Khutbah* Pearls], Surabaya: Indah, 108 pp. [12 *khutbah*]

In his introductory remarks, the author says:

> This book is composed in a simple way and in a short form as a basic guide for the *khatib*. However, it will need to be modified by the *khatib* in accordance with the situation and the conditions he faces while carrying out his duties. The book is intentionally simple and short in view of the Hadith suggesting that the time taken to deliver the *khutbah* should be shorter than that for the Friday prayer itself. It should be noted that the success of the *khatib* in bringing his mission into effect depends very much on his personal ability to deliver the *khutbah*. The main issue requiring his full attention is whether or not the material in the *khutbah* touches the depths of the hearts of a diversity of listeners. In other words, the *khutbah* needs to address a variety of listeners from different backgrounds—from educated people to lay people, civil servants and traders—who sometimes get sleepy (during the *khutbah*) because they are exhausted from work. All *khatib* have to take this important issue into consideration in order to get a hearing from the congregation. As important as keeping the attention of the audience is that the content of the *khutbah* be useful as a driving force to sustain and orient the life of the listeners towards God's path.

Contents
1   The Role of Religion in Cultivating Good Character
2   Total Submission to God Alone
3   Balanced Life
4   The Harmonious Family
5   The Responsibility of Parents
6   Cultivating an Affectionate Society
7   The Path of Salvation
8   Seeking Life through Immoral Ways
9   Function of Knowledge in Rejecting Defamation
10   The Enemy and Ally of Satan
11   Those Who Are under the Shelter of God
12   The Destruction of Human Dignity

No. 19

Ustadz Labib Mz. (2003), *Himpunan Khutbah Jum'at Populer* [Collection of Understandable *Khutbah*], Surabaya: Bintang Usaha Jaya, 128 pp. [28 *khutbah*]

The author's preface is as follows:

> Thanks to God for His mercy, help and guidance, this book is made possible. Its aim is to fulfil the demand of the community of followers (*jama'at*) for a written

publication of *khutbah*. It is written in simple language so that the ordinary person can understand the content. Above all, it paves the way for the *jama'at* to increase its faith and devotion to God. I hope that Muslims may find it effective and so increase their faith and devotion. Also, I hope this book can be cited as a good conduct of mine before God.

Contents

No. 20

Kafrawi Hamzah (1994), *Ulama dan Tanggung Jawabnya* [The *'Ulamā'* and Their Responsibilities], Jakarta: Pedoman Ilmu Jaya, 109 pp. [16 *khutbah*]

In his introductory remarks, the author says:

This book is a compilation of my Australian sermons and *dakwah* scripts. When I attended Friday prayers in Jakarta and other regions in Indonesia, I found that in their sermons most *khatib* tended to serve the interests of the government rather than those of the religion and the audience. As a result, in delivering the truth, they often used implicit and ambiguous expressions that were not clearly understood by the audience, and that blurred the essence of the truth itself. Similarly, the truth was not fully addressed; therefore, the audience was not able to perceive the exact meaning of the *khutbah*. In addition to this phenomenon, in general the *khatib* preferred to choose topics that were irrelevant to the needs of contemporary Muslims. Based on my two months of observation in Indonesia and my other outreach experiences, I began to compile the Friday sermons that I had delivered in Australia in the hope that this contribution would revive my own awareness of Islam and at the same time encourage my colleagues to carry out outreach activities. However, this book of sermons does not represent the interests of any party except Islam. I stand for no group except Islam. You are welcome to criticize my book. Let us together contribute the best for the Muslim community in order to gain the reward from God in the hereafter.

Contents
1   Isra' and Mi'raj
2   The Importance of Ramadan
3   Practices in the Month of Ramadan
4   The Month of Sya'ban
5   Welcoming the Month of Ramadan
6   Prayer Is the Most Important Element of Worship
7   Balance in Life
8   Religious Tolerance in Islam
9   The *'Ulamā'* and Their Responsibilities
10 Preventing Pregnancy and Islamic Law
11 AIDS Is God's Punishment for Human Beings in the Twentieth Century
12 *Khutbah* for Idul Fitri
13 The Concept of Leadership in Islam
14 The Predictions of the Prophet for the Fate of Muslim Society
15 Islam in Modern Times
16 Examples of the Second *Khutbah*

No. 21
Abdullah Rasyid, MA (1990), *Himpunan Khutbah Jum'at Pilihan* [Collection of Selected *Khutbah*], Bandung: Husaini, 142 pp. [27 *khutbah*]

In his introductory remarks, the author explains the purpose of the compilation as follows:

> This book, a compilation of the *khutbah* texts that I have delivered, is published as complementary material for the *khatib* and *muballigh* in their outreach activities, as well as for the public. It is my intention to discuss the *khutbah* materials in this book in a simple way, in modest, short but complete language, so that people from all backgrounds will easily be able to understand them. As is apparent from this compilation, in the *khutbah* I have deliberately chosen themes that can build the good character of Muslims. Central to this character building is the religious imperative for Muslims to increase the quality of their faith and piety towards God. In addition, the rationale behind this selection is to convey advice and guidance to sustain the spirit of Islamic solidarity.

Contents
1   Celebrating the First Day of Muharram
2   Celebrating the Birthday of the Prophet Muhammad
3   Rajab
4   Three Types of People Who Pray
5   Social Piety in Islam

6   The Greatness of Ramadan
7   The Qur'ān as the Way of Life
8   The Perfection of Islamic Teachings
9   The Advantages of Patience
10 The Essence of Life
11 The Advantages of Upholding the Ties of Kinship (*Silat al-Rahm*)
12 Self-control
13 Interaction between Muslims
14 Moral Diseases
15 The Character of Divinity
16 A Modest Life Pattern
17 Initiative and Resignation (*Tawakkal*)
18 Guidance and Digression
19 The Signs of a Religious Hypocrite
20 Kinds of Sins
21 Repentance
22 Respectfulness as Part of Faith
23 The Barriers to Prayer (*Do'a*) that Will Be Heard by God
24 *Khutbah* for Idul Fitri
25 Keeping the Divine Mandate
26 Second-stage *Khutbah* for Idul Adha
27 Second-stage *Khutbah* for Every Friday Prayer

No. 22
Drs. Sholihin Syaqiq and Drs. Ii Sufyana M. Bakri (2003), *Khotbah Jumat I* [Friday *Khutbah* I], Bandung: Sinar Baru Algensindo, 238 pp. [39 *khutbah*]

The authors note that people have different personalities and characters, leading to different needs and interests, including varying degrees of interest in religion. The *khatib* and *muballigh* need to be aware of these differences and choose topics that are appropriate to the targeted audience. The book is intended to help the *khatib* in this task by providing *khutbah* on a wide variety of topics. The *khatib* is expected to modify and strengthen them in accordance with need.

Contents
1   Punishment as a Way of Self-evaluation
2   Punishment or Ordeal
3   The Spirit (Meaning) of Hijrah
4   Patriots (Heroes) of Development
5   The Standard of Heroism
6   The Essence of Youth Pledge Day
7   The Generation that Doubted the Prophet
8   Nurturing Youth
9   Inheriting the Heroic Spirit
10 The Role of Women in Development
11 Encouraging Fraternity
12 Unity and Togetherness
13 Achieving Unity
14 The Cooperative Life

15 Life Is Challenge and Sacrifice
16 Moving Forwards, not Backwards
17 The *Ummah* Must Have an Identity
18 Umar Abdul Azis as a Role Model
19 The Path to Happiness
20 Developing the Perfect Human Being
21 Sustaining the Balance of Life
22 Noble Morals Protect the Life of the *Ummah*
23 The Muslim Way of Life
24 The Islamic Fraternity
25 Preserving the Bonds of Fraternity
26 The Responsibilities of the Faithful
27 The Muslim as an Example for Other Muslims
28 Muhammad as a Role Model
29 Islam Is Not Just the Confession of Faith
30 Prayer (*Shalat*), the Ascension (Mi'raj) of the Faithful
31 The Influence of Prayer in Life
32 Uncovering the Essence of *Azan*
33 Understanding Ourselves
34 The Characteristics of a Muslim
35 The Doctrine of the Unity of God (Ethics and Morality)
36 Faith in God and Judgment Day
37 Praiseworthy Deeds
38 Humanity Needs God
39 The Importance of Friendship and Wisdom

No. 23
Ustadz Labib Mz. (2003), *Himpunan Khutbah Jum'at Setahun 12 Bulan* [Collection of Friday *Khutbah* for 12 Months], Surabaya: Bintang Usaha Jaya, 584 pp. [129 *khutbah*]

In publishing this book, the author claims to offer a more comprehensive collection of *khutbah* than other publications. By providing *khutbah* for an entire year, arranged by month, he says that he has been able to cover the most important topics for the designated times and events.

Contents

I   The Month of Muharram
   a Jumat Wage
     1   Islamic New Year
     2   Belief in God
   b Jumat Legi
     3   The Importance of Fasting on 10 Muharram
     4   Being Conscious of Death
   c Jumat Pon
     5   Commemorating National Awakening Day (20 May)
     6   Congregational Prayer

d Jumat Kliwon
   7 Searching for Knowledge
   8 Implementing Knowledge
e Jumat Pahing
   9 The Religion of Islam
   10 Mutual Aid

II The Month of Shafar
a Jumat Wage
   11 Unity
   12 Educating Children
b Jumat Legi
   13 The Permitted and the Forbidden
   14 Faith
c Jumat Pon
   15 *Zakat*
   16 Work
d Jumat Kliwon
   17 Polytheism
   18 Interest [on money]
e Jumat Pahing
   19 Good Advice for Parents
   20 Rebelling against One's Parents

III The Month of Rabi'ul Awwal
a Jumat Wage
   21 Patience
   22 Commemorating Muhammad's Birthday
b Jumat Legi
   23 Good Conduct
   24 Struggle (*Jihad*)
c Jumat Pon
   25 Restoring Morality
   26 The Majesty of Friday
d Jumat Kliwon
   27 Doing Good Deeds and Refusing the Forbidden
   28 The Majesty of the *'Ulamā'*
e Jumat Pahing
   29 Charity
   30 The Importance of Charity

IV The Month of Rabi'ul Thani
a Jumat Wage
   31 Guarding against Carnal Desire
   32 Being Prepared for Death (Judgment Day)
b Jumat Legi
   33 Gratitude to God
   34 Indonesian Independence Day

X   The Month of Shawwal
  a Jumat Wage
    91 Visiting the Sick
    92 The Importance of Six Days of Fasting in Shawwal
  b Jumat Legi
    93 The Day of Muhammad's Death
    94 Neglecting God's Directives
  c Jumat Pon
    95 Accumulating Wealth
    96 Acting Justly
  d Jumat Kliwon
    97 Mankind on Judgment Day
    98 The Importance of the Recommended Midnight Prayer
  e Jumat Pahing
    99   The Importance of the Basmalah[38]
    100 The Importance of Friendship

XI   The Month of Dhu al-Qa'dah
  a Jumat Wage
    101 The World and Its Destruction
    102 Turning Away from the Qur'ān
  b Jumat Legi
    103 Betraying God's Message
    104 Unbelievers in Hell
  c Jumat Pon
    105 Asking the Angels to Intercede on Behalf of the Faithful
    106 Consistent Persons
  d Jumat Kliwon
    107 Avoiding Evil
    108 Judgment Day
  e Jumat Pahing
    109 Travelling in Obedience to God's Command
    110 Defamation

XII   The Month of Dzulhijjah
  a Jumat Wage
    111 The Obligation to Perform the *Hajj*
    112 The Importance of Sacrifice
  b Jumat Legi
    113 The Miracles of Muhammad
    114 Destiny
  c Jumat Pon
    115 Striving for God's Forgiveness
    116 The Qur'ān Is a Guide for Humanity

---

38 The invocation at the start of each chapter of the Qur'ān: 'In the name of Allah, most Gracious, most Compassionate'.

d Jumat Kliwon
  117 The Prophet as Role Model
  118 The Characteristics of a Muslim
e Jumat Pahing
  119 Faith as the Foundation of Human Life
  120 The Importance of Thought
  121 *Khutbah* on the Prayer for Rain (Istisqa') (I)
  122 *Khutbah* on the Prayer for Rain (Istisqa') (II)
  123 *Khutbah* on the Prayer at an Eclipse of the Sun/Moon (I)
  124 *Khutbah* on the Prayer at an Eclipse of the Sun/Moon (II)
  125 *Khutbah* for the Friday Prayer
  126 *Khutbah* for Idul Fitri (I)
  127 *Khutbah* for Idul Adha (I)
  128 *Khutbah* for Idul Fitri/Adha (II)
  129 *Khutbah* for the Marriage Ceremony

No. 24

H.A. Syafi'i Mufid and Munawar Fuad Noeh (eds) (1997), *Beragama di Abad Dua Satu: Serial Khutbah Kontemporer I* [Religiosity in the Twenty-first Century: Contemporary *Khutbah* Series I], Jakarta: Zikru'l Hakim, 234 pp. [15 *khutbah*]

The editors stress the importance of Muslim society playing an active role in modern history. The strategic positioning of Indonesian Islam is crucial in forming a new world order. This book is designed to be a manual and source of knowledge for the *khatib*. It brings a religious perspective to current events and realities, to aid understanding.

Contents
1 Empowering Society: Towards a Just, Open and Democratic State
   [by Nurcholish Madjid]
2 The Universal Islamic Mission in Developing a Religious Society
   [by Drs. Abul Basit]
3 Islam and an Ethics-based Society
4 The Role of Humanity in Developing Muslim Society in the Twenty-first
   Century
5 Building up the Image of Muslim Society
6 Muslim Ethics: Variety and Diversity
7 Developing a Spirit of Tolerance and Harmony [by Akhmad Roziqin]
8 The Responsibility of the Majority
9 The Religious Orientation of the Urban Class [by Mastuki]
10 The Moral Crisis in the Community
11 The Dynamics of Science in Muslim Society
12 Social Criticism for Justice
13 Islamic Leadership: A Reflection [by M. Samsul Hady]
14 Management of Life according to Islam [by Zaenudin BK]
15 Muslim Work Ethics Will Increase Mass Productivity [by Abdul Rozak]

5 Syariah in the Bureaucracy: The Department of Religion and the *Hajj*

Founded in 1946, the Department of Religion has been central to Indonesian Islam for the past 60 years. It administers the religious courts (or did so until 2004); supervises and provides curricula for religious education; administers registration of marriage and divorce; drafts and introduces important regulations such as the Compilation of Islamic Law (Kompilasi Hukum Islam; KHI); registers the wealth tax (*zakat*) and gifts (*wakaf*); is the location of the Indonesian Council of Ulama (Majelis Ulama Indonesia; MUI) (from 1975), administers the pilgrimage (*hajj*); and has an active research division. It is all-pervasive in Muslim affairs because, in practice, its procedures are a source of syariah—a 'bureaucratic syariah'—in the modern state.

One of the most important functions of the department is to organize the annual *hajj*. I have chosen this as an example of how the department functions because it demonstrates very clearly the importance of the bureaucratic element, that is, of regulated and systematized control of religious duty. This contrasts strongly with the divine imperative laying out the duty of the individual. My focus, therefore, is on what happens to the pilgrim.

There are three preliminary points to bear in mind. First, the *hajj* is compulsory for Muslims (means and health permitting), so it is vital that it be performed correctly and completely. The emphasis on orthopraxy is absolutely fundamental and the Department of Religion takes its duty of instruction very seriously. Second, the pilgrim is a citizen of Indonesia who is going abroad for a limited and specific purpose. Nevertheless, the formalities of passport, entry, stay and consular protection must be adhered to. Belief and piety on their own are no longer sufficient in the modern world. Finally, the *hajj* involves large amounts of money. The average pilgrim pays the Department of Religion about Rp 2.6 million (US$2,600) to make the *hajj* arrangements—probably more than this by now. The wealthy can make alternative arrangements though a licensed agent at a much higher cost. These comparatively large sums have obvious implications for family and local finances. From the point of view of the state, considerable sums have to be spent outside the country from which no financial return can be expected.

The *hajj* is a complex enterprise in which both the individual and the state have interests. The Department of Religion is the place where these interests meet.

1 THE PILGRIM AS SURRENDERED PERSON

Islam means surrender to God, but in the context of the *hajj* the Indonesian Muslim also surrenders to the state. It is not possible, once the decision to make the pilgrimage has been made, to undertake it without complying with the laws of the state—in effect, the laws and directives as administered by the Department of Religion. To obtain the necessary documents the pilgrim must surrender to the bureaucratic process.

Law No. 17/1999

Law No. 17/1999 on the Implementation of the Hajj is typical of all Indonesian legislation in being very general in its phrases. It states broad principles and aims, leaving much to subsequent subordinate regulations. As a result, it can only be read with its accompanying and supposedly derivative regulations. It is the latter that determine the reality of the law—how it actually works in practice—but even here there is uncertainty and room for multiple meanings. For example, Chapter XI of the law declares that the earlier Dutch Pilgrim Ondonnantie (Staatsblad No. 698/1922) and its amendments are no longer applicable. Despite this, the bureaucratic practices put in place by the Dutch continue into the present. This means that, in practice, it is still the colonially inherited bureaucratic procedures that determine the functioning of the law.

The text of the law itself is neither long nor, on the face of it, complex. Article 1 gives a series of definitions modelled directly on the Dutch original, but adding new elements reflecting the Indonesia of the 1990s. The pilgrim is an Indonesian citizen holding a '*hajj* passport' who has paid the requisite fees. Article 2 proclaims that every Muslim citizen 'has the right to perform the *hajj*' and article 3 requires the government, through the Department of Religion, to organize the pilgrimage. The department's actions must be based 'on justice, equality of opportunity and legal certainty in accordance with Pancasila and the 1945 Constitution' (article 4). The remaining articles set out the organization of the *hajj* division of the Department of Religion, including staffing levels and hierarchy. Pilgrims must register with the department. Provision is made for methods of payment (to named banks) and the organization of the annual quota of pilgrims by province and district.[1] The department is also charged with matters of health, emigration, and transport and accommodation.

Ministerial Decision No. 371/2002[2]

The purpose of Ministerial Decision No. 371/2002 is to state in formal terms how Law No. 17/1999 is to be implemented by the Department of Religion. It begins by setting out the hierarchies of authority for the *hajj*. In Indonesia, authority resides in the minister and is delegated to the director-general of the Department of Religion, the provincial governors and the district heads. In Saudi Arabia (the receiving state), authority resides in the Indonesian ambassador and is delegated to consular officials. The functions of the various levels of authority include the registration of pilgrims, providing receipts for payments, assisting with travel formalities and providing transport and accommodation. The lines of delegated authority are by no means consistently separated or even clear, with some functions allocated to the Ministry of Finance, the Ministry of Transport and even Garuda, the national airline.

Although there has been no legislative attempt to resolve the problem of overlapping responsibilities, the Department of Religion has issued instructions in its Guide to Implementation (Ditgen. D/377/2002).[3] Most of this guide is taken up with repeating the law and ministerial decision, but some elements of process are given. These cover four main topics: payment, organization, insurance and evaluation.

First, payment may be made to special accounts in specified banks either as a lump sum or, more commonly, in instalments. Because of the long-term nature of the savings, the guide provides for auditing and general account keeping to be carried out by provincial-level auditors under the direction of the auditor-general. However, the guide is not clear about the actual auditing process, and lack of transparency in the handling of *hajj* money is a subject of frequent complaint.[4] For example, the *hajj* candidates commonly do not know how their money is being spent or how the costs of travel, accommodation and so on are arrived at. Despite paying the upfront charge for the pilgrimage, pilgrims are

---

1 The quota for the whole of Indonesia is currently 205,000. This is allocated across the country on the basis of provincial population. Therefore, the most heavily populated areas have the greatest number of places (Java has about 50 per cent). The provincial allocation is made by way of ministerial decision, the most recent being Ministerial Decision No. 88/2005 for the year 2006. The enabling law is Law No. 17/1999 and Presidential Decisions No. 102/2001 and No. 45/2002. Allocation of quotas at the subprovincial (*kabupaten, kota* and *kecamatan*) level is also done by the department.
2 At the time of writing, amendments to this decision were under discussion.
3 Amendments and alterations were under discussion at the time of writing.
4 See generally the essays in Iskandar (2005).

commonly required to pay various extra fees. Any surplus funds held by the Department of Religion are supposed to be paid to the Islamic Community Perpetual Fund (Dana Abadi Umat) but there is no transparency in how this money is spent (Rahardjo 2005). The Indonesian procedures are often compared (unfavourably) with Malaysia's Tabung Haji, which is often held up as a model of *hajj* administration.[5] Clearly there are problems with *hajj* finances at the state (department) level with which the guide does not deal.

Second, the guide addresses the complex issue of organizing the *hajj* in Saudi Arabia itself. This is done by the Committee for the Operational Implementation of the Hajj (Panitia Pelaksanaan Operasional Haji; PPOH) located in the Indonesian consulate in Jeddah. The committee and the consulate answer directly to the Indonesian ambassador. The functions of the PPOH include the provision of advice and counselling to pilgrims as well as assistance with immigration formalities, health, accommodation and transport. The committee also supervises training courses for the staff in charge of the pilgrims. PPOH staff have minute control over the lives of Indonesian pilgrims while they are in Saudi Arabia. The implications of this are dealt with in detail below, but one aspect that is particularly important is accommodation. The guide sets out detailed instructions for the PPOH on the location and size of buildings and rooms, facilities, and the allocation of space to pilgrims. The average pilgrim has no choice but to surrender, although the wealthy can make other choices.

Third, the guide explains the two forms of insurance that have recently become available to pilgrims.[6] The first is individual insurance against death or permanent disability occurring while the pilgrim is on the *hajj*, arranged by the official *hajj* insurer. The amount claimable is 80 per cent of the total cost of the pilgrimage excluding air fares (clearly not a large sum). This type of contract is valid according to *fiqh* because the circumstances and amounts are known at the time of entering into the contract. Claims are lodged with the relevant provincial office of the Department of Religion along with evidence of the harm suffered, certified as correct by the Indonesian consulate in Jeddah. The second form of insurance is compensation (*dia* or *diyyah*)[7] for harm resulting in physical damage, whether caused intentionally or accidentally. This type of claim is administered by the Indonesian consulate in Jeddah. That is, insurance is another of its bureaucratic duties and is administered as such.

Finally, the guide sets out in great detail the chain of reports and evaluations required to show the successful completion of the *hajj*. Thus, the provincial and district-level offices of the Department of Religion report to the director-general,

---

5   For details of the Malaysian system, see Radia Abdul Kadir (1991).
6   Neither raises any of the controversial problems associated with other types of contract such as life insurance (see Hooker 2003a: 207–11).
7   Set amounts of financial compensation for homicide, assault or wounding. See Encyclopaedia of Islam (second edition): *diyyah*.

who reports to the minister, who reports directly to the president with a copy to the minister of social welfare. The consulate and embassy are also required to report to Jakarta, although the guide is not clear about where these reports are sent or who is responsible for evaluating them.[8]

The purpose of extensive reporting is to evaluate the success of the *hajj* in a particular year. But what is 'success'? This is a constant question put by the many critics of the department.[9] The department itself measures success by a very limited criterion: that the formalities of registration, payment and travel to and from Saudi Arabia are successfully concluded without loss or damage to the Indonesian participants. In the view of the critics this is far too narrow a basis on which to judge success. They point to poor accommodation (distant from the major sites, lacking in water and so on), chaotic travel arrangements within Saudi Arabia and general overpricing. Their major criticism, however, is that the Department of Religion is both the regulator and executor of the *hajj*. They argue that these are incompatible functions, leading to faulty execution. Moreover, the inconsistencies in Law No. 17/1999 are compounded by constant changes in departmental regulations, many of them implemented without notice or discussion (Mustoffa 2005; Marfuddin 2005).

The solution that is advocated is to leave the supervisory function with the department and put execution in the hands of the independent *hajj* travel agencies (*biro perjalanan haji*; BPH) that already handle some *hajj* business.[10] The critics point out that Law No. 17/1999 already provides for the licensing of such agent companies, which currently handle 12 per cent of the Indonesian national quota (now 205,000 per year). In 2003, 12,000 places were allocated to private agents and in 2004, 16,000.

This is clearly a business-oriented solution, but the *hajj* has always been a business.[11] The proponents of this course of action admit that the BPH option is more expensive but justify it on several grounds. First, it would attract the increasing number of wealthy middle-class pilgrims who wish to make the pilgrimage but do not want to put up with the rather Spartan amenities and services offered by the Department of Religion. Second, BPH pilgrims would not be bound by the rigid travel schedules of the department, allowing them to vary their times of

---

8   Enquiries indicate that the reports are sent to the Department of Religion and, in some instances, to the Ministry of Foreign Affairs (interviews with Department of Religion officials, Jakarta, June 2006).

9   For representative examples, see the essays in Iskandar (2005: 17–106). It is only fair to point out that many of the critics have vested interests; one is the general head of the Association of Agents for Umrah and Hajj Travel, for example (see Iskandar 2005: 35).

10 There are 200 such agencies licensed for the *hajj*, and 400 for the *umrah* (pilgrimages taken at other times of the year).

11 See Snouck Hurgronje (1931), Douwes and Kaptein (1997), Sarief (2005) and Vredenbregt (1962).

travel and take 'add-on' trips (to Cairo, Istanbul, Amman or even Europe). This is obviously a limited market but it is a valuable one; the add-on options start at US$3–4,000 and go up from there.[12] Third, because BPH pilgrims tend to travel business class and stay in good hotels near the main mosques—the Grand Mosque and the Prophet's Mosque (Masjid Haram and Masjid Nabawi)—they have the comfort and space to focus totally on the *hajj* and its significance. The proponents of the BPH model argue that wealthy Indonesians are choosing not to undertake the *hajj* because of the poor conditions—clearly an undesirable state of affairs. They propose to correct this by treating the pilgrim as a tourist, someone to be attracted and competed for. Of course it is only selected pilgrims—those with money—who fall into this category. It is impossible to say how serious the agencies would be about providing a lower-cost and better service to ordinary Indonesian pilgrims.

The Bureaucratic Profile of the Pilgrim

Mass transport, mass accommodation and mass health care are challenges that can only be met by tight administrative control. The inevitable result is that the individual is reduced to a passive object to be put through the appropriate process, becoming totally dependent on possessing the correct forms required by the bureaucracy. As we have seen, the pilgrim must register for the *hajj* and pay through an approved bank, which is required to provide five receipts of the final payment. The pilgrim must also have a certificate of medical fitness from either a registered practitioner or, in rural areas, a community health centre (*puskesmas*). There are additional requirements for women of child-bearing age, including a pregnancy test and (for women who are not pregnant) an inoculation against meningitis—the latter required by the receiving state, Saudi Arabia.

Having fulfilled these requirements, the pilgrim is eligible to receive a *hajj* passport: a travel document that can only be used at designated airports at specified times.[13] This document is in Indonesian and Arabic (although the Geneva Convention rules on international travel are in English). Like a regular passport, the opening pages give the name of the holder, registration details and the place of issue. But in the section headed 'Attention' we see the special nature of the document:

Attention

1   The Hajj Passport is the property of the State.
2   It is forbidden to alter and deface the Hajj Passport.
3   The Hajj Passport is to be kept safe in the bearer's pocket so as not to be lost or harmed.

---

12 They are heavily advertised in magazines and newspapers, especially *Republika.*
13 The peculiar form of the *hajj* passport is not mentioned in any of the standard accounts of passport studies, which remain wholly Euro-centric (see Torpey 2000).

4 If the Hajj Passport is lost, this must be reported to the Group Leader (*Ketua Kloter*) who must report the loss to the Hajj Office in Jeddah [that is, the consulate]

5 The Hajj Passport is valid for one person only and for one *hajj* season only.

6 The holder must present the Hajj Passport at the Airport Departure Hostel at the proper time.

7 If the holder dies in Saudi Arabia, he or she will be buried there.

8 The Hajj Passport has 12 detachable pages numbered A to L, for the purposes of *hajj* administration.

9 Page 3 is to be filled in by Saudi Arabian officials [this is the visa, now available online].

Numbers 1–3 are the usual warnings given to passport holders, but the remainder are specific to this document. In terms of illustrating surrender, perhaps the most important is No. 8: 'for the purposes of *hajj* administration'. The passport has a special explanatory page setting out the purpose of each of the 12 detachable pages:

Attached Pages to be Removed

At Time of Departure:

1 Page A (Pilgrim Identification), to be removed by the passport bearer and placed in the plastic pocket provided.

2 Page B (Embarkation Page), to be taken by the Hajj Management Committee (Panitia Penyelenggaraan Ibadah Haji; PPIH).

3 Page C (Departure Slip), to be taken by Immigration Official.

4 Page D: to be taken by Travel Group (*Kloter*) official on the aircraft and given to Hajj Affairs Section in Jeddah on arrival in Saudi Arabia.

On Arrival in Saudi Arabia:

5 Page E: to be taken by Saudi Immigration.

6 Page F: to be taken by an official of the Saudi Hajj Ministry.

7 Page G: to be taken by an official of the Saudi *hajj* authority in Jeddah on departure from Saudi Arabia.

8 Page H (Return Page), to be taken by Indonesian representative in Jeddah.

9 Page I: specifically to be filled in by an official of the Saudi *hajj* authority and the airline, and to be detached upon departure for home.

10 Page J: to be taken by Saudi Immigration when leaving for Indonesia.

11 Page K (Disembarkation Page), to be taken by *Kloter* official on the aircraft and handed to the PPIH.

On Arrival in Indonesia:

12 Page L (Immigration Re-entry Page), to be taken by Immigration Official.

The *hajj* passport is handed to the pilgrim in the *hajj* hostel (*asrama haji*), purpose-built accommodation located close to the designated airport from which the pilgrim is to depart.[14] Entry into the *asrama haji* requires production of a receipt from the bank showing that all fees have been paid, a health certificate, and an official letter of admission provided by the local Department of Religion

---

14 Until recently there were eight designated airports: Aceh, Medan, Batam, Jakarta, Surabaya, Solo, Makassar and Balikpapan. The number is soon to be increased.

office. The pilgrim is then provided with an identification tag. The *asrama haji* is run by the PPIH, which allocates rooms, supervises catering and deals with health problems. On paper the regime is quite strict (no food to be brought in, no cooking, no guests). The pilgrim is instructed 'to present a good appearance ... and build good relationships with other pilgrims'.

The requirement for individual pilgrims to prove their identity through a mountain of paperwork is therefore very high. The reader may see this observation as trite or obvious, and in a sense it is. But to leave the matter there would be a mistake, because this high level of documentation is only part of the department's bureaucratic profiling of pilgrims.

The Department of Religion has produced four short books on the *hajj* that it issues free to each pilgrim. They are: *Panduan Perjalanan Haji* [Guide for Hajj Travel]; *Bimbingan Manasik Haji* [Instruction Manual for the Hajj]; *Hikmah Ibadah Haji* [Insights into Religious Obligations for the Hajj]; and *Do'a dan Zikir Ibadah Haji* [Prayers and Invocations for the Hajj].[15] The first two are instruction manuals. The third aims to increase religious understanding. The last is a small book of the required prayers, in Arabic script, in Roman-letter transcription and in Indonesian translation. It contains all the prayers and recitations necessary for every stage of the *hajj*. It is designed to be hung from a cord around the neck where it is easily accessible without impeding movement. All four books have the same foreword (see Appendix A5.1). The list of contents of each book is given in Appendices A5.2–A5.5.

The first three of these texts are crucial for our purposes, because they deal with the interface between the obligation of the individual and the department's role (almost a guarantee) in the successful performance of that obligation. They may be read as representing further dimensions of the bureaucratic profiling of pilgrims—as traveller in the first book, and as instructed Muslim in the second and third books.

2   THE PILGRIM AS TRAVELLER[16]

Mass travel with its rigid disciplines and timetables is usually thought of as dehumanizing to a greater or lesser degree. One would expect the same to be true for the *hajj*, but there is evidence to show that such a sorry outcome is not necessarily inevitable. The first of the department's book, *Panduan Perjalanan Haji* (hereafter *Panduan*), is didactic but not minatory, and attempts to be 'user friendly' (see Appendix A5.2). Read alongside personal accounts of the *hajj*

---

15 My editions are departmental publications dated 2003. They are also available at <http://www.informasihaji.com>.

16 In this and the following section, I do not discuss the BPH (that is, private) pilgrim, who travels in greater comfort than the ordinary pilgrim.

experience, such as that by Haji Danarto (1989),[17] it is clear that the numinous informs mass travel, that is, that there is a difference between mass travel and the pilgrimage.

Travel to the Haramain

The Department of Religion handles the overseas travel arrangements for the *hajj* and delegates internal travel arrangements to its provincial and district offices. Groups are arranged on the basis of family, place of residence or domicile, ethnicity and, where possible, individual preference. A pilgrim may move from the allotted group to another. On the basis of the information provided by its regional offices, the department produces a final list (manifest) of *hajj* pilgrims. Domestic transport from the place of residence to the designated airport is organized at the provincial level. Accommodation at or near the airport is organized by a special body, the Board for Management of Hajj Accommodation (Badan Pengelola Asrama Haji; BPAH).[18]

Pilgrims are grouped into teams (*regu*) consisting of 10 persons plus a leader; units (*rombongan*) consisting of 45 persons; and travel groups (*kloter*) consisting of 7–11 units depending on the capacity of the aircraft. Each *kloter* has a head (*ketua kloter*), a doctor, paramedics and supporting administrative staff.

The *Panduan* provides detailed instructions for the pilgrim both before and after departure. Before leaving home pilgrims must have discharged all their obligations, including any debts owing, and ask forgiveness from family and friends for any faults or misconduct. The *Panduan* calls this 'spiritual preparation'. At the practical level, pilgrims are instructed to pack five changes of plain clothing (non-transparent in the case of women) and limit their luggage to one case weighing 30 kilograms plus a carry-on bag.

Before departure, pilgrims must go to the *asrama haji* where they will receive an ID bracelet, *hajj* passport and money for expenses. They are instructed to pray at least twice for a safe journey, just before departure. These prayers should be supplemented with chants (*zikir*) and other prayers (*do'a*). The *Panduan* also reminds pilgrims to recite the prayer of intention to undertake the pilgrimage (*talbiyah*)[19] on leaving their place of residence and while in the *asrama*. However, as travellers, pilgrims are permitted to shorten (*menggasar*) these prayers.[20]

---

17 For earlier as well as contemporary accounts, see Matheson and Milner (1984).

18 The BPAH acts in concert with the office for the National Development Program (Program Pembangunan Nasional; Propenas), which is responsible for building and maintaining pilgrim accommodation (Law No. 25/2000).

19 This is a prayer of surrender to God signifying the intention to perform the pilgrimage.

20 My own notes suggest that many (most?) pilgrims do not take the shorter option.

The *Panduan* also provides detailed instructions for pilgrims while on the aircraft. They are told to obey instructions, sit quietly, use the toilet properly and pay attention to lectures and instructional movies. The *Panduan* pays particular attention to the issue of prayer, warning that sufficient water is not available to carry out the usual ablutions. To quote from one traveller's account:

> Early the next morning, some passengers wanted water so they could complete the ablutions before the dawn prayers. ... Imagine how much water five hundred people would need. ... The *imam* recommended that we do what one does in the desert where there is sand but no water. Following this traditional alternative, we placed our palms on the wall and then rubbed our hands and our faces and forearms (Danarto 1989: 4).

Tayammum, the performance of ritual ablutions with sand or earth where water is not available, is a matter of dispute in Indonesian Islam, specifically with reference to air travel. The *Panduan* is scrupulous in stating the two main positions and leaving it up to the reader to decide between them. The first is that prayers said on board an aircraft are not valid because there is insufficient water and no 'proper' dust. The dust on an airplane is not from the earth and therefore lacks the cleansing quality of true dust. This position is supported by a *fatwā* issued by Nahdlatul Ulama (NU) in 1989 (see Hooker 2003a: 98). The second position is that such prayers are valid, because the necessity to pray at the proper times overrides the absence of water. Pilgrims should therefore perform *tayammum* by passing the palms of their hands over the back of the chair in front and/ or the walls of the aircraft and then wiping their face, hands and forearms. The prescribed ritual prayer (*salat*) should then be performed while seated. Those who pray without performing *tayammum* are advised to repeat their prayers on arrival at their destination.

These detailed instructions on *tayammum* recognize the anxiety of pilgrims to achieve correctness in ritual, including prayers. One of the chief functions of the *Panduan*, therefore, is to allay such anxieties. The *Panduan* also gives detailed instructions on the formalities of arrival: immigration, customs, accommodation and onward travel.

Travel in the Haramain

The travel program of pilgrims is highly condensed because of the time constraints: the *hajj* proper must be completed between the eighth and thirteenth days of the Muslim month of Dzulhijjah. The three most important areas to be covered are accommodation, health and the actual schedule of travel.

Accommodation is administered by the Department of Religion under the regulations accompanying Law No. 17/1999. The current practice is for the department to acquire leases on properties in Mecca and Medina under contracts governed by Saudi law. Property in Mecca is leased for up to 20 days during the *hajj* period; in Medina the period is nine days (that is, the eight days required for the *arbain* prayers[21] plus additional time for arrival and departure). The basic unit on which accommodation is based is the *kloter*, although it is not always possible to accommodate all members of the same *kloter* in the same building. Each building must have a minimum level of facilities, including water coolers, fans, air conditioning, electricity, bathing facilities, kitchens and comfortable sleeping quarters. Properties of four storeys or more must have a lift. The department's officers may cross-subsidize the cost of accommodation across buildings.[22]

The *Panduan* therefore informs pilgrims that their accommodation in Mecca and Medina will be in multi-storey buildings with lifts; however, they may need to queue and the able-bodied should take the stairs. The distance to the various mosques and other sites will vary, so pilgrims should take note of the location and address of their hostel. Each pilgrim will be allocated a space of 2.5×2 metres and provided with a thin mattress (*lihab*). The sleeping areas are also used to store personal possessions and take meals. The bathrooms are communal so queuing will be necessary. Water must be used carefully, and washing should be hung in the places provided, not in the corridors. This emphasis on 'domestic housekeeping', as it were, carries through into such details as the availability of food for purchase and cooking arrangements. The Arafah and Mina accommodation is in tents that are furnished with carpets but not with pillows. Food is provided. Toilets and bathrooms are limited so queueing and patience will be necessary. Some air conditioning is available.

The details provided in the *Panduan* are formalistic and take no account of the internal experience of the individual pilgrim. We are therefore fortunate in having several accounts of how the *Panduan* directions work in practice. One of the most interesting is that by Haji Danarto, written in 1989. The author is a talented writer whose command of language is sufficient to convey the emotional and religious aspects of the *hajj* as well as its practical aspects. He does not gloss over the often difficult daily experiences—overcrowding with its physical and mental toll—but in the end he does convey the numinous:[23]

> Despite the chaotic conditions, these crowded rooms often exuded a beautiful fragrance when we prayed together. Our clean white clothes separated us for a while from life's daily problems, as we all drew close to a truer understanding of the will of God. (Danarto 1989: 4–5)

Health is a significant and detailed component of the *Panduan*. The main theme is to encourage pilgrims to look after their own health, before and after leaving Indonesia. They are told to ensure that they are physically fit at least six months before departure. This can be attained by doing 'aerobic exercise or gym

---

21 The 40 *salat* that must be performed at Masjid Nabawi in Medina.
22 This is an important and, to the best of my knowledge, uninvestigated aspect of *hajj* financing.
23 See also Matheson and Milner (1984: 31 ff.). For South Asia, see Metcalf (1990).

work two or three times per week'. (No doubt this comment is intended for pilgrims from urban areas.) All pilgrims should attend the health education classes run by the *puskesmas*, the Department of Religion and privately run NGOs.

The *Panduan* also gives advice on nutrition. Pilgrims are advised to eat a balanced diet containing carbohydrates, protein, oil, vitamins and clean water. They should eat green vegetables and fruit containing vitamin C and avoid fatty / oily foods and sugar. There is specific advice for pilgrims who suffer from various medical conditions. For example, people with diabetes should eat regularly, take care not to consume excessive amounts of calories and avoid sweets, including condensed milk. Those with heart conditions should avoid sweets, fats and oils, fibrous matter such as spinach (*kangkong*) and stimulating spices such as chilli. Similar rules apply to those with high blood pressure. Women are advised to use contraception (method not specified) and regulate their periods through the use of oestrogen, progesterone or a combination of the two.

In the case of illness, the *Panduan* directs pilgrims to the head of the *kloter* or the Hall for the Medical Care of Indonesian Pilgrims (Balai Pengobatan Haji Indonesia; BPHI). Treatment is free, as is treatment at Saudi Arabian hospitals. There is general health advice to protect pilgrims against cold weather, which can cause muscle and bone problems, nosebleeds and chafed skin and lips, and aggravate problems such as diabetes, asthma and rheumatism. Precautions include keeping warm, eating properly, drinking warm water and wearing a face mask. Pilgrims are also advised to limit non-compulsory religious activities (*ibadah sunat*) to safeguard their health. Common illnesses among *hajj* pilgrims include heat stroke, meningitis and dysentery; the symptoms of each are listed and appropriate methods of care recommended. If a pilgrim dies, proper burial will be organized by Saudi officials without charge, unless the family requests prayers at Masjid Haram in Mecca or the Masjid Nabawi in Medina.

We turn finally to the actual mechanics of the times and places of travel. The *Panduan* puts this in diagram form (see Figure 5.1 overleaf).[24]

Returning to Indonesia

The *Panduan* has little of interest to say about the return trip to Indonesia, with two exceptions. First, it advises pilgrims that their documents will be checked on arrival, and that any person suspected of being ill will be detained for examination at no cost to them. Pilgrims who fall sick within 14 days of arrival must report to a medical authority such as a *puskesmas*. Second, the new Haji or Hajjah is reminded of the religious duty to perform certain prayers (*salat sunat mathlak* and *sujud syukur*) in the local mosque or prayer house (*mushalla*) before entering the home.

---

24 Many commercial publications offer similar advice; see, for example, Sarief (2005: 147).

3 THE PILGRIM AS INSTRUCTED MUSLIM (I): ORTHOPRAXY

Islam is sometimes described as a religion in which correctness of conduct (ortho-praxy) is more important than correctness of dogma (orthodoxy). A moment's thought shows this to be a false opposition—the two are connected. In theory there is a balance between the two but in practice this balance varies from place to place and over time. When judged against some ideal standard the connection may fall short of a pure congruence, but that is simply the nature of Islam. In fact, it is the 'ideal' itself that causes the difficulty. As we saw in Chapter 2, the ideal exists in the mind of a particular author, specifically in the questions that he or she asks. These are issues which do not concern the mass of ordinary pilgrims. For them, orthopraxy—correct performance of a pilgrimage acceptable to God (*hajj mabrur*)—is primary. That is why the *Panduan* devotes no less than five pages to the penalties (*dam/denda*) incurred by pilgrims who infringe any of their ritual obligations.

The purpose of the second book issued by the Department of Religion, *Bimbingan Manasik Haji* (hereafter *Bimbingan*), is to ensure such correctness (see Appendix A5.3). The department itself says its function is:

> To provide assistance and instruction to build the character of the [pilgrim] by focus-ing on the revitalization and sustainability of religious strength ...

The *Bimbingan* has 117 pages plus another 15 pages of tables and appendices.[25] It has six chapters, including a chapter on definitions (Chapter II), one on prepa-ration and procedures (Chapter IV) and one on commonly asked questions and answers (Chapter V). This is a very modern arrangement that owes nothing to the past, even though it is informed by the rules derived from the Qur'ān and Sunnah. But is the *Bimbingan* significant in other ways as well? To answer this question, we need to look at its actual content.

Definitions

This section has 20 entries. The department has made what it obviously feels to be an appropriate selection of the terms requiring definition, even though it does not specify the criteria for its choice. The explanations that follow are minimal but accurate, in keeping with the needs of the reader who, by definition, is in need of instruction. However, from an analytical point of view the *process* of definition is quite complex. Broadly speaking the terms chosen are of three types: those concerned with real events; those describing an inner state; and

---

25 The latter include a schedule of prayers and the places where these are to be per-formed; a table comparing the required duties for each of the four Sunni schools; and a table setting out the penalties (*dam/denda*) for errors in performing one's ritual obligations.

Figure 5.1   Process of Implementing the Hajj via Garuda Airlines

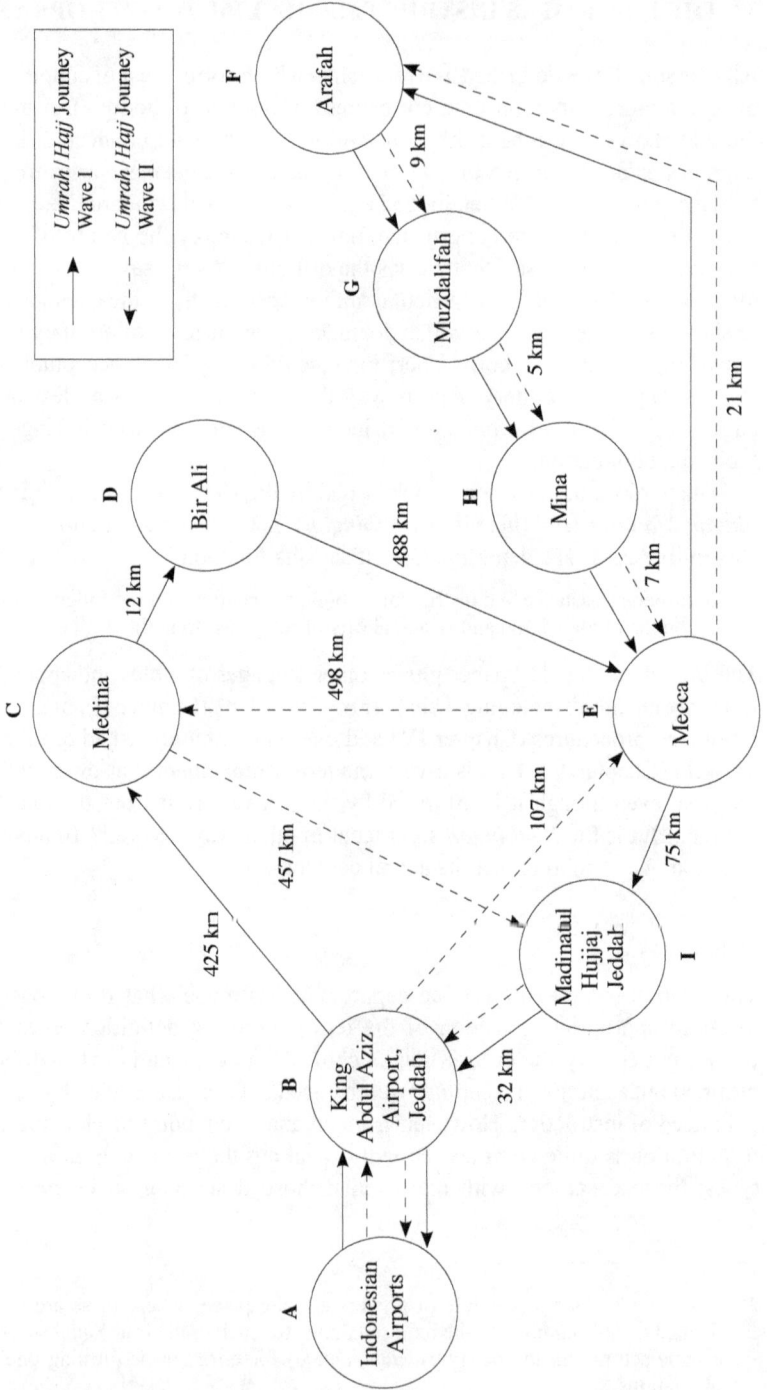

A
1 Bring letter of admission to embarkation hostel (SPMA)
2 Weigh baggage
3 Receive accommodation card and food coupon
4 Final health check
5 Participate in group prayer, lecture on health procedures and practice of *hajj*
6 Receive passport, money for living expenses and ID bracelet
7 Board bus and plane

B
At King Abdul Aziz Airport, Jeddah
A Wave I
1 Go to waiting room
2 Passport check
3 Health check
4 Baggage collection
5 Baggage inspection
6 Proceed to rest place
7 Prepare for Medina, collection of passports, board bus in groups
B Wave II
1–6 As above
7 Prepare for Mecca, perform ablutions (*wudu*), recite *ihram* prayer
8 Bus to Mecca, recite intention (*niat*) to undertake *umrah/hajj*

C
At Medina
A Wave I
1 On arrival proceed to accommodation
2 Visit the Prophet's grave; women from 7.00 to 10.00 and between Zuhur and Asar prayers
3 Recite *arbain* prayers in Masjid Nabawi; men and women separately
4 Visit historical sites
5 After 8 days prepare for *hajj/umrah* (*ihram*, 2 units of *ihram* prayers), board bus to Bir Ali
B Wave II
1–4 As above
5 After 8 days go to Jeddah

D
At Bir Ali
1 Those who have not yet recited *niat* to undertake *umrah/hajj* do so here
2 Bus to Mecca

E
At Mecca
Wave I
1 On arrival from Jeddah/Medina proceed to accommodation and prepare for the required rituals
2 Before going to Arafah, recite set prayers in the hostel and mosque
3 On 8 Dzulhijjah in the afternoon prepare for Arafah
4 Board bus to Arafah
At Mecca (after performing wukuf)
1 Return to accommodation
2 Perform *tawaf ifadah* and *sa'i* (if not yet done)
3 All perform the farewell circumambulation (*tawaf wada'*) together; Wave I leaves for Jeddah and Wave II for Medina

F
At Arafah
1 Go to tents allocated by school
2 Rest at night and prepare for staying (*wukuf*) at Arafah the next morning
3 Perform *wukuf* on 9 Dzulhijjah from zenith until sunset
4 Listen to *wukuf* sermon, recite requisite prayers, recite Qur'an
5 At night prepare to leave by bus for Muzdalifah and Mina

G
At Muzdalifah
1 Recite waiting (*mabit*) prayers, gather pebbles for stone-throwing ritual (*jamrah*)
2 Take bus to Mina after midnight

H
At Mina
1 Go to tents allocated by school, rest
2 On 10 Dzulhijjah perform *jamrah*, cut/shave hair
3 On 11–13 Dzulhijjah perform *jamrah*
4 Those in *nafar awal* leave Mina before sunset on 12 Dzulhijjah, those in *nafar tsani* leave on 13 Dzulhijjah

I
At Jeddah
(time to return home)
1 Wait with the appropriate travel group (*kloter*)
2 Receive passport, rest
3 Depart from King Abdul Aziz Airport

Source: Adapted from Department of Religion (2003), *Panduan Perjalanan Haji*, Jakarta.

those describing actions. The best way to explain these three categories is to give examples from the *Bimbingan*.

The first group comprises the defined places (*miqat makani*) and defined times (*miqat zamani*) at which the events of the *hajj* take place. These include Tarwiyah, the eighth day of Dzulhijjah (the day on which the Prophet ensured that pilgrims had sufficient water for their journey to Arafah); Arafah, the ninth day of Dzulhijjah (the day on which pilgrims gather on the plain of Arafah); Nahar, the tenth day of Dzulhijjah (the day of sacrifices); and Tasyriq, the eleventh to thirteenth days of Dzulhijjah (the days on which the *jamrah* stoning and *mabit* waiting rituals take place at Mina).

The second group describes inner states of being. The *hajj* itself is defined as 'visiting Baitullah' (that is, the Ka'bah) in accordance with God's call, in the hope of receiving His grace or blessing (*ridha*). The definition of *umrah* also contains the same basic reference to *ridha*. *Istita'ah* meaning 'capable' is defined as the physical, financial and, most importantly, spiritual capacity to undertake the *hajj*. The latter means 'having a healthy mind that comprehends the [meaning of] the *hajj* and is prepared to carry out the journey'. The emphasis throughout is on the necessity for the individual to both understand and wholly commit to the pilgrimage. This is repeated in a variety of ways to reinforce the message.

The last group consists of actions that the pilgrim must perform, beginning with the religious obligation to perform the *hajj* (*wajib hajj*), the compulsory duties (*amalan*) the pilgrim must carry out during the *hajj*, and the penalties (*dam*) for incorrect performance of these duties. The latter are based on the sacrifice of various types of animals (goats, camels, cows). The specific actions that a pilgrim must perform while on the *hajj* include *tawaf* (circling the Ka'bah seven times counterclockwise, starting and finishing at the Black Stone, or Hajar Aswad); *sa'i* (running or walking seven times between the two hills of Safa and Marwa, just outside the walls of Masjid Haram); *wukuf* (staying on the plain of Arafah at the set times); *mabit* (waiting at Arafah on 10 Dzulhijjah and overnight at Muzdalifah and Mina on 11–13 Dzulhijjah); and finally, *lontar jamrah* (the stoning ritual performed on 11–13 Dzulhijjah).

Although the definitions provided in this section are short and to the point, they are repeated in later pages of the *Bimbingan* in much greater detail, with an emphasis on correct performance of ritual.

Preparation and Procedures

This 32-page section of the *Bimbingan* consists of stipulations for the *hajj* and *umrah*. Each of its sections is preceded by *hukum*, which in this context means 'rules' rather than 'law'. The stipulations in this section expand on and reinforce the definitions given earlier. For example, on the subject of correct clothing and behaviour (*ihram*), the *Bimbingan* stipulates the following:

Men must wear two unsewn pieces of clothing—one around the lower part of the body, such as a sarong, and one over the shoulders. They may not wear shirts or trousers. When circumambulating the Ka'bah, the left shoulder should be exposed. Clothing should preferably be white.

Men are not permitted to wear normal clothes or shoes that cover the heels; or to cover their heads (unless it is very cold or they have a wound).

Women must wear clothes that cover their whole bodies, except their hands from the wrists to the tips of the fingers.

Women are forbidden to wear gloves or cover their faces.

Both men and women are forbidden to wear perfume, cut their fingernails or shave or pluck hair from their bodies; chase wild animals to eat them; kill animals (except dangerous ones); marry or propose marriage; flirt or have sex; or quarrel or swear.

Other stipulations continue to describe in minute detail the conduct prescribed for all aspects of the required rituals. The pilgrim is thus presented with a step-by-step manual of instruction.

Considerable attention is paid to the problems of female pilgrims, especially to menstruation and the period of sexual abstinence after childbirth (*nifas*):

It is possible for a woman to undertake the *hajj* while menstruating or during *nifas*, except for *tawaf*, where it is a condition that people be free from both large and small impurities (*hadats*). Women may prevent menstruation by taking pills.

These short extracts bring us back to the pairing of stipulation and law (*ketentuan* and *hukum*) with their unmistakable emphasis on conformity to rules, that is, the performance of specific duties at specified times and places. Failure to follow these rules incurs a penalty (*dam*). In short, the duty of the individual performing the *hajj* takes the form of positive sovereign commands.[26]

Questions and Answers

This is the longest section in the *Bimbangan*, comprising about two-thirds of the whole. It is arranged in 16 sections numbered (A) to (P), taking the pilgrim from the initial stages of the *hajj* through to its completion. Each step in this progression is explained through simple questions accompanied by short, clear answers. This method of instruction is very effective: it is legally authoritative, simple and logical. The topics covered by the question and answer section are as follows:

A   Understanding the syariah and the *hajj* principles and obligations
    (17 questions)

---

26 At this point the reader will rightly anticipate the epistemological problem: that because the positivism of ritual duty is based on historical precedent (that is, the Prophet's acts), then it is possible to derogate from the certainty of positivism depending on the truth or falsity of the historical evidence. This is of no concern to the ordinary Muslim undertaking instruction in the *hajj*. Along the same lines, it has recently been suggested in Indonesia that the timing of the *hajj* rituals should be changed in the interests of public safety (see Abdallah 2005). Of course that is impossible.

B   Putting oneself in a state of ritual purity (*ihram*) and the places where this is required (*miqat*) (28 questions)
C   Circumambulation (*tawaf*) (29 questions)
D   Surrendering to God (*munajat*) at Multazam and prayers (*shalat*) at Maqam Ibrahim and Hijir Ismail (30 questions)
E   Running between Safa and Marwa (*sa'i*) (10 questions)
F   Staying (*wukuf*) (9 questions)
G   Waiting (*mabit*) at Muzdalifah (7 questions)
H   Stoning (*jamrah*) (11 questions)
I   Waiting (*mabit*) at Mina and Nahar (the day of sacrifices) (11 questions)
J   Coming out of *ihram* (*tahallul*) (7 questions)
K   Penalties (*dam*) (10 questions)
L   Pilgrimage done in the name of or for another (*badal haji*) (2 questions)
M   Women pilgrims (8 questions)
N   The *hajj* for pilgrims who are ill (9 questions)
O   Prayers at Masjid Nabawi and Masjid Haram (4 questions)
P   Prayers on the plane (6 questions)

I have room here for only a few examples. I have chosen to use a passage from (A), because it describes the basic structure of the pilgrims' obligations; all of (D), because it emphasizes personal devotion; and all of (K), because it describes the positive law penalties for incorrect or omitted acts.[27] These three categories should be read with the earlier discussion of definitions in mind.

A   Understanding the syariah and the *hajj* principles and obligations

What are the essential conditions for carrying out the *hajj* or *umrah*?
There are five conditions. The person must (a) be a Muslim; (b) be an adult; (c) be healthy of mind; (d) be free (not a slave); and (e) be capable (*istita'ah*).

What is meant by *istita'ah* in connection with the *hajj*?
Istita'ah means (a) being healthy in body and mind; and (b) having sufficient finances for yourself and the family you leave behind.

How many *hajj* principles (*rukun haji*) are there?
There are six *rukun haji*: (a) being in a state of ritual purity (*ihram*) with the intention (*niat*) to perform the *hajj*, (b) staying (*wukuf*) in Arafah, (c) circumambulation (*tawaf*); (d) running between Safa and Marwa (*sa'i*); (e) shaving / cutting one's hair; (f) behaving appropriately (*tertib*) in accordance with the *hajj* obligations (*manasik haji*). If one of these *rukun haji* is not carried out, then the *hajj* is invalid.

How many *hajj* obligations (*wajib haji*) are there?
There are six *wajib haji*: (a) being in *ihram* at each place (*miqat*) where this is required; (b) waiting (*mabit*) at Muzdalifah; (c) *mabit* at Mina; (d) stoning (*jamrah*); (e) avoiding forbidden acts while in *ihram*; and (f) the farewell circumambulation

---

27   I am very grateful to Ms Helen Pausacker, Asian Law Centre, University of Melbourne, who did the initial translations.

(*tawaf wada'*) for those who are leaving Mecca. If one of these obligations is left out, the *hajj* can still be made legal by paying *dam*. If *tawaf wada'* is left out by a pilgrim who is sick or menstruating (*uzur*), there is no need to pay *dam*.

What is meant by behaving appropriately (*tertib*) in carrying out the *hajj*?
What is meant by *tertib* in carrying out the *hajj* is carrying out the *hajj* in accordance with the rules and regulations.

How many *umrah* principles (*rukun umrah*) are there?
There are six *rukun umrah*: (a) *ihram / niat*; (b) *wukuf* at Arafah; (c) *tawaf*; (d) *sa'i*; (e) shaving / cutting one's hair; and (f) *tertib*.

D Surrendering to God (*munajat*) at Multazam and prayers (*shalat*) at Maqam Ibrahim and Hijir Ismail

What is surrendering to God (*munajat*)?
Munajat is 'pouring out one's heart' (*mencurahkan isi hati*) and surrendering oneself in order to be close to God.

Where is Multazam?
Multazam is between Hajar Aswad and the gate of the Ka'bah.

What is the law regarding the performance of *munajat* at Multazam?
It is desirable (*sunat*) if circumstances permit it.

How does one perform *munajat* at Multazam?
If possible, get close to (*merapatkan badan*) Multazam. If that is not possible, then take a step in the direction of Multazam.

When should *munajat* at Multazam be carried out?
Munajat at Multazam should be performed after *tawaf* but it can be carried out at any time.

What and where is Maqam Ibrahim [the tomb of the Prophet Abraham]?
Maqam Ibrahim is the stone on which the Prophet Ibrahim stood when building the Ka'bah. It lies between Hajar Aswad and Rukun Syami and has the shape of a birdcage. Above it is a stone imprinted with the two footprints of the Prophet Ibrahim.

What religious acts of devotion (*ibadah*) are carried out at Maqam Ibrahim?
The voluntary *tawaf* prayer (*shalat sunat tawaf*) and praying (*berdoa*) behind Maqam Ibrahim.

When should the voluntary prayer (*shalat sunat*) behind Maqam Ibrahim be performed?
After *tawaf*, unless the compulsory prayer (*shalat fardhu*) is about to be performed.

What and where is Hijir Ismail?
Hijir Ismail is the part of the Ka'bah that lies between Rukun Syami and Rukun Iraqi. It has a semi-circular-shaped wall.

What religious acts of devotion (*ibadah*) are carried out in Hijir Ismail?
Voluntary prayer (*shalat sunat*), praying (*berdoa*) and invocations (*dzikir*). The *shalat sunat* in Hijir Ismail has no connection with *tawaf*.

What is the importance of prayer (*shalat*) in Hijir Ismail?
It has the same importance as *shalat* in the Ka'bah.

When is voluntary prayer (*shalat sunat*) carried out in Hijir Ismail?
At any time except when the compulsory prayer (*shalat fardhu*) is about to be performed.

K   Penalties (*dam*)

What is *dam*?
Dam means 'blood'. It is the blood of the slaughtered animals used to fulfil the conditions of the *hajj*.

What are the two types of *dam*?
(a) *Dam nusuk*—for people who are performing the *hajj tamattu'* or *hajj qiran* (not because they have done wrong).[28]

(b) *Dam isa'ah*—for pilgrims who have either broken the rules of the *hajj/umrah* or omitted one of the *hajj/umrah* obligations (*wajib*), by not performing *mabit* at Mina, for example.

When should the sacrificial animals (*hewan dam*) be slaughtered?
The sacrificial animals should be slaughtered after a compulsory duty (*amalan*) has not been performed properly or, in the case of *hajj tamattu'*, after carrying out the *umrah*.

What is the correct way to carry out *dam*?
By slaughtering a goat or, for those with insufficient finances, fasting for 10 days: three in Mecca after *wukuf* in Arafah and seven upon return to one's own country. If it is not possible to fast in Mecca, then the person should fast for three days and then seven days [in his or her own country], separated by four days.

What is the difference between *qurban* and *dam*?
Qurban is slaughtering in connection with the days of sacrifice (Qurban and Tasyriq), both for the *hajj* and for other purposes, and can be carried out in the home country. *Dam* is slaughtering in connection with the *hajj* and must be carried out in the Holy Land.

What can be done instead of paying *dam*?
(a) Fasting (as above); (b) for breaking the regulations on hair cutting etc., it is possible to give alms to the poor; (c) for killing a wild animal, it is possible to pay with basic food to the same value as the animal, or by fasting; (d) for having sexual intercourse at the wrong time, then a camel or cow or seven goats should be slaughtered, or food to the same value as a camel should be given to the poor, or [the person should pay by] fasting.

What is the difference between a husband and wife having sexual intercourse before and after the first stage in coming out of *ihram* (*tahallul awal*)?

---

28 The former refers to the *hajj* combined with the *umrah*, with the pilgrim allowed to come out of *ihram* between the two. The latter refers to the *hajj* combined with the *umrah* without coming out of *ihram*.

If they have sexual intercourse before *tahallul awal*, then their *hajj* is not legal and they must make expiation (*kifarat*). If they break the prohibition after *tahallul awal*, their *hajj* remains legal but they must still make expiation.

There is nothing very special about the content of these three sections of the *Bimbingan*. Their significance lies, rather, in what they say about the formal structure of the *Bimbingan*—in its character as a guide for pilgrims, whose duty to God must be explained to them. The *Bimbingan* gives pilgrims the constituent concepts and appropriate actions and prayers to enable them to carry out their duty to God. It is therefore much more than a set of dictionary definitions. It conveys, or attempts to convey, the reality of revelation in specific ways—those set out in the question and answer section above. Mostly this means the re-enactment of historical events and the recognition of important historical places. The *Bimbingan* brings that past into the present though a formal description of *duty* (syariah). It also provides an organized corpus of *practice* (again, syariah) in a comprehensive Indonesian-language text. Duty and practice are therefore equated, in yet another affirmation of syariah as positive law.

4 THE PILGRIM AS INSTRUCTED MUSLIM (II): BUREAUCRATIC INTERPRETATIONS

The third book in the Department of Religion series, *Hikmah Ibadah Haji* (here-after *Hikmah*), consists of passages from the Qur'ān and Hadith chosen to be appropriate for each stage of the pilgrimage (see Appendix A5.4). The texts are given in Arabic, followed by an Indonesian translation and a commentary and explanation. The *Hikmah* elaborates on earlier material on the inner state of the pilgrim. Like the *Panduan* and *Bimbingan*, it is a highly structured text stressing that the *hajj* is a sacred journey requiring mental and physical preparation. In this section I concentrate on the second of its three chapters and letter (O) of the third chapter. There is a considerable degree of repetition both within the *Hikmah* and between it and the preceding two books in the series. While I have tried not to allow this to dominate, *it is important for readers to realize just how important repetition is in the construction of these manuals*. The same points are made over and over again; the Department of Religion clearly believes that the audience needs constant reinforcement in *hajj* practice and understanding.

Definitions and General Descriptions[29]

Chapter II of the *Hikmah* concerns definitions and descriptions, beginning with the *hajj* itself. The prologue explains that the *hajj* is one of the five pillars of

---

29 In this and the following subsection, I have collapsed the actual subdivisions in the *Hikmah* to make a readable narrative in a way that I hope does not corrupt the text.

Islam. It is therefore imperative that all Muslims who are financially, physically and mentally capable of performing the *hajj* do so at least once:

> ... Pilgrimage is a duty owed to God by people who are able to undertake it. Those who reject this should know that God has no need of anyone. (Q3:97)

> 'O people! The *hajj* has been made incumbent upon you, so perform the *hajj*.' A man inquired: 'O Messenger of God, is it prescribed every year?' He remained silent till the man repeated it thrice. Then he said, 'Had I replied in the affirmative, it would surely become obligatory, and you would not have been able to fulfil it'. (Narrated by Abu Hurairah)[30]

Next, the prologue explains that the *hajj* was commanded in 4 AH, and that the Prophet himself performed it only once, not long before his death. The *hajj* is therefore a precious and most worthy act of worship to God:

> Whoever performs the *hajj* and does not have sexual relations (with his wife) nor commits sin nor disputes unjustly, then he will return from the *hajj* as pure and free from sin as on the day on which his mother gave birth to him. (Narrated by Bukhari and Muslim)

But although the *hajj* is primarily an act of devotion to God, it may also affect the life journey of the individual. When properly understood and performed, the *hajj* not only fulfils one of God's commands but may result in the transformation of the individual, because the rituals themselves are so deeply profound. For that reason the Prophet's wife Aisha performed the ritual every year:

> Aisha asked the Prophet, 'We find that *jihad* is the best deed, so shouldn't we do *jihad*?' The Prophet replied, 'Rather, the best *jihad* is a proper *hajj* (*hajj mabrur*)!' Aisha later said, 'I will never stop performing the *hajj* after hearing that from the Messenger of God'. (Narrated by Bukhari and Muslim)

Nevertheless, the spiritual experience of the individual varies from person to person. Much depends on the circumstances of the particular *hajj*—possibly meaning such things as the weather, the time of year and the level of organization. However, leaving these (unspecified) circumstances aside, the *Hikmah* asserts that even for people in the same group undertaking the *hajj* at the same time, the experience may vary from one person to another. At this point the *Hikmah* cites a verse from Q22, the chapter of the Qur'ān specifically on the *hajj*:

> ... [They will come to you] to attain benefits and celebrate God's name, on the specified days, over the livestock He has provided for them—feed yourselves and the poor and unfortunate. (Q22:28)

The prologue ends by reiterating that although the *hajj* provides lessons for life in this world, the spiritual gain is the primary benefit. The *hajj* increases devotion to God, and it is for this reason that the instructions and prohibitions have

---

30 The Hadith sources are given as they appear in the *Hikmah*. Some appear to be incorrectly ascribed. I leave it to colleagues more expert than I am to say whether thay are correct or not.

been prescribed. They are a demonstration of God's care for the welfare of His people.

The second section of Chapter II discusses the concept of *hikmah* itself. *Hikmah* signifies the essential meaning that informs the meaning and purpose of ritual. Syariah is the external form of devotion, but devotion also has an inner, real meaning: 'Like salt, its essence is water from the sea'. That is, every act of worship has both an external and internal character. It is the internal reference that makes possible a true transformation in the spiritual life of the individual. It is this essence that must be grasped by the individual, by way of ritual. At this point the following Hadith is cited:

> *Hikmah* may increase the status of the slave to equal that of kings. (Narrated by Abu Nu'aim and Ibn 'Addi)

This is followed by Q2:32:

> They [the angels] said may You be glorified! We have knowledge only of what You have taught us. You are the All Knowing and All Wise.

This verse is interpreted as meaning that human beings should not be passive but rather submit actively to God and worship Him, both physically (by obeying the prescribed *ibadah*) and spiritually (by understanding the meaning of the forms of the rituals).

There is an increasing emphasis on the inner transformation of the individual throughout the first two sections of Chapter II. This is to be achieved by following the detailed instructions that follow in the rest of the chapter describing the 'essence' of obligation and of performing the *hajj*.

The third section of the chapter begins with some general observations. The syariah is essentially rules in the form of commands and prohibitions and is based on the Qur'ān and Sunnah. It includes some elements of worship that cannot be changed or omitted. These are specific instructions from God and the Prophet and are essentially summed up in the five pillars of Islam. But why are certain actions required and others forbidden? It can only be because God intended these actions to have a particular purpose and significance. If pilgrims understand what the actions signify, then they will be able to understand the real essence of worship:

> All this [is ordained by God]; anyone who honours God's rites shows the piety of his heart. (Q22:3)

In fact, many people perform the required rituals to fulfil God's commands without properly understanding the real essence of worship or the real message symbolized by the acts of worship. For example, why should one face the Ka'bah when praying, why does one go to Mecca for the *hajj*,[31] and why are *tawaf, sa'i,*

---

31 Almost all deviant sects in Southeast Asia refuse to accept the primacy of Mecca and instead have their own places of pilgrimage.

wukuf and so on performed? These actions have meanings that are not immediately apparent. The human intellect is unlikely ever to be able to comprehend or rationalize the purpose of some of these actions, while others may seem illogical or unreasonable. Nevertheless they should be carried out unquestioningly, because all of the *hajj* rituals are performed as symbolic acts of complete submission to God and His commands:

> I perform the *hajj* to show my utmost devotion to and worship of God. (Narrated by al-Bazzar and Thabrani)

The words used in this Hadith, *ta'buddan wariqqa*, mean that the act of devotion takes place on a higher level than other actions. The *hajj*, therefore, structures the entire spiritual life of the sincere Muslim, as well as having deep significance for the entire Muslim community.

At this point the *Hikmah* itemizes the essence of the *hajj*. First, the *hajj* manifests submission to God alone. Performing the *hajj* requires the pilgrim to remove any luxurious clothing and wear only *ihram*, indicating humility before God and the intention to leave all worldly life behind in seeking to worship God. The *hajj* is a chance to seek forgiveness for one's sins and obtain God's blessing. When standing (*wukuf*) at Arafah, the pilgrim shows not only submission to God but also gratitude for His blessings. In the same way, the pilgrim may seek forgiveness for the sins of his or her family. In performing *tawaf*, the pilgrim is seeking protection from the temptations of Satan.

Second, the *hajj* is a manifestation of the pilgrim's gratitude for God's precious gift of health and wealth. In addition, it symbolizes the physical and spiritual struggle to dispose of one's wealth in a way that obeys God's commands, and thus become closer to God. Gratitude is easily understood by the human intellect and is a constant feature in Islamic teaching.

Third, and importantly, the *hajj* develops the individual's sense of discipline and self-worth. It tests a pilgrim's patience, endurance, good manners and commitment to fellow pilgrims. Simply reaching Mecca involves a long and arduous journey. But regardless of the difficulties, pilgrims must be ready to perform their *hajj* obligations (*manasik hajj*) wholeheartedly on the eighth day of Dzulhijjah. The *hajj* is God's gathering; with His guidance, the devotional acts of millions of pilgrims take place successfully. It is difficult to comprehend the magnitude of this movement of people. Looked at logically, it proves that Islam is the highest pattern for the struggles in human life.

Fourth, the *hajj* enables Muslims from all over the world to come together in the spiritual centre of Islam in order to know and love each other. All differences of status—wealth, gender, colour, race, ethnicity—disappear. The pilgrims willingly join in the greatest gathering of human beings and, in the spirit of mutual affection, show their devotion to God.

Finally, the *hajj* generates an ability for human beings to worship perfectly in obedience to God's commands. It signifies true faith in God.

The final section of Chapter II goes further into what it means to perform the *hajj*. It concentrates on two features: the place of Islam in the wider sphere of revealed religions; and the *hajj* as a manifestation of universal Islamic brotherhood. The text emphasizes, first, that Islam is the religion revealed to all Prophets, from Adam to Muhammad; it is therefore the one true religion for all peoples in all ages. Prophet Muhammad is the seal and confirmation of revelation; he stands at the end of the chain of revelation. All the Prophets taught that there is only one God, who is the creator and controller of the universe, and He alone can be worshipped. This—the doctrine of monotheism—is the main legacy of the Prophetic inheritance. The prescriptions for the *hajj* contained in the 'syariah Islam' of the Prophet Muhammad are a continuation of those contained in the syariah Islam of the Prophet Abraham; that is, the religion of Prophet Muhammad is not new but a continuation of the religion of Prophet Abraham. The doctrine of monotheism that runs through the Prophetic teachings is exemplified in the recitation of the prayer of surrender (*talbiyah*) by pilgrims from the time they assume *ihram* for their journey to Masjid Haram.

The text then stresses the universal and communal nature of the *hajj*. At this yearly gathering, Muslims can share their experiences, discuss their visions for and perceptions of Islam, and devise and implement programs to advance Islam when they return home. The gathering brings together peoples of all political persuasions and all schools (*mazhab*) of faith and law for a common purpose that does not include disputes over differences. This sense of brotherhood or fellowship is the essence of the *hajj*. The gathering also provides an opportunity for each individual to gain the knowledge or instruction necessary to achieve true happiness in this world and the hereafter. The supporting references are as follows:

> Proclaim the Pilgrimage to all people. They will come to you on foot and on every kind of swift mount, emerging from every deep mountain pass to attain benefits and celebrate God's name, on specified days, over the livestock He has provided for them—feed yourselves and the poor and unfortunate. (Q22:27–28)

This passage is interpreted as a commitment to the Prophet Abraham's call to faith in one God. Several Hadith follow:

> Islam rises and is not risen over. (Narrated by HR ad Daraquthni and al-Baihaqi)

> The Prophet was asked, 'Which is the best deed?' He said, 'To believe in Allah and His Messenger'. He was then asked, 'Which is the next?' He said, 'To participate in *jihad* in the path of God'. He was then asked, 'Which is the next?' He said, 'To perform a proper pilgrimage (*hajj mabrur*)'. (Narrated by Muttafaq 'Alahi / Bukhari and Muslim)

> Those who approach God are of three types: the warrior (*gazi*) who joins combat in the path of God, the one who performs the *hajj*, and the one who performs the *umrah*. (Narrated by an-Nasa'i and Ibn Hiban)

The *Hikmah* interprets the latter Hadith as meaning that to perform the *hajj* is to be a special guest of God.

The definitions and descriptions given in Chapter II cover subjects ranging from basic theology to the significance and underlying symbolism of ritual to the psychological state of the pilgrim. The whole is unified by belief in God, who alone can be worshipped. It is notable, too, that the unity of the Islamic community (*ummah*) is constantly stressed, both as a reality (that is, discarding differences of status and race) and as a practical ideal from which nothing but good can arise. The chapter also stresses the importance of syariah, and even raises the difficult question of understanding what may seem to be pointless ritual. The Department of Religion recognizes that the ordinary pilgrim is unlikely ever to comprehend or understand certain elements of the *hajj*. Its answer—that rituals are symbolic acts signifying total submission to God—is justified by citations from the Qur'ān and Hadith, thus emphasizing the centrality of each. In particular the symbolic references indicate the timelessness of Islam, stretching from the early Prophets (Adam and Abraham) to the present.

The Significance of the *Hajj*

As well as summarizing the rest of the chapter, the concluding section (O) of Chapter III of the *Hikmah* distils the Department of Religion's thinking on the significance of the *hajj*. There are five aspects to this.

First, the *hajj* is a sacred journey. All the activities of the *hajj* can be considered acts of worship. It is no ordinary journey:

> There is no journey so exalted except that to the three mosques: Masjid Haram [in Mecca], Masjid Nabawi in Medina and Masjid Aqsa in Jerusalem. (Narrated by Bukhari and Muslim)

The *hajj* is different from other journeys in having a set ritual that begins with the intention (*niat*) to perform the pilgrimage and bear the cost of travel. This, as well as the other *hajj* activities, will be counted and rewarded by God:

> Every expense for the *hajj* is counted as equal to [the actions of] those who struggle in the path of God (*jihad fi sabilillah*). One *dirham* will be increased seven hundred times. (Narrated by Ahmad and Tirmidzi)

Second, the *hajj* is an annual gathering where Muslims from all over the world can worship, share their knowledge, learn from each other and understand other cultures without hesitation or prejudice. The *hajj* unifies Muslims through their common worship of God. This sense of unity (brotherhood), peace and commonality is most likely to be felt during *wukuf* at Arafah, where all stand equal before God and worship Him simultaneously. At this time, in this place, the pilgrim commemorates the Prophet's own *hajj*, during which he preached loyalty and commitment to Islam, respect for the Holy Land, observance of the month of Dzulhijjah and fellowship within the *ummah*:

> No doubt, your blood and your properties are sacred to one another like the sanctity of this day of yours and of this month of yours. And I have left among you a thing which,

if you adhere to it, you will never be misguided after me, the Book of God. You will be asked about me. So what will you say? They said: 'We shall testify that you have certainly conveyed and fulfilled the message from God, and given admonition'. Then he said with his forefinger raised up towards heaven and pointing towards men: 'O God, be witness to what they have said'. (Narrated by Jabir)

The *Hikmah* comments that the pilgrim is likely to hear sermons on a similar theme while waiting (*mabit*) in the dry and arid deserts of Mina. The intention is to increase the pilgrim's awareness of the purpose, the real meaning, of being part of the *ummah*. In particular, the pilgrim can learn (*tadabbur*) from people of other cultures, who provide real proof of the power of God, and from the history of previous civilizations to be found in the Holy Land. Such lessons not only enhance awareness but lead to total submission to God:

> People, We created you all from a single man and a single woman, and made you into nations and tribes so that you should know one another. In God's eyes, the most honoured of you are those most aware of Him ... (Q6:11)

The *Hikmah* widens this reference to say that the brotherhood, religious homogeneity and personal interactions among millions of people from various backgrounds are an effective tool for the mutual transformation of customs and culture. Moreover, there is no barrier to trade while on the pilgrimage:

> ... but it is no offence to seek some bounty from your Lord ... (Q2:198)

While only part of this verse is given, the *Hikmah* points out that it should be read in conjunction with Q2:197–198:

> The pilgrimage takes place during the prescribed months. ... Provide well for yourselves; the best provision is to be mindful of God ... but it is no offence to seek some bounty from your Lord ...

For centuries pilgrims have made use of the *hajj* for trade and the mutual communication of ideas and literature. The international aspect of the gathering is important in widening the personal perspectives of Indonesians as well as being a valuable aspect of the individual's common identity as a member of the *ummah*.

Third, the *hajj* is a mass glorification of God. The millions of pilgrims who pray together have the same intention and say the same prayers:

> All this [is ordained by God]; anyone who honours God's rituals shows the piety of his heart. (Q22:32)

> So let the pilgrims perform their acts of cleansing, fulfil their vows and circle the Ka'bah. (Q22:29)

Purity of body and soul is a prerequisite for the worship of God:

> So go out ... and struggle in God's way with your possessions and your persons. (Q9: 41)

It is essential that the pilgrim be strong, willing, pious and sincere (Q2:197).

Fourth, the *hajj* signifies total submission to God and is the last of the five pillars of Islam. But as well as having the religious obligation to undertake the *hajj*, the pilgrim must also have the financial means to do so:

> What is the meaning of 'being able to afford' [the *hajj*]? He [the Prophet] said it means sustenance and the means to pay for the journey. (Narrated by Tirmidzi)

The *hajj* symbolizes a physical and spiritual struggle. Pilgrims must therefore be strong enough, both physically and mentally, to endure the physical rigours associated with travel and the various *hajj* rituals, as recommended by the *'ulamā'*.[32]

Finally, the *hajj* is significant for the rewards it bestows on pilgrims. One of these is forgiveness for one's sins:

> Whoever performs the *hajj* and does not have sexual relations (with his wife) nor commits sin nor disputes unjustly, then he will return from the *hajj* as pure and free from sin as on the day on which his mother gave birth to him. (Narrated by Bukhari and Muslim).

Another is entry into Paradise:

> There shall be no reward for a proper pilgrimage (*hajj mabrur*) except Paradise. (Narrated by Ahmad and Thabrani)

The expenses incurred while on the *hajj* will also be rewarded:

> Every expense for the *hajj* is counted as equal to [the actions of] those who struggle in the path of God (*jihad fi sabilillah*). One *dirham* will be increased seven hundred times. (Narrated by Ahmad and Tirmidzi).

The *hajj* is the highest form of *jihad* and will be rewarded as such:

> Aisha asked the Prophet, 'We find that *jihad* is the best deed, so shouldn't we do *jihad*?' The Prophet replied, 'Rather, the best *jihad* is a proper *hajj* (*hajj mabrur*). (Narrated by Bukhari)

Death on the *hajj* is equated to death in the service of God (*syahid*):

> If a person sets out from his home as a pilgrim and then dies, he is granted a reward equal to those who die in the path of God. (Narrated by Muslim)

Another reward for the pilgrim is that God will grant the prayers and petitions said on behalf of others:

> If [the pilgrim] makes requests (*syafa'at*) on behalf of others, He will grant them. (Narrated by Abu Nu'aim)

God also bestows various blessings on those who have performed the *hajj*:

> If someone sets out from his home as a pilgrim, his every step is rewarded by God as righteousness and his sins are forgiven. When he stands (*wukuf*) in Arafah, God will

---

32 Nevertheless, provision is made for the sick and disabled in both the *Panduan* and the *Bimbingan*.

acknowledge him in front of the angels, saying, 'Look at my servant! He comes to me with hair uncombed. I testify to you that I will forgive his sins even if they are as many as the stars in the sky or the pebbles in the desert. And if he throws the stones (*jamarat*) then no one will know the reward for him until his resurrection on Judgment Day. And if he cuts his hair, he will have blessings as many as the hairs falling from his head. And if he finishes the *tawaf* in the Ka'bah, he will return as pure and free from sin as on the day on which his mother gave birth to him.' (Narrated by Habban from Umar)

This brings us to the end of our discussion of the *Hikmah* as a tool of bureaucratic instruction directed towards the pilgrim. It presents a straightforward exposition of the doctrine of syariah Islam, supported by the obvious selections from the Qur'ān and Hadith. The essence of this doctrine is to achieve an inner state (of submission to God) as a reflection of correct orthopraxy. The only special feature (perhaps?) is the emphasis on the *ummah*, where the *Hikmah* could be writing a universal text for all Muslims.

5   CONCLUSION: THE FACES OF SYARIAH ISLAM

Together the four books published by the Department of Religion describe what is consistently referred to as 'syariah Islam'. The books are a package and are meant to be read together. To borrow a phrase from Schacht (1950: 77–81), though in a different context, they are 'an organized corpus of received practice', with the emphasis, here, on 'organized'. The pilgrim captured in these books can be thought of as a Department of Religion construction—as a surrendered person, as a traveller and as an instructed individual. This instruction extends not just to orthopraxy but also to what the Department of Religion believes to be the true significance of the *hajj*.

New Texts for a New Age

The texts governing the *hajj* are Law No. 17/1999 on the Implementation of the Hajj, Ministerial Decision No. 224/1999 and Ministerial Decision No. 371/2002. These have been reformulated for the ordinary Indonesian in the *Panduan*, *Bimbingan*, *Hikmah* and *Do'a*—the new *hajj* texts. This package is tied together through a common preface and foreword that appear in each book. To quote from the preface:

> The *hajj* is a sacred journey that requires physical and mental preparation as well as adequate knowledge of the basic elements and rituals of the *hajj*, including travel.
>   Law No. 17/1999 states that the government [through the Department of Religion] has the obligation to provide and publish a package of standard instructional books on the *hajj*. To fulfil this obligation [the department] has prepared four instruction books which those who wish to perform the *hajj* can obtain from local offices of the Department of Religion.

The package is designed for a new type of readership, one made up of the consumers of mass print culture, the majority of whom are increasingly literate in standard Indonesian. The texts come with state imprimature, as one would expect in a country where religion is such an important part of the national system of education.

At the same time, it is also true that the Department of Religion's texts are not accepted uncritically, and that there has been considerable criticism of its practices. For example, in a recent publication on *hajj* management, Nidjam and Hanan (2001) argue that there is a need for a more educated workforce and modern management techniques to overcome the 'slave mentality of civil servants' and the all too common absence of ethics in the bureaucracy, where 'many officials abandon their conscience to obtain commissions ... If they are civil servants with progressive thinking they are usually hampered by internal factors in the bureaucracy' (Nidjam and Hanan 2001: ix–xii). While these criticisms are no doubt founded in fact, it is difficult to see how modern management techniques would change the fact of endemic corruption.

The Pilgrimage as Commodity

One strongly argued alternative to departmental regulation is for the government to allow a greater degree of privatization of the *hajj*—in fact, to turn it into a commercial commodity. This would simply recognize the reality that the *hajj* has always been a business offering its own commercial opportunities. Indeed, the Department of Religion already has competition, though this is limited by government reluctance to allow it unrestrained opportunity. Given the sums involved, one can understand why the department would be reluctant to give up its control; on average the 205,000 pilgrims who performed the *hajj* in 2006 paid $US2,600 each, or $US533 million in total—possibly more. But despite the magnitude of the sums, no real economic benefit flows to the country as a whole—religion, after all, is not an economic activity. According to the critics, it is time the department faced up to the fact that pilgrims are customers with individual needs and preferences, and should be treated as such.

The department is often accused of undue profiteering, particularly by those who are themselves engaged in private *hajj* businesses. They argue (a) that the department does not cope satisfactorily with the travel and accommodation needs of the mass pilgrim market, and (b) that it does not cope at all with the new market of wealthy pilgrims who want to perform the *hajj* in comfort and do a bit of travel on the side. The easiest way to demonstrate this 'new need' is to read the advertisements in papers such as *Republika*, where wealthy potential pilgrims are offered accommodation in five-star hotels and apartments, luxury bus transfers, add-on destinations (Cairo, Istanbul, Amman, Spain, Damascus, Yemen), a choice of airlines, and well-known scholars as tour guides. Prices range from $US4,000 to $US7,000 for the various packages: Hajj, Hajj Plus, Umrah, Umrah Plus, Umrah Ramadan, Umrah Lailatul Qadr and so on.

At the moment this form of private enterprise is not free from Department of Religion control. The private agency must be an Indonesia-domiciled company with experience in travel to Saudi Arabia. It must have an agent or connected company in Saudi Arabia and possess a valid trade and business licence issued by the Department of Tourism, Art and Culture. A letter of recommendation from the Department of Religion is also required. The company is responsible for pilgrim registration, complying with the quota, obtaining the *hajj* passport, providing guides and medical staff, and arranging transport and accommodation.

A second source of profit from the *hajj* is the commercially available texts that compete with the department's publications. They include DVDs and videos made by well-known scholars such as KH Mustofa Bisri ('Gus Mus') as well as a wide range of books, some in *komik* form (for example, Sarief 2005), on all aspects of the *hajj*, including a minor genre on health.

Finally, there is a thriving niche market in instructing intending pilgrims across all price brackets. A striking example can be found in West Sumatra, where a small-scale replica of the sacred sites of the Holy Land has been built in the grounds of the newly constructed Masjid Zikrullah about 30 kilometres from Padang. For the not inconsiderable sum of Rp 1 million (US$1,000), intending pilgrims can receive instruction in the practice of the *hajj* by means of guided tours and lectures.[33] So far as I am aware, no nationwide survey of the financial aspects of such *hajj* services has been carried out.

At the official state level, the modern *hajj* is as much about money and control of the individual as it is about individual duty to God. This is not to deny the numinous, but rather to point out that surrender, travel and instruction overlay that duty. We must therefore be aware that these, too, are part of syariah Islam.

---

33 Field notes, West Sumatra, June 2006.

APPENDIX A5.1   FOREWORD TO THE DEPARTMENT OF RELIGION'S *HAJJ* MANUALS

In the Name of God the Compassionate and Merciful

Praise be to God, and due to His guidance and His help, the service, supervision and safety provided for pilgrims are gradually being improved.

The Indonesian Government as the managerial organ for administering the *hajj* will always continue to improve *hajj* management. This includes providing laws as well as implementing procedures.

The issuance of Law No. 17/1999 on the Implementation of the Hajj as well as Minister of Religious Affairs Decision No. 224/1999, with its addendum No. 371/2002 on Regulation of the Hajj and Umrah, are among the many efforts aimed at providing a strong legal basis for the management of the *hajj* and its practical implementation.

Those efforts have contributed towards developing a steady and transparent system for Indonesian *hajj* management.

Supervision and guidance for prospective pilgrims is one of the main elements in the Law on the Implementation of the Hajj. This has been achieved through the package of books given to all prospective pilgrims before their departure to the Holy Land. It consists of four books:

1 Guide for Hajj Travel
2 Instruction Manual for the Hajj
3 Insights into Religious Obligations for the Hajj
4 Prayers and Invocations for the Hajj

These books are written to be in line with the development of Indonesian *hajj* policy and also in response to various suggestions from the Muslim community.

This book is only among many others available from other publishers. The content of these other books vary and differ one from another. Nevertheless, in order to provide a better service for pilgrims, based on the [laws and regulations], *this book is expected to be the main source of instruction for every pilgrim* [emphasis added].

It is hoped that these four books will help pilgrims perform the *hajj* properly in accordance with syariah Islam, in order to achieve spiritual enlightenment.

APPENDIX A5.2   CONTENTS OF THE *PANDUAN*

Chapter I   Introduction

Chapter II   Preparation
A   Registration, grouping and counselling
   1   Registration
   2   Grouping
   3   Counselling
B   Medical examination
   1   First medical examination
   2   Second medical examination

Chapter III   Departure
A   Preparation
   1   Mental and spiritual preparation
   2   Material preparation
B   Departure
   1   At home before departure
   2   From home to the *hajj* embarkation hostel
   3   At the *hajj* embarkation hostel
   4   In the airplane

Chapter IV   Activities in Saudi Arabia
A   At King Abdul Aziz Airport, Jeddah
B   In Medina before standing (*wukuf*) in Arafah (for Flight Group I)
C   In Mecca before *wukuf*
D   In Arafah
E   In Muzdalifah
F   In Mina
G   In Mecca
H   In Mecca before *wukuf*
I   In Medina after *wukuf* (for Flight Group II)

Chapter V   Returning [to Indonesia]
A   At Madinatul Hujjaj, Jeddah
B   At King Abdul Aziz Airport, Jeddah
C   In Indonesian airports
D   In the *hajj* hostel
E   Medical examination on arrival and in the region of origin
F   At home

Chapter VI   Medical Counselling and Care
A   Medical counselling in Indonesia
B   Medical care in Saudi Arabia

APPENDIX A5.3 CONTENTS OF THE *BIMBINGAN*

Chapter I Introduction
A Prologue
B Aims
C Objectives
D Outline of contents

Chapter II Definitions and General Provisions on the *Umrah* and *Hajj*
A. Definitions
B General provisions on the *umrah* and the *hajj*

Chapter III *Hajj Tamattu', Hajj Ifrad* and *Hajj Qiran*[34]
A Procedure for *hajj tamattu'*
B Procedure for *hajj ifrad*
C Procedure for *hajj qiran*

Chapter IV Preparation and Procedures for the *Umrah* and the *Hajj*
A Preparation before departure
B Procedures for the *umrah* and the *hajj*

Chapter V Questions and Answers on *Hajj* Matters

Chapter VI Epilogue

Appendices [tables of dates, times and places, and the actions that the pilgrim must perform at each place]

---

34 On *hajj tamattu'* and *hajj ifrad*, see footnote 28. *Hajj qiran* refers to a pilgrimage undertaken before the person becomes an adult.

APPENDIX A5.4   CONTENTS OF THE *HIKMAH*

Chapter I   Introduction

Chapter II   Concept and General Significance of *Hikmah*
A   Prologue
B   The concept of *hikmah*
C   The essence of obligation
D   The essence of performing the *hajj*

Chapter III   Insights into the *Hajj*
A   *Ihram* dress
B   Wearing *ihram*
C   Surrender to God (*talbiyah*)—answering God's call
D   The meaning of circumambulation (*tawaf*)
    1   Ka'bah
    2   Hajar Aswad
    3   Multazam
    4   Rukun Yamani
    5   Maqam Ibrahim
    6   Hijir Ismail
    7   [The well of] Zamzam
E   The essence of *sa'i*
F   The significance of hair cutting / shaving
G   Staying (*wukuf*)
H   Waiting (*mabit*) in Muzdalifah
I   Waiting (*mabit*) in Mina
J   Throwing the stones (*jumrah* / *jamarat*)
K   Penalties (*dam*)
L   Sacrifice (*qurban*)
M   *Nafar*
N   *Tawaf wada'*
O   The significance of the *hajj*

APPENDIX A5.5 CONTENTS OF *DO'A DAN ZIKIR*

I *Do'a* on Departure
A Prologue
1 *Do'a* when leaving home
2 *Do'a* after performing the recommended prayer before departure
B *Do'a* while sitting in a vehicle
C *Do'a* when the vehicle starts moving
D *Do'a* when arriving at one's destination
E Intention to perform the *umrah* and *hajj*
F Surrender to God (*talbiyah*), invocation for the Prophet (*shalawati*) and *do'a*
G *Do'a* when entering Mecca
H *Do'a* when entering Masjid Haram
I *Do'a* when sighting the Ka'bah
J *Do'a* when passing Maqam Ibrahim

II *Do'a* when Performing *Tawaf*
A *Do'a* for the first to seventh rounds of the *tawaf*
B *Do'a* after *tawaf*
C *Do'a* after performing the recommended prayer at Maqam Ibrahim
D *Do'a* when drinking the water of Zamzam
E *Do'a* after performing the recommended prayers in the enclosure of the Prophet Ismail (Hijir Ismail)

III Do'a when Performing *Sa'i*
A *Do'a* when climbing Mount Safa before performing *sa'i*
B *Do'a* on the top of Mount Safa looking towards the Ka'bah
C *Do'a* for the first to seventh rounds of *sa'i*
D *Do'a* on Mount Marwa after performing *sa'i*

IV Intention: *Do'a* when Leaving for Arafah and *Do'a* when Performing *Wukuf*
A Intention to perform the *umrah* and *hajj*
B *Do'a* when departing for Arafah
C *Do'a* when entering Arafah
D *Do'a* when seeing Mount Rahmah
E *Do'a* when performing *wukuf*

V *Do'a* when waiting (*mabit*) in Muzdalifah and Mina
A *Do'a* when arriving in Muzdalifah
B *Do'a* when arriving in Mina
C *Do'a* when throwing the stones (*jamrah*)
D *Do'a* after performing *jamrah* three times

VI *Do'a* **when Performing the Farewell Circumambulation (***Tawaf Wada'***) and** *Do'a* **after Performing** *Tawaf Wada'*

A   *Do'a* when performing *tawaf wada'*

B   *Do'a* after performing *tawaf wada'*

VII *Do'a* **when Visiting Medina**

A   *Do'a* when entering Medina

B   *Do'a* when entering Masjid Nabawi

C   *Do'a* at the Prophet's Tomb

D   *Do'a* for Abu Bakr

E   *Do'a* for Umar Ibn Khattab

F   *Do'a* in the Raudah

G   *Do'a* when visiting Baqi Cemetery

H   *Do'a* for Utsman Ibn Affan

I   Greeting to Hamzah and Mu'ab Ibn Umar

J   Greeting to all martyrs of the Battle of Uhud

K   *Do'a* when leaving Medina

VIII *Do'a* **when Arriving Home**

IX   Simple *Do'a*

A   *Do'a* when leaving the house

B   *Do'a* while sitting in a vehicle

C   *Do'a* when the vehicle starts moving

D   *Do'a* when arriving at one's destination

E   *Do'a* when entering Medina

F   *Do'a* when entering Masjid Nabawi

G   Intention to perform the *umrah* and *hajj*

H   *Do'a* for *ihram*

I   *Do'a* when entering Mecca

J   *Do'a* when entering Masjid Haram

K   *Do'a* when sighting the Ka'bah

L   *Do'a* when performing *tawaf*

M   *Do'a* when performing *sa'i*

N   *Do'a* when cutting one's hair

O   *Do'a* when arriving at Arafah

P   *Do'a* when performing *wukuf*

Q   *Do'a* when arriving at Muzdalifah

R   *Do'a* when arriving at Mina

S   *Do'a* when throwing the stones (*jamrah*)

T   *Do'a* for coming home

U   *Do'a* when gathering with the family

V   *Do'a* for sick pilgrims

6 Syariah Values in the Regions: A New *Ijtihad* for a 'Sick' Society

In this chapter I examine four regional syariah law texts that collectively illustrate a new stream of independent judgment (*ijtihad*) in Indonesian syariah. They are the Aceh Qanun, the South Sulawesi draft syariah code, the West Sumatra regional regulations and the MMI draft criminal code. The appearance of such texts over the past few years raises questions about the relationship of the new codes with Pancasila, the current laws and regulations of the state, and the Constitution. The texts also provide insights into the new forms syariah might take in the Indonesian state.

All four texts reflect the syariah values of their proponents, so a preliminary word on what these values are may be in order. Chapter 4 on the public transmission of syariah suggested that these values are based on the Qur'ān and include an affirmation of Islam, orthopraxy, public propriety and the maintenance of core values in a time of unprecedented social and political change. In the texts examined here, these values are distilled into forms ready for adoption by regional governments. These regional expressions of syariah values now inform the debate on a national school of legal thinking (*mazhab*) on syariah. However, this raises its own problem: of how such widely differing interpretations of syariah values can be integrated into a national *mazhab* and, indeed, whether they should be integrated at all.

Contemporary debate on the new syariah codes focuses on three issues in particular. The first concerns the extent to which the first principle of Pancasila—belief in one God—can be made to accommodate the imposition of syariah values in the wider community. The proponents of the new codes argue that they are justified because they express the essential nature of belief in one God and are, therefore, merely practical manifestations of it. This argument is commonly extended further to claim that the mass of Indonesians agree with the new texts because they defend a general social morality to which all citizens—regardless of religion—subscribe. Those who oppose the codes claim that they exceed the boundaries of Pancasila and are contributing to a 'creeping Islamization' of

Indonesian society. They are, in short, an attack on the secular foundations of the Indonesian state. The debate must remain inconclusive so far as positive law is concerned, because the ideology of Pancasila allows for multiple interpretations. To be sure, both sides are able to present evidence to support their respective cases, but the techniques used to obtain this evidence are so obviously deficient as to prove nothing.[1] Nevertheless, the public argument about Pancasila cannot entirely be ignored. Pancasila is both a sword and a shield; it is a context for positive law but does not constitute positive law.

The second focus of debate concerns the relationship between regional laws (including the new syariah codes) and national laws and regulations. With the demise of the New Order regime in May 1998 and the start of a new era of reform (*reformasi*), a fresh opening of the gates to *ijtihad* became possible. The Regional Autonomy Laws (No. 22/1999 and No. 25/1999) provide the formal positive-law expression for regional laws.[2] They devolve law-making power to the regions (*kabupaten*) and cities (*kota*), which have become the operative units of local government. The regions' areas of responsibility now include finance, trade, public works, land, investment, health and environment, but not defence, public order or—importantly—religion. The national autonomy laws also require the regions to formulate regulations (*peraturan*) that conform with national practice and are in the required form. In short, devolution is not total, nor without formal restraint.

Formal restraint means two things. First, to be valid a law must be in the appropriately drafted form. By its nature this is restrictive. The standard text begins with a reference to the Constitution of 1945 and other appropriate laws. A typical formulation is: '... in order to [here follows the purpose of the law] there is a need for [the law] ... bearing in mind [then follow linked or related laws]'. It is this complex of references that sets the agenda for syariah. In other words, the new syariah text does not stand alone but is part of a complex web of non-syariah laws, regulations and instructions. It is part of the national, regional and district laws. Second, the law must not contravene superior laws. In the case of the regional syariah codes, this means the Regional Autonomy Laws. However, the status of syariah within these laws is by no means clear or consistent, given that religion was not devolved to the regions. Each of the four syariah texts must therefore be approached differently and on its own terms. I do this in detail below, but as a general introduction it is clear that: (1) the Aceh Qanun is valid in terms of positive law, because the Special Autonomy Law for Aceh (No.

---

1   For media reports of this debate, including reports on the surveys on syariah implementation carried out by both sides, see *Gatra*, No. 25, 6 May 2006, pp. 21 ff.

2   For an exhaustive survey of the Regional Autonomy Laws and regional regulations, see Bratakusuma and Solihin (2004).

18/2001) specifically permits local regulations on syariah; (2) the validity of the West Sumatra regional regulations is debatable; (3) the South Sulawesi code has no status in positive autonomy law; and (4) the MMI code also has no status in positive autonomy law.

Syariah implementation in positive law is not, therefore, a simple proposition. Each of the texts discussed in this chapter has its own unique context and arose out of a different set of conditions and circumstances. Regional autonomy does not mean that the state now permits unrestrained *ijtihad*, although it does permit alternative law texts to exist (as in Aceh) as well as allowing room for the discussion of others (as in West Sumatra). The essential point is that discussion on its own is a huge advance for Indonesian syariah, even if it does draw us into a world of competing texts. On the other hand, this is perfectly within the tradition of Islam—a history of syariah could actually be a history of competing texts. What has changed is the state's claim to limit or forbid alternative law texts, because central government control over the regions is diminishing. The state's claim to limit alternatives is expressed in the positive law, and enforced by the bureaucracy.

The final area of debate concerns the constitutionality of the regional syariah texts. The Constitution of 1945 is the basic law on which the Indonesian state rests. Originally a rather minimalist document, it has been amended several times in the past few years. Of the four major amendments since 1999, one is of particular relevance here.[3] Article 28(A–J) of Chapter XV has been amended to provide for an extensive set of individual rights, including the right to form and maintain a family, the right to personal development and education, the right to security provided by the law, the right to freedom to profess one's religion, the right to freedom of thought and expression, the right to physical and spiritual welfare, and the right to cultural identity and freedom from discrimination on any ground. These provisions are broadly drafted and wide ranging. They have not been tested judicially with reference to the new syariah texts at either the local or the national level. At first reading these texts seem to restrict the rights of freedom of conduct, movement and expression guaranteed by article 28. The Constitution, then, throws considerable uncertainty in the way of the texts, a difficulty that neither the Constitutional Court nor the Supreme Court has been called upon to resolve.

To sum up: the status of the syariah texts is uncertain in terms of Pancasila, the Regional Autonomy Laws and the Constitution. All have an impact on the texts but the effect is very much a work in progress.

---

3   I am grateful to Professor Timothy Lindsey and his colleagues at the Asian Law Centre, University of Melbourne, for providing the text relied on here.

1   THE ACEH QANUN[4]

Although usually referred to in the singular, the Aceh Qanun[5] actually consists of nine separate regulations (*qanun*) plus a presidential decision. This public expression of syariah values is administered through the religious courts.

The Special Autonomy Law for Aceh (No. 18/2001) gives the Aceh regional assembly (Dewan Perwakilan Rakyat Daerah; DPRD) the authority to make laws 'based on syariah'. This recognizes the perceived special position of Aceh as a particularly 'Islamic' province—although some in Aceh see it merely as a way of deflecting attention from the real problems afflicting the province of poverty and poor standards of public order (see, for example, Fealy and Hooker 2006: 191–3). Nevertheless, there are limits on the power of the regional government to make syariah laws; for example, the syariah laws must be consistent with the national system of law, although 'syariah' and 'consistent' are not defined. In addition, while the Aceh legislature has the authority to establish a Syariah Court (Mahkamah Syariah), the Supreme Court of Indonesia has ultimate authority via cassation. The Ministry of Justice retains the authority to appoint, transfer and dismiss judges, a process that also involves the chief justice of the Supreme Court. Aceh's system of religious courts was originally established in 1989 under Law No. 7/1989 on Religious Justice and is now governed by new national legislation enacted in 2006 (Law No. 3/2006).

Although the syariah provisions in the Special Autonomy Law are rather confined, this has not prevented the local legislature from drafting *qanun* with the express purpose of expressing and implementing 'syariah values' in Aceh. A list of these *qanun* together with a brief description of their content is given in Table 6.1.

The first of these, Qanun No. 3/2000, establishes a Consultative Council of Ulama (Majlis Permusyawaratan Ulama; MPU) comprising *'ulamā'* and city/district representatives. Its purpose is to provide 'opinions, guidance and suggestions [to the regional assembly] from the perspective of syariah'. It also has a consultative role; under article 3(2) it is described as an 'equal partner [with] the Regional Government and the DPRD ... to provide an opinion, whether requested or not, to government on the development of Islamic society and economy'. The MPU has interpreted this as giving it the authority to promote or veto regulations depending on their consonance with 'Islam'.[6]

---

4   Material for this section is taken from an earlier draft based on fieldwork conducted in Aceh in 2003–04 by the author and Timothy Lindsey, whose input I gratefully acknowledge.

5   From the Arabic *qānūn* meaning a secular law text. Although distinct from the classical syariah texts, it may refer to or even contain elements of *fiqh*.

6   Interview with Dr Muslim Ibrahim, chair of the MPU, Banda Aceh, February 2003 (interviewed by the author and Timothy Lindsey).

Table 6.1   An Overview of the Aceh Qanun

No.	Description of Content	Comment
3/2000	Establishes the MPU.	Increases the political and legal functions of earlier bodies. Issues *fatāwā* (Komisi Fatwa 2000) and provides guidance and suggestions for policy on law and government administration based on Islamic principles. Potential for it to have considerable power through direct input into government policy and practice.
5/2000	Describes the implementation of Islamic syariah in Aceh (introduction + nine provisions). Establishes the Syariah Office (Dinas Syariah) and a special body (Wilayatul Hisbah) that, in conjunction with the police, investigates and prosecutes breaches of the *qanun*.	Constitutes the core of syariah in Aceh. States that Islam is central to Aceh and its Muslim population and is the basis of justice, prosperity and moral well-being. The sources for the law are the Qur'an, Hadith and the 1945 Constitution. Muslims must follow correct doctrine (*aqidah*) according to the Sunni schools.
7/2000	Concerns the customary laws (*adat*) of Aceh and how they relate to the syariah.	In general terms, *adat* institutions are integrated into government and supported by its agencies, but syariah has overriding authority.
43/2001	Refines the administration of the MPU and establishes the Plenary Council.	Addresses bureaucratic issues concerning the MPU.
10/2002	Establishes the Syariah Court (Mahkamah Syariah) of Aceh.	Preserves the structure and procedures of the existing religious courts (*pengadilan agama*) and recognizes the overriding jurisdiction of the Supreme Court (Mahkamah Agung). The intention is to widen the jurisdiction of the existing religious courts from family law and trusts to include criminal and commercial law.
11/2002	Sets out rules for the implementation of syariah in the areas of doctrine (*aqidah*), devotion (*ibadah*) and public expression (*syi'ar*).	Families are responsible for ensuring family members perform the daily and Friday prayers; no government or other agency may obstruct this. All Muslims must observe the fast and wear Islamic dress (not rigidly defined). Penalties for breaches are at the discretion (*ta'zir*) of the judge. *Hudud* and *qisas* punishments are specifically excluded. *Ta'zir* penalties include fines, imprisonment for up to 2 years and public caning (up to 12 strokes).

(continued)

Table 6.1 (continued)

No.	Description of Content	Comment
23/2002	Law for a religious education system based on the Qur'an and Hadith but also following the objectives of the national education system.	The aim is to provide an education for the holistic development of Muslims and to equip them for employment. The curriculum must include Islamic studies as well as secular subjects. Arabic and English are compulsory.
7/2004	Concerns the management of *zakat*; establishes a system for the collection and distribution of *zakat*.	The law provides for the definitions of those who must pay *zakat*, the recipients of *zakat* and the rates of *zakat*. Collection, distribution and enforcement refers to Qanun No. 5/2000 and Qanun 10/2002.
11/2004	Sets out the tasks and duties of the national police, including with reference to syariah.	Attempts to define the respective spheres of authority of the Wilayatul Hisbah and the national police, and, more generally, to integrate the enforcement provisions of the national and local criminal codes.

Source: Fealy and Hooker (2006: 189).

Qanun No. 43/2001 essentially explains and expands on Qanun No. 3/2000. Its purpose is wholly bureaucratic—to detail the workings of the various committees through which the MPU exercises its functions. It provides for committees on community harmony, women and family, syariah, *fatāwā* and political studies. Oversight of the work of these committees is vested in a Plenary Council which 'plans and implements the relevant operational programs'. In effect this council is the executive body of the MPU. Nevertheless the Plenary Council and, more generally, the MPU attempt to strike a balance between individual and collective authority in Islamic matters by allowing individual *'ulamā'* to express their opinions and consult widely.

The history of the MPU over the past five years seems to show a consistent attempt to promote itself as an independent authority in matters of religion. In 2000 it published a collection of *fatāwā* issued by it and its predecessor organizations between 1965 and 1999 (Komisi Fatwa 2000). This was clearly intended to establish its authority as the primary source of syariah in the province. Perhaps more importantly, in its introduction to the collection the MPU is consciously historical. It claims to be the successor to the Ulama Association (?–1965), which became the Ulama Council in 1967 and merged with the national Indonesian Council of Ulama (Majelis Ulama Indonesia; MUI) in 1975. The point of this bureaucratic claim of succession is that the authority of the Acehnese *'ulamā'* can be shown to derive from 1965, when they claim to have saved the province and its people from the communists.[7] This allows them to claim that they represent an Islam that is 'pure' and protective of the people. It is the function of the *'ulamā'* to ensure that the values of the past are made manifest in the present. The 2000 *fatāwā* collection does this through close argument from the Qur'ān and Sunnah, with little or no recourse to the formal rules of classical law (*fiqh*) or reasoning by analogy (*qiyas*). The MPU has therefore managed to stamp its own version of syariah onto Islam as practised in Aceh. Qanun No. 43/2001 places the *'ulamā'* firmly in the provincial bureaucracy and so adds government fiat to their particular view.

To the outside observer, Qanun No. 3/2000 and Qanun No. 43/2001 would seem to provide an adequate framework for the *'ulamā'* to be able to perform their *fatwā*-giving function. However, Qanun No. 5/2000 goes further in providing for the establishment of a Syariah Office (Dinas Syariah) in the governor's office itself. Staffed by civil servants and some *'ulamā'*, its function is to oversee all aspects of syariah administration in the province. Its main emphasis is on enforcing 'proper' Islamic conduct in public. The *qanun* therefore contains provisions on appropriate dress, especially for women (article 15); observance of prayer times, directed especially towards private employers (articles 13 and 16); immoral behaviour such as consumption of alcohol and unlawful proximity of the sexes (article 11); insulting behaviour towards religion (article 17); and the appropriate punishments for breaches of these rules. Article 20 establishes a religious police authority, the Wilayatul Hisbah, to supervise the enforcement of the provisions just described. Its powers are limited to investigating and questioning individuals suspected of improper behaviour; actual power to enforce is in the hands of the national police.

Qanun No. 11/2004 specifies that the national police in Aceh have a dual function: first, to enforce the ordinary criminal law (*norma hukum*); and second, to support the Wilayatul Hisbah in implementing syariah (articles 6 and 14). This means that the national police are subject to two authorities: the superior national authority in the province and, ultimately, Jakarta in the case of criminal law; and the governor of Aceh in the case of syariah law (as stated in the elucidation to the *qanun*).[8] The assumption seems to be that there is no conflict between these dual functions but whether this is true or not remains to be shown. What is obvious is that together Qanun No. 5/2000 and Qanun No. 11/2004 provide for a state syariah. Although ultimate authority does not lie with the *'ulamā'*, this does not mean that the syariah is defined wholly by its bureaucracy.[9] That may be the public perception but it is only partly true.

---

7   This claim is based on a *fatwā* against communism issued in the mid-1960s by a predecessor to the MPU (Hasjmy 1985: 706).

8   The elucidation is a feature of all laws (*undang*). It is intended to be read in conjunction with the main text.

9   As we saw in Chapter 5 on the *hajj*, the bureaucracy can define the parameters of duty but not, perhaps, the duty itself.

Qanun No. 11/2002 covers the same ground as Qanun No. 5/2000 with the same intention of defining a substantive syariah for Aceh. It contains detailed provisions on correct doctrine (*aqidah*), prescribed ritual duty (*ibadah*), the public glorification of Islam (*syi'ar Islam*) and, of course, punishments for breaches.

Article 6 of Qanun 5/2000 obliges Muslims to exhibit *aqidah* in their personal, family and community behaviour. Article 7 of Qanun No. 11/2002 goes further in requiring the regional government and community institutions to support the development of *aqidah* among Muslims and preserve it against deviance, atheism and superstition. Article 6 of the *qanun* gives the MPU the power to declare what is or is not correct doctrine by issuing *fatāwā*. This is a significant extension of the power of the *'ulamā'*.

Qanun No. 5/2000 treats *ibadah* as a purely administrative matter. The government must create the appropriate conditions for Muslims to properly perform prayers, the pilgrimage and the fast (articles 8 and 9). *Ibadah* is undefined but clearly understood. Qanun No. 11/2002 goes into greater detail, specifying the duty of parents to supervise their children's prayers and fasting, that of employers to provide an appropriate environment for Muslims to practise their religion, and that of government to ensure compliance (articles 7–10). Individual Muslims also have a duty to carry out their religious obligations, with breaches (such as absence from Friday prayers or eating or drinking during the fast) subject to punishment (see below).

Syi'ar Islam covers a variety of activities that demonstrate public respect for Islam and acknowledge the greatness of revelation (celebration of holy days, use of the Jawi script and the Muslim lunar calendar, dressing correctly and so on). In practice, *syi'ar Islam* is public orthopraxy. Initially the power to define *syi'ar Islam* was placed in the hands of the governor (Qanun No. 5/2000, article 162) but Qanun No. 11/2002 relocated this in the DPRD. The regional assembly then proceeded to place great emphasis on the necessity for correct Islamic dress (article 13), promoting it in government offices, educational institutions and business organizations. The purpose was to ensure modesty and, thus, respect for religion—a constant theme in Indonesian Islam. Although the requirement for Islamic dress applies to both sexes, it certainly applies more than equally to women, who are required to wear a headscarf (*jilbab*) and avoid 'transparent' or 'tight' clothing. Modesty as exemplified by dress is, of course, a Qur'ānic injunction; to dress modestly is to show the proper Qur'ān-based moral behaviour. As a direct public statement of personal virtue, one can speculate that the *'ulamā'* see dress as a positive expression of syariah.[10]

Article 2 of Qanun No. 11/2002 explains the purpose of *syi'ar Islam* as being:

---

10 A point made by Dr Alyashar Abu Bakar, a member of the Syariah Office, when interviewed in Banda Aceh by Timothy Lindsey and myself in February 2002.

... to develop the faith and consciousness of God (*taqwa*) of individuals and the community and protect them from the influence of misguided teachings, to improve the understanding and performance of *ibadah* and the provision of facilities for it, *and to enliven and celebrate activities in order to create an Islamic atmosphere and environment.* [Emphasis added]

This is not just symbolism; both Qanun No. 5/2000 and Qanun No. 11/2002 provide for punishments—fines, imprisonment and public caning—for breaches. There are two interesting features about these punishments. First, they are all discretionary (*ta'zir*) punishments that give the judge a wide degree of freedom to impose penalties according to the individual circumstances. There is no mention in the *qanun* of the (harsher) *hadd* form of punishment (mandatory punishment for contravention of limits set by God) or *qisas* (compensation for voluntary or involuntary killing or wounding). Second, there is a clear attempt to achieve proportion and balance in the punishments. For example, failure to attend Friday prayers on three consecutive Fridays carries a penalty of six months in prison or three strokes of the cane (article 8(1) of Qanun No. 11/2002) while the more serious offence of disseminating deviant doctrines carries a penalty of two years in prison or 12 strokes of the cane. Other offences follow a similar pattern.

Qanun No. 11/2002 describes the purpose of the punishments as being to warn and re-educate:

... the punishment of caning for those who commit criminal offences is intended to make offenders realize their error and to be a warning for the community not to commit criminal offences. The punishment of caning is expected to be more effective because the convicted person feels ashamed and it does not create a risk for that person's family.[11]

Ta'zir punishments will be handed down if contraventions are committed repeatedly and [the offender] has received warnings from the Wilayatul Hisbah, or are committed flagrantly so that they conflict with propriety and the community's sense of decency. Even this *ta'zir* punishment should begin at the lightest level possible.

It is difficult to know what to make of 'moral policing' in the name of religion but in general it has an unhappy history.[12] Just as serious, this sort of policing raises human rights issues arising out of the new article 28 of the Indonesian Constitution. While the Special Autonomy Law for Aceh may be relatively clear, the jurisdiction of the religious courts is open to dispute. It is to this issue that I now turn.

---

11 In other words, caning does *not* mean flogging to the point of physical incapacity; its purpose is to humiliate—but see ICG (2006) on excesses in the application of the laws in Aceh.

12 For example, the 'preventors of immorality' (*pencegah maksiat*) in some states in Malaysia are considered to be incompetent and corrupt and are generally despised. It would be a pity to see Aceh and other parts of Indonesia go the same way in the name of religion. The temptation for rent seeking is, after all, very strong.

The religious court system in Aceh is complex. As noted earlier, Indonesia's religious courts were originally established in 1989 and are now governed by legislation enacted in 2006. The state's experience with judicial syariah administration is therefore short.[13] The Special Autonomy Law enacted in 2001 contains its own specific provisions on Aceh's religious courts. Article 25 says:

> ... the jurisdiction of the religious courts is based on Syariah Islam as found within the system of national laws, and is further regulated by the *qanun*, which apply to the followers of Islam.

Two elements of this article are worthy of notice. First, syariah is defined to mean the syariah of 'national laws', namely the 1989 Law on Religious Justice, the 1991 Compilation of Islamic Law (Kompilasi Hukum Islam; KHI) and the 1974 Marriage Law. Second, the Aceh DPRD may issue *qanun* but these must not contravene the 'national [syariah] laws'. Obviously, the concurrence of *qanun* provisions with national syariah laws was always going to be a matter of dispute.

The DPRD has already attempted to extend the jurisdiction of Aceh's newly created Syariah Court beyond the traditional domain of family and inheritance law to economic and criminal matters, through articles 49 and 53–54 of Qanun No. 10/2002. The jurisdiction of the religious courts in civil law (*ahwal al-shakhisiyah*) is generally restricted to family law as defined in the provisions of Law No. 7/1989 on Religious Justice. The revised Law on Religious Justice (No. 3/2006) extends this jurisdiction to adoption. How this fares in Aceh is yet to be determined.

The range of contracts (*mu'amalat*) covered by the elucidation to Qanun No. 10/2002 includes sales and purchases, loans, debts, partnerships, banking and insurance. This is a vastly increased jurisdiction. At the time of writing there was no evidence that the Syariah Court was either willing or able to deal with such matters—quite the contrary, in fact. These matters are already governed by secular laws and drawn up on secular principles. In the one field that might appear to involve Islam directly—Islamic banking—the typical contract specifically *excludes* the religious courts in favour of arbitration. There is no *technical* syariah input. However, Law No. 3/2006 extends the jurisdiction of the religious courts to Islamic economics (*ekonomi Islam*), including contracts. Whether the arbitration provisions usual in such contracts will prevent the religious courts from exercising their new jurisdiction is not yet known.

In the area of criminal law (*jinayah*), Qanun No. 11/2002 extends the range of penalties to include fines, caning and imprisonment in that order. These are described as *ta'zir* punishments to be handed down by the religious courts. The *qanun* specifically rejects *hadd* and *qisas* punishments.

---

13 Compare, for example, the 200 years of experience in British and independent India, 150 years in Malaysia and Singapore, 100 years in Brunei, well over 50 years in the Middle East and North Africa and 70–80 years in Muslim southern Africa.

There is one innovation in the Aceh Qanun that may prove to be significant in practice. This is the consistent use of the classical syariah classes (such as *jinayah* and *mu'amalat*) as the basis for law making. The casual reader of the *qanun* is apt to ignore the importance of classes of action, but their use indicates another way of thinking about individual duty and how the individual Muslim is perceived by the state. That person is not primarily a citizen as defined in state law but a Muslim as defined in syariah. He or she is a *'fiqh* person' and as such is outside the ambit of the national secular authority. The problem, of course, is that this position denies the sole authority of the secular state. Fundamentally it has the potential to re-introduce conflicts of law back into Indonesian law—an extreme example being the MMI code discussed in section 4 of this chapter. As a matter of principle the state has made a point of resisting internal conflicts of law since the 1940s and continues to do so today. The best that syariah proponents can hope for, then, is managed compromise. The classical classes occupy an area where compromise will be necessary. Resolving such difficulties will essentially be a matter of state political policy.

That policy is legislatively clear. Under MPR Decree III/2000 on the Sources of Law and Hierarchy of Laws and Regulations, laws (*undang*) made by the People's Representative Council (Dewan Perwakilan Rakyat; DPR) take precedence over DPRD regulations. Therefore, the Special Autonomy Law for Aceh ranks higher than the Aceh Qanun. However, there is a complicating factor. Presidential Decision No. 11/2003, which officially establishes the new Syariah Court for Aceh, affirms the jurisdiction of the religious courts as set out in Law No. 7/1989 and, by implication, the KHI but includes the words:

... [jurisdiction] over the life of the people in religious worship and the greater good of Islam as provided for in the Qanun. (Article 3(1))

The 'life of the people' and the 'greater good' are not defined in the presidential decision. On one construction, the 'life of the people' is restricted to ritual (*ibadah*) and the 'greater good' to the public manifestation of Islam (*syi'ar Islam*). The assumption is that these are private or at best semi-public expressions of orthopraxy. But the Acehnese *'ulamā'* hold this to be false; for the *qanun* to make any sense, both *ibadah* and *syi'ar Islam* have to be enforced. This is the whole point of Qanun No. 11/2002 and the purpose of having a Syariah Court (Qanun No. 10/2002). The prospects for a resolution between these two opposing points of view seem poor, at least in the immediate future.

In the meantime, the practice of syariah in Aceh is ruled by an inconsistent and overlapping set of texts that are open to multiple interpretations and, unfortunately, political chicanery at the national and local levels. These texts are:

• The Autonomy Laws of 1999 and 2001;
• MPR Decree III/2000 on the Sources of Law and Hierarchy of Laws and Regulations;
• Presidential Decision No. 11/2003;

- The 1989 and 2006 Laws on Religious Justice; and
- Qanun No. 10/2002 (establishing the Syariah Court).

Because all these texts are relatively new, there is no tradition for the Acehnese courts or the Supreme Court to fall back on. Indeed, the timeframe is so short that any comments must be largely speculative.

Nevertheless, one positive-law interpretation of the question of legal precedence would be that the Special Autonomy Law for Aceh (an *undang*) is the basic law defining the jurisdiction of the religious courts in Aceh and takes precedence over both the presidential decision and the Aceh Qanun. The latter are therefore valid only to the extent that they are 'based on Syariah Islam as found within the system of national laws'. The presidential decision is superior to the Aceh Qanun; where there is any inconsistency between them, it should be the determining law.

This is not an acceptable answer for many in Aceh. Their objections focus on the presidential decision. They argue that the decision is either invalid or pointless given that the Special Autonomy Law—an *undang*—gives the regional government the authority to regulate syariah. The capacity to develop *qanun* is one of the things that makes Aceh 'special' under the Special Autonomy Law. It and the *qanun* therefore not only outrank the presidential decision, but negate its influence altogether.

This is all very well from a strict language-construction point of view, but in fact the Special Autonomy Law is far less clear about the status of *qanun* than is implied by this argument. It should be remembered, first, that MPR Decree III/2000 on the hierarchy of laws puts the Aceh Qanun at a lower level; and second, that article 3(2) of Presidential Decision No. 11/2003 may prove to be *practically decisive*. It says:

> The other powers and authority [of the religious courts] shall be implemented in stages in accordance with the ability, competence and availability of human resources in the framework of the national court system.

This means that the Supreme Court continues to have effective administrative control over the Aceh courts. The issue of competing jurisdictions therefore remains unresolved and can only be decided by the Supreme Court,[14] although so far no application has been made to it. In any case, article 26 of the Special Autonomy Law gives the Supreme Court the right of cassation over the Aceh courts. Now that the religious courts have been transferred from the Department of Religion to the Supreme Court,[15] the latter is administratively and financially responsible for all of Indonesia's courts, including appointments and promotions. That is, The judicial system remains firmly under central government con-

---

14 Under article 24 of the Constitution and article 29 of Law No. 24/2003.
15 Under Law No. 5/1999; the effective date of transfer appears to have been September 2004.

trol. The extension in 2006 of the jurisdiction of the religious courts to include adoption and economic matters reinforces the dependent status of the Syariah Court established by Qanun No. 10/2002, because the *qanun* is effective only within the scope of Law No. 3/2006. On a plain reading this *qanun* adds nothing; a local practice may develop but that is a matter for the unpredictable future.

The effects of some other *qanun* are equally uncertain. The general intent of the *qanun* is to ensure the penetration of syariah into the social life of Aceh. As such, they considerably exceed their narrow legal remit.

First, the elucidation to Qanun No. 23/2002 on the Implementation of Education explains its purpose as follows:

> Special status in the field of education along with special status in the implementation of Islamic syariah, customary law (*adat*) and the expansion of the role of the '*ulamā*' are all part of a whole that is integral to the effort to realize once more an Islamic Acehnese community. For that reason, the system of education in Aceh is based on the Qur'ān and the Hadith and is packaged with an Acehnese culture that is infused with Islam, in a framework of engendering a Muslim personal character and an Acehnese community that has faith and consciousness of Almighty God, that has a command of science and technology and is skilled in putting it to good use, that is noble in ethics (*akhlak*), healthy in body and spirit, independent, and capable of facing global challenges. In order to realize the system of education described above, a renewal of the education system is required, towards a system that is capable of increasing quality, that is not separate from the national education system, and that is in line with the demands of modern life and the expansion of globalization.

What is being proposed here is total Islamic education for the Aceh Muslim population. It is, however, to be integrated into the national system. Specifically, it has to enable the student to cope with 'globalization'. To quote from the *qanun*:

> NAD [Nanggroe Aceh Darussalam] emphasizes education that is Islamic in nature, with the following characteristics:
> a. The number of hours for the study of Islam is to comprise about 20 per cent of the total, with the lessons to cover the Qur'ān, Hadith, Doctrine (*Aqidah*), Ethics (*Akhlak*), Law (*Fiqh*), the History of Islamic Civilization, and Ritual (*Ibadah*).
> b. [There is to be] an integration in subject matter and in the process of study, particularly between elements of *imtaq* [*iman dan taqwa*—faith and God-consciousness] and *iptek* [*ilmu pengetahuan dan teknologi*—science and technology] education in all subjects.
> c. [There is to be] a living environment in the schools (*madrasah* and *dayah*)[16] that has an Islamic flavour.

The core subjects in the curriculum at all levels are Islamic Studies, Languages (Indonesian, English, Arabic), Science (including Social Science), Citizenship Education, Mathematics, Regional Language, *Adat* and Culture, Physical Education, and Arts and Crafts.

---

16 A *madrasah* is an Islamic school; a *dayah* is the Acehnese equivalent of a Javanese *pesantren* or Malaysian *pondok*.

Qanun No. 7/2000 on the Implementation of *Adat* Life also attempts to integrate a 'foreign' subject into the syariah framework. *Adat* is not, of course, 'foreign' in the same sense that the secular curriculum is, but it does represent an alternative value system. As we know, *adat* came to have almost sacerdotal status under Dutch colonial legal policy. In the 1950s and 1960s it was put forward seriously as a basic principle in the creation of a national system of Indonesian law (Koesnoe 1969, 1970). In the end, however, the most that was achieved was a rather limited symbolic status for *adat*.[17] In practice it remained confined to matters of dispute settlement, with varying degrees of formal acceptance at the official state level (Lev 1965; von Benda-Beckman 1984). During the New Order period a number of regulations and instructions[18] were promulgated re-emphasizing this approach, which was also to be found in Acehnese regulations.[19] Qanun No. 7/2000 was supposed to replace these earlier regulations, but the formal structures for dispute resolution remain much the same. The *qanun* is simple and rather formulaic, although, as Bowen (2003: 22 ff.) has demonstrated, the actual process of dispute resolution itself is anything but simple.

However, our interest here is in the nexus between syariah and *adat*. Article 1(19)—the definition section of the *qanun*—says that:

> *Adat* customs and traditions (*adat istiadat*) are rules or actions *based on Islamic Syariah* that have long been generally followed, respected and honoured, and that form the foundation of life. [Emphasis added]

Articles 2 and 3 say:

> The *adat* law, *adat* customs, and traditions and customs that continue to apply, live and develop in the Acehnese community must be maintained, so far as *they do not conflict with Islamic Syariah* [Emphasis added].

> Islamic Syariah is *the yardstick for the implementation of adat life in the region* [Emphasis added].

These passages state that syariah has a greater value than *adat*. On its own this principle is not decisive, because the ability to negotiate according to circumstance is clearly available. However, what 'available' means is constrained by the bureaucratic nature of the function of Qanun No. 7/2000—which is to provide an exclusive mechanism for dispute resolution at the village (*gampong*) level. Whether or not exclusiveness is actually achieved remains to be seen, but there is no denying the primacy of the bureaucratic form.

Qanun No. 7/2004 regulates the collection and distribution of the wealth tax (*zakat*). Consisting of 50 articles, essentially it is a short form of the national Zakat Management Law (No. 38/1999). It establishes boards at the provincial,

---

17 For example, in article 5 of the Basic Agrarian Law (No. 5/1960).
18 Regulations No. 11/1984 and No. 3/1997, Minister of Home Affairs Instruction No. 17/1989.
19 Regional Regulations No. 5/1996 and No. 2/1999.

district and village levels to collect and distribute *zakat*. The Syariah Court has general oversight of these boards as well as extensive powers to prosecute corruption. The definitions of who must pay *zakat*, how the amounts should be calculated, the types of property that should be included in the calculations and where the payments should go are the same as in the existing national law. In short, the *qanun* merely provides a higher level of detail on local *zakat* administration. Data on how the system works in practice are not available as far as I am aware.

What, then, can we conclude about the Aceh Qanun? Is it a new stream of *ijtihad*? This is a difficult question to answer. The Aceh regulations meet the internal *fiqh* definition of *ijtihad* in that they do not transgress the principle of certainty (*qaṭ*) and are based on expert knowledge. This is essential for the credibility of the regulations. But fundamental as it is, the internal view is not wholly sufficient. The regulations must also be valid in the eyes of the state, and that means conforming with a state-imposed form of syariah. The result is uncertainty as to which standard or set of criteria is prior: the 'Islamic' or the 'secular'.

This is one of those unfortunate cases where selection becomes necessary but is not decisive. The reason may well be that the deeply held belief in the historical significance of Islam in Aceh has now become bound up in the wider issue of regional autonomy. The latter raises its own difficulties, some secular (regarding the ownership of natural resources, the distribution of finances and the alleviation of poverty, for example) and some religious (such as the basic religious question of the status of Islam in public life). The elucidation to Qanun No. 5/2000 says:

> *Adat* is alive and developed in the life of the community, and is accumulated and summarized in the statement '*Adat bak Poteu Meureuhom, Hukom bak Syiah Kuala, Kanun bak Putro Phang, Reusam bak Laksamana*', which means, '*Adat* Law is in the hands of the government and Syariah Law is in the hands of the '*ulamā*''. This expression constitutes a reflection of the manifestation of Islamic Syariah in the practices of daily life.

There appears to be a manifest opposition between the secular and the religious, but is this inevitable, and what are the implications for a new stream of *ijtihad*? There are two overlapping answers, neither of them decisive on its own.

First, while giving the regional legislature the power to make laws concerning syariah, the Special Autonomy Law for Aceh does not give it unrestrained discretion in this area. Moreover, the central bureaucratic institutions retain ultimate authority over the 'new' Syariah Court. To be sure, the Special Autonomy Law allows for the formal symbols of autonomous government—article 10 provides for a head of state (*wali nanggroe*) and council of elders (*tuha nanggroe*), for example—but so far this has had little effect on the local political structure. More important than any such symbolic gestures is the authority to create institutions for the definition and implementation of syariah principles and values. Two such have been established: the MPU created by Qanun No. 3/2000 and the

Syariah Office created by Qanun No. 5/2000. The MPU is both a consultative assembly of *'ulamā'* providing 'opinions, guidance and suggestions' and 'an equal partner to the Regional Government and the DPRD' (article 3(2) of Qanun No. 3/2000). The *'ulamā'* have interpreted this rather vaguely drafted clause as giving the MPU a *de facto* right to veto laws it considers to be 'un-Islamic'. The real authority of the MPU is located in its executive body, the Plenary Council created by Qanun No. 43/2001. The Syariah Office provides a secular counter-balance to the MPU/Plenary Council. Located in the governor's office, its function is to draft *qanun* and coordinate government activity on Islamic matters. Its responsibilities overlap with those of the MPU but its priorities lie in state administration. The laws of the state, not the 'pure' syariah, are its primary reference. In short, the Special Autonomy Law: (a) allows the province to make determinations on and apply syariah; and (b) creates a bureaucracy in which the MPU and Syariah Office compete to establish an appropriate framework for syariah. In this framework, the new stream of *ijtihad* is found in the rules of the bureaucracy.

Our second attempt at locating *ijtihad* takes us to the substance of the Aceh Qanun, and the extent to which it represents substantive *fiqh*. Again, our answer must be inconclusive with one exception: the Aceh *fatāwā*. The collected *fatāwā* for 1965–99 (Komisi Fatwa 2000) show about a 30 per cent reference rate to the standard Shafi'i texts, with the majority based on the Qur'ān and Hadith. There is nothing exceptional about this but for one thing: about 13 per cent of the Aceh *fatāwā* are on deviance or deviant sects, compared with a national average of 1 per cent. Doctrine is clearly contested but that is all one can say. Coming back now to the substance of *fiqh*, we find that the two core texts, No. 5/2000 and No. 11/2002, actually focus on doctrine (*aqidah*), ritual (*ibadah*) and public Islam (*syi'ar Islam*). In short, the emphasis is on orthopraxy and its enforcement by a special body, the Wilayatul Hisbah. The *qanun take for granted* the existing jurisdiction of the religious courts in family law, donations (*wakaf*) and *zakat*, although other *qanun* provide local regulations for the latter. The emphasis on doctrine is interesting given the high percentage of *fatāwā* on deviance.

On *aqidah*, article 6(1) of Qanun No. 5/2000 says:

> Every Muslim is obliged to strengthen and fulfil Islamic *Aqidah* based on the doctrine of *ahlus sunnah waljamaah*, in the proper manner, personally, and in family and community behaviour.

Article 7 of Qanun No. 11/2002 states that it is the responsibility of the government to see that this is carried through:

> ... the Governments of the Province and the Districts (*Kabupaten*) and Cities and community institutions are obliged to guide and develop the *aqidah* of the religious community (*ummah*) and guard it from the influence of misguided interpretations and/or sects.

In their approach to both *ibadah* and *syi'ar Islam*, these two *qanun* focus mainly on public events: attendance at Friday prayers and fasting during Ramadan in the case of *ibadah*, and correct dress and being respectful of religion (Islam) in the case of *syi'ar Islam*. Qanun No. 23/2002 provides for the reinforcement of *ibadah* by means of a graded system of instruction. Overall, therefore, one can see that there is very little substantive *fiqh* in the Aceh Qanun. That is left to the courts and the KHI.

The new stream of *ijtihad* is primarily focused on public law, resulting in a selective orthopraxy based on syariah values. The Aceh Qanun does not attempt to replace the existing secular bureaucracy, which continues to operate on secular principles, issuing its own instructions and circular letters (Dinas Syariat Islam Aceh 2005: 359 ff.). The uncertainty surrounding this form of syariah leaves it open to the vagaries of politics and social attitudes. There is anecdotal evidence to suggest that many Acehnese see the Aceh Qanun as a trivialization or secularization of divinely inspired law.

2   THE SOUTH SULAWESI DRAFT SYARIAH CODE

In December 2001 a self-appointed committee produced a draft special autonomy law for the implementation of syariah in South Sulawesi. Initially called the Committee for the Preparation of Enforcement of Islamic Syariah (Komite Persiapan Penegakan Syari'at Islam; KPPSI), it later became known as just the Committee for the Enforcement of Islamic Syariah (Komite Penegakan Syari'at Islam; KPSI).

As well as being self-appointed, it appears to have consisted mainly of local *'ulamā'* and politicians seeking to take advantage of the uncertain political climate of the time. The spark for its formation seems to have been a congress held in August 2000 (Kongres Mujahidin) calling for the Indonesia-wide implementation of syariah.[20] A local congress on the same theme was then held in South Sulawesi in October of the same year.[21] Those behind the push for syariah in the province seem to have shared some ideological common ground with the MMI, whose code is discussed in section 4 of this chapter. They also claimed a degree of legitimating inheritance from predecessors such as Abdul Kahar Muzakkar, who had attempted to establish an Islamic state in South Sulawesi in the 1950s and 1960s. His son, Abdul Aziz Kahar Muzakkar, was named chair of the KPPSI. Prominent local politicians who had unsuccessfully lobbied Jakarta for some form of autonomy for South Sulawesi were also on the committee (Junedding

---

20 For a full account, see Suharyadi (2001).

21 Hj. Abdul Hadi Hj. Awang, then chief minister of the Malaysian state of Terengganu, attended the congress. He was responsible for introducing the Syariah Criminal Offence (Hudud and Qisas) Bill (2002) in that state (see the extracts in Fealy and Hooker 2006: 181–4). The importance of the Malaysian connection will become apparent later in the chapter when the MMI code is discussed.

and Pradadimara 2000). It was in this context that the South Sulawesi draft code was drawn up.

The timing is important: *reformasi* was well under way; the new Regional Autonomy Laws had been implemented; Aceh had been given special autonomy in which syariah was an important component; and Islamic politics were in a state of flux at the local and national levels. The syariah card was an obvious one to play but it did not go uncontested. For example, one member of a party with an avowed Islamic platform described the South Sulawesi draft code as a 'syariah Islam [which is] a conception of Islam by a group of Islamic activists not yet in power'. The same author claimed that its authors 'do not represent the Muslim community' (M. Qasim Mathar, cited in Fealy and Hooker 2006: 186–7). I am in no position to make a judgment on the motives and intentions of the competing political claims. What I can say, however, is that the text itself is very well drafted.

The code is drafted as if it were a law (*undang*). Indeed, the casual reader might think it were an *undang* if it were not for the absence of dates and signatures! It is a clever document based on the Special Autonomy Law for Aceh, as its first page illustrates.[22] As the following extract shows, the draft law is both ambitious and technically correct. It is presented in the standard legal form, even to the point of leaving room at the end for a presidential signature and gazette entry number and date. It makes the case for syariah in South Sulawesi in a thoroughly professional manner. And in a clear parallel with the Special Autonomy Law for Aceh, the elucidation at the end of the draft provides detailed justifications for the code.

People's Representative Council of the Republic of Indonesia
Draft Law of the Republic of Indonesia No. ...... of 2002
Concerning Special Autonomy for the Implementation of
Islamic Syariah for the Province of South Sulawesi
Through the Grace of Almighty God,
The President of the Republic of Indonesia

Considering that:

a The 1945 Constitution acknowledges, honours and protects all believers in following their own religions, both individually and in the life of the community, the nation and the state;

b The Government of the Unitary Republic of Indonesia, according to the 1945 Constitution, acknowledges and respects the uniqueness of the Regional Government, which has particular characteristics and/or is special according to law;

c The religious life of the South Sulawesi community is a system of values and is a part of the democratic life of the nation and state;

---

22 The translations that follow are the work of the Asian Law Centre, University of Melbourne. It has kindly given permission for their use here.

d The desire for religious life (Islamic life) of the community of South Sulawesi is to implement Islamic law in all state or government matters in the Province of South Sulawesi as a life which is guaranteed by the Unitary State of the Republic of Indonesia;

e In the implementation of Regional Government, it is necessary to have a guarantee of legal certainty and to implement the business and matters which are recorded in (a), (b), (c) and (d) above, so that it is necessary to determine Laws for the Granting of Special Autonomy for the Implementation of Islamic Syariah for the Province of South Sulawesi.

The elucidation begins by describing the 'philosophical basis' of the code. It argues that decentralization and/or regionalism must: (a) be democratic: (b) be in line with the Constitution;[23] and (c) recognize syariah values. More specifically, decentralization means a recognition of local values and the characteristic features of local society. Islam, and in particular syariah, is an essential component of local culture and values. Decentralization must therefore recognize syariah and allow it to be implemented in the province.

The supporting arguments for the code are based on both history and the contemporary situation. The elucidation points out that the traditional inhabitants of the province, the Bugis, Makassarese and Mandarese, have long been known as devout Muslims. Indeed, South Sulawesi merits the honour of being called the Verandah of Medina (Serambi Madinah) just as Aceh is called the Verandah of Mecca (Serambi Mekkah). The Islamic status of the province was diminished by Dutch colonialism, enjoyed a revival in the 1950s and was suppressed once again during the New Order period. Now, under *reformasi*, true syariah based on the proper values for legal, social and political life may flourish once again. The elucidation stresses in several paragraphs—(f), (i) and (h)—that a recognition of these values would strengthen the relationship between the province and the unitary state of Indonesia. Paragraphs (a) and (d) of the introduction (above) also emphasize this point.

The contemporary argument for the code starts with the failure of present laws to bring peace, justice and prosperity to the region. Syariah would provide a solution to these ongoing problems of mismanagement. Paragraphs 6 and 7 of the elucidation sum up the position as follows:

> It is essential that the government respond positively to these very strong aspirations of the community of South Sulawesi, because they are an endeavour to maintain and protect the Unitary State of the Republic of Indonesia, and because these aspirations are carried out in a peaceful and constitutional manner. If [the government does not respond positively], the voices or aspirations [of those who] wish to separate themselves will become stronger, [growing] like a snowball, and eventually it will not be easy to overcome them;

> The granting of Special Autonomy for the implementation of Islamic Syariah is a perfect solution because it is cohesive for the nation as well as being an endeavour to

---

23 Presumably articles 18A and 18B of the Constitution of 1945, as revised in 2001.

broaden the participation of the community of South Sulawesi in building a special nation in South Sulawesi.

This rather complex justification for syariah in the history of the province, the desire to preserve the unitary state and the need to improve public morality is reflected in the content of the draft code. Two aspects are worthy of notice. First, autonomy means that government, education, the economy, customs (*adat*) and the judicial system would all be regulated by syariah. This would be done by issuing '*qanun* yet to be written'. This means that important areas of substantive law are missing. It is possible that South Sulawesi already has regional regulations that attempt to regulate some of these areas. Their validity does not depend on the draft code but rather on whether or not they conform with the national government's Regional Autonomy Laws. The point to stress here is that the draft lacks practical detail. This deficiency extends to the appointment and functions of its proposed Council of Ulama. The draft gives the council a supervisory role in government but does not define its exact jurisdiction or the qualifications of members.

Second and, I think, uniquely, articles 22–24 give the Council of Ulama a direct supervisory role in the economy and trade of South Sulawesi. Trade is to be based on syariah, although what this means remains to be 'further regulated by *qanun*' (article 22(2)). Articles 23 and 24 provide for the participation of the '*ulamā*' in the economy and trade at all levels of government—from district to provincial—in the form of the right to give opinions. Again, the binding force, if any, of these opinions is undefined. In an obvious parallel to the MPU in Aceh, the Council of Ulama is to be an independent body with the 'function of passing judgment and supervising regional policy' (article 30(1)). The national police are to have a role in enforcing syariah (article 31), as they do in Aceh.

The two most interesting features of the South Sulawesi draft syariah code are its correctness as a formal document and its stated intention to shift the economy and trade of the area from a secular to syariah basis. In addition, the draft devotes considerable space to creating institutional structures in which the '*ulamā*' would take a dominant position. Some attention is paid to public orthopraxy (prayer, observance of the fast) but this is a minor aspect of the code. In short, the draft looks towards the creation of an Islamic state (*negara Islam*) in the region, and in this sense is attempting to rewrite the failures of the 1950s. It also justifies the need for the code on the basis of the perceived parlous state of the Republic of Indonesia in the late 1990s, and South Sulawesi's unsubstantiated claim to be the Verandah of Medina.

Does this justification simply amount to political opportunism? The draft clearly intends to place the '*ulamā*' (undefined) at the centre of law making in South Sulawesi. However, it does not provide the detail necessary to enable one to come to any conclusion about the coherence or practicality of the proposed syariah, because in too many instances practical matters are left to '*qanun* yet to be written'. This phrase leaves the draft code hostage to politics and an unpredictable future, and in this respect is reminiscent of the syariah as sufficient school (see Chapter 2). On a strict construction it can be read as a wilful refusal to discuss efficacy and, hence, an unjustifiable politicization of the concept of syariah.[24]

Of course, that criticism is itself representative of a political position. It should also be noted that the KPSI does not deny the politics of syariah. Some representative comments from members and supporters follow. They are taken from an undated paper by Muhammad Adlin Sila based on research conducted in 2001–02.[25]

> If Democracy is indeed something that is good, then where is the proof? Throughout the Old Order and the New Order, which used the system of democracy (even though it was only fake democracy), the Islamic community, as the majority, suffered discriminatory and unjust treatment in the areas of law, economics, social [life] and politics. The people are still immature, because they adhere to laws and government that are repressive, and it is therefore evident that crime is now rampant. Apart from that, law enforcement, administered incorrectly in the past, has now lost its bite. As a result there is no social order and the community does not feel safe. If democracy is to be carried out at its best, the democracy that we will support must be based on Islamic syariah. (Chair of the Makassar branch of the KPPSI, 2002)

> We have deliberately left the concept of the enforcement of Islamic syariah to be defined by the Islamic community together with its leaders. If we make an agreement, it would bring about wide social unrest. For that reason, the KPPSI has limited its struggle to the political field only, that is, how South Sulawesi can gain special autonomy from the central government to implement Islamic syariah in every field. (Secretary-general of the KPPSI, 2001)

> The greatest constraint to be faced in realizing the introduction of Islamic syariah in a formal fashion in South Sulawesi is the factor of misunderstanding by the Islamic community itself. Thus, I consider that the first step to be taken in implementing Islamic syariah in a formal fashion is socialization of the understanding of the meaning and essence of Islamic syariah among Muslim communities themselves, particularly in the circles of the South Sulawesi elite. (Prominent public prosecutor, 2001)

> Endeavours in this direction [that is, integrating syariah into the national legal system] should be not only formal but also cultural. Cultural efforts should be carried out by individual Muslim men and women, families and the community. This can be through education. The aim is to create a community which understands and carries out Islamic syariah in a total (*kaffa*) way. In the meantime, the formal method is to spread the movement to a number of social, political, bureaucratic and governmental institutions. This would involve fighting for Islamic values in both legislative and executive institutions in an endeavour to influence policies. These efforts will certainly experience opposition, particularly concerning viewpoints, thoughts and per-

---

24 See, for example, M. Qasim Mathar (cited in Fealy and Hooker 2006: 186–7) and Junedding and Pradadimara (2002).
25 See Sila (n.d.). The original Indonesian version is held in the Asian Law Centre, University of Melbourne. I am grateful to the translators, Professor Timothy Lindsey and Ms Helen Pausacker at the Asian Law Centre, University of Melbourne, for allowing me to use their translation.

ceptions in viewing the future of Indonesia. Both types of approaches can become one if they are synergetic and mutualistic. (Leading local scholar, 2002)

Don't imagine that if Islamic syariah (read: Islamic criminal law) were enacted today, tomorrow people's hands would be chopped off. Is the purpose of chopping off hands to make the Islamic community disabled or to reduce the incidence of robbery? The proof is that Umar bin Khattab did not cut off the hands of thieves if it was a dry season or a famine. *This means that Islam also cannot reject the prevailing reality. Islam teaches that the situation and conditions should be examined before laws are applied.* [Emphasis added] (Deputy chair of the KPPSI, 2002)

These remarks indicate the political nature of the syariah underpinning the draft. But they also show an awareness of the need to convince the population that syariah is necessary, and that it provides the solution to the all-too-evident ills of society. Nevertheless, the syariah on offer is not a positive program, because the details of how it would work are not specified. The authors of the draft attempt to avoid this dangerous lacuna by specifically rejecting the 'extreme' forms of syariah applied elsewhere. For example, Sila (n.d.) quotes the secretary of the KPPSI as saying in 2002:

If indeed the Taliban is convinced that this [that is, extreme Islamism] is what the Prophet Muhammad set as an example, then the Taliban has misinterpreted the prescriptions of the Qur'ān and the Hadith. What the Prophet gave as the example was not like that. If in the future South Sulawesi obtains special autonomy for the enactment of Islamic syariah, we will not use as an example the enforcement of Islamic syariah which is in operation in other Islamic countries [but] which is not in accordance with the essence of Islam and the culture of the community of South Sulawesi.

In effect the debate is circular: to manifest purity Muslims need to live in an Islamic society; but the creation of an ideal Islamic society requires, first, individuals who manifest purity. As Ahmad Hassan lamented in the 1930s and 1940s, and Mohammad Natsir in the 1960s to 1980s, neither of these things has yet happened. To act politically—that is, opportunistically—is (apparently?) an attractive solution, but the circle cannot be broken by such means. Political acts may postpone but cannot solve the problem. The only solution, as both Hassan and Natsir recognized, is to create or encourage the creation of 'proper Muslims' (however defined). The assumption is that there are very few of these—that society is indeed 'sick'.

3   THE WEST SUMATRA REGIONAL REGULATIONS

From the new stream of *ijtihad* in Aceh and South Sulawesi to the attempt to cure a 'sick' society in West Sumatra is not a large step; both put their faith in the implementation of syariah values. The journey has at its end a better and more pure society and thus a better Muslim individual. The motive is to cure the 'sickness of society' (*penyakit masyarakat*) as manifested by immodesty, immorality, crime and, more generally, a failure to fulfil one's duty as a Muslim.

The mechanism adopted in West Sumatra has been to issue a large number of (Islamic) regional regulations (*peraturan daerah; perda*)—numbering 27 as of August 2006.[26] An overview of the regulations issued through to the end of 2004 is given in Table 6.2.

Regional regulations on religion raise an important issue. The Regional Autonomy Laws reserve religious matters for the central government. On a plain reading of the law, regional authorities lack the authority to write and implement regulations on Islam. The issue, therefore, is whether the regional regulations on Islam contravene the Regional Autonomy Laws, or, more broadly, are unconstitutional. This is not relevant to the situation in Aceh, where the provincial government does have the authority to manage Islam; the question there is the *extent* rather than *the fact* of jurisdiction. However, public debate, especially in the media, commonly confuses the Aceh and non-Aceh cases and, indeed, subsumes them under the catchy soubriquet of 'creeping Islamization'. This sort of language merely confuses the legal issues at stake.[27] Nevertheless, it has succeeded in shaping the public debate in terms of public morality and, by an easy progression, 'Islamic' public morality. The terms of the debate have remained remarkably consistent over the last five years, at least in the case of the West Sumatra *perda*.

In April 2001 a draft regulation on the prevention and elimination of immorality, one of the main categories of *perda*, was presented to the West Sumatra DPRD in Padang for discussion.[28] The mayor spoke against the draft, maintaining that while the proposal was lawful, it was unnecessary because the substance of the document merely repeated the existing criminal law provisions. He defined lawfulness in terms of the Regional Autonomy Laws, although, as I have pointed out elsewhere, this is not a safe assumption. The mayor argued that the function of *perda*, at least those concerning public morality, was to correct deficiencies in the existing (criminal) law where there was a clear necessity to do so. That need could only be demonstrated by assessing *local* conditions and the character of *local* society. He cited the well-known phrase: '*Adat* [here the matrilineal social structure] rests on Syariah, Syariah rests on the Scripture of God ('*Adat basandi Syarak, Syarak basandi Kitabullah*'). The mayor thought that local conditions were already sufficiently well served by the criminal law, although wider debate about the justice system was also necessary.

---

26 West Java, South Sulawesi, South Kalimantan, Madura, West Nusa Tenggara and no doubt other regions as well have issued similar regulations. The number of regulations issued in West Sumatra is 25 or 27 depending on how they are counted. A comprehensive list of the West Sumatra regulations is being compiled by the Asian Law Centre, University of Melbourne and should be available in due course.

27 The rather sensationalist debate on Indonesia's proposed Anti Pornography Bill is another example. The bill is almost certainly unnecessary; most of the proposed rules are already in the existing criminal code, which is itself under revision.

28 Copies of the original document are in the author's possession.

Table 6.2   An Overview of the West Sumatra Regional Regulations

Regulation No.	Description of Content

Regulations on the Prevention and Elimination of Immorality

No. 11/2001, Province of West Sumatra	Consists of 7 chapters plus an elucidation. Lists the legal bases of the regulation, namely the national Regional Autonomy Laws, parts of the criminal code, and letters / instructions issued by the provincial governor. The elucidation sets out the purpose of the regulation, namely to protect society, in particular religion and customs. Districts are required to use this text as a model for their own regulations (article 4).
No. 9/2001, Kota Bukit Tinggi	Follows No. 11/2001.
No. 20/2003, Kota Bukit Tinggi	An elaboration of No. 9/2001, it contains new definitions of immorality and provides for increased penalties and revised investigative procedures.
No. 3/2004, Padang Panjang	Contains same definitions of immorality as above and provides for heavy penalties of up to Rp 5 million or 6 months imprisonment.
No. 2/2004, Padang Pariaman	Same as above.
Letter No. 460/311 of the Office of the District Head, Tanah Datar, June 2002	Prohibits pornography.

Regulations on Reciting the Qur'ān

No. 10/2001, Solok	Requires all schoolchildren and engaged couples to be able to recite selected passages from the Qur'ān to a standard appropriate to their age and status. Students may not proceed to a higher class or graduate without the appropriate certificate. A marriage may not be solemnized if either party does not have the required level of competence.
No. 8/2004, Pesisir Selatan	Same as above.
No. 6/2003, Lima Puluh Kota	Same as above.
No. 21/2003, Pasaman	Same as above but with expanded penalties. School principals may be fined or imprisoned for issuing false certificates. An officer of the Religious Affairs Office (Kantor Urusan Agama; KUA) may be dismissed for allowing a marriage if either one of the parties cannot recite the Qur'ān.

Table 6.2 (continued)

Regulation No.	Description of Content
No. 1/2003, Sawahlunto Sijunjung	If a person engaged to be married does not have the required level of competence in the Qur'ān, the marriage may be delayed or the marriage may be solemnized but no marriage certificate provided until the required level of competence has been achieved.

Regulations on Proper Dress

No. 6/2002, Solok	Article 29 of the Constitution of 1945 guarantees freedom of religion; this means that Muslims must behave as their religion requires, hence the need for proper/modest dress.
No. 5/2003, Lima Puluh Kota	Same as above.
No. 22/2003, Pasaman	Same as above but without the constitutional reference.
No. 2/2003, Sawahlunto Sijunjung	Same as above.
2004, Agam	No regulation at the time of writing, but a draft regulation (*ranperda*) was produced in 2004.

Regulations on *Zakat*

No. 29/2004, Kota Bukit Tinggi	Essentially copies the national Zakat Management Law (No. 38/1999). A *mufti* is to sit on the local board and give *fatāwā* as required.
No. 13/2003, Solok	Same as above but *zakat* recipients are confined to the Qur'ānic classes and payments for public purposes such as schools and hospitals are specifically prohibited. The poorest are to be given priority for payments.
No. 31/2003, Pesisir Selatan	Wholly administrative, based on Law No. 38/1999.
No. 26/2003, Lima Puluh Kota	Permits a broader scheme of payments for general Muslim advancement and social welfare. In other respects follows Law No. 38/1999.

The opposing view in favour of the draft was quite simple. It was lawful for the DPRD to draft and implement the *perda* under the Regional Autonomy Laws. The *perda* was justified on social, philosophical and legal grounds. The present disturbed state of society and religion (as evidenced by activities such as gambling, drug and alcohol abuse, prostitution and other sexual offences) amply justified the proposed law.

The draft *perda* was not accepted but a later one based on it did succeed, in November 2001 (Perda No. 11/2001 of the Province of West Sumatra, discussed below). The arguments put forward in the debate then are exactly the same now.[29] Thus, social immorality is rampant and the police and public prosecutor (*jaksa*) either cannot or do not wish to control it. The only other source of author- ity is Islam; hence, such *perda* are necessary. Moreover, people of all religions, Muslims and non-Muslims, agree that public immorality must be eliminated for the general good. The general good is more important than legal argument about the lawfulness of the *perda*. But in any case, the *perda* are properly drawn up by the DPRD, do not contravene any superior laws and, indeed, reinforce the spirit of the Constitution. Despite such assertions, the fact remains that the validity of the *perda* is an important issue, as contemporary opponents of the regulations, especially women's groups, point out.[30]

At the time of writing no authoritative resolution to the question of the validity of the *perda* had been reached. Clearly it would be a matter for the Supreme Court to consider the regional regulations involving 'Islam' *vis-à-vis* the Regional Autonomy Laws.[31] In a recent newspaper interview, the chair of the Supreme Court stated that 'such material must be in accordance with autonomy principles' (*Media Indonesia*, 10 June 2006: 14). But how this opinion would be reflected in a substantive decision is another matter.

The 14 regions in the province of West Sumatra all issue (Islamic) *perda*. In addition, the districts (*nagari*) issue *perna* (*peraturan nagari*) that repeat, sum- marize or sometimes elaborate on the *perda*. Although the *perda* and *perna* tend to be 'works in progress', going in and out of existence, we know enough about them to be able to say two things.

First, like the Aceh Qanun, they are presented in a standard legal form, as required by Presidential Decision No. 44/1999. A fault in formal presentation would invalidate the text, so drafting in the correct form is essential. But as discussed above, even if the *form* is correct, this does not settle the question of validity.

Second, there seem to be four main categories or classes of (Islamic) *perda*. They are:

---

29 Interviews in June–July 2006. None of the interviewees wished to be identified by name but they all held academic or civil service positions.
30 For extracts and sources, see Fealy and Hooker (2006: 191–3).
31 Essentially under article 24A(1) of the Constitution.

1   regulations on the prevention and elimination of immorality (*pencegahan dan pemberantasan maksiat*);
2   regulations on reciting the Qur'ān (*pandai baca huruf al-Qur'an*);
3   regulations on proper dress (*berpakaian Muslim dan Muslimah*); and
4   regulations on compulsory charitable payments (*zakat*).

As one would expect, there is a high degree of overlap and repetition between the *perda* from different districts. In the discussion that follows I have chosen to concentrate on representative examples from two districts, Padang and Solok, dating from 2001 to 2006. Not only were they the first places to draw up *perda*, but they have succeeded in doing very good and consistent drafting. For that reason other districts have clearly copied their texts when drawing up their own *perda*.

The intention of the *perda* is to implement syariah values, that is, to convert syariah values into public duty. Many Muslims view them as a justified attempt to create 'better' Muslims. Others say that the *perda* are pointless or even offensive because religious commitment cannot be imposed on the individual by enforcing public orthopraxy; all such laws do is satisfy the craving of zealots for a certain kind of public order and behaviour. As with other conflicting assertions surrounding the *perda*, we can only wait for data to emerge from sociological and criminological surveys on the effectiveness of the regulations in changing behaviour—if, indeed, such surveys are ever done.

Regulations on the Prevention and Elimination of Immorality

This topic attracts a great deal of national and international attention, for two reasons. First, the regulations tend to focus on the conduct of women in public, as well as the conduct of both sexes in and around places of public entertainment (hotels and so on), especially at night. Second, the provisions are usually enforced by ill-trained and aggressive young men regarded by many as little better than vigilantes. The issues are therefore often construed in terms of human rights and the ways in which public order should be maintained. This is a potent mix, because inserting syariah (always undefined) into public perceptions about proper behaviour leaves the field wide open for political opportunism as well as the harassment of women.

I look first at the 'mother' text, Perda No. 11/2001 of the Province of West Sumatra.[32] Its elucidation reads:

> The prevention and eradication of immorality (*maksiat*) regulated by this Regulation includes various efforts to stem the outbreak (*maraknya*) of sinful (*munkar*) acts, now often termed 'social ills' (*penyakit masyarakat*). Immoral behaviour (*perbuatan maksiat*) in this region (*daerah*) has begun to disturb society and disrupt the harmony of family and social life, and has undermined (*merusak*) the foundation (*sendi-sendi*)

---

32   Peraturan Daerah, Propinsi Sumatera Barat, 14 November 2001.

of Minangkabau [that is, traditional West Sumatran] social life, which is based on [the principle that] *'Adat* rests on Syariah, Syariah rests on the Scripture of God'. If this matter is not speedily checked, it is feared that future generations will lose their culture: 'Syariah legislates, *Adat* is used, Nature is the teacher' (*Syarak mangato, Adat memakai, Alam takembang jadi guru*). Thus the primary aim of this Regulation is to stem the decline in the morals of society in general, and of the coming generations in this region in particular. Thus the implementation of this Regulation consistently refers to religious teachings, *adat* norms and the regulations and laws in force, so that the moral decline resulting from various forms of immoral acts will speedily be overcome.[33]

'Immoral acts' are defined in five ways. First, social immorality is behaviour that disturbs the foundations of social life and is considered contrary to the norms of *adat* and religion. The specific offences are defined in article 2(2). Second, unlawful sex is intercourse between two people who are not married to each other, whether it takes place voluntarily or by force, and whether or not payment is made. Article 5(2) extends the offence to facilitating the act, for example by providing materials (books, photos, entertainment) designed to 'trigger desire'. Third, gambling is defined as the intention to gain a financial benefit through games of chance—a rather loose definition that is not helped by the limited examples provided. The main focus of the provisions (articles 7–10) is on preventing premises or facilities from being used for gambling. In addition civil servants (undefined) and the military are specifically forbidden to take part in gambling-related activities (article 9(1)). Fourth, articles 11–14 prohibit the consumption of alcohol and drugs, as well as the manufacture, store and supply of alcohol and narcotic substances. There are two exceptions: the consumption of alcohol for medical reasons is permitted under the supervision of a doctor (article 12(2)); and 'authorized institutions' (undefined) may provide drugs and alcohol (article 12(3)). The definition of a 'drug' is drawn directly from national laws.[34] Finally, article 15 prohibits the manufacture and distribution of pornography, with the definitions once again being drawn from existing national laws.[35]

The remainder of the regulation reinforces the idea of generalized social control. Thus, the members of society are required to assist the authorities by supporting law enforcement agencies and participating in the elimination of social immorality (article 3). Members of the community have a responsibility and a duty to report immoral behaviour to the appropriate authority (article 16(1–3)). Those doing so are entitled to protection and need not report immoral behaviour

---

33 The syariah–*adat* dualism in this passage has a long history in West Sumatra. On the first phase of this history, see Hooker (1972: 35) citing customary sayings from the Malaysian state of Negeri Sembilan, and Hooker (1986: 391–4) on the written Minangkabau (West Sumatra) and Sungei Ujong (Malaysia) law texts.

34 Laws No. 23/1992, No. 5/1997 and No. 22/1997.

35 Laws No. 24/1997 and No. 40/1999.

if such protection is not available (article 16 (4–5)). An individual may issue a warning to those acting immorally or providing the premises for immoral behaviour (article 17). Once a report has been received, the 'authorized institution' must act on it; failure to do so is a punishable offence (article 18). In addition, the local government is obligated to take the initiative in preventing and eliminating social immorality (articles 20 and 21).

As this brief summary shows, Perda No. 11/2001 is a rather minimalist document, lacking in detail. To demonstrate this, we need only compare it with the draft on which it is based.[36] In the latter, public order is defined in terms of the necessity to maintain public safety and peace. Immorality is therefore a threat to public security. It is not dealt with adequately by the existing criminal law (which is nevertheless listed at the front of the draft). Immorality is defined widely to include obvious offences such as sexual misconduct, offences against religion such as breaking the fast, and offences against customary practices such as inappropriate dress and impolite behaviour. The draft goes into considerable detail about the places where immoral behaviour is likely to occur; the list includes such places as hotels, guesthouses, student dormitories, cafes, restaurants, billiard parlours, beauty salons, video rental venues, massage parlours, parks, tourist and beauty sites, taxis and other forms of transport. Specific offences include unlawful sex, consumption of drugs and alcohol (including eating food in public during Ramadan, or even pushing a food barrow along the road) and the provision of pornography in any form. Persons who facilitate any of these activities are also guilty of an offence.

The draft also contains considerably more detail on the enforcement process. Offences are to be investigated by police officers or specially appointed civil service investigating officers (*penyidik pegawai negri sipil*; PPNS), who may receive reports or complaints, carry out inspections, examine identity documents, confiscate items or documents, take fingerprints and photographs, and cross-examine suspects or any other person (article 7). These wide-ranging powers are subject to police control, in that an investigation must be terminated if the police decide that no crime has been committed or that there is insufficient evidence for them to take action. However, even in such cases the public prosecutor and the family of the suspect may still be informed that an investigation has taken place. As we have seen, these powers did not make it into Perda No. 11/2001. The latter does, however, give the governor of West Sumatra the power to make implementing regulations on enforcement, a variety of which have been produced. In addition, it should be noted that article 17 of the national Law No. 32/2004 concerning Regional Regulations gives governors, mayors and district heads wide powers to make regulations covering the areas within their jurisdictions. These include the authority to guard public ethics and morals and preserve

---

36 Rancangan tentang Penertiban Pelarangan dan Penindakan Penyakit Masyarakat, March/April 2001, Walikota Padang.

the health of society, and would be understood to include enforcement of Perda No. 11/2001.

The civil service investigating officers function under the umbrella of the Civil Service Police (Polisi Pamong Praja). In June 2006 the mayor of Padang published a general paper on the role of the civil police in maintaining order and enforcing regulations in the city.[37] Like Perda No. 11/2001, it is long on rhetoric but short on detail. It begins with a survey of the history of the Civil Service Police during the colonial period, the period of Japanese occupation and the troubled early years of the Republic of Indonesia. The thrust of the argument is that this institution has always been necessary to the maintenance of public order and social stability. The unstated implication is that the national police were and still are incapable of fulfilling this role. Similar regulations issued by other districts in West Sumatra proceed from the same position.

However, there still remain serious unknowns. The functions of the civil police are very broadly stated in the Padang paper as well as in Perda No. 11/2001. There are no clear limits on their behaviour, and complaints about excesses are constant in the Padang media. The qualifications required for employment are not specified—unlike in Aceh, where a minimum standard of education is required (ICG 2006: 9)—and civil police receive minimal training of just a few weeks. Finally, as in Aceh, the respective powers and jurisdictions of the civil police and the national police are not clear. They are supposed to cooperate in public order matters but initial observation would suggest something closer to competition. Nevertheless the system is in place, has a bureaucratic structure and offers a new career path for aspiring police officers. It has been adopted by most districts in West Sumatra as well as the city of Padang.

Regulations on Reciting the Qur'ān

The example used in this subsection is a regulation from the district of Solok (Perda No. 10/2001). Its elucidation says:

> The traditional Minangkabau philosophy stating that '*Adat* rests on Syariah, Syariah rests on the Scripture of God' has been close to the hearts of the community for a long time and is often quoted on various occasions by both formal and informal leaders as well as other community members.
>
> However, it is clear that this philosophy has not been adopted fully by the community. This is evidenced by the fact that many school students and people engaged to be married are unable to read the Qur'ān. Because of this, and in the interests of improving knowledge and understanding of the Qur'ān throughout the community, the Regional Government feels it is necessary to implement Regional Regulations regarding literacy in the Qur'ān for school students and people engaged to be married.

---

37 Peranan Satuan Polisi Pamong Praja dalam Menegakkan Peraturan Daerah dan Memilihara Ketertiban Umum, Padang, 28 June 2006. A copy is held by the Asian Law Centre, University of Melbourne.

It is important to be aware that issues of religion and piety are not simply a matter of the relationship between the individual and God, but also relate to the relationship between human beings and the way life is ordered, both in this life and the hereafter.

With this in mind, to improve faith and piety in the community and create a harmonious and joyful community, it is necessary to implement regulations that will serve to motivate the community to improve its level of faith and piety by improving literacy in the Qur'ān. It is expected that the implementation of these Regional Regulations will motivate school students and those engaged to be married to study the Qur'ān and eventually to understand and practise the lessons correctly.

Aside from this, in implementing these Regional Regulations regarding literacy in the Qur'ān, the Regional Government will have a legal basis for its efforts to motivate the community.

On the one hand, the Regional Government has a program of Nine Years of Compulsory Education that aims to assist school students to graduate to the next stage of education. On the other hand, it is feared that without equipping students with a knowledge of the Qur'ān from an early age, a generation that is intelligent but lacking in faith may develop. The ideal community is one that is faithful and pious, intelligent, creative, skilled and disciplined, has a high work ethic, and is physically and mentally healthy.

Because of this, the Regional Government feels it is necessary to implement these Regional Regulations regarding literacy in the Qur'ān.

One could not get a much clearer statement of values than this. The initial 'considerations' to the text make the same point: that the function of the national education system is 'to create the perfect human being (Muslim) who has the characteristics of a well-rounded person ... and an Indonesian society that is faithful and pious towards God'. This is not especially new; a similar initiative was attempted nationally in 1982, for example.[38]

The regulation defines literacy as the ability to recite the Qur'ān fluently (depending on age and capacity) in accordance with the rules for correct pronunciation, intonation and rhythm. It focuses on two groups: schoolchildren and engaged couples. Schoolchildren from primary school through to senior high school age are required to attend classes in the Qur'ān in addition to fulfilling the requirements of the secular curriculum. Study of the Qur'ān is just one subject in the Qur'ānic studies curriculum. Schools are required to provide the equipment and facilities necessary to implement the Qur'ānic studies program (article 7), although the content may vary depending on which authority—the Department of Education, the Department of Religion or the regional government—is in charge of the school. The Solok regulation simply specifies that the basic subjects in the Qur'ānic studies curriculum should include Ritual (Ibadah), Ethics (Akhlak), History/Chronicles (Tarikh) and Correct Recitation of the Qur'ān

---

38 Joint Decision of the Minister of Home Affairs No. 128/1982 and the Minister of Religion No. 44A/1982 to Improve Qur'ān Literacy for the Muslim Community in the Interest of Full Comprehension and Practice of the Qur'ān in Daily Life. Gade (2004) and especially Headley (2000: 234 ff.) deal authoritatively with the related and very complex issues surrounding recitation of the Qur'ān in South Sulawesi and Java respectively.

(Tajwid). Students are to be tested and receive a grade as in the secular subjects (article 8(4)) and will receive a certificate on completion of the course. Without this they may not proceed to a higher level of schooling (articles 11 and 18). There are heavy penalties of up to six months in prison or a fine of Rp 5 million for issuing false certificates.[39] The enforcement of these sanctions is in the hands of the civil service investigating officers, who have wide-ranging powers to stop, search, interrogate, seize documents and so on (article 14) identical to those in the prevention of immorality legislation. However, formal criminal proceedings are subject to national police procedures.

Regulations on Proper Dress

The example used here is Perda No. 6/2002, again from Solok. The elucidation says:

> Wearing Muslim attire is one of the ways to reflect and represent one's Muslim identity. This identity can grow and develop through various channels, such as education and development. It is expected that the wearing of Muslim attire will encourage people to remember their faith and piety to God.
>
> Wearing Muslim attire is part of Minangkabau society because, in general, West Sumatra/Solok District is an Islamic society. This is strengthened by the traditional philosophy '*Adat* rests on Syariah, Syariah rests on the Scripture of God', which means that our culture also supports the wearing of Muslim attire.
>
> While not everybody wears Muslim attire, on the most important religious occasions the community always wears Muslim attire. Workers in Solok District have increasingly been inclined to wear Muslim attire at work. This is due to their personal awareness and because of the efforts made to encourage the wearing of Muslim attire.
>
> We are now in an era of globalization and must protect ourselves and the generations to follow from cultural influences that are not in accordance with the teachings of Islam and our own culture. One form of cultural colonization is through attire; thus, it is possible that we may inadvertently wear attire that is not in accordance with our religious and cultural teachings.
>
> In relation to this issue, it is apparent that Solok society, particularly the state apparatus and students, must wear Muslim attire in their everyday lives.
>
> If every Muslim civil servant and student wears Muslim attire, it is hoped that this will set a good example for the rest of society and encourage everyone to wear Muslim attire.
>
> Because of these factors, in order to provide a legal basis for the wearing of Muslim attire in Solok, particularly in state and private offices, in the school environment and at official events, it is necessary to have Regional Regulations regarding the wearing of Muslim attire.
>
> In implementing these Regional Regulations it is expected that the attempt to create a society that reflects a faithful and pious Muslim identity will not merely be an effort but something that has a legal basis that will motivate the community.

---

39 Despite this there is a thriving trade in false certificates (field notes, West Sumatra, June 2006).

Proper dress has always been of immense social significance, and acquired an extra dimension for the Muslim world during the past 200 years of European contact.[40] In Indonesia, the debate about dress that originated in the Dutch colonial period has continued into the present day.[41] For Muslims, correct dress is partly a question of modesty (Q33:59) and partly a question of demonstrating a distinct 'Islamic' persona.[42] In the Solok regulation, one of the functions of dress is to create an environment 'that reflects one's Muslim personality'. Dress also has the function of 'preserving Minangkabau culture' and 'traditional customs' (article 3) and 'protecting one's self-worth as a Muslim and avoiding threats from others' (article 4).

Those who are required to wear Muslim dress are school and university students as well as civil servants. Muslim dress is to be worn on official occasions. The general public is also requested to wear Muslim attire, particularly at public events. The stipulated clothing is long trousers and a long or short-sleeved top for men; and a long top covering the hips, a dress or slacks extending to the feet, and a scarf covering the hair, ears, neck, shoulders and chest for women. None of these items may be transparent or tight fitting. Sanctions for non-compliance include disciplinary action for public employees and, in the case of students, verbal and written warnings, informing the student's parents, refusing entry to classes and, finally, expulsion. These provisions apply only to Muslims; non-Muslims may dress 'in accordance with their own religion'.

Regulations on *Zakat*

The obligation to pay *zakat* is one of the five pillars of Islam but, with the exception of *fitrah* payable at the end of Ramadan, has historically been widely avoided. Successive governments in the Dutch and postwar administrations tended to ignore the issue, leaving collection and payment to private institutions such as Nahdlatul Ulama (NU) and Muhammadiyah. Since the 1980s, however, there has been a consistent trend towards state intervention in *zakat* as part of a general trend for the government to try to control 'Islamic money'. Indonesia now has national *zakat* legislation in place,[43] and all regions of West Sumatra (and Aceh) have *zakat* regulations.

---

40 See, for example, Lewis (2002: 73–6; 138–9) on the significance of dress in Ottoman Turkey.

41 See Hooker (2003a: 126–8; 130–4) for *fatāwā* on dress.

42 See the extracts in Fealy and Hooker (2006: 326–8) on the headscarf.

43 Law No. 38/1999 on Zakat Management, Minister of Religion Decision No. 581/1999 implementing this law and the Law on Income Tax No. 7/1983, amended by Law No. 17/2000 with reference to *zakat*.

The example used here is a standard one: Perda No. 13/2003 from Solok. It is based closely on the national laws, even to the extent of repeating most of the opening phrase of Law No. 38/1999: '... based on the principles of faith and piety, clarity and legal certainty in accordance with the Pancasila and the 1945 Constitution'. The full passage reads:

> With sound management, *zakat* funds are a vast potential resource to be used for the benefit of the community. *Zakat* funds are used to reduce poverty and social inequality but professional and accountable management is necessary to achieve this, and this is the responsibility of the community and the Regional Government. The Regional Government is responsible for providing protection, advocacy and services for Muslim individuals and bodies (*muzakki*) as well as for the rightful recipients of *zakat* (*mutahiq*) and *zakat* managers. Thus, it is necessary to implement Regional Regulations on the management of *zakat*, based on the principles of faith and piety, with the aim of achieving social justice, the common good, clarity and legal certainty in accordance with the Pancasila and the 1945 Constitution of the Republic of Indonesia. (Article 2)

While the Qur'ānic classes (Q2:177) of *zakat* recipients are described in the regulation, the bulk of it is taken up with setting out the management system necessary to accomplish the expanded aims. Essentially this system is the same as that described in the national Zakat Management Law (No. 38/1999). All regions in West Sumatra have adopted its provisions with minor variations, thus ensuring that a formal nationwide system is in place. We are a long way from understanding how the provisions actually work at the regional level, but it is undeniable that *zakat* has now been translated from a personal value to an objective state value. We shall have to wait and see whether the logic of capitalization of *zakat* via state or state-approved bodies will prevail. In positive law terms it should, and the national and regional regulations are all clearly directed towards that end. Moreover, it is worth noting that *adat* values have no place in the matter; they are totally excluded.

What can we conclude from the West Sumatra regulations? We know that their purpose is to cure the ills of a 'sick' society. The proposed remedies are to prevent immorality, increase basic religious knowledge (especially competence in the Qur'ān), require proper dress as an indicator of identity (especially for women) and regulate the payment of *zakat*, one of the five pillars of Islam. These remedies are simply selections from a much vaster expanse of syariah values. They have been elevated above others in the expectation that they will provide *the* answer to the perceived ills of contemporary society. Selection is well within the tradition of Indonesian Islam, but in the instances just described it diminishes the real complexities of contemporary Indonesian syariah. Perhaps that is not so serious from a formal point of view; after all, (selected) *fiqh* principles are present in the KHI and the religious courts, and the selections in the regional regulations are in addition to, not a derogation from, the classical inheritance.

But a balance between the classical *fiqh* and its contemporary interpretations has not been established, in West Sumatra as in Aceh.

The regional regulations emphasize individual responsibility, thus rejecting hierarchies of wealth and status. This is, of course, completely in line with the syariah emphasis on personal duty to God. But at the same time the regulations reinforce existing formal inequalities, most notably in the provisions on the conduct and appearance of women. This immediately raises the issue of constitutional equality, that is, between a 'citizen of the Republic' and a 'Muslim woman'. Which of these two statuses is prior? So far, no answer has been forthcoming.

The constitutional issue has two further aspects, both of them disputed. First, are the regional regulations legal? They would appear to lie outside the scope of the Regional Autonomy Laws, although no judicial determination on this matter has been made. Second, the enforcement provisions are confused, not to say chaotic. This has serious implications for the administration of public law.

4   THE MMI DRAFT CRIMINAL CODE

The Council of Indonesian Mujahideen (Majelis Mujahidin Indonesia; MMI) was founded in August 2000 at a national conference held to discuss the form and function of syariah in Indonesia (Fealy 2004: 113–14). Its draft criminal code is the major outcome for present purposes.[44] Essentially the code proposes to implement syariah values by imposing punitive sanctions; indeed, the entire text is devoted to this subject. In a very real sense it is the logical next step for the syariah as sufficient school (see Chapter 2), and thus falls into the same class of document as the regional regulations. The common factor between the MMI code and the syariah regional regulations is compulsion. Like them, the MMI code is at pains to justify itself, as the following preamble shows:

> In the effort to bring about the supremacy of law and bring order to the community social life of the people of Indonesia, there are many things that have been attempted by various groups that feel they have an interest in this matter; however, they have not shown any meaningful improvements thus far. What actually happened has in fact been the opposite of what was hoped for.
>
> The secular system of laws and legislation that has been applied by the government has in fact caused there to be a multiplicative increase in criminality, disharmony of life, moral decadence and the decay of human values. A further consequence, which has gone hand in hand with the increasing weakness of the law enforcement authorities, is the occurrence of brutality and anarchy by the community in punishing those who commit criminal acts. This shows among other things that secular law is not capable of providing shelter and protection, peace, justice and a sense of security to the community, because the edifice of the secular legal system is based only on

---

44 I leave aside its place in Islamic politics. Its *emir* (commander) is Abu Bakar Ba'asyir; see Fealy and Hooker (2006: 442–5).

empirical rationality, which can never stretch to reach the psychic aspect of humanity that is so very wide and complex.

Therefore, as long as the legislation that orders the life of the community is not based on law that is in harmony with the primordial essence of man and humanity, that legislation will damage the equilibrium of human life, because it will be unable to fulfil the basic demands of human life itself. And there is no law whatsoever in this world that is capable of fulfilling this matter, except if man submits to the law of Allah and His Prophet totally and comprehensively.

As a religion that is universal in nature and *rahmatan lil alamin* [a mercy for all the worlds], the sharia of Islam does not only speak about matters of law and punishment; on the contrary, it also functions to guide, shelter and protect, and guarantee the safety, security and prosperity of mankind, as individuals, as a community, as a nation and as a state. The sharia of Islam guarantees and gives the protection of law, at the very least, to five fundamental needs of human life.

First, it guarantees the freedom of human beings to have religion (*hifdzud din*). Second, it protects the faculty of reason from influences that damage its function in life (*hifdzul 'aql*). Third, it guarantees purity of descent, so that there can be no doubts about the familial ties between a person and their parents (*hifdzun nasl*). Fourth, it shelters and guarantees the safety of human life, both as an individual and as a species (*hifdzun nafs*). And fifth, it guarantees and protects the property rights of human beings, both as personal rights and as communal rights (*hifdzul mal*).

The firm and clear guarantees of sharia such as those enumerated above can never be matched by secular laws. With sharia guarantees such as those, man has been given a basic reference to make regulations and laws that are necessary if there is no *nash* [clear stipulation] in the Qur'an and the Sunnah, with his own *ijtihad* [independent reasoning], as long as they continue to refer to the principles above. This means that Islam does not nullify man's initiative in making laws and regulations that are necessary on the basis of the situation and conditions of his times, as long as they are intended to guarantee the above five basic principles.

On the basis of the reasons above, the institution of Majelis Mujahidin, which has the objective of upholding the sharia of Islam in the lives of individuals, families, the community and the state, has prepared a Criminal Code adjusted to accord with the sharia of Islam, as a contribution to the reform of the Criminal Code [*KUHP*] that is the colonial legacy of the Dutch and has become outdated and no longer in line with the spirit of *reformasi*, yet strangely continues until now to have its applicability in Indonesia maintained.

May Allah send down His grace on the publishing of this Criminal Code adjusted to accord with the sharia of Islam, so that it may bring benefits and make a contribution to the effort to bring about justice and prosperity for all people. Amen, O Answerer of Those Who Ask. (Cited in Fealy and Hooker 2006: 168–9)

The reasoning expressed here is the same as that found in the Aceh Qanun and West Sumatra *perda*: that secular laws have failed, leaving syariah as the only recourse. 'Syariah' in this context means punishment for offences that are committed in public and can be classed as wrongs (as defined by *fiqh*), and must therefore be dealt with publicly. These offences are murder and manslaughter, theft and unlawful sex, all of which must be eliminated. This very narrow view of syariah is not confined to Indonesia but occurs throughout the Muslim world. Indeed, the genesis of the MMI code lies in a code drafted by the Malaysian state of Kelantan, which was itself based on the Hudood Ordinances introduced in

Pakistan between 1978 and 1982 by then president Zia al-Haqq.[45] The example given in Table 6.3 of a few of the parallel provisions of the Kelantan and MMI codes reveals the similarity between them. Note that the translations from Malay and Indonesian respectively were done by two different people, making the concordance between them even more remarkable.

The Kelantan and MMI codes are unusual in expressing syariah values in terms of *ideology*. Their authors, as well as being ideologues, certainly knew (or knew of) each other. Hj. Abdul Hadi Hj. Awang, then chief minister of the Malaysian state of Terengganu, was the prime mover behind that state's Syariah Criminal Offence (Hudud and Qisas) Bill (2002)—a successor to the Kelantan bill—and had been present at the South Sulawesi congress in 2000. Like all ideologies, both the Kelantan and MMI codes deal in absolutes that are unattainable in the present but will be achieved at some point in the future 'when people understand and accept the truth' and adjust their behaviour accordingly.[46] They have another and more important feature in common: they are not consistent with the state legal system and are therefore impractical. For the proposed laws to work, the ideology underlying them would have to be accepted by the state. But this is not the case in either Malaysia or Indonesia. As a result, the proposed ideology-laws have no possible point of connection with the processes of the general legal system.

The MMI draft criminal code (and, indeed, all ideologically based law texts) raises two issues for the contemporary Indonesian legal system. First, the code is very narrow in being focused on punishment, in particular penalties for sexual misconduct. Admittedly this is not its whole focus, but at the same time, punishment does inform and restrict its content. Such a narrow view obscures the subtleties of the comprehensive code of behaviour (*'adhāb*) underpinning the proposed laws, which should include not only the mandatory (*hadd*), retaliatory (*qisas*), compensatory (*diya*) and discretionary (*ta'zir*) forms of punishment, but also the subtleties of *fiqh* commentary. In particular, the types and (more importantly) standards of proof for imposing the various forms of punishment are not addressed. This is a serious deficiency so far as historical *fiqh* theory is concerned, as well as being unacceptable in *contemporary* Arabic scholarship. There is no evidence that the authors of the Kelantan and MMI codes have consulted this scholarship (Hallaq 1997: 168 ff., 214 ff.), even though it is absolutely germane to syariah criminal code construction. Avoiding it wilfully ignores (or denies by default) recent analyses of contemporary syariah functions (*maqasid al-syariah*) *from within the classical tradition*. It is true that the preamble to the

---

45 On the Hudood Ordinances, see Fealy and Hooker (2006: 177, note 51). The Malaysian bill did not succeed in becoming law because it was unconstitutional.

46 In this sense the Kelantan and MMI codes are, in terms of structure, rather like Marxism, although the adherents of each would be unhappy with the comparison. Perhaps they might like to refute this?

Table 6.3   A Comparison of Sample Clauses in the Malaysian Kelantan Code and Indonesian MMI Code

The Kelantan Code	The MMI Code
Clause 10	Article 15
<u>Zina</u>	
1 Zina is an offence which consists of sexual intercourse between a man and a woman who are not married to each other and such intercourse does not come within the meaning of 'wati syubhah' as defined in subsection (3).	1 *Zina* is a crime that consists of sexual intercourse between a man and a woman who are not husband and wife and that sexual intercourse does not fall under the definition of '*wati syubhah*' as stated in subsection (3).
2 where an offender is validly married and has experienced sexual intercourse in such marriage, such offender is called 'mohsan', but where an offender is not married, or is already married but has not experienced sexual intercourse in such marriage, such offender is called 'ghairu mohsan'.	2 If the person who commits *zina* has been married and has had sexual intercourse in that marriage, that person who commits *zina* is called '*muhshan*', but if the person who commits it has not yet married or has married but has not had sexual intercourse in that marriage, that person who commits *zina* is called '*ghairu muhshan*'.
3 Wati syubhah is sexual intercourse performed by a man with a woman who is not his wife and such intercourse took place–	3 *Wati Syubhah* is sexual intercourse that is committed by a man with a woman who is not his wife and that sexual intercourse is committed:
a in doubtful circumstances in which he thought that with [*sic*] the woman whom he had sexual intercourse was his wife, when in fact she was not; or	a in doubtful circumstances where he believes that the woman with whom he is having sexual intercourse is his wife, whereas the woman is not his wife; or
b in doubtful circumstances in which he believed that his marriage to the woman with whom he had sexual intercourse was valid according to Syariah law, when in fact his marriage to her was invalid.	b in doubtful circumstances where he believes that the marriage with the woman with whom he is having sexual intercourse is valid according to sharia law, whereas in truth that marriage is not valid according to sharia law.

Source: The translations originally appeared in Fealy and Hooker (2006: 179–80). The Malay extract is from Sisters in Islam (1995: 14, appendix 1).

MMI code cited earlier does set out the intentions of the code, but without taking into account that these are now negotiable. In contemporary Indonesia as elsewhere in the Muslim world, syariah provisions vary in intensity and suitability. The duty of those drafting such codes, therefore, is to move beyond a pre-modern 'taxonomy of interests' (Hallaq 1997: 169). The KHI provides one example of how this can be done. The MMI code does not.

The second issue concerns the compatibility of the proposed code with existing laws—a subject already touched on above. Two sets of existing laws are of particular interest: the current criminal code (Kitab Undang-Undang Hukum Pidana), which is currently under revision; and the religious court laws (Laws No. 7/1989 and No. 3/2006). Even on the most generous reading of the MMI code, there are serious structural inconsistencies between it and the KUHP, most notably in the areas of evidence, procedure and penalties. The code would also appear to be inconsistent with the second set of laws, specifically those relating to the jurisdiction of the religious courts. This issue also directly involves the Supreme Court, which has overriding jurisdiction. These compatibility issues have not been addressed. Nor has the related problem of transition: the MMI code proposes to make substantial changes to the intention and substance of the criminal law but does not give any attention to the period of transition during which the shift from the present criminal code to the MMI code would take place. Given this state of affairs, the only possible outcome would be chaos.

In short, the MMI code has no credibility in terms of either the classical jurisprudence or contemporary Indonesian circumstances.

5 CONCLUDING REMARKS

The syariah values described in this chapter do not exist in a vacuum; they are articulated in a modern state. The state has values of its own, the most important one being the maintenance of public order through a monopoly over policing or, at the very least, the efficient administration of positive law. It is now commonplace to say that Indonesia has been less than successful in these matters. However, the syariah laws introduced by some regions do nothing to help. On the contrary, by introducing ill-trained 'para-police' with equally ill-defined powers, the Aceh Qanun (through the Wilayatul Hisbah) and the West Sumatra *perda* (through the civil service investigating officers) simply compound the problem. The intensity of the debate surrounding the syariah and state criminal law systems is forcing Indonesians to choose between them. This is unfortunate, because they are not necessarily mutually exclusive. It is also unfortunate that the debate so far has been driven by emotion rather than reason.

The case in favour of the *qanun* and *perda* can be summarized as follows:

- Syariah values are primary for the individual and society because they are revealed values.

- The state has failed in its duty to implement or even protect these values, as demonstrated by the widespread incidence of immorality, improper dress, ignorance of the Qur'ān and failure to pay *zakat*.
- Because of the failure of the local and national authorities to enforce correct behaviour, the *qanun* and *perda*, as well as local enforcement bodies, are necessary.

While admitting that syariah values are real, the secular or state argument holds instead:

- The Pancasila already sufficiently incorporates syariah values.
- The regional regulations may contravene the Regional Autonomy Laws and, perhaps, the Constitution.
- Laws on their own cannot make people behave morally; enforcing some sort of outward show of morality on the public does not ensure the existence of inner morality.
- Insistence on public orthopraxy alone is a distortion of both law and religion.
- Special enforcement bodies inevitably lead to corruption and political opportunism, further debasing public order values.
- Social ills exist, but they cannot be cured just by introducing syariah laws. A syariah defined in this way is not a true or full definition of syariah.[47]

The debate over values is clearly divisive and at first sight may appear irreconcilable given its highly politicized nature; politicians on both sides have appropriated an undefined 'syariah' to prop up their own positions. What is not disputed is that 'syariah values' must be responsive to the Constitution, Pancasila, the Regional Autonomy Laws and positive state laws. The syariah has become a polarizing mechanism separating the individual's view of the state from that person's faith in God. But when values are translated into actual practice, they are always debatable. Application does not necessarily deny the absoluteness of values, although this is often made to seem the case.

If we understand the two opposing sets of values in this way, we can see that they are not necessarily in opposition. The law texts examined in this chapter are actually on the margins of what we might call 'mainstream law', that is, family law, commercial law, and laws involving public order and government. Of course they impinge on these areas but they are not essential to the whole law system. If these texts disappeared tomorrow, then neither the proper intention of syariah (*maqasid al-syariah*) nor the Constitution of Indonesia would in any way be affected. The respective basic functions—public good or public benefit in the case of syariah and strict neutrality in the case of secular law—would remain the same. But there is another factor that does have potentially serious consequences

---

47 For extracts on these opposing positions, see Fealy and Hooker (2006: 137–206).

for syariah. We can call this public perceptions of law—specifically of syariah values. There is considerable public disquiet about the application of Aceh's *qanun* and other regions' *perda*, and as any sociology of law would show, that could easily translate into rejection. The extra factor here is that while the values are ostensibly objective (God-given), the 'rational' imperatives of application are very much subjective. The *qanun* and *perda* therefore carry within them the seeds of incoherence and contradiction.[48]

Contradiction is always implicit when law is used as an instrument to change values. So far as Islam is concerned, this has mainly been a history of failure. During the period of European dominance in Indonesia (and elsewhere for that matter), Islam, broadly construed as a value system, was wholly rejected as a basis for public law. This policy continued for the first 50 years of Indonesian independence. What we are seeing now is a renewed attempt, through regional autonomy, to reverse that status, that is, to place syariah values once again at the forefront of public (legal) life.

The four texts examined in this chapter provide interesting insights into what such a system might look like. It could co-exist alongside the existing religious law system (as in Aceh); it could replace the existing criminal law (as in West Sumatra or as proposed by the MMI draft criminal code); or it could establish a totally new system, including economics, that is integrated into the existing legal system (as proposed by the South Sulawesi draft syariah code). There are difficulties with each version, but they all claim to be true to syariah values and, as such, to exemplify the vitality of revelation and reinforce its relevance for contemporary life. Secular critics, on the other hand, see these efforts as avoidance of the real problems of poverty, corruption and government incompetence; a retreat into pointless defensiveness for which 'Islamic values' are just a cover for local political interests; and an unjustifiable manipulation of religion.

Whatever one's views might be, it is clear that, as used in the ways described in this chapter, syariah laws are a rather blunt instrument. Without exception all the examples show the contradictions inherent in translating syariah values into an effective legal program for contemporary Indonesian society.

---

48 That this is not just speculation is shown by the example of Pakistan, whose Hudood Ordinance (1979) was repealed in December 2006 as (a) unworkable and (b) a distortion of *fiqh* (Masud 2006). Given that the MMI code is indirectly based on the Pakistan material (via the Kelantan code), this is important (Fealy and Hooker 2006: 176 ff.).

7 Epilogue: Syariah on the Edge

Indonesian syariah is *sui generis*—it is not the syariah of the Middle East, North Africa or other parts of Southeast Asia. It does, however, share a common classical (Arabic) heritage with Muslim states in other regions, including the great technical *fiqh* heritage. All states have had to work through that heritage since the nineteenth century, and in doing so have stretched the historically derived doctrine to the edge. For example, modern medical science and modern forms of finance now pose questions that force syariah techniques to their limits (Hooker 2003a: 227 ff.). More recently, Bulliet (2004: 135 ff.) has used 'edge' to mean periphery—in the sense of the differences that have emerged between the traditional centre of Islam (the Middle East) *vis-à-vis* the geographical edge of Islam (Africa and Asia). Both meanings are appropriate for Indonesia and it is in them that the notion of syariah as a work in progress finds its context.

'Work in progress' can mean just a continuing activity, but it has also acquired connotations of improvement or advancement. From the Western point of view 'progress' has a favourable resonance. But this is not a universally held position in Muslim states, where the modernization of syariah is often rejected as just another version of orientalism (see, for example, Mahdi 1990). Here I use 'progress' in the minimal sense of work that is proceeding. In this sense Indonesian syariah can be described as having progressed to the point where it is suitable for local and temporal conditions—a real achievement. Progress on the localization and rationalization of syariah (see Chapter 2) is also advancing into new ('edge') territory. Of course one may object that the syariah is no longer an independent variable but merely an object to which the state gives a form in some law or regulation. *Fiqh* has totally disappeared. The state sets the agenda and conducts an ongoing process of selection directed towards the creation of a national school of legal thought (*mazhab*).

What, therefore, is the true state of syariah in contemporary Indonesia? I approach this question first through an examination of syariah definitions and then through a discussion of syariah as a vital expression of universal legal values. The picture that emerges is of a distinctive form of syariah forged by the pressure of edge issues and Indonesia's position on the geographical periphery of Islam—a syariah that is still very much a work in progress.

1   DEFINITIONS

It is apparent that there are multiple definitions of syariah. It is equally apparent that syariah has no *a priori* meaning in contemporary Indonesia. Instead it depends on context, and that in turn depends on purpose—it is the latter which must be established as the initial premise. The syariah heritage, therefore, is mined for a purpose; the selections made from it are prioritized over others, which then drop away because they are not suitable for whatever that purpose might be.

Before giving some examples, it is worth pointing out that the well-known Middle Eastern scholar Yusuf Qardhawi reached a similar conclusion, but at a rather theoretical level.[1] His work—including his *fatāwā* (see Qardhawi 1995)— is extensively translated into Indonesian and may well have been effective in at least reinforcing the notion of priorities.[2] But there is no question of the practice of selection having been invented for Indonesian syariah—it has a long history and the Qardhawi proposals are really nothing new for the heartland or the edge of Islam. Indonesia has made its own contribution to syariah selections in at least three areas: philosophy of law, positive law and legal values.

Syariah in the Philosophy of Law

In Indonesia philosophy of law means (a) the principles on which the 1945 Constitution rests and (b) the place of syariah (if any) in the state. It has been 60 years since Indonesia achieved independence, but the debate about the philosophical basis of the legal system continues in the media and in the Muslim world more generally. In contrast, this subject receives little attention in the Western media except when some sort of scandal erupts. Why the difference? The obvious answer is that Islam represents a real alternative to the secular Constitution. It says that the primary duty of the individual is to God and only secondarily to the Constitution. Governments of Muslim states do not agree with this proposition or, at best, pretend to agree while implementing laws that ignore the divine imperative. Indonesia, to its great credit, has faced the issue of philosophy of law in a very direct manner over the past 60 years.

Many—perhaps most—Western comparative lawyers fail to realize just how important religion is in the Muslim world. But how could they when most of them are theologically illiterate? This is not altogether their fault; it is perfectly possible to have a philosophy of law that does not include religion. That issue was fought out in Europe in the eighteenth and nineteenth centuries and was resolved in favour of secular law systems, which are now considered 'normal' in the West.

---

1   For Yusuf al-Qardhawi's views, see his internet site: <http://www.islamonline.net/>.

2   See the commentary and extract in Fealy and Hooker (2006: 161–2).

This is not the situation in Indonesia, where no proper or working legal system is in place and where Islam is a fact of life, including political life, to a degree that requires the philosophy of law to be of central interest at all levels of society. It is important to remember that the individual Muslim is not a passive consumer of law but a person who has to think about and engage with personal duty *from* Islam but also *within* the state (including all its infrastructure). It is quite wrong to dismiss this with a sense of *déjà vu* as some historians do; the fact of the matter is that this is the lot of the individual Muslim and he or she must put up with it.

The syariah as sufficient school argues that this is an abnormal situation that could be rectified by the restoration of the caliphate as the only real alternative to the Constitution. But this is to confuse cause and conditions, when the conditions of life in contemporary Indonesia are not, of themselves, a sufficient cause to demand a caliphate. Such an all-or-nothing solution confuses conditions with mere occasions. Occasions are ephemeral and subject to unpredictable change. Such a change may be brought about simply by a swing in fashion or by political opportunism, that is, by choices that can easily be reversed. This is clearly the case with the syariah-coloured regional regulations (*perda* and *qanun*) discussed in Chapter 6, which attempt to translate occasions (immorality, improper dress and so on) into cause for the new regulations. However, the choice of target for the regulations is entirely arbitrary, making this halfway step towards a caliphate illogical. It cannot work. That is not to say that a certain amount of emotional satisfaction or even political advantage cannot be derived from such an exercise, but it comes at the price of restricting behaviour that would otherwise be guaranteed (by the Constitution) or dealt with by a law of higher status (for example, the criminal code).

Both localized syariah and rationalized syariah approach the abnormal circumstances in which syariah must co-exist with the Indonesian state by trying to remove or at least diminish the perceived abnormality (see Chapter 2). But can the abnormal be a point of departure, and by what test is it to be identified? For Western jurisprudence lack of certainty is abnormal, but we have already seen that certainty is not a high or absolute value in Indonesian legal thinking, where opaqueness and variousness are the preferred forms of acting. Of course, there is certainty in the classical *fiqh* texts, although the relevance of these is now questioned. But there is no certainty in the new hermeneutics of the last 50 years, and it is on this that the rationalized and localized syariah rests. Certainty is only one test but it does not deal adequately with Indonesian syariah.

Contextualized syariah provides another way of dealing with the abnormal situation in which syariah finds itself in Indonesia. Its strength is that it proposes a historical link between the time of revelation and the conditions of the present. However, the assumptions on which it rests are rather large ones, the most problematic one being that history can be shown to be objective—in short, that there is an objective condition that allows one to formulate a 'suitable syariah'. But as we know, the motive of the historian for stating a historical case is decisive, because the 'facts' of history are a matter of choice; there will always be others that are equally possible or valid. This is an especially acute problem in Indonesia where the state legal system is a failed one. But is failed an abnormality and is failed really the right word?

This brings us back to context. Context is much more than occasion; because it encompasses the institutions of state, it is a condition for syariah. This makes some sort of objectivity possible. But it still has to be explained, and this is where the curricula of Indonesia's State Islamic Universities (UIN), State Islamic Institutes (IAIN) and State Islamic Colleges (STAIN) are important (see Chapter 3). All curricula have two purposes. The first purpose of the Indonesian syariah curricula is to teach the basics of *fiqh*. The second is to contextualize the *fiqh* in a form suitable for contemporary Indonesia. This whole package is called 'syariah'. In the 1960s and 1970s, the more traditional *'ulamā'* found this latter aspect of the legal curriculum to be abnormal—a view that still persists today. Despite being correct from a classical position, this is to overlook the fact that the context for establishing conditions and, especially, cause has now changed. The present context is the state as both the source of authority and the definer of syariah. The state is now an essential condition *and* the cause of contemporary syariah forms, as the various curricula make clear.

The importance of the syariah curricula lies not so much in their content as in their structure, which is modelled directly on the secular tertiary education system. Both the syariah and national curricula are based on three tiers of subjects: Basic General Subjects, Basic Skills Subjects and Specialist Skills Subjects. These are taken in a graded progression with examinations at each level. The educational philosophy underlying this system is directed towards framing a localized syariah suitable for the Indonesian context. The bulk of the required texts are in Indonesian, but Arabic and English-language texts are also used. Significantly, there now seems to be a move towards prioritizing English over Arabic in all except the basic core *fiqh* subjects. A closer examination of the syariah reading lists shows, first, that most of the readings for state positive law are in Indonesian; second, that the majority of those for economics and related subjects are in English; and third, that most of those for *fiqh* and, to some degree, philosophy of law are in Arabic (with English increasing in the latter case). The sources are therefore diverse, and becoming more so. The only section of the curriculum where sources have remained relatively stable is localized and rationalized syariah, which is taught as part of positive law.

The really difficult area of the curriculum is contextualized syariah, where a variety of sources (Arabic, Indonesian and English) compete for priority. This is not surprising given that students are required to approach the study of contextualized syariah through both exegesis (*tafsir*) (in Arabic) and hermeneutics (in English and Indonesian). Indonesian scholarship is divided on the validity of each of these methods, with no prospect of agreement. In short, debate on the concept of syariah and how to explain and transmit it is a work in progress. The terms of this debate have shifted over time and it will continue to throw up alternative views. In only one case, the syariah as sufficient position, is syariah put forward as a direct alternative to the Indonesian Constitution.

Syariah as Positive Law

Positive law is man-made law. It does not depend on divine inspiration but is grounded in some other authority. This may be a constitution that sets out the criteria for the validity of the law and the rules by which it may be changed, and is binding on both its subjects and the officers of state charged with its administration. This is a minimalist definition, but it does encapsulate Indonesian syariah. In practice Indonesian syariah refers to the religious courts, the Compilation of Islamic Law (KHI), the regulations on gifts (*wakaf*) and the wealth tax (*zakat*), Islamic forms of money and the regulations of the Department of Religion. These owe nothing to revelation in terms of authority, although they are connected to it through words like 'Islamic' and 'syariah'. It is therefore essential not to confuse authority with connectedness—just as cause and conditions should not be confused. In this case, the confusion commonly arises from the assumption that because a law deals with an 'Islamic' matter then it must itself be either Islamic or derived from syariah. This is not the case for the positive laws of the state. Their authority, formulation and administration are quite different, not to say remote, from syariah-derived laws. The error is endemic in the syariah as sufficient position and is an ever-present danger in contextualized syariah. The former argues not only that positive law is not authentic as syariah (which is true) but also that it is a betrayal of syariah principles. This conveniently ignores the entire history of syariah administration in the Muslim world. Contextualized syariah also has historical problems, specifically in allowing an unrestrained individual intellectual initiative that can easily lead to an amorphous relativism.

The Indonesian version of syariah as positive law has so far avoided these difficulties (but see below on syariah values). My explanation for this is that Indonesian legal practitioners have always made a practice of selecting the aspects of syariah that are most suitable for Indonesia. The appropriation of the useful and practical is no doubt inspired by faith, but it is also an admission of the constraints on the wholesale adoption of dogma. The legal history of Islam in Indonesia thus exactly parallels the history of canon law or Hindu law, to name but two. One can even be somewhat sympathetic to the often feckless politics of religion, which may be regarded as a necessary process in weeding out extremes of dogma while also revealing the degrees of (in)comprehension of syariah in the political world.

Syariah selection in positive law has had a varied history. In pre-modern Indonesia selections from syariah were minimal. Instead, the main focus was on selecting from state practice in the Middle East with the purpose of establishing legitimate sovereignties ('Muslim' states) in the region. The Dutch, equally concerned with sovereign legitimacy, selected syariah out—it had no place except at the most minimal level. The story since independence is more complex. True selection did not really begin until the late 1980s. Until this time the Dutch system of minimal syariah influence in the legal system was maintained. The only new initiative was the founding of the Department of Religion in 1946.

When discussing the nexus between syariah and Indonesian positive law, the religious courts are the obvious place to start. In form, structure and procedure they are the same as the secular courts, but they have a far more limited jurisdiction. The jurisdiction of the religious courts is confined to family law, trusts and, since 2006, 'Islamic' contracts of finance. As well as having a limited jurisdiction, the religious courts have a dependent status. That dependency was emphasized by the transfer of these courts from the Department of Religion to the Supreme Court in 2004. It is important to acknowledge that the procedural element of the religious courts owes nothing to any classical definition of syariah. For purposes of practice, they are subject to the same rules and discipline as any other court. From the individual petitioner's point of view, this means that any claim will essentially stand or fall on its procedural correctness. We often forget the importance of procedure—that is, of the bureaucratic formalities—perhaps because it tends to be honoured more in the breach than in the practice. In short, the religious courts are selected *into* the national secular system and are thus bound by it.

Selection *in* is not the end of the matter. There is also selection *out*—of the *fiqh*. Until 1989 it was open to religious court judges to refer to a standard set of Shafi'i *fiqh* texts (Hooker 1984: 279–80). While the KHI does not forbid recourse to *fiqh* texts, in practice this has become uncommon. That the KHI 'provides all we need' is an Indonesia-wide judicial view.[3] The exceptions are minor so far as I am aware.[4]

From selection *in* and selection *out* we turn to selection *with a purpose*. All selections have a purpose. However, the KHI expresses its purposes consciously and in detail—a new development in contemporary Indonesian syariah.[5] The first and most obvious purpose of the KHI is to provide a working text for judges in the religious courts. It uses relatively simple language and is arranged in books, chapters and articles so as to provide a comprehensive guide. It is based on a presidential instruction and is therefore a formal positive-law text.

---

3   Field notes, Jakarta, Yogyakarta, Surabaya, Banda Aceh and Medan, 2003–05.
4   A note of caution: a full-country or even province-based survey has not been carried out, so there may be local trends of which I am not aware. It is important that this possibility be investigated as soon as possible.
5   But not unknown in the past; the Minangkabau and classical Malay texts also reveal a consciousness of directed selection (see Hooker 1986: 389–94).

If we look at the text a little more closely with selection for purpose in mind, we can see that an even more fundamental purpose of the KHI is to ensure that its provisions are compatible with existing laws, especially the Marriage Law of 1974. The KHI is in fact a special version of the Marriage Law and is dependent on it, as the frequent references to it in the KHI show. To see this, we need look no further than the formalities for marriage, specifically the certificate of marriage. Issued by the district or city office of the Department of Religion, the marriage certificate authorized by the KHI is in fact an exact copy of that authorized by the Marriage Law. The register of marriage—the formal state archive of marriage—is also an exact copy of the secular register. Compatibility with secular law is the essence of the KHI.

The same is true of other areas of law. For example, the laws in the KHI on *zakat* must be read alongside the Regional Autonomy Laws (No. 22/1999 and No. 25/1999) and the laws and regulations on taxation. In the case of *wakaf*, the Basic Agrarian Law of 1960 and its later amendments and regulations are referred to as the key texts in determining registration and land use. The new Islamic banking laws are subject to the national banking and finance laws. In all cases, the syariah laws stand or fall on their compatibility with secular laws.

At this juncture, one might well ask what has become of the *fiqh* texts. The answer is that they have been selectively reduced to a very minimal component of the KHI. The ostensible purpose of selecting *fiqh* for inclusion in the KHI was to eliminate differences between the *mazhab* and so achieve uniformity of practice. But in the process the *fiqh* was reduced to a set of banal reference points. If this was not the purpose all along, then no matter—the result was still the virtual selection out of *fiqh* so that it became just a point of reference in the text.

Like *zakat*, the *hajj*—another of the five pillars of Islam—has become a creature of positive law. It is no longer possible to discuss it without reference to the laws and forms required by the Department of Religion. It is no exaggeration to say that the structure of the *hajj* is now defined by the *hajj* passport and the department's instruction manuals; the state, through the department, lays down the rules for the *hajj*.

Syariah Defined as Values

Syariah values are, by their nature, ill defined and therefore open to political abuse. This has led to unrestrained, not to say reckless, selections of what syariah 'is' in public life. This trend has been supported by the widespread perception that the state has failed in its duty to preserve a decent standard of public behaviour in daily life. Those who hold this view point to the high incidence of crime, corruption, drug taking and sexual immorality, all of which are contrary to syariah values. The 'cure' proposed for this 'illness' is to enforce syariah values, that is, to insist on Islamic public orthopraxy. The belief is that adherence to proper dress, reciting the Qur'ān and so on will lead to a more moral society that has absorbed syariah values. Punishment for transgressions is an integral part of the process, with some advocating the more extreme *hadd* punishments.

The syariah-based regional regulations adopted by Aceh and West Sumatra raise two issues, one practical and one theoretical. The first concerns the fragmentation of public authority. Enforcement is split between a specialized religious police authority (or civil servants with police powers) and the national police force. While some attempt has been made to demarcate the respective spheres of authority, the delineation is not sufficiently clear. The result is likely to be overlapping jurisdictions. To complicate matters, the religious police are poorly trained and even more poorly disciplined. We also have to remember that the West Sumatra *perda* may or may not be valid; no court, including the Supreme Court, has made any ruling on this matter as yet. In short, the new regulations provide a sure recipe for confusion and chaotic administration.

At the theoretical level, the old question arises once again of whether values or morality based on religion can be enforced by law. Do laws change behaviour? And if so, how and according to what standard is change for the better to be assessed? More fundamentally, the new syariah regulations must pass the efficacy test (that is, they must extract a basic level of compliance from the population); they must state the criteria by which their validity can be tested (including the rules for transition from one principle to another); and they must be capable of effective implementation by public officials. The *perda* and *qanun* fail these tests. To explain what this means in practice, I take two examples from opposite ends of the spectrum of expression of syariah values.

The first is the criminal code drafted by the Council of Indonesian Mujahideen (MMI) in July 2002 (see Chapter 6). It begins by emphasizing the poor state of public morals in Indonesia:

> The secular system of laws and legislation that has been applied by the government has in fact caused there to be a multiplicative increase in criminality, disharmony of life, moral decadence and the decay of human values. A further consequence, which has gone hand in hand with the increasing weakness of the law enforcement authorities, is the occurrence of brutality and anarchy by the community in punishing those who commit criminal acts. This shows among other things that secular law is not capable of providing shelter and protection, peace, justice and a sense of security to the community, because the edifice of the secular legal system is based only on empirical rationality, which can never stretch to reach the psychic aspect of humanity that is so very wide and complex. (Hooker and Hooker 2006: 168)

The solution proposed by the MMI is purely to administer punishments, including the more extreme *hadd* punishments of stoning to death and amputation. The code has two other interesting features. First, it is proposed as a national code for the whole of Indonesia and it is in excess of the current *perda* and *qanun* provisions. Second, its list of offences and penalties is drawn directly from similar codes proposed for Malaysia, demonstrating that syariah values have an international dimension (Fealy and Hooker 2006: 179–84). In this instance 'values' means physical violence. So much for the 'psychic aspect of humanity'!

My second example of the expression of syariah values is the Friday sermon (*khutbah*) (see Chapter 4). The *khutbah* is at the same time simpler and more complex than the MMI code: simpler because no state law is involved, but more complex because it presents a range of syariah values—or, better, a range of values that can be called 'syariah'. Although the *khutbah* involves values rather than laws, it would be foolish indeed to ignore it just because it is not in the approved legal form. To do so would be to take the form of the law (*undang, peraturan* and so on) as stating the entirety of the law, when syariah does not recognize a distinction between 'law' and 'values'.

Khutbah comment on, feed off, respond to and translate state syariah for the congregation in the mosque at Friday prayer. They are also becoming increasingly widely available through printed texts, audiotapes and videos. The state is always present in this public articulation of syariah as either a benign or oppositional force. The essential part of the *khutbah*, the citation from the Qur'ān, must now be interpreted against the background of an intrusive bureaucratic state. All *khutbah* are therefore relational, and in this sense can be seen as articulations of the 'crisis of modernity'. This somewhat hackneyed phrase directs us to the inevitable tension between state authority and revealed authority. Moreover, most *khutbah* are delivered in simple language directed towards the ordinary person. They may mention punishment, but more usually they urge the values of tolerance and humility.

2 UNIVERSAL LEGAL VALUES

The syariah is one of the world's great legal traditions with a highly respected classical canon. In addition many countries have developed their own localized syariah canons. The focus of this book has been the localization of syariah in Indonesia. The forms, expressions and character of syariah are of course influenced by the times and, more importantly, by the disciplinary fashions of the day. Each generation of scholarship produces its own version, although Islam still exists and goes on as an eternal truth. The place of these various expressions of syariah in the state is therefore an important edge issue in all Muslim states— and even in European countries that have significant Muslim minorities.[6]

Part of the answer to the place of syariah in the state must be to recognize that the syariah is now as well known in Western discourse as it is in the classical Arabic discourse of the past 1400 years. The Indonesian material shows this in the various forms described in the preceding chapters. However, the balance—if there can be one—between the classical and Western disciplines is by no means established. Hence the characterization of Indonesian syariah as a

---

6 For a range of references covering the United States, Canada and the United Kingdom, see Glenn (2000: 198–9), especially footnotes 221 and 222.

'work in progress'. For Indonesia at least, we now have a sufficient accretion of knowledge and experience to enable us to see the main issue. It is the absence of an agreed agenda for discussion. The only possible mutual ground is the common acceptance that secularism is the issue—that is, whether God is or is not the Prime Mover and whether syariah should or should not have priority in public law. Compromise on 'priority' is the only possibility.

In fact very few Indonesians take a strong position on this matter at either extreme; the constraints imposed on syariah by local conditions make this impossible. The state syariah does have a presence in family law, trusts, *wakaf* and *zakat*. At the lower level of *qanun* and *perda* it has an increasing public profile (*not* general public acceptance). At the national level the syariah is not the national law, nor is Islam the state ideology. These are the conditions of time and place, although actual practice varies widely. Perceptions of syariah are in constant flux, and this has been the history of the past 200 years.

A New *Qiyas*?

Reasoning by analogy (*qiyas*) is one of the ways in which Muslim scholars have traditionally attempted to deal with change, using it to bridge the gap between a known and a new set of circumstances. Two techniques are integral to this process: establishing a sufficient cause for extending an existing principle to a new case (*'illa*), and determining the underlying rationale (*hikmah*) for doing so. The problem, of course, is to identify *'illa* and *hikmah* with sufficient rigour so that some infinite regress resulting in an unrestrained *ijtihad* does not occur.

The proposition I am suggesting is that the new circumstances in which syariah finds itself in Indonesia—of a nation-state that controls the substance and form of law—require a new *qiyas*. The question is whether a classical technique like *qiyas* can be applied to contemporary material such as that covered in the preceding chapters of this book. Scholars like Hazairin, Nasution and Madjid stressed the necessity of *ijtihad* for resolving the difficulty in which syariah finds itself, but unfortunately this term has become so generalized as to become practically meaningless. If a new *qiyas* could be arrived at, then it follows that the classical jurisprudence as well as the modern manifestations of syariah would become part of the same discussion on the validity and use of syariah in the contemporary age. Such a result would have the tremendous advantage of justifying contemporary forms of syariah while reversing the trend of jettisoning 1400 years of scholarship. It would create a common structure for the classical and contemporary forms of syariah, helping to avoid the present mutually self-destructive recourse to flatly opposing options and paving the way for the emergence of a uniquely Indonesian form of syariah. I do not minimize the difficulties of communicating this alternative to both positivist syariah lawyers and the wilder theorists. However, not to attempt to do so would merely prolong the 'crisis of modernity' that is occurring with respect to the role of syariah in the state.

We begin with *hikmah*. The reasoning justifying the extension of an existing rule to new circumstances is as much about the epistemology of rules as about the practicality of extension. Ideally these two things would be conjunctive, but in practice, especially in the context of the need to 'modernize' syariah, often they are not. In Indonesia practicality has become the dominant working principle, although this does not mean that epistemology is totally ignored. It is not.

The formal state syariah structures described in Chapter 1 show us syariah selected out and selected in. The focus in both cases is *fiqh*. Selection from *fiqh* would continue to occur under the new *qiyas*, but it would be conducted through the modern administrative methods that constitute the new circumstances. The danger, of course, is that the latter may become dominant, as in fact appears to be happening. The KHI and the IAIN/UIN curricula are the obvious examples, as, to a lesser degree, are the *hajj* and *zakat* regulations. We can conclude, therefore, that in the new *qiyas*, *hikmah* is not so much a program for linking *fiqh* and contemporary manifestations of syariah as a point at which the strictly classical can be demonstrated to be deficient. But at least a common dialogue would be established. One might even speculate a Qur'ānic reference for this dialogue; for example Q5:48:

> For each of you We have appointed a Divine law and way of conduct.

Perhaps, as a starting point, a rationale could be developed for a specific local syariah law, using the new *qiyas*?

Turning now to *'illa*, and continuing this line of possibilities for a common dialogue, we can find examples of attempts to locate a sufficient cause for the extension of an existing principle to a new case in the *fatwā* form (Chapter 1), the *khutbah* (Chapter 4) and the regional expressions of syariah values (Chapter 6). They formulate longstanding issues in new ways, with varying degrees of success. For example, contemporary *fatāwā* discuss insurance in terms of both contract theory and the Qur'ānic prohibition on gambling without establishing a clear case (*'illa*) for extrapolating from one to the other. On the other hand, the issues covered by the *qanun* and *perda* do refer to known individual duty, making both *hikmah* and *'illa* easily locatable elements in the values debate.

As these comments suggest, a new *qiyas* would have to acknowledge a method of selection that is conscious of state laws, because these laws themselves claim to be a version of *fiqh*. It is the *fact* of this claim, not its truth or falsity, that is important. Much therefore depends on the motive for selection. That motive must acknowledge different sources (revelation, history, state laws) and rank them for a specified purpose. The purpose is crucial, because it directly determines the underlying rationale. It is here that *hikmah* may easily be distorted, as has in fact happened in the *qanun* and *perda* (Chapter 6). The result has been to diminish the efficacy of the whole system.

However, the fact remains that *qiyas* has no *formal* place as a decisive mechanism for judging the validity of the new *fiqh*; its presence is a behind-the-scenes one. The comments of M. Yahya Harahap on the drafting of the KHI provide a good example (see pp 56–7). Perhaps we can say that there is a sort of *qiyas*, not in the narrow sense of reasoning strictly by analogy but in the sense of attempting a 'systematic reasoning in a broader sense'. This phrase is taken from Joseph Schacht's comment on Imam Shāfi'ī's approach to *qiyas* (Schacht 1950: 126), and it seems appropriate here. Indonesia has chosen to remove the differences existing between *fiqh* texts in the Sunni *mazhab*. This is a kind of 'systematic reasoning' that does not do violence to *fiqh* but may ultimately end up leaving only *fiqh* of the lowest common denominator. On the other hand, systematic reasoning (in the Shāfi'ī via Schacht sense) plays a positive role in the process of selection, localization and contextualization. This is Indonesian syariah's answer to the challenge of efficacy—of creating an effective legal system that successfully encompasses both positive law and syariah values and, thus, a new *qiyas*. It puts the focus on the two necessary conditions: sustainable connecting factor (*'illa*) and rationale (*hikmah*). In doing so it provides room for the substance of classical reasoning within the contemporary syariah context, thus permitting and explaining the emergence of coherent localization.

Localization can be identified in a number of areas, including the new *fiqh* (Chapter 1), the syariah curricula (Chapter 3) and the *hajj* regulations (Chapter 5). These can be construed as representing a conscious attempt at *'illa* and *hikmah*. This is not the case with the transmission of syariah values (through *khutbah*) and their enforcement (through regional regulations) (Chapters 4 and 6), where conditions are dominant and probably always will be. Having said this, the new *qiyas* should rule out extremes, such as some fantasy of a return to seventh-century Arabia, as well as reducing the opportunities for short-term political opportunism.

The Objectification of Syariah

The Orientalist Debate

At the end of Chapter 2, I anticipated a further discussion of objectified syariah. It was described as the Western claim to a monopoly of method in defining and classifying all laws for all times and all places. The sustainability of this claim is not my direct concern here. I am more interested in trying to understand how such a claim came to be made with particular reference to Indonesian syariah. The Indonesian experience of objectified syariah is that it undermines the certainty of faith-based laws. Indonesian scholars have long argued that whereas Islam defines the duty of the individual as being primarily to God and only secondarily to mankind, Christianity defines duty as being dual in nature ('Render unto Caesar the things which are Caesar's, and unto God the things that are God's'). This dualism necessarily diminishes spiritual obligation to the point of loss of faith, thus inevitably leading to the rise of secularism.

This is a persistent background theme in Indonesian syariah studies. In its latest version it is described as 'Christian hegemony' or 'secular–liberal domination [of Islam and Islamic studies]' (Husaini 2006). That argument goes on to claim that a key element in the triumph of secularism in the West was the development of critical textual studies of the Old and New Testaments. Proceeding as they did from a non-faith perspective, these studies were essentially destructive of faith. Their claims to bring a rigorous 'scientific' approach to, for example, philology or history were spurious, because science is not and never will be value-free. To seek to apply such methods to Islam is, therefore, to deny faith-based values and constitutes a direct attack on faith (see pp. 82–3 on hermeneutics). In short, so far as Islam is concerned, the Western claims to correctness of method are simply exercises in 'orientalism'. Since its redefinition in the 1970s by Edward Said, this term has become common currency in the debate on the relationship between Islam and the West—and much abused through polemics. The main tenet of the anti-orientalist position—that Western scholarship shows a clear bias against the Middle East—is located in three main streams of Western thinking on Islam.

The first had its roots in medieval polemic. The classic description of this was written by Daniel (1966).[7] From this and other works[8] written in the 1960s (which pre-date the more public debates sparked by Edward Said's *Orientalism*, discussed below), it is clear that the medieval and early modern material was initially concerned to deploy Christian theology against the threat to Europe ('Christendom') from the expanding Ottoman power. The theology of the time conflated the religion of Islam with Muslim military superiority and economic dominance. Its defence was to denigrate the foundations of Islam by denying that Muhammad was the Prophet of God, thus reducing Islam to (at best) a Christian heresy. Traces of this remain today in the more extreme Christian circles. By the late eighteenth century, when the balance of power had shifted to the European side, conversion had become the main focus of Christianity. This required a knowledge of those being converted and, hence, of Islam. At the same time the new Christian exegesis was gathering momentum. It was not long before Semitic studies, including study of Islam, became a fundamental part of Bible studies.

The development of an increasingly critical attitude towards Islam and, later on, other scriptural religions formed the second part of the orientalist legacy. There can be no doubt that much of the eighteenth and nineteenth-century commentary was hurtful to Muslim historians because of its inaccuracy and bias, not to mention questionable motives. However, paradoxically, much of it was not so much a direct attack on Islam as an attack on the foundations of European Christianity itself. For example, in eighteenth-century France—then the intellec-

---

7   For a more popular and rather polemical account, see Irwin (2006).

8   See, for example, Southern (1962).

tual exemplar for Europe—the great Voltaire, a ferocious opponent of organized religion (Catholicism), alternately praised and denigrated Islam and the Prophet. But his real target was the Catholic Church and especially the Papacy, and his views on Islam have to be read in this light. The device of using a foreign religion to attack European Christianity was common in the political circumstances of the time (Smith 1977). This fact has not always been fully grasped by today's Muslim scholars.

Third, the nineteenth and twentieth-century orientalist scholarship on Islam and other religions attracted the ire of many Muslim commentators because of its association with Western imperialism. This association, by definition, involved not just distortion of the truth (of Islam) but a wholesale and totally false reconstruction of the 'orient'. The best-known proponent of this argument was the late Edward Said, who wrote the hugely influential *Orientalism* (Said 1978). Although not himself a Muslim, Said was a fluent advocate of the case against orientalism. There has been a lot of polemic since this time—the latest initiated by Irwin (2006)—but from the point of view of those interested in syariah, both the original and subsequent critiques are rather disappointing. The main texts concentrate on literature and history, addressing syariah issues only tangentially. This does not mean that they are unimportant—far from it. For example, they demonstrate the necessity of distinguishing the motive for study of the Christian and Jewish testaments—biblical exegesis—from the methods adopted to explain them. Initially Islam was studied through the prism of study of the Old and New Testaments. That emphasis changed in the late nineteenth century, and by the early years of the twentieth century Islam was considered a subject worthy of study in its own right. Unfortunately, however, polemics was always an integral part of the debate, and remains so.

The crucial component of the orientalist legacy is the methods—not the individual opinions—of the various authors. It is easy to confuse the two, but as we have seen, the test of the validity of any method is its persistence and usefulness over time. Said's work ranges widely across the eighteenth to twentieth centuries, with special emphasis on the nineteenth century—the century of imperialism triumphant. He rightly points out the baleful influence of imperialism at that time. But that is not to say that the philological and historical methods invented then are equally harmful. At this distance Said should have been able to sort the gold from the dross, but he pays only ritual obeisance to Goldziher's acclaimed nineteenth-century work on Hadith (Goldziher 1967–71) and entirely neglects that of Schacht (1950), who not only built on Goldhziher's work but corrected the huge misunderstandings (still persisting) about what he actually said. Perhaps that is because of the nature of the discipline pursued by Schacht—law.

It is often observed that the syariah *is* Islam, but many commentators on Islam still fail to fully appreciate this fact. Perhaps the complexities of *fiqh* have something to do with it. Said's critiques may suffice for history, literature and the social sciences, but they do not do well in law. Not only does Said fail to mention Schacht but he also overlooks the late Noel Coulson, whose technical work on succession (Coulson 1971) is matched only by his broader study on *ijtihad* (Coulson 1969). These are monuments of scholarship. Moreover, when Said does touch on law, he often falls into error.

This brings us to Indonesian syariah and the role of the scholars and administrators—an additional and specifically Indonesian element of the orientalist debate. Said's example is Christiaan Snouck Hurgronje (1875–1936), a correspondent of Goldziher, a founder of *Encyclopaedia Islam* and a Dutch colonial civil servant in the Netherlands East Indies. His major works (Snouck Hurgronje 1899, 1931) are regarded as classics to this day, in modern Indonesia as well as in the wider world of Islamic scholarship. Nevertheless, the anti-orientalist position is that this scholarship is 'tainted' because of its close connection with imperialism—that it is a distortion of Islam. For law, however, the picture is not quite so simple, although non-legal scholars do not always realize this. The problem is the nature of law itself; there is no universal definition of 'law' and never will be. Instead, 'law' can mean private duty, public order, ethics and values, or, in the case of syariah, duty to God. Until the late nineteenth century each legal tradition was a self-contained world. But at the height of colonialism the concept of 'hybrid' laws deriving from two or more traditions emerged.[9] These persist today in large parts of the world, usually in the form of 'legal pluralism' (Hooker 1975, 1986). The scholars and administrators were perhaps the most important agent in this development.

The difficulties of the discipline of law and the development of hybrid systems of law pose serious problems for the orientalist debate. Said's (mis)interpretation of Snouck Hurgronje provides a good example. He cites the latter on the importance for Europe and European government in the Orient of understanding Islam and Islamic law (Said 1978: 255–6). He then says:

> Although Hurgronje allows that something so abstract as 'Islamic law' did occasionally yield to the pressure of history and society, he is more interested than not in retaining the abstraction for intellectual use because in its broad outline 'Islamic law' confirms the disparity between East and West. For Hurgronje the distinction between Orient and Occident was no more academic or popular cliché: quite the contrary. For him it signified the essential, historical power relationship between the two. Knowledge of the Orient either proves, enhances, or deepens the difference by which European suzerainty (the phrase has a venerable nineteenth-century pedigree) is extended effectively over Asia. To know the Orient as a whole, then, is to know it because it is entrusted to one's keeping, if one is a Westerner. (Said 1978: 256)

To make sense of this comment we need to know what the 'Islamic law' referred to actually was at the time. Said's subject, Snouck Hurgronje, was active in scholarship and government from the 1890s until his death in 1936. By that time Islamic law in no way 'confirm[ed] the disparity between East and West'.

---

9 For the idea of 'traditions', see Glenn (2000).

The reason is obvious: there was no such thing as classical Islamic law in existence in the Muslim world (except in Saudi Arabia). Either it had been formally abolished (as in the Czarist and later Russian Empires) or, more commonly, it had been rewritten into European civil code forms or (English) common law precedent. These new 'laws for Muslims' were hybrids (as they remain today), as Snouck Hurgronje was well aware.

This process had begun at the end of the eighteenth century in British India. It continued at an increasing rate throughout the next century and even well into the twentieth century (Hooker 1975). While it is true that these reformulations were imposed by force, either through the colonial enterprise or, from the 1960s onwards, through the pressure of globalization, the fact remains that they have largely been successful and now form the personal law in many states where religious adherence determines the law applicable to the individual. These hybrid personal laws have taken on a life of their own and are now thoroughly internalized in the many states in which religion has a public law significance. There can be no question of appropriation or representation in these instances.[10]

The (English) common law tradition allows for the incorporation of other laws subject to some restriction, namely that they are 'not repugnant to justice, equity and good conscience' (the standard imperial phrase). As a consequence, the syariah became part of the common law and evolved through precedent (some of it now 200 years old) in countries throughout Africa and Southeast Asia. It was and is a successful working system, but it cannot be described as 'oriental' or 'Eastern'. It is neither; instead it is a 'personal' law for a particular time and place.

The syariah has taken a quite different form in countries with a civil law tradition. The civil law system posits a single sovereignty; it is exclusive in its construction. The Dutch in Indonesia, faced with syariah and customary law (*adat*), selected syariah out but created a separate and special legal universe for *adat*. The result was an internal conflict of laws. Critics of orientalism generally seem to be unaware of the importance of these differences in legal theory—they do not seem to realize that there is no blanket 'colonial law'. It is for this reason that Said's comments on Islamic law are so seriously flawed. He is correct in saying that the colonial powers were motivated by a desire to maintain domination by providing legal representation, but that is not an adequate explanation for the adoption of hybrid systems of law. Such systems can only be understood in their own terms, including their grounding in a civil or common law construction. They can and frequently do ignore other discourses, whether these be philosophical, literary–historical or whatever. Said's failure to engage with

---

10 For example, the 'Anglo-Muslim' laws of India and Malaysia/Singapore are just as much 'Muslim' as they are 'Anglo'; see Fyzee (1964) and Hooker (1984, 1999) on the connections between common law and the Qur'ān, Hadith and *fiqh* in these countries.

Goldziher's Hadith studies is therefore a serious omission, if perhaps an extreme example of the limitations of orientalist critique.[11] Neither is it appropriate to use the language of appropriation for the KHI. Its sources are eclectic; it is motivated by the need for administrative clarity; and its authors include Muslim authorities from all streams of Islamic educational traditions in Indonesia. To be sure, if one tries hard enough one can find Western intellectual imperialism in the KHI, but this is by no means uncontested.

Another aspect of the colonial and post-colonial legal history of Indonesia that further complicates the idea of orientalism—more specifically the objectification of syariah—is the debate on 'laws for natives'. These were the *adat*-based laws established from the end of the nineteenth century. At issue was whether there should be a codified law suitable for the whole population, on the grounds that European law was superior to *adat* in utility and value. This proposal was rejected on the basis that *adat* represented the Indonesian people's 'inner sense of justice'. This is an example of a successful defence of an 'oriental law' against a state-suggested positive law. The defence was conducted in the first decades of the twentieth century by Dutch scholars and academics—people whose motives cannot be impugned given that this was the high point (perhaps the beginning of the decline) of Western imperialism.[12]

Moreover, the Dutch found, as a matter of *fact*, that the operable laws in Indonesian peasant society were governed by *adat*, not syariah, except to a very limited extent in some areas. There can be no doubting the scholarly authority of these findings.[13] But they also proved useful from the colonial government's point of view, because they lent credibility to the effective suppression of syariah—its selection out. The post-independence period brought its own paradoxes. *Adat* was ignored in practice in the new laws of the Republic of Indonesia, although it did retain a symbolic presence as an expression of 'Indonesian values'. Until the late 1980s syariah, too, retained essentially the same status as it had had in the Netherlands East Indies. Perhaps in reaction to this, a considerable literature developed on the significance of syariah and what place it should have in the Indonesian legal system (see Chapter 2 for a summary). The example of Hazairin is illustrative of the limitations of orientalism. Hazairin was a Dutch-trained specialist in *adat* and a judge in the pre-war judicial system. He was also a devout Muslim, although with no formal syariah training. This did not deter him from entering the syariah field and proposing a 'national *mazhab*' for Indonesian syariah. He brought his secular legal training to bear on this issue, even though this way of approaching law contradicted his stated aims for syariah. This is not

---

11 Despite quite heroic efforts by Dabashi (2006: lviii ff.) to defend the omission.

12 See Burns (1988) and Hooker (1978: 56 ff., 76 ff.).

13 They are contained in two massive collections: *Adatrechtbundel* (1911–55) and *Pandecten van het Adatrecht* (1914–36). Parts of the first were translated into Indonesian and were still used in the district courts in rural areas as recently as the 1970s.

to say that he was 'wrong', but it does seem unlikely that orientalism would be able to explain the thought processes of someone like Hazairin.

The comments above are not intended as an *ad hominem* attack on Said but rather as an illustration that orientalism is in fact an empty class for so-called 'oriental' law. As I hope the preceding chapters have shown, there is no such thing as oriental law in Indonesian syariah; it is certainly not 'oriental'.

Secular Methodologies

We are seemingly on safer ground if we approach the objectification of syariah without the intervening orientalist filter. But is it safe to rely on the secular methodologies that have sprung up over the past few decades? These have given us a plethora of labels to describe certain streams of Islam—modernist versus traditionalist, conservative versus liberal, or reformist versus real/nominal, for example. More recently, the debate on syariah has thrown up terms such as 'mainstream positions', 'spirit of the law', letter of the law', 'syariah as symbol of Islamist ideology', 'syariah as ethno-nationalism', 'syariah as local politics' and 'syariah in practice' (Hooker and Hooker 2006). This propensity for labels must be treated with considerable caution; they may be useful for a particular time and purpose but that is about all. As method, labelling leaves much to be desired. It is too subjective. On the other hand, the discipline of law does allow for a degree of objective description (while not entirely eliminating the subjective element). Thus, the facets of syariah covered in the first three chapters of this book—the new *fiqh*, syariah philosophies and the syariah curricula—deal with known classes in an international legal language that is comprehensible to both syariah and non-syariah legal theorists. The bureaucratically formulated syariah discussed in Chapter 5 and the regional law texts discussed in Chapter 6 can similarly be described as specific instances of accepted legal forms. These show us that the syariah debate is essentially an international one. Two features of this debate need to be mentioned here.

First, Indonesian syariah is not quarantined from developments in the wider world of syariah scholarship. The idea of transmission from the centre to the edge is a familiar one, although it should not be emphasized to the extent of obscuring local originality.[14] Modern methods of communication have greatly increased the pace and intensity of transmission. For example, the concept of the purposes of syariah (*maqasid al-syariah*) is as common in Indonesia as it is internationally, and is universally interpreted to include nationalism, human rights, feminism, democracy and good governance. The descriptions and methods of analysis developed in these forums have even penetrated syariah reason-

---

14 See Hooker (1983: 1–22). More generally, see Chapter 2 of this book on localization and contextualization. For a recent specific example of transmission, see Azra (2003).

ing itself, to the extent of displacing the traditional historiographies of Islam.[15] One might even suggest a 'pan-syariah' tendency. For example, the new *qiyas* suggested earlier seems to share more than a passing resemblance to Hasan al-Turābī's new *fiqh* (see al-Turābī 1980), although each was arrived at independently. What they have in common is a recognition that conventional methods have proved inadequate for contemporary legal life and new methods are required. What these are to be is the real challenge for modern syariah studies. It seems more than likely that local circumstances and needs will provide the answers. This is certainly the case for Indonesia.

Second, the international syariah debate has forced a recognition of syariah in comparative law. Until very recently this subject was almost wholly Euro-American-centric; the laws of 'the East' received very little space in the standard textbooks. Fortunately this has now changed and these laws, including syariah, are now acknowledged as core expressions of universal legal values (Glenn 2000: 157–204). This is a major advance. However, the fact of variation among national syariahs, as these exist in Muslim states, is still not sufficiently acknowledged. The syariahs of the Middle East are not the syariahs of Pakistan, India, Malaysia or Indonesia. There is a good case for distinguishing broadly between the syariah of the Middle East and the syariah practised in other regions. But even within a region it is possible to distinguish families of syariah: the Anglo-Muslim family in the case of Pakistan, India, Malaysia, Singapore and Brunei, for example. Moreover, it is perfectly possible today for someone with no Arabic or classical syariah training to read, understand and administer the rules in this family. All that is required is a training in (English) common law.

The new *fiqh* in Indonesia clearly belongs to the civil law family and so must be read in the light of the formal civil law structures. These include the theories of state and state sovereignty on which the Constitution rests, court structures, and the systems in place for drafting and implementing legislation and subordinate regulations (Chapter 1). The philosophies of syariah (Chapter 2) are responses to and explanations of these principles. In its 60 years of existence, Indonesian syariah has developed a new *fiqh* (Chapter 1) and bureaucratic process (Chapter 5) that can only be understood in the light of its civil law origins. But it has also developed uniquely Indonesian characteristics, as the material on the syariah curricula (Chapter 3), the *khutbah* (Chapter 4), the *hajj* (Chapter 5) and regional syariah values (Chapter 6) shows. These Indonesian definitions of syariah certainly challenge any notion of a grand theory of comparative law. For example, modernization and globalization theories make no sense at all in the Indonesian context because they do not do justice to local originalities. It is the latter that constitute the faces of syariah in Indonesia—the new *fiqh*, the syariah philosophies, the syariah curricula, the public transmission of syariah and the

---

15 For a striking example, see Robinson (2003: 90–1).

values expressed in regional syariah texts. Indonesian syariah is *sui generis* and must therefore be taken on its own terms.

The striking originality of Indonesian syariah needs to be appropriately valued in the international Islamic-law context. Too often the Southeast Asian materials are ignored or glossed over in contemporary studies, whose focus is the Middle East, Iran and India/Pakistan.

So far as comparative law is concerned, Indonesian syariah calls into question such fundamental issues as the definition of law and the philosophy of law. These issues cannot be evaded by any 'general theory' that hopes to encompass contemporary political–legal realities. Islam and syariah are very much on the international political–legal agenda, a fact further complicated by the movement of large numbers of Muslims into Western countries. These individuals and communities define themselves through their faith, unlike individuals in secular Western society. In short, the practitioners of comparative law have an urgent public duty to explain what law is, how it is to be defined, and what the philosophies of traditions such as syariah mean for policy makers and law makers.

The preceding chapters attempt to do this by drawing lessons from a detailed study of syariah in one nation-state, Indonesia. It is important to realize that the state is both the focus as well as the starting point of syariah; to a greater or lesser degree, the various facets of syariah described in this book all interact with the laws of the state. This means that comparative lawyers with no previous knowledge (of Arabic or the classical texts) can enter into one modern syariah world through the forms of law with which they are already familiar (courts, compilations, legislation, bureaucratic regulations, curricula). This approach makes universal comprehension, even dialogue, possible. When seemingly insuperable obstacles such as faith in God and the truth of the message revealed to the Prophet become givens in defining law, they no longer pose an insurmountable barrier to understanding of syariah. Once these givens are accepted for what they are, then it becomes possible to acknowledge both the timelessness of belief and its various manifestations throughout history. Indonesian syariah provides one concrete example of how this has been done. It is of truly international significance.

References

Abdallah, Ulil Abshar (2005), 'Saatnya Memikirkan Kembali Ibadah Haji', in Iskander (ed.), *Haji: Dari Aroma Bisnis Hingga Pergulatan Spiritual*, Bekasi: Al-Kautsar Prima, pp. 172–80.

Abdurrahman (1995), *Kompilasi Hukum Islam di Indonesia*, Jakarta: Akademika Presindo.

Ahmad, Mirzar Tahir (1998), *Revelation, Rationality, Knowledge and Truth*, Surrey: Islam International Publications.

Ahmad, Zainal Abidin (2001), *Membangun Negara Islam*, Yogyakarta: Pustaka Iqra.

Antonio, Muhammad Syafi'i (2001), *Bank Syariah*, Jakarta: Gema Insani.

Antoun, Richard T. (1989), *The Muslim Preacher in the Modern World*, Princeton NJ: Princeton University Press.

Archer, Simon and R.A.A. Karim (eds) (2007), *Islamic Finance*, Singapore: John Wiley and Sons.

Ash-Shiddieqy, Hasbi (1966), *Shari'at Islam Menjawab Tantangan Jaman*, Jakarta: Bulan Bintang.

Assyaukanie, Luthfi (2004), 'Perlunya Mengubah Sikap Politik Kaum Muslim', *Media Indonesia*, 19 March; partial translation in G. Fealy and V. Hooker (2006), *Voices of Islam in Southeast Asia*, Singapore: Institute of Southeast Asian Studies, pp. 240–1.

Azra, Azyumardi (1999a), 'The Transmission of *Al-Manar*'s Reformism to the Malay–Indonesian World', *Studia Islamika*, 6(3): 75–100.

Azra, Azyumardi (1999b), *Pendidikan Islam*, Jakarta: Logos.

Azra, Azyumardi (2003), *The Origins of Islamic Reformism in Southeast Asia*, Sydney: Allen & Unwin, and Honolulu: University of Hawai'i Press.

Azra, Azyumardi (2005), 'Islamic Legal Education in Indonesia', unpublished paper, Jakarta: PPIM-UIN, 4 January.

Bowen, John R. (1995a), 'The Forms Culture Takes: A State-of-the-Field Essay on the Anthropology of Southeast Asia', *Journal of Asian Studies*, 54(4): 1,047–78.

Bowen, John R. (1995b), 'Western Studies of Southeast Asian Islam: Problems of Theory and Practice', *Studia Islamika*, 2(4): 69–86.

Bowen, John R. (1999), 'Legal Reasoning and Public Discourse', in D.F. Eickelman and J.W. Anderson (eds), *New Media in the Muslim World: The Emerging Public Sphere*, Bloomington IN: Indiana University Press, pp. 80–105.

Bowen, John R. (2003), *Islam, Law and Equality in Indonesia*, Cambridge: Cambridge University Press.

Bratakusuma, D.S. and Dadang Solihin (2004), *Otonomi Penyelenggaraan Pemerintahan Daerah*, Jakarta: Gramedia.

Bucaille, Maurice (1979), *The Bible, the Quran and Science*, translated from French by A.D. Pannel, Indianapolis IN: North American Trust Publication.

Bulliet, Richard W. (2004), *The Case for Islamo-Christian Civilization*, New York NY: Columbia University Press.

Burhanudin, Jajat and Dina Afrianty (eds) (2006), *Mencetak Muslim Modern*, Jakarta: PT Raja Grafindo Persada.

Burns, Peter (1988), 'The Netherlands East Indies: Colonial Legal Policy and the Definitions of Law', in M.B. Hooker (ed.), *Laws of South-east Asia, Volume II: European Laws in South-east Asia*, Singapore: Butterworths, pp. 148–282.

Burton, John (1977), *The Collection of the Qur'an*, Cambridge: Cambridge University Press.

Butt, Simon (1999), 'Polygamy and Mixed Marriage in Indonesia', in T. Lindsey (ed.), *Indonesia: Law and Society*, Sydney: Federation Press, pp. 122–44.

Cammack, Mark (1997), 'Indonesia's 1989 Religious Judicature Act: Islamization of Indonesia or Indonesianization of Islam?', *Indonesia*, 63: 143–68.

Cammack, Mark (2002), 'Islamic Inheritance Law in Indonesia: The Influence of Hazairin's Theory of Bilateral Inheritance', *Australian Journal of Asian Law* 4:(3), 295–315.

Chalil, Moenawar (1970), *Definisi dan Sendi Agama*, Jakarta: Bulan Bintang.

Collingwood, R.G. (1946), *The Idea of History*, Oxford: Clarendon Press.

Coppel, Charles (2002), 'The Indonesian Chinese', in M.B. Hooker (ed.), *Law and the Chinese in Southeast Asia*, Singapore: Institute of Southeast Asian Studies, pp. 131–49.

Coulson, N.J. (1969), *Conflict and Tensions in Islamic Jurisprudence*, Chicago IL: University of Chicago Press.

Coulson, N.J. (1971), *Succession in the Muslim Family*, Cambridge: Cambridge University Press.

Crone, Patricia and Martin Hinds (1986), *God's Caliph: Religious Authority in the First Centuries of Islam*, Cambridge: Cambridge University Press.

Dabashi, Hamid (2006), 'Ignaz Goldziher and the Question Concerning Orientalism', new introduction to Ignaz Goldziher, *Muslim Studies*, edited by S.M. Stern, translated from German by C.R. Barber and S.M. Stern, NY and London: Aldine Transaction, pp. ix–xciii.

Danarto (1989), *A Javanese Pilgrim in Mecca*, translated from Indonesian by Harry Aveling, Working Paper on Southeast Asia No. 58, Clayton: Monash Centre of Southeast Asian Studies.

Daniel, N. (1966), *Islam, Europe and Empire*, Edinburgh: University of Edinburgh Press.

Departemen Agama (1982), *Pedoman Pelaksanaan P-4 Bagi Umat Islam*, Jakarta: Departemen RI.

Dhofier, Zamakhsyari (1994), *Tradisi Pesantren: Studi Tentang Pandangan Hidup Kyai*, Jakarta: LP3ES.

Dinas Syariat Islam Aceh (2005), *Himpunan Undang-Undang, Peraturan Daerah/Qanun, Instruksi Gubenur, Edaran Gubenur*, fifth edition, Bandar Aceh: Dinas Syariat.

Douwes, Dick and N. Kaptein (eds) (1997), *Indonesia dan Haji*, Jakarta: INIS.

Ellen, Roy F. (1983), 'Social Theory, Ethnography and the Understanding of Practical Islam in South-east Asia', in M.B. Hooker (ed.), *Islam in South-east Asia*, Leiden: Brill, pp. 50–91.

Esposito, John L. (1991), *Islam: The Straight Path*, New York NY: Oxford University Press.

Fasseur, C. (1993), *De Indologen: Ambtenaren Voor de Oost 1825–1950*, Amsterdam: Bert Bakker.

Fealy, Greg (2004), 'Islamic Radicalism in Indonesia', *Southeast Asian Affairs 2004*, Singapore: Institute of Southeast Asian Studies, pp. 104–24.

Fealy, Greg and Virginia Hooker (eds) (2006), *Voices of Islam in Southeast Asia*, Singapore: Institute of Southeast Asian Studies.

Feener, R. Michael (2001), 'Indonesian Movements for the Creation of a "National Madhhab"', *Islamic Law and Society*, 9(1): 83–115.

FK3 (Forum Kajian Kitab Kuning) (2003), *Wajah Baru Relasi Suami–Istri: Telaah Kitab 'Uqud al-Lujjayn*, Lembaga Kajian Islam dan Sosial in cooperation with FK3 and the Ford Foundation, Yogyakarta (first published 2001).

Foulcher, Keith (2000), 'Sumpah Pemuda: The Making and Meaning of a Symbol of Indonesian Nationhood', *Asian Studies Review*, 23(3): 377–410.

Fox, James J. (2002), 'Toward a Social Anthropology of Islam in Indonesia', in F. Jabali and Jamhari (eds), *Islam in Indonesia: Islamic Studies and Social Transformation*, Montreal and Jakarta: Indonesia–Canada Islamic Higher Education Project, pp. 73–84.

Fyzee, A.A. Asaf (1964), *Outlines of Muhammadan Law*, third edition, London: Oxford University Press.

Gade, Anna M. (2004), *Perfection Makes Practice*, Honolulu: University of Hawai'i Press.

Geertz, Clifford (1960), 'The Javanese Kijaji: The Changing Role of a Cultural Broker', *Comparative Studies in Society and History*, 2: 228–49.

Ghazali, Aidit bin (1991), 'Zakat Administration in Malaysia', in Mohamed Ariff (ed.), *The Islamic Voluntary Sector in Southeast Asia*, Singapore: Institute of Southeast Asian Studies, pp. 85–117.

Glenn, H. Patrick (2000), *Legal Traditions of the World*, New York NY: Oxford University Press.

Goldziher, Ignaz (1967–71), *Muslim Studies*, 2 volumes, translated from German by C.R. Barber and S.M. Stern, Albany NY: State University of New York Press.

Haleem, M.A.S. Abdel (2004), *The Qur'an*, Oxford: Oxford University Press.

Halim, Abdul (ed.) (2001), *Teologi Islam Rasional*, Jakarta: Ciputat Pers.

Hallaq, Wael B. (1984), 'Considerations on the Function and Character of Sunni Legal Theory', *Journal of the American Oriental Society*, 104(4): 679–89.

Hallaq, Wael B. (1997), *A History of Islamic Legal Theories*, Cambridge: Cambridge University Press.

Hallaq, Wael B. (2005), *The Origins and Evolution of Islamic Law*, Cambridge: Cambridge University Press.

Hamim, Toha (1997), 'Moenawar Chalil: The Career and Thought of an Indonesian Muslim Reformist', *Studia Islamika*, 4(2): 1–54.

Harahap, M. Yahya (1992), 'Informasi Materi Kompilasi Hukum Islam: Mempositifkan Abstraksi Hukum Islam', *Mimbar Hukum*, 3(5): 21–63.

Hasjmy, Ali (1985), *Semangat Merdeka*, Jakarta: Bulan Bintang.

Hazairin (1951), *Ilmu Pengetahuan Islam dan Masyarakat*, Jakarta: Tintamas.

Hazairin (1958), *Hukum Kewarisan Bilateral Menurut Qur'an dan Hadith*, Jakarta: Tintamas.

Hazairin (1960), *Hendak Kemana Hukum Islam?* Jakarta: Tintamas.

Hazairin (1968), *Hukum Kekeluargaan Nasional*, Jakarta: Tintamas.

Headley, Stephen C. (1989), *La Prière à Java: Trois Styles sur le Corps, avec des Offrandes et dans la Mosquée*, Paris: CNRS.

Headley, Stephen C. (2000), 'The Mirror in the Mosque', in D. Parkin and S. Headley (eds), *Islamic Prayer across the Indian Ocean*, London: Curzon, pp. 213–38.

Hisyam, Muhammad (2000), 'Islam and Dutch Colonial Administration', *Studia Islamika*, 7(1): 91–118.

Hoadley, M.C. and M.B. Hooker (1986), 'The Law Texts of Java and Bali', in M.B. Hooker (ed.), *Laws of South-east Asia, Volume I: The Pre-modern Texts*, Singapore: Butterworths, pp. 241–346.

Hoodbhoy, Pervez (1992), *Islam and Science: Religious Orthodoxy and the Battle for Rationality*, London: Zed Books.

Hooker, M.B. (1972), *Adat Laws in Modern Malaya*, Kuala Lumpur: Oxford University Press.

Hooker, M.B. (1975), *Legal Pluralism*, Oxford: Clarendon Press.

Hooker, M.B. (1978), *A Concise Legal History of South-east Asia*, Oxford: Clarendon Press.

Hooker, M.B. (1983) (ed.), *Islam in South-east Asia*, Leiden: Brill.

Hooker, M.B. (1984), *Islamic Law in South-east Asia*, Kuala Lumpur: Oxford University Press.

Hooker, M.B. (1986), 'The Law Texts of Muslim South-east Asia', in M.B. Hooker (ed.), *Laws of South-east Asia, Volume I: The Pre-modern Texts*, Singapore: Butterworths, pp. 347–434.

Hooker, M.B. (1999), 'Qadi Jurisdiction in Contemporary Malaysia and Singapore', in M.A. Wu (ed.), *Public Law in Contemporary Malaysia*, Kuala Lumpur: Longman, pp. 57–75.

Hooker, M.B. (2003a), *Indonesian Islam: Social Change through Contemporary Fatāwā*, Sydney: Allen & Unwin; Honolulu: University of Hawai'i Press.

Hooker, M.B. (2003b), 'Submission to Allah?', in V.G. Hooker and N. Othman (eds), *Malaysia: Islam, Society and Politics*, Singapore: Institute of Southeast Asian Studies, pp. 80–98.

Hooker, M.B. and Virginia Hooker (2006), 'Sharia', in G. Fealy and V. Hooker (eds), *Voices of Islam in Southeast Asia*, Singapore: Institute of Southeast Asian Studies, pp. 137–206.

Hooker, M.B. and Tim Lindsey (2002), 'Public Faces of Syariah in Contemporary Indonesia', *Australian Journal of Asian Law*, 4(3): 259–94.

Huntington, Samuel P. (1996), *The Clash of Civilizations and the Remaking of World Order*, New York: Simon & Schuster.

Husaini, Adian (2005), *Wajah Peradaban Barat*, Jakarta: Gema Insani.

Husaini, Adian (2006), *Hegemoni Kristen Barat dalam Studi Islam di Perguruan Tinggi*, Jakarta: Gema Insani.

ICG (International Crisis Group) (2006), 'Islamic Law and Criminal Justice in Aceh', Asia Report No. 117, Jakarta/Brussels, 31 July.

Ihza, Yusril (1995), 'Combining Activism and Intellectualism: The Biography of Mohammad Natsir', *Studia Islamika*, 2(1): 111–47.

Irwin, Robert (2006), *For Lust of Knowing: The Orientalists and their Enemies*, London: Allen Lane.

Iskandar, Dudi (2005), *Haji: Dari Aroma Bisnis Hingga Pergulatan Spiritual*, Bekasi: Al Kautsar Prima.

Ismail Faisal (2004), *Islam vis-à-vis Pancasila*, second edition, Jakarta: Mitra Cendekia.

Jabali, Fu'ad and Jamhari (2002), *IAIN: Modernisasi Islam di Indonesia*, Jakarta: Logos.

Jabali, Fu'ad and Jamhari (eds) (2003), *The Modernization of Islam in Indonesia*, Montreal and Jakarta: Indonesia–Canada Islamic Higher Education Project.

Jellinek, G. (1900), *Das Recht des Modernen Staates*, Berlin: O. Haring.

Johns, A.H. and Abdullah Saeed (2004), 'Nurcholish Madjid and the Interpretation of the Qur'an', in Suha-Taji Farouki (ed.), *Modern Muslim Intellectuals and the Qur'an*, Oxford: Oxford University Press, pp. 67–96.

Jones, Gavin W. (1994), *Marriage and Divorce in Islamic South-east Asia*, Kuala Lumpur: Oxford University Press.

Junedding, B. and Dias Pradadimara (2000), *Latar Belakang Sosial dan Politik Gerakan Islam Kasus KPPSI Sulawesi Selatan*, Jakarta: Media Dakwah.

Juynboll, Th.W. (1930), *Handleiding tot de Kennis van de Mohammedaansche Wet*, Leiden: Brill.

Kaptein, Nico (1995), 'Meccan Fatwās from the End of the Nineteenth Century on Indonesian Affairs', *Studia Islamika*, 2(4): 141–60.

Katz, J.S. and R.S. Katz (1975), 'The New Indonesian Marriage Law', *American Journal of Comparative Law*, 23: 653–81.

Keeler, Ward (1998), 'Style and Authority in Javanese Muslim Sermons', *Australian Journal of Anthropology*, 9(2): 163–78.

Kelsen, Hans (1989), *Pure Theory of Law*, translated from German by M. Knight, Gloucester MA: Peter Smith.

Kennedy, Charles (1988), 'Islamization in Pakistan', *Asian Survey*, 28(3): 307–16.

Kerr, Malcolm (1966), *Islamic Reform*, Berkeley CA: University of California Press.

Koesnoe, Moh. (1969), 'Menetapkan Hukum dari Adat', *Hukum Nasional*, 3: 3–11.

Koesnoe, Moh. (1970), 'Hukum Adat dan Pembangunan Hukum Nasional', *Hukum dan Keadilan*, 3: 32–43.

Kollewijn, R.D. (1929), 'International Private Law', in B. Schrieke (ed.), *The Effect of Western Influence on Native Civilizations in the Malay Archipelago*, Batavia: Royal Batavia Society of Arts and Sciences.

Komisi Fatwa Hukum Majelis Daerah Istimewa Aceh (2000), *Kumpulan Fatwa: Fatwa Majelis Ulama Daerah Istimewa Aceh*, Banda Aceh.

Lambton, Anne K.S. (1962), 'Justice in the Medieval Persian Theory of Kingship', *Studia Islamica*, 17: 91–120.

Lapidus, Ira M. (1988), *A History of Islamic Societies*, Cambridge: Cambridge University Press.

Lev, Daniel S. (1965), 'The Lady and the Banyan Tree', *American Journal of Comparative Law*, 14: 282–307.

Lev, Daniel S. (1972a), 'Judicial Institutions and Legal Culture in Indonesia', in C. Holt, B.R.O'G. Anderson and J. Siegel (eds), *Culture and Politics in Indonesia*, Ithaca NY: Cornell University Press, pp. 246–318.

Lev, Daniel S. (1972b), *Islamic Courts in Indonesia*, Berkeley CA, University of California Press.

Lewis, Bernard (2002), *What Went Wrong?* London: Weidenfeld and Nicolson.

Lindsey, Tim (ed.) (1999), *Indonesia: Law and Society*, Sydney: Federation Press.

Lindsey, Tim (2000), 'Black Letter, Black Market and Bad Faith: Corruption and the Failure of Law Reform', in C. Manning and P. van Diermen (eds), *Indonesia in Transition*, Singapore: Institute of Southeast Asian Studies, pp. 278–92.

Llewellyn, Karl N. (1940), 'The Normative, the Legal and the Law Jobs', *Yale Law Journal*, 49: 1,355–400.

Lubis, Abdur-Razzaq (1996), *Tidak Islamnya Bank Islam*, Penang: PAID Network.

Lubis, Nur Fadhil (1997), 'Islamic Legal Literature', *Studia Islamika*, 4(4): 33–92.

Lucas, Anton and Carol Warren (2003), 'The State, the People and Their Mediators', *Indonesia*, 76: 87–126.

Madjid, Nurcholis (1979), 'The Issue of Modernization among Muslims in Indonesia', in Gloria Davis (ed.), *What Is Modern Indonesian Culture?* Athens OH: University of Ohio Press, pp. 143–55.

Madjid, Nurcholis (1987), *Islam, Kemodernan dan Keindonesiaan*, Bandung: Mizan.

Madjid, Nurcholis (1994), 'Islamic Roots of Modern Pluralism: Indonesian Experience', *Studia Islamika*, 1(1): 55–78.

Madjid, Nurcholish (1997), *Tradisi Islam: Peran dan Fungsinya dalam Pembangunan di Indonesia*, Jakarta: Paramadina.

Madjid, Nurcholis (2004), 'Menyambung Matarantai Pemikiran yang Hilang', in Agus Edi Santoso (ed.), *Tidak Ada Negara Islam: Surat-Surat Politik Nurcholis Madjid–Mohamed Roem*, Jakarta: Penerbit Djambatan, pp. 12–41.

Mahdi, Muhsin (1990), 'Orientalism and the Study of Islamic Philosophy', *Journal of Islamic Studies*, 1: 73–98.

Maine, Sir Henry (1861), *Ancient Law*, London: John Murray.

Makdisi, George (1981), *The Rise of Colleges,* Edinburgh: Edinburgh University Press.

Makdisi, John (1985), 'Legal Logic and Equity in Islamic Law', *American Journal of Comparative Law*, 33: 63–92.

Man, Zakariya (1988), 'Islamic Banking: The Malaysian Experience', in Mohamed Ariff (ed.), *Islamic Banking in Southeast Asia*, Singapore: Institute of Southeast Asian Studies, pp. 67–102.

Mansurnoor, Iik Arifin (1990), *Islam in an Indonesian World*, Yogyakarta: Gadjah Mada University Press.

Marcoes, Lies (1992), 'The Female Preacher as a Mediator in Religion', in S. van Bemmelen et al. (eds), *Women and Mediation in Indonesia*, Leiden: KITLV Press, pp. 203–28.

Marfuddin, Ade (2005), 'Penyelenggaraan Haji Terus-Menurus Menyisakan Masalah', in Iskander (ed.), *Haji: Dari Aroma Bisnis Hingga Pergulatan Spiritual*, Bekasi: Al-Kautsar Prima, pp. 24–9.

Masud, Khalid (2006), *Hudood Ordinance 1979 (Pakistan): An Interim Brief Report*, Council of Islamic Ideology, Government of Pakistan, available at <http://www.cii.gov.pk/hudood/HOO_1979.pdf>.

Matheson, V. and A.C. Milner (1984), *Perceptions of the Haj: Five Malay Texts*, Singapore: Institute of Southeast Asian Studies.

Mattei, Ugo (1997), 'Three Patterns of Law', *American Journal of Comparative Law*, 45: 5–44.

Mawardi, Ahmad Imam (2003), 'The Political Backdrop of the Enactment of the Compilation of Islamic Laws in Indonesia', in A. Salim and A. Azra (eds), *Shari'ah and Politics in Modern Indonesia*, Singapore: Institute of Southeast Asian Studies, pp. 125–47.

Metcalf, Barbara D. (1990), 'The Pilgrimage Remembered: South Asian Accounts of the Hajj', in D.F. Eickelman and J. Piscatori (eds), *Muslim Travellers*, Berkeley CA: University of California Press, pp. 85–110.

Moore, Sally Falk (1978), *Law as Process: An Anthropological Approach*, London: Routledge and Kegan Paul.

Mudzhar, M. Atho (2003), *Islam and Islamic Law in Indonesia*, Jakarta: Department of Religion.

Muhaimin, A.G. (1999), 'The Morphology of Adat', *Studia Islamika*, 6(3): 103–30.

Mulia, Siti Musdah (2004), *Islam Menggugat Poligami*, Jakarta: PT Gramedia.

Muslehuddin, Muhammad (1977), *Philosophy of Islamic Law and the Orientalists*, Lahore: Islamic Publishing Ltd.

Mustoffa, M. Farid (2005), 'Penyelenggaraan Haji Tidak Memiliki Blue Print', in Iskander (ed.), *Haji: Dari Aroma Bisnis Hingga Pergulatan Spiritual*, Bekasi: Al-Kautsar Prima, pp. 17–23.

Muzani, Saiful (1994), 'Mu'tazilah Theology and the Modernization of the Indonesian Muslim Community: Intellectual Portrait of Harun Nasution', *Studia Islamika*, 1(1): 91–132.

Nasution, Harun (1977), *Islam Ditinjau dari Berbagai Aspeknya*, 2 volumes, Jakarta: Bulan Bintang.

Nasution, Harun (1986a), *Teologi Islam: Aliran-Aliran Sejarah Analisa Perbandingan*, Jakarta: University of Indonesia Press.

Nasution, Harun (1986b), *Akal dan Wahyu dalam Islam*, Jakarta: University of Indonesia Press.

Nasution, Harun (1987), *Muhammad Abduh dan Teologi Rasional Mu'tazilah*. Jakarta: University of Indonesia Press.

Nasution, Harun (1995), *Islam Rasional: Gagasan dan Pemikiran*, Bandung: Mizan.

Nidjam, Achmad and Alatief Hanan (2001), *Manajemen Haji*, Jakarta: Zikrul Hakim.

Noer, Deliar (1973), *The Modernist Muslim Movement in Indonesia, 1900–1942*, Kuala Lumpur: Oxford University Press.

Noer, Deliar (1997), *Pemikiran Politik di Negeri Barat*, Jakarta: Mizan.

Oakeshott, Michael (1962), *Rationalism in Politics and Other Essays*, London: Methuen.

Pompe, S. (1988), 'Mixed Marriages in Indonesia: Some Comments on the Law and the Literature', *Bijdragen tot de Taal-, Land- en Volkenkunde*, 144: 259–75.

Pompe, S. (1991), 'A Short Note on Some Recent Developments with Regard to Mixed Marriages in Indonesia', *Bijdragen tot de Taal-, Land- en Volkenkunde*, 147: 261–72.

Qardhawi, Yusuf (1995), *Fatwa-Fatwa Kontemporer I*, Jakarta: Gema Insani Press.

Quine, Willard van Orman (1960), *Word and Object*, Cambridge MA: Technology Press of Massachusetts Institute of Technology and J. Wiley.

Radia Abdul Kadir (1991), 'The Malaysian Pilgrims Management and Fund Board and Resource Mobilization', in M. Ariff (ed.), *The Islamic Voluntary Sector in Southeast Asia*, Singapore: Institute of Southeast Asian Studies, pp. 138–67.

Rahardjo, M. Dawam (ed.) (1974), *Pesantren dan Pembaharuan*, Jakarta: LP3ES.

Rahardjo, M. Dawam (1988), 'The Question of Islamic Banking in Indonesia', in M. Ariff (ed.), *Islamic Banking in Southeast Asia*, Singapore: Institute of Southeast Asian Studies, pp. 137–63.

Rahardjo, M. Dawam (2005), 'Pemberdayaan Ekonomi Umat Melalui Dana Haji', in Iskandar (ed.), *Haji: Dari Aroma Bisnis Hingga Pergulatan Spiritual*, Bekasi: Al Kautsar Prima, pp. 94–104.

Rahman, Fazlur (1984), *Islamic Methodology in History*, Islamabad: Islamic Research Institute.

Ramsay, Jacob (2006), 'Cambodia and Vietnam', in G. Fealy and V. Hooker (eds), *Voices of Islam in Southeast Asia*, Singapore: Institute of Southeast Asian Studies, pp. 31–8.

Rasjidi, H.M. (1977), *Koreksi terhadap Dr Harun Nasution tentang Islam Ditinjau dari Berbagai Aspeknya*, Jakarta: Bulan Bintang.

Rawls, John (1996), *Political Liberalism*, second edition, New York NY: Columbia University Press.

Raz, Joseph (1970), *The Concept of a Legal System*, Oxford: Clarendon Press.

Raz, Joseph (1994), *Ethics in the Public Domain*, Oxford: Clarendon Press.

Richards, Matt (2003), 'Islamic Contracts of Finance in Malaysia', *Studia Islamika*, 10(1): 161–200.

Rifa'i, A. Bachrun and M. Fakhruroji (2005), *Manajemen Masjid*, Bandung: Benang Merah.

Robinson, Chase F. (2003), *Islamic Historiography*, Cambridge: Cambridge University Press.

Rosenthal, E.I.J. (1965), *Islam in the Modern National State*, Cambridge: Cambridge University Press.

Rosidi (ed.) (2003), *Kumpulan Khotbah*, Jakarta: PPSDM–Universitas Islam Negeri.

Ruthven, Malise (2006), *Islam in the World*, third edition, London: Granta Books.

Saeed, Abdullah (1996), *Islamic Banking and Interest*, Leiden: Brill.

Sa'id, Busthami Muhammad (1984), *Mafhum Tajdid al-Din*, Kuwait: Dar al-Da'wah.

Said, Edward (1978), *Orientalism*, New York NY: Pantheon Books.

Salim, A. (2003), 'Zakat Administration in Politics of Indonesian New Order', in A. Salim and A. Azra (eds), *Sharia and Politics in Modern Indonesia*, Singapore: Institute of Southeast Asian Studies, pp. 181–92.

Salim, A. and A. Azra (eds) (2003), *Sharia and Politics in Modern Indonesia*, Singapore: Institute of Southeast Asian Studies.

Santoso, Agus Edi (ed.) (2004), *Tidak Ada Negara Islam: Surat-surat Politik Nurcholish Madjid–Mohamed Roem*, Jakarta: Penerbit Djambatan.

Sarief, H. Sukri (2005), *Cara Mudah Melaksanakan Ibadah Haji*, Jakarta: Laba 2.

Schacht, Joseph (1950), *The Origins of Muhammadan Jurisprudence*, Oxford: Clarendon Press.

Schwarz, Adam (2004), *A Nation in Waiting*, Singapore: Talisman.

Shahrabi, H. (1970 *Arab Intellectuals and the West, 1875–1914*, Baltimore MD: Johns Hopkins.

Sila, Muhammad Adlin (n.d.), 'Otonomi Khusus Syariat Islam: Perjuangan Politis–Historis Yang Belum', Jakarta: PPIM-UIN.

Sisters in Islam (1995), 'Appendix 1: Kelantan Syariah Criminal Code (II) Bill 1993', in *Hudud in Malaysia: The Issues at Stake*, Kuala Lumpur: SIS Forum (Malaysia) Berhad, pp. 105–42.

Sjadzali, H. Munawir (1991), *Islam and Governmental System*, Jakarta: INIS.

Skovgaard-Petersen, Jakob (1997), *Defining Islam for the Egyptian State*, Leiden: Brill.

Smith, Byron P. (1977), *Islam in English Literature*, second edition, Delmar NY: Caravan Books.

Snouck Hurgronje, C. (1899), 'Muhammedanisches Recht Nach Schafiitischer Lehre von Eduard Sachau', *Zeitschrift der Deutschen Morgenländischen Gesellschaft*, 53: 125–67.

Snouck Hurgronje, C. (1931), *Mekka in the Latter Part of the Nineteenth Century*, translated from Dutch, Leiden: Brill (first published in 1888).

Solus, H. (1927), *Traité de la Condition des Indigènes en Droit Privé*, Paris: Sirey.

Southern, Richard (1962), *Western Views of Islam in the Middle Ages*, Cambridge MA: Harvard University Press.

Stevens, Alan M. and A. Ed. Schmidgall-Tellings (2004), *A Comprehensive Indonesian–English Dictionary*, Athens OH: Ohio University Press.

Subekti, R. and J. Tamara (1965), *Kumpulan Putusan Mahkamah Agung Mengenai Hukum Adat*, Jakarta: Gunung Agung.

Subhan, Arief (1999), 'Prof. Dr. Harun Nasution Penyemai Teologi Islam Rasional', in Azra Azyumardi and S. Umam (eds), *Tokoh Pemimpin Agama: Biografi Sosial-Intelektual*, Jakarta: PPIM and Departemen Agama, pp. 41–58.

Suharyadi, I.S. (2001), *Risalah Kongress Mujahidin dan Penegakan Syariah Islam*, Yogyakarta: Wihdah Press.

Syihab, Habib Rizieq (2000), *Dialog Piagam Jakarta: Kumpulan Jawaban Seputar Keraguan terhadap Penegakan Syari'at Islam di Indonesia*, Jakarta: Pustaka Ibnu Sidah.

Taufik, Abdullah (1991), 'Zakat Collection and Distribution in Indonesia', in Mohamed Ariff (ed.), *The Islamic Voluntary Sector in Southeast Asia*, Singapore: Institute of Southeast Asian Studies, pp. 50–84.

Taylor, E.N. (1929), 'The Customary Law of Rembau', *Journal of the Royal Asiatic Society: Malayan Branch*, 7(1): 1–55.

Taylor, E.N. (1937), 'Malay Family Law', *Journal of the Royal Asiatic Society: Malayan Branch*, 15(1): 1–78.

Ter Haar, B. (1948), *Adat Law in Indonesia*, New York NY: Institute of Pacific Relations.

Thalib, Sajuti (1976), *Pembaharuan Hukum Islam di Indonesia*, Jakarta: University of Indonesia Press.

Thanthawi, Sy. (1998), *Fatwa-Fatwa Populer*, Jakarta: Intermedia.

Torpey, John (2000), *The Invention of the Passport*, Cambridge: Cambridge University Press.

Turābī, Hasan al- (1980), *Tajdid 'Usūl al-Fiqh al Islāmī*, Khartoum: Dar al-Fikr.

Ubaidillah, A. et al. (2000), *Pendidikan Kewargaan Demokrasi, HAM dan Masyarakat Madani*, Jakarta: Puslit IAIN.

van Bruinessen, M. (1990), 'Kitab Kuning', *Bijdragen tot de Taal-, Land- en Volkenkunde*, 146: 226–69.

van Bruinessen, M. (1995), 'Muslims of the Dutch East Indies and the Caliphate Question, *Studia Islamika*, 2(3): 115–40.

von Benda-Beckman, Keebet (1984), *The Broken Stairways to Consensus*, Dordrecht: Foris.

Vredenbregt, Jacob (1962), 'The Haddj', *Bijdragen tot de Taal-, Land- en Volkenkunde*, 118(1): 91–154.

Waddell, Sarah (2005), 'Shifting Visions of the Social and Legal Order in Indonesia: Implications for Legislative Style and Form', *Australian Journal of Asian Law*, 7(1): 43–59.

Wahid, Abdurrahman (1983), 'Islam: Punyakah Konsep Kenegaraan?' *Tempo*, 26 March, p. 20.

Wahid, Abdurrahman (1996), 'Foreword', in Greg Barton and Greg Fealy (eds), *Nahdlatul Ulama: Traditional Islam and Modernity in Indonesia*, Melbourne: Monash Asia Institute, pp. xiii–xvii.

Watt, W. Montgomery (1988), *Islamic Fundamentalism and Modernity*, London: Routledge.

Wilson, R.K. (1907), 'Modern Ottoman Law', *Journal of Comparative Legislation and International Law*, 8(1st series): 41–50.

Wolters, O.W. (1982), *History, Culture and Region in Southeast Asian Perspectives*, Singapore: Institute of Southeast Asian Studies.

Yousuf Ali, Abdallah (1934), *The Glorious Kur'an*, Lahore: Call of Islam Society.

Yusanto, Muhammad Ismail (2003), 'Selamatkan Indonesia dengan Syariah', in Burhanuddin (ed.), *Syariat Islam: Perdangan Muslim Liberal*, Jakarta: Jaringan Islam Liberal/Asia Foundation, pp. 139–72.

Yusanto, Muhammad Ismail (2004), 'Towards a Resumption of an Islamic Way of Life through the Re-establishment of the Caliphate and the Application of Shariah', paper presented to a conference on Islamic Perspectives on State, Governance and Society, Canberra, 30–31 August; partial translation in G. Fealy and V. Hooker (2006), *Voices of Islam in Southeast Asia*, Singapore: Institute of Southeast Asian Studies, pp. 236–9.

Zahro, Ahmad (2004), *Tradisi Intelektual NU: Lajnah Bahtsul Masa'il*, Yogyakarta: LKiS.

Zein, H. Satria Effendi (1991), 'Maqashid al-Syari'at dan Perubahan Sosial', *Dialog*, 33 29–40.

Zein, H. Satria Effendi (2004), *Problematika Hukum Keluarga Islam Kontemporer*, Jakarta: UIN Jakarta and Balitbang DEPAG RI.

INDEX

Page numbers in bold type (e.g. **175–8**) indicate detailed discussion of the topic.
Alternative spellings and translations are indicated in brackets, e.g. family (*keluarga*).

A

abangan ('nominal' Muslims), 2, 4, 78, 302
'Abd al-Qadir' 'Awdah, 115
Abdallah, Ulil Anshar, 221
Abduh, Muhammad, 45, 71, 73, 124
Abdurrahman, 21
abortion, 95
Abraham, Prophet, 133, 166, 189, 223, 229–30
Abu Bakar, Dr Alyashar, 250
Abū Hanīfa, 111
Abu Huraira, 226
Abu Nu'aim, 227, 232
acceptance: *see* validity of laws
accountability, 112
accounting, 118–19
accretions: *see* corrupted law
Aceh
    hajj, 211
    regional government, 246, 258
    religious courts, 11, 16, 57, 290
    Special Autonomy Law (No.
        18/2001), 41, 245–6, 251–4,
        257–8, 260
    universities, 101, 104, 106, 110, 120,
        187
    Verandah of Mecca, 261
Aceh Qanun, x, 243–5, **246–59**, 262,
    264–5, 275, 277–8, 281, 283
    courses on 110, 120
Acehnese language, 134, 255
action, will to (*ikhtyār*), 45

adat (customary law)
    colonial period, 3–5, 75, 300–301
    Counter Legal Draft, 25
    courses on, 94, 96, 109–10
    handbook (*Adatrechtbundel*), 75–6,
        301
    KHI, 25
    philosophy of syariah, 51–2, 79–80
    pre-modern texts, 2
    regional syariah law texts, 247, 255–
        7, 262, 265, 270, 272, 274, 276
    religious courts, 11
administration: *see* bureaucracy
adoption (*anak angat*), 25, 252, 255
adultery: *see* sexual relations
aesthetics, 104
Al-Afghani, 115
Afghanistan, 49
Afrianty, Dina, 86
Africa, 91, 102, 252, 285, 300
AFTA, 49
agents (*amil*), 32, 205–6, 209, 234–5
agrarian cultures, 91
agrarian law, 96
agribusiness, 120
agriculture, 35–6
Agus Salim, Haji, 124
ahl al-Kitab (People of the Book), 22
Ahmad, cited, 230, 232
Ahmad, Mirza Tahir, 9
Ahmad, Zainal Abidin, 59–60
Ahmadiyya, 9
AIDS, 110, 196

collections, 174–203
printed collections, as models, **130–31**, 139, 168–9, 172
public transmission of syariah, x, **129–73**, 293, 303
published form, 129, **130–32**, 137, 139–40, 168, 173, 186–7, 189, 294
qiyas, 295–6
text as literary composition, **131**, 168–9
topic-based collections, 132, 136, **137–40**, 168–9, 172–203
'ulamā', **132–3**, 134, 146, 166, 168–9, 195
knowledge (*ilmu*), 65–6, 166
Koesnoe, Moh., 11, 256
Kollewijn, R.D., 76
Kompilasi Hukum Islam: *see* 'Compilation of Islamic Law'
Kongres Mujahidin (2000), 259
Konstituante (Constituent Assembly, Bandung, 1956–59), 64
Kota Bukit Tinggi (West Sumatra), 266–7
KUA: *see* Religious Affairs Office
KUHP: *see* Civil Code; Criminal Code
kyai, 132–3

L

Labib Mz., Ustadz, 136, 146–7, 149, 152, 157, 160, 162, 165, 194–5, 198–203
Lambton, Anne, 115
land law, 22, 36–7, 109–10, 112, 117, 244, 291
languages
courses, 90–91, 95, 108, 127
khutbah, 129–30, 134
Persis *fatwā* method, 29
regional syariah law texts, 255
See also Arabic language; English language; Indonesian language; regional languages
Lapidus, Ira M., 81, 110
law administration, 114, 277, 281
Law No. 22/1946, 19
Law No. 32/1954, 19
Law No. 5/1960 (Basic Agrarian Law), 37, 109, 256, 291
Law No. 14/1970 on Judicial Powers, 7, 21

Law No. 1/1974: *see* Marriage Law
Law No. 7/1983 on Income Tax, 275
Law No. 14/1985, 21
Law No. 7/1989: *see* Law on Religious Justice
Law No. 7/1992, 38
Law No. 23/1992, 270
Law No. 5/1997, 270
Law No. 22/1997, 270
Law No. 24/1997, 270
Law No. 10/1998, 38
Law No. 5/1999, 254
Law No. 17/1999 on the Implementation of the Hajj, **206–7**, 209, 214, 233, 236
Law No. 35/1999, 16
Law No. 38/1999 (Zakat Management Law), 33, 256, 267, 276
Law No. 40/1999, 270
Law No. 17/2000, 275
Law No. 25/2000, 213
Law No. 18/2001: *see* Special Autonomy Law for Aceh
Law No. 24/2003, 254
Law No. 4/2004, 16
Law No. 10/2004, 18
Law No. 32/2004, 271
Law No. 41/2004, 34
Law No. 3/2006: *see* Law on Religious Justice
Law on Religious Justice (No. 7/1989), 10–11, 13, 18–19, 39, 107, 246, 252, 254, 281
Law on Religious Justice (No. 3/2006), 16, 39, 246, 252, 254–5, 281
law schools: *see* curricula
law texts: *see* undang
leadership, 138, **140–53**, 172
Lebanon, 27
legal history, 58, 72–5, 77, 113, 121, 289
legal opinion: *see* fatāwā
legal precedence, 253–4
legal precedent, 11, 79, 108, 300
legal reasoning, 2, 12–13, 30–31, 80, 111, 127
legal research methods, 88, 94, 121–3
legal studies, 87–8, 93, 108, 114–16
legislation, 93, 303–4
Lembaga Amil Zakat (LAZ; Zakat Collection Agencies), 33–4
Lembaga Ilmu Pengetahuan Indonesia (LIPI, Indonesian Institute of Sciences), 163

philosophy of syariah, 46–9, 68, 71,
74
syariah, 285–6, 289, 303–4
syariah administration, 252
See also the names of countries
military: *see* armed forces
Mill, J.S., 115
millenarianism (curricula), 92
Milner, A.C., 213, 215
Minangkabau, 2, 270, 272, 274–5, 290
mining & extraction, 35
Minister of Home Affairs Instruction No.
17/1989, 256
Ministerial Decisions, 40
No. 224/1999 (Minister of Religious
Affairs), 233, 236
No. 581/1999 (Minister of Religion),
33, 275
No. 1/2001, 34
No. 371/2002 on Regulation of the
Hajj & Umrah, **207–10**, 233, 236
No. 88/2005, 207
Ministers/Ministries, 16, 30
Education, 86–7, 273
Finance, 35, 207
Foreign Affairs, 61, 209
Health, 30
Interior, 15
Justice, 15, 246
Religious Affairs: *see* Department of
Religion
Social Welfare, 209
Transport, 207
MMI: *see Majelis Mujahidin Indonesia*
model sermons: *see khutbah*
'modernist' Islam (*salafi*), 5, 17, 20, 28,
30, 302
curricula, 92, 125
khutbah, 164
philosophy of syariah, 44, 53–5, 61,
68, 70
See also Muhammadiyah
modernity/modernization
khutbah, 135, 155, **165–7**, 170, 172,
191, 203, 293
philosophy of syariah, 48
syariah, 285, 294–5, 303
modesty, 155, 264, 267, 275
money, **31–40**
curricula, 111, 117, 120, 125
hajj, 205–11, 230, 232, 234–5
regional syariah law texts, 275

religious courts, 10
See also banking; interest on money;
wakaf; zakat
monotheism (*tauhid*), 8, 63, 150, 229
Moore, Sally Falk, 79
morality: *see* ethics; immorality
mortgages (curricula), 94, 117
mosques, 36, 130–32, 168–9, 173, 181,
189, 216, 293
motherhood, 138, 154–7, 159, 186
MPR: *see* People's Consultative
Assembly
MPRS (Interim People's Consultative
Assembly), 109
MPU: *see* Consultative Council of
Ulama
mu'amalat: *see* contract law
mubah (permissible or indifferent), 29
muballigh; muballighah (itinerant or lay
preachers), 132–3, 181, 196–7
Mudzhar, M. Atho, 26, 86
Mufid, H.A. Syafi'i, **168–72**, 203
mufti, 10, 267
Muhaimin, A.G., 78
'Muhammadan law' courses, 4
Muhammadiyah, 20, 27, **28–9**, 34, 86, 98,
165, 275
MUI: *see Majelis Ulama Indonesia*
Muin, Abdul, 144–6, 189
Muin, Haidayatul, 155, 190
Mulia, Siti Musdah, 25, 58
Mulyadi, H., 138, 190
Murjiah, 124
murtad (apostasy), 15, 113
Muslehuddin, Muhammad, 105
Muslim, cited, 226, 229–30, 232
Muslim calendar, 134–7, 250
Muslim Code: *see* 'Compilation of
Islamic Law'
Muslim community: *see ummah*
Muslim history: *see* historical syariah;
Islamic civilization
Muslims' relations with other Muslims:
see fellow Muslims
Mustoffa, M. Farid, 209
Mu'tazilites, 62, 124
Muthohar, Aries, 167, 190
Mutiara Khadijah (journal), 181
Muttafaq, 'Alahi, 229
Muzani, Saiful, 61, 96
mysticism: *see* Sufism

www.ingramcontent.com/pod-product-compliance
Lightning Source LLC
Chambersburg PA
CBHW020811100426
42814CB00001B/16